Wireless Home Networking

FOR

DUMMIES®

3RD EDITION

Wireless Home Networking

FOR DUMMIES®

3RD EDITION

by Danny Briere, Pat Hurley, and Edward Ferris

WILEY

Wiley Publishing, Inc.

Wireless Home Networking For Dummies®, 3rd Edition

Published by
Wiley Publishing, Inc.
111 River Street
Hoboken, NJ 07030-5774

www.wiley.com

Copyright © 2008 by Wiley Publishing, Inc., Indianapolis, Indiana

Published by Wiley Publishing, Inc., Indianapolis, Indiana

Published simultaneously in Canada

For general information on our other products and services, please contact our Customer Care Department within the U.S. at 877-762-2974, outside the U.S. at 317-572-3993, or fax 317-572-4002.

For technical support, please visit www.wiley.com/techsupport.

Wiley also publishes its books in a variety of electronic formats. Some content that appears in print may not be available in electronic books.

Library of Congress Control Number: 2008923598

ISBN: 978-0-470-25889-7

Manufactured in the United States of America

10 9 8 7 6 5 4 3 2

WILEY

About the Authors

Danny Briere founded TeleChoice, Inc., a telecommunications consulting company, in 1985 and now serves as CEO of the company. Widely known throughout the telecommunications and networking industry, Danny has written more than 1,000 articles about telecommunications topics and has authored or edited eight books, including *Smart Homes For Dummies,* 3rd Edition, *HDTV For Dummies,* 2nd Edition, *Windows XP Media Center Edition 2004 PC For Dummies, Wireless Network Hacks & Mods For Dummies,* and *Home Theater For Dummies,* 2nd Edition (all published by Wiley). He is frequently quoted by leading publications on telecommunications and technology topics and can often be seen on major TV networks providing analysis on the latest communications news and breakthroughs. Danny lives in Mansfield Center, Connecticut, with his wife and four children.

Pat Hurley is director of research with TeleChoice, Inc., specializing in emerging telecommunications technologies, including all the latest access and home technologies: wireless LANs, DSL, cable modems, satellite services, and home networking services. Pat frequently consults with the leading telecommunications carriers, equipment vendors, consumer goods manufacturers, and other players in the telecommunications and consumer electronics industries. Pat is the co-author of *Smart Homes For Dummies,* 3rd Edition, *HDTV For Dummies,* 2nd Edition, *Windows XP Media Center Edition 2004 PC For Dummies, Wireless Network Hacks & Mods For Dummies,* and *Home Theater For Dummies,* 2nd Edition (all published by Wiley). He lives in San Diego, California, with his wife, beautiful daughter, and two smelly and unruly dogs.

Edward Ferris is a consultant and director of information systems with TeleChoice, Inc., specializing in information management, wired and wireless networking, and security technologies. He has extensive experience with all the latest VOIP technologies: SIP, vPBX, Hybrid PBX, QoS, and packet labeling and switching. Ed frequently consults with companies looking to tighten information security, develop scalable technology plans, and expand network and client support operations. He has written many training and technology manuals for corporate use and has created custom training materials and seminars for numerous applications and business processes. He lives in Norwood, Massachusetts, with his wife and three children.

Authors' Acknowledgments

Danny wants to thank his wife, Holly, and kids, for their infinite patience while he and Pat wrestled with this book toward the finish line. He agrees that the wireless Webcam in the shower was not a good idea. (Just kidding.) He also wants to thank his sister, Michelle, for all her hard work over the years that has made it possible to continue to survive in this crazy business environment — we could not have made it without her. He also wants to note that he has a 42-inch LCD HDTV and even has a 108-inch screen for playing with the Wii.

Pat, as always, thanks his wife, Christine, for providing her impeccable judgment when he asks, "Can I write this wisecrack and not get in trouble?" and for her ability to restrain her desire to knock him over the head with a big frying pan when deadlines and late-night writing intrude on their domestic tranquility. He also wants to thank her for letting him hog the computers *and* the sofa while writing. He also thanks Annabel for not "playing my computer" (in the typing-over-a-just-finished-paragraph way that only a three-year-old can manage) during crucial writing moments — Daddy will take you to In-N-Out for a hamburger and french fries to celebrate the completion of this edition and let you get back to your computer explorations!

Ed wants to thank his wife, Maureen (Moe), and the kids, for letting him take all the extra time to write and for digging him out of the basement now and then so he remembers what sunlight really looks like. He even got to play a few soccer games this time around thanks to the kids. He also wants to thank Moe for all her support as a test subject and pre-editor of everything he types. Without her to say "Okay, now it makes sense to me," much of the instructional material in this book would not have been finished.

Danny, Pat, and Ed want to thank the following people and organizations for their support in writing this edition of the book: Bill Bullock, at Witopia; Melody Chalaban and Jonathan Bettino at Belkin; Shira Frantzich from Sterling PR (for NETGEAR); David Henry at NETGEAR; Karl Stetson at Edelman (for the Wi-Fi Alliance); and Mindy Whittington and Ana Corea at Red Consultancy (for Eye-Fi).

We also can't forget folks who have helped us for the two previous editions, including (but by no means limited to): Doug Hagan and Mehrshad Mansouri, at NETGEAR; Dana Brzozkiewicz, at Lages & Associates, for ZyXEL; Trisha King, at NetPR, for SMC Networks, Fred Bargetzi, at Crestron; Shawn Gusz, at G-NET Canada (still waiting to try Auroras in our cars!); Karen Sohl, at Linksys; Keith Smith, at Siemon; Darek Connole and Michael Scott, at D-Link; Jeff Singer, at Crestron: Amy K Schiska-Lombard, at Sprint; Brad Shewmake, at Kyocera Wireless; James Cortese, at A&R Partners, for Roku; Bryan McLeod, at Intrigue Technologies (now part of Logitech); Stu Elefant, at Wireless Security Corporation (now part of McAfee); Craig Slawson, at CorAccess (good luck, too!); and others who helped get the content correct for the readers.

Our team at Wiley — Steve Hayes and Tiffany Ma on the corporate side of the house — and especially our exceptionally patient and wise project editor Susan Pink all get a well-deserved round of applause from us. We'd also like to thank our technical editor, Dan DiNicolo, for helping us look good. Finally, we want to thank Melody Layne, who's moved on to a different and exciting job at Wiley, but who we suspect is always keeping an eye out on what we're up to.

Publisher's Acknowledgments

We're proud of this book; please send us your comments through our online registration form located at www.dummies.com/register/.

Some of the people who helped bring this book to market include the following:

Acquisitions, Editorial, and Media Development

Project Editor: Susan Pink

(Previous Edition: Rebecca Whitney)

Acquisitions Editor: Tiffany Ma

Technical Editor: Dan DiNicolo

Editorial Manager: Jodi Jensen

Editorial Assistant: Amanda Foxworth

Sr. Editorial Assistant: Cherie Case

Cartoons: Rich Tennant
(www.the5thwave.com)

Composition Services

Project Coordinator: Lynsey Stanford

Layout and Graphics: Reuben W. Davis, Alissa D. Ellet, Joyce Haughey, Stephanie D. Jumper, Ronald Terry

Proofreaders: Laura Bowman, Jessica Kramer

Indexer: Potomac Indexing, LLC

Publishing and Editorial for Technology Dummies

Richard Swadley, Vice President and Executive Group Publisher

Andy Cummings, Vice President and Publisher

Mary Bednarek, Executive Acquisitions Director

Mary C. Corder, Editorial Director

Publishing for Consumer Dummies

Diane Graves Steele, Vice President and Publisher

Joyce Pepple, Acquisitions Director

Composition Services

Gerry Fahey, Vice President of Production Services

Debbie Stailey, Director of Composition Services

Contents at a Glance

Table of Contents

Introduction

∙∙

*W*elcome to *Wireless Home Networking For Dummies,* 3rd Edition. Wireless networking for personal computers isn't a new idea; it has been around since the late 1990s. The emergence of an industry standard, however, has caused the use of wireless networking technology to explode.

One of the most appealing things about the current crop of wireless networking equipment is the ease with which you can set up a home network, although its reasonable price may be its *most* attractive aspect. In some cases, setting up a wireless home network is almost as simple as opening the box and plugging in the equipment; however, you can avoid many "gotchas" by doing a little reading beforehand. That's where this book comes in handy.

About This Book

If you're thinking about purchasing a wireless computer network and installing it in your home — or if you have an installed network and want to make sure it's operating correctly or want to expand it — this is the book for you. Even if you've already purchased the equipment for a wireless network, this book will help you install and configure the network. What's more, this book will help you get the most out of your investment after it's up and running.

With *Wireless Home Networking For Dummies,* 3rd Edition, in hand, you have all the information you need to know about the following topics (and more):

- Planning your wireless home network
- Evaluating and selecting wireless networking equipment for installation in your home
- Installing and configuring wireless networking equipment in your home
- Sharing an Internet connection over your wireless network
- Sharing files, printers, and other peripherals over your wireless network
- Playing computer games over your wireless network
- Connecting your audiovisual gear to your wireless network
- Securing your wireless network against prying eyes
- Discovering devices that you can connect to your wireless home network

System Requirements

Virtually any personal computer can be added to a wireless home network, although some computers are easier to add than others. This book focuses on building a wireless network that connects PCs running the Windows operating system (Windows XP and Vista) or Mac OS X. You *can* operate a wireless network with Windows 98, Me, or 2000 or with Mac OS 9, but these systems are less and less able to handle the rapidly increasing requirements of applications and the Internet. As a result, we focus mostly on the most recent operating systems — the ones that have been launched within the past five years or so. Wireless networking is also popular among Linux users, but we don't cover Linux in this book.

Because wireless networking is a relatively new phenomenon, the newest versions of Windows and the Mac OS do the best job of helping you quickly and painlessly set up a wireless network. However, because the primary reason for networking your home computers is to make it possible for all the computers (and peripherals) in your house to communicate, *Wireless Home Networking For Dummies,* 3rd Edition, gives you information about connecting computers that run the latest versions of Windows and the most widely used version of the Mac OS. We also tell you how to connect computers that run some of the older versions of these two operating systems.

How This Book Is Organized

Wireless Home Networking For Dummies, 3rd Edition, is organized into twenty chapters that are grouped into five parts. The chapters are presented in a logical order — flowing from planning to installing to using your wireless home network — but feel free to use the book as a reference and read the chapters in any order you want.

Part 1: Wireless Networking Fundamentals

Part I is a primer on networking and on wireless networking. If you have never used a networked computer — much less attempted to install a network — this part of the book provides background information and technogeek lingo that you need to feel comfortable. Chapter 1 presents general networking concepts; Chapter 2 discusses the most popular wireless networking technology and familiarizes you with wireless networking terminology; and Chapter 3 introduces you to several popular complementary and alternative technologies to wireless networking.

Part II: Making Plans

Part II helps you plan for installing your wireless home network. Chapter 4 helps you decide what to connect to the network and where to install wireless networking equipment in your home, and Chapter 5 provides guidance on making buying decisions.

Part III: Installing a Wireless Network

Part III discusses how to install a wireless network in your home and get the network up and running. Whether your have Apple Macintosh computers running the Mac OS (see Chapter 8) or PCs running a Windows operating system (see Chapters 6 and 7), this part of the book explains how to install and configure your wireless networking equipment. In addition, Part III includes a chapter that explains how to secure your wireless home network (see Chapter 9). Too many people don't secure their wireless network, and we want to make sure you're not one of them!

Part IV: Using a Wireless Network

After you get your wireless home network installed and running, you'll certainly want to use it. Part IV starts by showing you the basics of putting your wireless network to good use: sharing files, folders, printers, and other peripherals (see Chapter 10). We discuss everything you want to know about playing multiuser computer games wirelessly (see Chapter 11), connecting your audiovisual equipment (see Chapter 12), using your wireless network to make phone calls (see Chapter 13), and doing other cool things over a wireless network (see Chapter 14).

Bluetooth-enabled devices are becoming more prevalent these days, so you don't want to miss Chapter 15 — or Chapter 16, for that matter, where we describe how to use wireless networking to connect to the Internet through wireless *hot spots* (wireless networks you can connect to for free or a small cost when you're on the road) in coffee shops, hotels, airports, and other public places. How cool is that?

Part V: The Part of Tens

Part V provides three top-ten lists that we think you'll find interesting — ten frequently asked questions about wireless home networking (Chapter 17); ten troubleshooting tips for improving your wireless home network's performance (Chapter 18); ten devices to connect to your wireless home network — sometime in the future (Chapter 19); and the top ten sources for more information about wireless networking (Chapter 20).

Icons Used in This Book

All of us these days are hyperbusy people, with no time to waste. To help you find the especially useful nuggets of information in this book, we have marked the information with little icons in the margin.

As you can probably guess, the Tip icon calls your attention to information that saves you time or maybe even money. If your time is really crunched, you may try just skimming through the book and reading the tips.

This icon is your clue that you should take special note of the advice you find there — or that the paragraph reinforces information provided elsewhere in the book. Bottom line: You will accomplish the task more effectively if you remember this information.

Face it, computers and wireless networks are high-tech toys, er *tools,* that make use of some complicated technology. For the most part, however, you don't need to know how it all works. The Technical Stuff icon identifies the paragraphs you can skip if you are in a hurry or just don't care to know.

The little bomb in the margin should alert you to pay close attention and tread softly. You don't want to waste time or money fixing a problem that could have been avoided in the first place.

Where to Go from Here

Where you should go next in this book depends on where you are in the process of planning, buying, installing, configuring, or using your wireless home network. If networking in general and wireless networking in particular are new to you, we recommend that you start at the beginning, with Part I. When you feel comfortable with networking terminology or get bored with the lingo, move on to the chapters in Part II about planning your network and selecting equipment. If you already have your equipment in hand, head to Part III to get it installed — and secured (unless you *like* the idea of your neighbor or even a hacker being able to access your network).

If you were thinking of skipping Part I, know that a new standard for wireless networking — 802.11n — will dramatically affect your planning. If you are not up to speed on this new standard, we recommend that you at least take a quick view of Chapter 2 first.

The wireless industry is changing fast. We provide regular updates for this book at www.digitaldummies.com.

Happy wireless networking!

Part I
Wireless Networking Fundamentals

The 5th Wave — By Rich Tennant

"Okay – did you get that?"

In this part . . .

If you've never used a networked computer or you're installing a network in your home for the first time, this part of the book provides all the background info and down-and-dirty basics that will have you in the swing of things in no time. Here, you can find general networking concepts, the most popular wireless networking technology, wireless networking terminology, and the latest alternatives in wireless networking. We also delve into cool new options for complementing your wireless network with peripherals networking and home control and home automation standards. Now that's whole-home networking the wireless way!

Chapter 1

Introducing Wireless Home Networking

*W*elcome to the wireless age! Nope, we're not talking about your grandfather's radio — we're talking about almost everything under the sun — truly. What's not going wireless? Wanna say your refrigerator? Wrong — it is. How about your stereo? Yup, that too. Watches, key chains, baby video monitors, high-end projectors — even your thermostat is going wireless and digital. It's not just about computers any more! Your entire world is going wireless, and in buying this book, you're determined not to get left behind. Kudos to you!

A driving force behind the growing popularity of wireless networking is its reasonable cost: You can save money by not running network wiring all over your house, by spending less on Internet connections, by sharing peripherals (such as printers and scanners), and by using your PC to drive other applications around your home, such as your home entertainment center. This book makes it easier for you to spend your money wisely by helping you decide what you need to buy and then helping you choose between the products on the market. Wireless networks are not only less expensive than more traditional wired networks but also much easier to install. An important goal of this book is to provide you with "the skinny" on how to install a wireless network in your home.

Whether you have one computer or more, you have several good reasons to want a personal computer network. The plummeting cost of wireless technologies, combined with their fast-paced technical development, has meant that more and more manufacturers are getting on the home networking bandwagon. That means that more applications around your house will try to ride your wireless backbone — by talking among themselves and to the Internet. So, wireless is here to stay and is critical for any future-proofed home.

Nothing but Net (work): Why You Need One

Wireless home networking isn't just about linking computers to the Internet. Although that task is important — nay, critical — in today's network-focused environment, it's not the whole enchilada. Of the many benefits of having wireless in the home, most have one thing in common: sharing. When you connect the computers in your house through a network, you can share files, printers, scanners, and high-speed Internet connections between them. In addition, you can play multiuser games over your network, access public wireless networks while you're away from home, check wireless cameras, use Internet Voice over IP (VoIP) services, or even enjoy your MP3s from your home stereo system while you're at work — really!

Reading *Wireless Home Networking For Dummies,* 3rd Edition, helps you understand how to create a whole-home wireless network to reach the nooks and crannies of your house. The big initial reason that people have wanted to put wireless networks in their homes has been to "unwire" their PCs, especially laptops, to enable more freedom of access in the home. But just about every major consumer goods manufacturer is hard at work wirelessly enabling its devices so that they too can talk to other devices in the home — you can find home theater receivers, music players, and even flat-panel TVs with wireless capabilities built right in.

File sharing

As you probably know, computer *files* are created whenever you use a computer. If you use a word processing program, such as Microsoft Word, to write a document, Word saves the document on your computer's hard drive as an electronic file. Similarly, if you balance your checkbook by using Quicken from Intuit, this software saves your financial data on the computer's drive in an electronic file.

A computer network lets you share those electronic files between two or more computers. For example, you can create a Word document on your computer, and your spouse, roommate, child, sibling, or whoever can pull the same document up on his or her computer over the network. With the right programs, you can even view the same documents at the same time!

But here's where we get into semantics: What's a computer? Your car has more computing and networking capability than the early moon rockets. Your stereo is increasingly looking like a computer with a black matte finish. Even your refrigerator and microwave are getting onboard computing capabilities — and they all have files and information that need to be shared.

The old way of moving files between computers and computing devices involved copying the files to a floppy disk and then carrying the disk to the other computer. Computer geeks call this method of copying and transferring files the *sneakernet* approach. In contrast, copying files between computers is easy to do over a home network and with no need for floppy disks (or sneakers).

What's interesting is that more computers and devices are getting "used to" talking to one another over networks in an automated fashion. A common application is *synchronization,* where two devices talk to one another and make the appropriate updates to each other's stored information so that they're current with one another. For example, Microsoft's Zune portable media player (www.zune.net) is in many ways similar to Apple's iPod, with one big exception: the Zune's wireless capabilities. Whenever you put your Zune in its charger base, it connects across your wireless network and automatically syncs new content (music, audiobooks, podcasts, and videos) from your PC. This means you always have that new content at your fingertips — literally — without having to lift a finger.

Printer and peripheral sharing

Businesses with computer networks have discovered a major benefit: sharing printers. Companies invest in high-speed, high-capacity printers that are shared by many employees. Sometimes an entire department shares a single printer, or perhaps a cluster of printers is located in an area set aside for printers, copy machines, and fax machines.

Just like in a business network, all the computers on your home network can share the printers on your network. The cost-benefit of shared printers in a home network is certainly not as dramatic as in a business, but the opportunity to save money by sharing printers is clearly one of the real benefits of setting up a home network. Figure 1-1 depicts a network through which three personal computers can share the same printer.

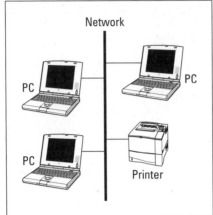

Figure 1-1:
Share and
share alike:
Share one
printer via
your home
network.

Other peripherals, such as extra hard drive storage for your computers or for all those MP3s that someone in the household might be downloading, also are great to share. Anything connected to your PCs or that has a network port (we talk about these in great detail throughout the book) can be shared anywhere on your wireless network.

Internet connection sharing

Another driving reason behind many homeowners' interest in wireless home networking is a desire to share an Internet connection. Let's face it, the Internet is a critical part of day-to-day living — from kids doing their homework to you managing your bank account — so it's only natural that more than one person in the household wants to get online at the same time. And, with the proliferation of *broadband Internet connections* — cable, digital subscriber line (DSL), fiber optics, and satellite modems — we can know that the demand at home has only soared.

High-speed *(broadband)* Internet service is appealing. Not only is the connection to the Internet 50 times or more faster than a dial-up connection, with sharing enabled over your wireless network, all the computers connected to the network can access the Internet at one time through the same broadband service for one monthly fee. (The fee can be as low as $14.95 per month in some areas.) And you can surf and talk on the phone at the same time. No more having your dial-up connection tie up your phone line!

Modem types

Your wireless network helps you distribute information throughout the home. It's independent of the method you use to access your outside-of-home networks, like the Internet. Whether you use a dial-up connection or broadband, your wireless home network will be applicable.

- **Dial-up modem:** This device connects to the Internet by dialing an Internet service provider (ISP), such as America Online (AOL) or EarthLink, over a standard phone line.

  Fewer and fewer wireless networking equipment manufacturers support a dial-up connection on their equipment, because the majority of homes (and the *vast majority* of networked homes) use broadband these days. We mention dial-up here only for completeness; not because we recommend that you use it.

- **Cable modem:** This type of modem connects to the Internet through the same cable as cable TV. Cable modems connect to the Internet at much higher speeds than dial-up modems and can be left connected to the Internet all day, every day.

- **DSL modem:** Digital subscriber line modems use your phone line, but they permit the phone to be free for other purposes — voice calls and faxes, for example — even while the DSL modem is in use. DSL modems also connect to the Internet at much higher speeds than dial-up modems and can be left connected 24/7.

- **Broadband wireless modem:** The same wireless airwaves that are great for around-the-house communications are great for connecting to the Internet as well. Although the frequency may be different and the bandwidth much less, broadband wireless modems give you connectivity to your home's wireless network, in a similar fashion as DSL and cable modems.

- **Satellite modem:** Satellite modems tie into your satellite dish and give you two-way communications even if you're in the middle of the woods. Although they're typically not as fast as cable modems and DSL links, they're better than dial-up and available just about anywhere in the continental United States.

- **Fiber-optic modem:** We're at the front end of the fiber-fed revolution as the telephone and cable companies push to outcompete each other by installing extremely high-capacity lines in homes to allow all sorts of cool applications. (The biggest example of this in the U.S. is Verizon's FiOS system — www.verizon.com — which is connecting millions of homes to the Internet by using fiber-optic connections.) Until now, the broadband access link has been the limiting bottleneck when wireless networks communicate with the Internet. With fiber optics, you could see broadband access capacity equal to that of your wireless network.

Phone jacks versus a network

Most homes built in the past 20 years have a phone jack (outlet) in the wall in every room in the house where you would likely use your computer. Consequently, connecting your computer to the Internet via a dial-up modem over a telephone line doesn't require a network. You simply run a phone line from your computer's modem to the phone jack in the wall and you're in business.

However, without a network or without Internet connection sharing turned on at the computer, the connection cannot be shared between computers; only one computer can use a given phone line at any given time. Not good.

With a wireless home network, we can help you extend that modem connection throughout the home. The same is true with your broadband modem — it can be shared throughout the home.

When configuring your PCs on a network, you can buy equipment that lets you connect multiple computers to a regular or high-speed modem through the phone lines — or even through the coaxial wiring or the power lines — in your house. No matter what the physical connection is among your networked devices, the most popular language (or *protocol)* used in connecting computers to a broadband modem is a network technology known as Ethernet. *Ethernet* is an industry standard protocol used in virtually every corporation and institution; consequently, Ethernet equipment is plentiful and inexpensive. The most common form of Ethernet networking uses special cables known as *Category 5e/6 UTP* (or unshielded twisted pair). These networks are named after their speed — most are 100 Mbps (much faster than alternative networks that run over powerlines or phone lines) and are called 100BaseT. You also find 1000BaseT (gigabit Ethernet) networks, which run at 1 *giga*bit per second. Figure 1-2 illustrates a network that enables three personal computers to connect to the Internet through a DSL or cable modem. (This network model works the same for a satellite or fiber-optic connection.)

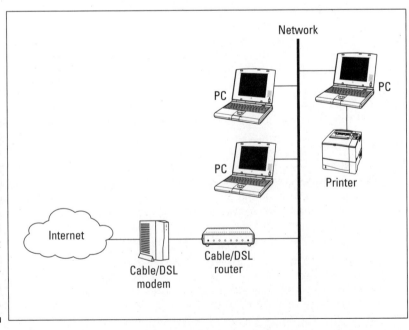

Figure 1-2:
Internet for all: Set up a network that enables many PCs to connect to the Internet through a DSL or cable modem.

See Chapter 4 for more information about planning and budgeting for your network and Chapter 5 for help in selecting your wireless networking equipment.

Phone calling for free

With some new wireless phone capabilities, you can get rid of the static of your cordless phone and move digital over your wireless home network, thus saving money on calls by using less-expensive, Internet-based phone calling options (Voice over IP, or VoIP). What started as a hobbyist error-prone service has grown into a full-fledged worldwide phenomenon. Phone calling over the Internet is now ready for prime time:

- ✔ **Free and for-fee services are available.** Services such as Vonage (www. vonage.com) and Skype (www.skype.com) allow you to use your regular phones to call over the Internet for free or for a low monthly cost.

- ✔ **Add-ons to popular software programs are available.** Internet calling and even videoconferencing have been added to instant messaging programs such as AOL Instant Messenger (AIM) so that you can talk to the people you used to only IM.

- ✔ **New devices make it simple.** New devices, such as the Olympia Dual-Phone (www.dualphone.net), ease access to these Internet calling services — so you don't have to don a headset every time you want to make a phone call.

The best part is that VoIP services are all moving toward wireless too. Throw away that old cordless phone and replace it with a new wireless handset or a neat Wi-Fi phone that you can take on the road to make free calls from any Wi-Fi network you happen to have access to.

The convergence of wireless and Voice over IP is one of the major megatrends going on in the telecommunications and Internet markets today — you can bet that you want it in your home too!

Home arcades and wireless to go

If you aren't convinced yet that a wireless home network is for you, we have four more points that may change your mind. Check them out:

- ✔ **Multiuser games over the network:** If you're into video games, multiplayer card games, or role-playing games, you may find multiuser games over the network or even over the Internet fascinating. Chapter 11 discusses how to use your wireless network to play multiuser games.

✔ **Audio anywhere in the household:** Why spend money on CDs and keep them stacked next to your stereo? Load them on your PC and make them wirelessly available to your stereo, your car, your MP3 player that you take jogging, and lots more. Check out Chapter 12 for more info on how to use your wireless network to send audio and video signals around the house.

✔ **Home wireless cam accessibility:** You can check out your house from anywhere in the house — or the world — with new wireless cameras that hop on your home network and broadcast images privately or publicly over the Internet. Want to see whether your kids are tearing apart the house while you're working in your office downstairs? Just call up your wireless networked camera and check them out. (In our generation, we always said, "Mom has eyes in the back of her head"; this generation will probably think that Mom is omniscient!)

✔ **Wireless on the go:** This concept is great if you have a portable computer. Many airports, hotels, malls, and coffee shops have installed public wireless networks that enable you to connect to the Internet (for a small fee, of course) via hot spots. See Chapter 16 for more about using wireless networking while away from home.

Wired versus Wireless

Ethernet is the most-often-used method of connecting personal computers to form a network because it's fast and its equipment is relatively inexpensive. In addition, Ethernet can be transmitted over several types of network cable or sent through the air by using wireless networking equipment. Most new computers have an Ethernet connection built in, ready for you to plug in a network cable. The most popular wireless networking equipment transmits a form of Ethernet by using radio waves rather than Category 5e/6 cables.

Installing wired home networks

Even though we're talking mostly about wireless networks and how great they are, we would be misleading you if we told you that wireless is the only way to go. Wireless and wired homes each have advantages.

Wired homes are

✔ **Faster:** Wired lines can reach speeds of 1000 Mbps, whereas wireless homes tend to be in the 20 Mbps to 200 Mbps range. Both wireless and wired technologies are getting faster and faster, but for as far as our crystal balls can see, wired will always be ahead.

✔ **More reliable:** Wireless signals are prone to interference and fluctuations and degrade quickly over short distances; wired connections typically are more stable and reliable all over your home.

✔ **More secure:** You don't have to worry about your signals traveling through the air and being intercepted by snoopers, as you do with unsecured wireless systems.

✔ **Economical over the long term:** The incremental cost of adding CAT-5e/6 voice and data cabling and RG-6 coaxial cabling into your house — over a 30-year mortgage — will be almost nothing each month.

✔ **Salable:** More and more home buyers are not only looking for well-wired homes but also discounting homes without the infrastructure. As good as wireless is, it isn't affixed to the house and is carried with you when you leave. Most new homes have structured wiring in the walls.

If you're building a new home or renovating an old one, we absolutely recommend that you consider running the latest wiring in the walls to each of your rooms. That doesn't mean that you won't have a wireless network in your home — you will. It just will be different than if you were wholly reliant on wireless for your networking.

If you choose to use network cable, it should ideally be installed in the walls, just like electrical and phone wiring. Network jacks (outlets) are installed in the walls in rooms where you would expect to use a computer. Connecting your computer to a wired network is as easy as plugging a phone into a phone jack — after the wiring is in place, that is.

Without question, the most economical time to install network cable in a home is during the home's initial construction. In upscale neighborhoods, especially in communities near high-tech businesses, builders often wire new homes with network cable as a matter of course. In most cases, however, the installation of network cable in a new home is an option or upgrade that's installed only if the new owner orders it and pays a premium. Installing a structured wiring solution for a home can cost at least $2,000–$3,000, and that's for starters.

Although the installation of network cable in an existing home certainly is possible, it's much more difficult and expensive than installing cable during construction. If you hire an electrician to run the cable, you can easily spend thousands of dollars to do what would have cost a few hundred dollars during your home's construction. If you're comfortable drilling holes in your walls and working in attics and crawl spaces, you can install the cabling yourself for the cost of the cable and outlets.

The reality is that no home will ever be purely wireless or wireline (wired). Each approach has benefits and costs, and they coexist in any house. If you're building a new house, most experts tell you to spend the extra money on a structured wiring solution because it adds value to your house and you can better manage all the wiring in your home. We agree. But no wiring solution can be everywhere you want it to be. Thus, wireless is a great complement to your home, which is why we advocate a whole-home wireless network for your entire home to use.

Installing wireless home networks

If you're networking an existing home or are renting your home, wireless has fabulous benefits:

- ✔ **Portable:** You can take your computing device anywhere in the house and be on the network. Even if you have a huge house, you can interconnect wireless access points to have a whole-home wireless network.

- ✔ **Flexible:** You're not limited to where a jack is on the wall; you can network anywhere.

- ✔ **Cost effective:** You can start wireless networking for a few hundred dollars. Your wiring contractor can't do much with that!

- ✔ **Clean:** You don't have to tear down walls or trip over wires when they come out from underneath the carpeting.

What's more, there's really no difference in how you use your networked computer, whether it's connected to the network by a cable or by a wireless networking device. Whether you're sharing files, a printer, your entertainment system, or the Internet over the network, the procedures are the same on a wireless network as on a wired network. In fact, you can mix wired and wireless network equipment on the same network with no change in how you use a computer on the network.

It's time for the fine print. We would be remiss if we weren't candid and didn't mention any potential drawbacks to wireless networks compared with wired networks. The possible drawbacks fall into four categories:

- ✔ **Data speed:** Wireless networking equipment transmits data at slower speeds than wired networking equipment. Wired networks are already networking at gigabit speeds, although the fastest current wireless networking standards (in theoretical situations) top out at 248 Mbps. (The real-world top speed you can expect will be under 100 Mbps.) But, for almost all the uses we can think of now, this rate is plenty fast. Your Internet connection probably doesn't exceed 10 Mbps (though lucky folks who have fiber-optic lines running to their homes may exceed this rate by a big margin!), so your wireless connection should be more than fast enough.

✔ **Radio signal range:** Wireless signals fade when you move away from the source. Some homes, especially older homes, may be built from materials that tend to block the radio signals used by wireless networking equipment, which causes even faster signal degradation. If your home has plaster walls that contain a wire mesh, the wireless networking equipment's radio signal may not reach all points in your home. Most modern construction, however, uses drywall materials that reduce the radio signal only slightly. As a result, most homeowners can reach all points in their home with one centralized wireless *access point* (also called a *base station*) and one wireless device in or attached to each personal computer. And, if you need better coverage, you can just add another access point — we show you how in Chapter 18 — or you can upgrade to a newer technology, such as 802.11n, which promises farther coverage within your home.

✔ **Radio signal interference:** The most common type of wireless networking technology uses a radio frequency that's also used by other home devices, such as microwave ovens and portable telephones. Consequently, some wireless home network users experience network problems (the network slows down or the signal is dropped) caused by radio signal interference.

✔ **Security:** The radio signal from a wireless network doesn't stop at the outside wall of your home. A neighbor or even a total stranger could access your network from an adjoining property or from the street unless you implement some type of security technology to prevent unauthorized access. You can safeguard yourself with security technology that comes standard with the most popular wireless home networking technology. However, it's not bulletproof, and it certainly doesn't work if you don't turn it on. For more information on wireless security, go to Chapter 9.

For our money, wireless networks compare favorably with wired networks for most homeowners who didn't have network wiring installed when their houses were built. As we mention earlier in this chapter, even if you do have network wires in your walls, you probably want wireless just to provide the untethered access it brings to laptops and handheld computers.

Choosing a Wireless Standard

The good news about wireless networks is that they come in multiple flavors, each with its own advantages and disadvantages. The bad news is that trying to decide which version to get when buying a system can get confusing. The even better news is that the dropping prices of wireless systems and fast-paced development are creating dual- and tri-mode systems on the market that can speak many different wireless languages.

You may run into gear using one of two older standards. For the most part, manufacturers aren't making gear using these systems anymore (at least not for the home — some industrial and commercial network gear still on the market use these systems), but you will still hear about these systems as you explore wireless networking:

- **802.11a:** Wireless networks that use the Institute for Electrical and Electronics Engineers (IEEE) 802.11a standard use the 5 GHz radio frequency band. Equipment of this type is among the fastest wireless networking equipment widely available to consumers.

- **802.11b:** Wireless home networks that use the 802.11b standard use the 2.4 GHz radio band. This standard is the most popular in terms of number of installed networks and number of users.

Following are the two major wireless systems that have pretty much replaced 802.11b and 802.11a:

- **802.11g:** The current member of the 802.11 wireless family to hit the mainstream, 802.11g has rapidly taken over the market. In many ways, 802.11g offers the best of both worlds — backward compatibility with the older 802.11b networks discussed in the next section (they too operate over the 2.4 GHz radio frequency band) and the speed of the older 802.11a networks also discussed in that section. And the cost of 802.11g has dropped so precipitously that it's now less expensive than the older and slower 802.11b. (You can buy an 802.11g network adapter for less than $20 and a home router for less than $50.) For these reasons, 802.11g has become the de facto solution that most users now buy.

- **802.11n (draft standard):** 802.11g is still the default, but it is rapidly being replaced by a newer and faster system called 802.11n. 802.11n (like 802.11g before it) is backward compatible, which means that older 802.11b and 802.11g systems can work just fine on an 802.11n network. 802.11n systems can also support the 5 GHz frequencies (though not all do; more on this in Chapter 3), and may therefore be backward compatible with 802.11a as well. A lot of new technology in 802.11n extends the range of the network and increases the speed as well — 802.11n can be as much as *five times* faster than 802.11g or 802.11a networks.

You'll note the words *draft standard* in the preceding description of 802.11n. The group that ratifies the technical specifications of wireless networks (the IEEE, discussed in Chapter 3) has not completely finished agreeing on the 802.11n system standard. What they have in place (and what manufacturers are building their systems around) is a draft of the final standard that's about 99 percent of the way there (the final isn't expected to be ratified until 2009). Normally we would recommend that people wait for a final standard to be in place, but 802.11n is so far along (and working so well) that we don't hesitate to recommend it for folks who could use the extra range or speed.

Equipment supporting all three finalized standards — 802.11a, 802.11b, and 802.11g — as well as the draft standard for 802.11n can carry the Wi-Fi logo that's licensed for use by the Wi-Fi Alliance trade group based on equipment that passes interoperability testing. You absolutely want to buy only equipment that has been Wi-Fi certified, regardless of which 802.11 standard you're choosing.

The terms surrounding wireless networking can get complex. First, the order of lettering isn't really right because 802.11*b* was approved and hit the market before 802.11*a*. Also, you see the term *Wi-Fi* used frequently. (In fact, we thought about calling this book *Wi-Fi For Dummies* because the term is used so much.) Wi-Fi refers to the collective group of 802.11 specifications: 802.11a, b, g, and n. You may sometimes see this group also named *802.11x* networking, where x can equal a, b, g, or n. To make matters more confusing, a higher-level parent standard named 802.11 predates 802.11a, b, g, and n and is also used to talk about the group of the three standards. Technically, it's a standards group responsible for several other networking specifications as well. For simplicity in this book, we use 802.11 and Wi-Fi synonymously to talk about the four standards as a group. We could have used 802.11x, but we want to save a lot of *x*s (for our wives).

For the most part, 802.11a and 802.11b equipment is being phased out. If you're buying all new gear, 802.11g or 802.11n are your real choices. You can still find a few bits of 802.11a or b gear, but it's mostly sold to fit into older networks. If you already have some gear that's 802.11b, don't despair — it still works fine in most cases, and you can upgrade your network to 802.11g or 802.11n bit by bit (pun intended!) without worrying about compatibility. In this section, we still discuss 802.11a and b, even though they're increasingly not something you're likely to consider.

The differences between these four standards fall into five main categories:

- **Data speed:** 802.11a and 802.11g networks are almost five times faster than the original 802.11b networks — 802.11n is five times faster still! For the most part, any current Wi-Fi gear (whether it be 802.11g or 802.11n) will be faster than the Internet connection into your house, but the extra speed of 802.11n may still be worthwhile if you're trying to do things such as transfer real-time video signals around your home wirelessly.

- **Price:** 802.11g networking gear (the standard system today) has been on the market for three years as we write — accordingly, the price for this gear is quite low (less than $20 for an adapter). The new 802.11n adapters can cost two to four times as much.

- **Radio signal range:** 802.11a wireless networks tend to have a shorter maximum signal range than 802.11b and g networks. The actual distances vary depending on the size and construction of your home. In most modern homes, however, all three of the older standards should provide adequate range. Because it uses a new technology called MIMO, 802.11n can have two or more times the range in your home, so if you have a big house, you might gravitate toward 802.11n.

✔ **Radio signal interference:** The radio frequency band used by both 802.11b and 802.11g equipment is used also by other home devices, such as microwave ovens and portable telephones, resulting sometimes in network problems caused by radio signal interference. Few other types of devices now use the radio frequency band employed by the 802.11a standard. 802.11n gear can use either frequency band (though not all gear does — some uses only the more crowded 2.4 GHz frequency range).

✔ **Interoperability:** Because 802.11a and 802.11b/g use different frequency bands, they can't communicate over the same radio. Several manufacturers, however, have products that can operate with both 802.11a and IEEE 802.11b/g equipment simultaneously. By contrast, 802.11g equipment is designed to be backward compatible with 802.11b equipment — both operating on the same frequency band. The forthcoming 802.11n products will interoperate with each other after the standards are finalized, but will support backward compatibility to 802.11b/g if the standard falls in the 2.4GHz range as expected. 802.11n is backward compatible with all three previous standards, though the 802.11a backward compatibility is available only on 802.11n gear that operates in the 5 GHz frequency range.

Think of dual-mode, multistandard devices as being in the same vein as AM/FM radios. AM and FM stations transmit their signals in different ways, but hardly anyone buys a radio that's only AM because almost all the receiving units are AM/FM. Users select which band they want to listen to at any particular time. With an 802.11a/b/g (or 2.4/5 GHz 802.11n) device, you can also choose the band that you want to transmit and receive in.

We expect that 802.11g products will be, at minimum, the standard device deployed in most home networks. 802.11a has never made much of an inroad into the home network, but the advent of 5 GHz capable 802.11n devices may finally bring 5 GHz networks into more homes.

For most home networks, 802.11g wireless networks are the best choice because they're relatively inexpensive, offer the best data speed, and provide a more than adequate range for most homes. As we discuss in the next chapter, however, if you have some higher performance networking requirements (such as trying to transmit video around your home wirelessly), you may want to invest in the newer 802.11n standard.

Planning Your Wireless Home Network

Installing and setting up a wireless home network can be ridiculously easy. In some cases, after you unpack and install the equipment, you're up and running in a matter of minutes. To ensure that you don't have a negative experience, however, you should do a little planning. The issues you need to consider during the planning stage include the ones in this list:

- Which of your computers will you connect to the network (and will you be connecting Macs and PCs or just one or the other)?

- Will all the computers be connected via wireless connections, or will one or more computers be connected by a network cable to the network?

- Which wireless technology — 802.11a, 802.11b, or 802.11g — will you use? (Or will you use all of them? Or will you move right into the new 802.11n standard?)

- Which type of wireless adapter will you use to connect each computer to the network?

- How many printers will you connect to the network? How will each printer be connected to the network — by connecting it to a computer on the network or by connecting it to a print server?

- Will you connect the network to the Internet through a broadband connection (cable or DSL) or dial-up? If you're sharing an Internet connection, will you do so with a cable/DSL/satellite/dial-up router or with Internet connection-sharing software?

- What other devices might you want to include in your initial wireless network? Do you plan on listening to MP3s on your stereo? How about downloading movies from the Internet (instead of running out in the rain to the movie rental store!)? Will you be using VoIP with your network?

- How much money should you budget for your wireless network?

- What do you need to do to plan for adequate security to ensure the privacy of the information stored on the computers connected to your network?

We discuss all these issues and the entire planning process in more detail in Chapter 4.

Choosing Wireless Networking Equipment

For those of us big kids who are enamored with technology, shopping for high-tech toys can be therapeutic. Whether you're a closet geek or (cough) normal, a critical step in building a useful wireless home network is choosing the proper equipment.

Before you can decide which equipment to buy, take a look at Chapter 4 for more information about planning a wireless home network. Chapter 5 provides a more detailed discussion of the different types of wireless networking equipment. Here's a quick list of what you need:

✔ **Access point:** At the top of the list is at least one wireless *access point* (AP), also sometimes called a *base station.* An AP acts like a wireless switchboard that connects wireless devices on the network to each other and to the rest of the network. You gotta have one of these to create a wireless home network. They range from about $30 to $300, with prices continually coming down (prices predominantly are in the $40–$60 range for 802.11g and in the $100–$175 range for 802.11n). You can get APs from many leading vendors in the marketplace, including Apple (www.apple.com), D-Link (www.d-link.com), Linksys (www.linksys.com), NETGEAR (www.netgear.com), and Belkin (www.belkin.com). We give you a long list of vendors in Chapter 20, so check that out when you go to buy your AP.

For wireless home networks, the best AP value is often an AP that's bundled with other features. The most popular APs for home use also come with one or more of these features:

- **Network hub or switch:** A *hub* connects wired PCs to the network. A *switch* is a "smarter" version of a hub that speeds up network traffic. (We talk more about the differences between hubs and switches in Chapter 2.)

- **DHCP server:** A *Dynamic Host Configuration Protocol* (DHCP) server assigns network addresses to each computer on the network; these addresses are required for the computers to communicate.

- **Network router:** A *router* enables multiple computers to share a single Internet connection. The network connects each computer to the router, and the router is connected to the Internet through a broadband modem.

- **Print server:** Use a *print server* to add printers directly to the network rather than attach a printer to each computer on the network.

In Figure 1-3, you can see an AP that also bundles in a network router, switch, and DHCP server. You may increasingly see more features added that include support for VoIP routing as well. We talk about more features for your AP in Chapter 5.

✔ **Network interface adapters:** As we mention earlier in this chapter, home networks use a communication method *(protocol)* known as Ethernet. The communication that takes place between the components of your computer, however, doesn't use the Ethernet protocol. As a result, for computers on the network to communicate through the Ethernet protocol, each of the computers must translate between their internal communications protocol and Ethernet. The device that handles this translation is a *network interface adapter,* and each computer on the network needs one. Prices for network interface adapters are typically much less than $30, and most new computers come with one at no additional cost.

A network interface adapter that's installed inside a computer is usually called a *network interface card* (NIC). Virtually all computer manufacturers now include an Ethernet NIC as a standard feature with each personal computer.

✔ **Wireless network interface adapter:** To wirelessly connect a computer to the network, you must obtain a wireless network interface adapter for each computer. Prices range between $10 and $150. A few portable computers now even come with a wireless network interface built in. They're easy to install; most are adapters that just plug in.

Figure 1-3:
Look for an AP that bundles a network router, switch, and DHCP server.

The three most common types of wireless network interface adapters are

- **PC or Express Card:** This type of adapter is often used in laptop computers because most laptops have one or two PC Card slots. Figure 1-4 shows a PC Card wireless network interface adapter.

- **USB:** A *Universal Serial Bus* (USB) adapter connects to one of your computer's USB ports; these USB ports have been standard in just about every PC built since the turn of the millenium.

- **ISA or PCI adapter:** If your computer doesn't have a PC Card slot, or USB port, you have to install either a network interface card or a USB card (for a USB wireless network interface adapter) in one of the computer's internal peripheral expansion receptacles (slots). The expansion slots in older PCs are Industry Standard Architecture (ISA) slots. The internal expansion slots in newer PCs and Apple Macintosh computers follow the Peripheral Component Interconnect (PCI) standard.

Figure 1-4:
A PC Card wireless network interface adapter.

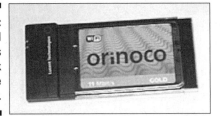

 More and more PDAs, laptops, and other devices are shipping with wireless already onboard, so you don't need an adapter of any sort. These devices just come with the wireless installed in them. We tell you how to get your wireless-enabled devices onto your wireless backbone in Part II.

Chapter 2

From a to n and b-yond

*I*n the not-so-distant past, networked computers were connected only by wire: a special-purpose network cabling. This type of wiring has yet to become a standard item in new homes, but we're getting closer, with more people asking to have a home wired from the start. That's a different book: *Smart Homes For Dummies* (also from Wiley and which we hope you consider when you're buying a new home). The cost of installing network cabling after a house is already built is understandably much higher than doing so during initial construction. By contrast, the cost of installing a wireless network in a particular home is a fraction of the cost of wiring the same residence — and much less hassle. As a result, because more and more people are beginning to see the benefits of having a computer network at home, they're turning to wireless networks. Many of us can no longer recall life without wireless phones; similarly, wireless computer networking has become the standard way to network a home.

That's not to say that it's easy, though. Face it: Life can sometimes seem a bit complicated. The average Joe or Jane can't even order a cup of java any more without having to choose between an endless array of options: regular, decaf, half-caf, mocha, cappuccino, latté, low fat, no fat, foam, no foam, and so on. Of course, after you get the hang of the lingo, you can order coffee like a pro. That's where this chapter comes in: to help you get used to the networking lingo that's slung about when you're planning, purchasing, installing, and using your wireless network.

Like so much alphabet soup, the prevalent wireless network technologies go by the names 802.11a, 802.11b, 802.11g, and now 802.11n; employ devices such as APs and Express cards; and make use of technologies with cryptic abbreviations (TCP/IP, DHCP, NAT, MIMO, WEP, and WPA). Pshew. Whether you're shopping for, installing, or configuring a wireless network, you will undoubtedly run across some or all of these not-so-familiar terms and more. This chapter is your handy guide to this smorgasbord of networking and wireless networking terminology.

If you're not the least bit interested in buzzwords, you can safely skip this chapter for now and go right to the chapters that cover planning, purchasing, installing, and using your wireless network. You can always refer to this chapter whenever you run into some wireless networking terminology that throws you. If you like knowing a little bit about the language that the locals speak before visiting a new place, read on.

Networking Buzzwords You Need to Know

A computer *network* is composed of computers or network-accessible devices — and sometimes other peripheral devices, such as printers — connected in a way that they transmit data between participants. Computer networks have been commonplace in offices for nearly 20 years, but with the advent of reasonably priced wireless networks, computer networks are becoming increasingly common in homes. Now, we mere mortals can share printers, surf the Internet, play multiplayer video games, and stream video like the corporate gods have been doing for years.

A computer network that connects devices in a particular physical location, such as in a home or in a single office site, is sometimes called a *local area network* (LAN). Conversely, the network outside your home that connects you to the Internet and beyond is called a *wide area network* (WAN).

In a nutshell, computer networks help people and devices share *information* (files and e-mail) and expensive *resources* (printers and Internet connections) more efficiently.

Workstations and servers

Each computer in your home that's attached to a network is a *workstation,* also sometimes referred to as a *client* computer. The Windows operating system (OS) refers to the computers residing together on the same local area network as a *workgroup.* A Windows-based computer network enables the workstations in a workgroup to share files and printers visible through *Network Neighborhood* (or *My Network Places*). Home networks based on the Apple Macintosh OS offer the same capability. On a Mac, just use Finder to navigate to *Network.*

Some networks also have *servers,* which are special-purpose computers or other devices that provide one or more services to other computers and devices on a network. Examples of typical servers include

- **Windows Home Server:** Microsoft and its hardware partners (companies such as HP) have created a new specification for hardware and software known as Windows Home Server. Essentially, Windows Home Server is a stripped-down version of the Windows OS that is designed to run on a small device that sits in your network and provides file and media storage for all the computers in your home (and remote access to your stuff over the Internet while you're out of the house). Windows Home Servers are a lot like the NAS devices discussed in the next bullet point, but use a special Windows OS. You can read more at www. microsoft.com/windows/products/winfamily/windowshomeserver/ default.mspx.

- **Network Attached Storage (NAS) Server:** A specialized kind of file server, an *NAS* device is basically a small, *headless* (it doesn't have a monitor or keyboard) computing appliance that uses a big hard drive and a special operating system (usually Linux) to create an easy-to-use file server for a home or office network. The Buffalo Technology LinkStation Network Storage Center (www.buffalotech.com) is a good example of an NAS device appropriate for a home network.

- **Print server:** A *print server* is a computer or other device that makes it possible for the computers on the network to share one or more printers. You don't commonly find a print server in a home network, but some wireless networking equipment comes with a print server feature built in, which turns out to be very handy.

- **E-mail server:** An *e-mail server* is a computer that provides a system for sending e-mail to users on the network. You may never see an e-mail server on a home network. Most often, home users send e-mail through a third-party service, such as America Online (AOL), EarthLink, MSN Hotmail, and Yahoo!.

- **DHCP server:** Every computer on a network, even a home network, must have its own, unique network address to communicate with the other computers on the network. A *Dynamic Host Configuration Protocol* (DHCP) server automatically assigns a network address to every computer on a network. You most often find DHCP servers in another device, such as a router or an AP.

You can find many types of client computers — network-aware devices — on your network, too. Some examples include

- **Gaming consoles:** The Microsoft Xbox 360 (www.xbox.com), Sony PlayStation 3 (www.playstation.com), and Nintendo Wii (www.nintendo. com) have adapters for network connections or multiplayer gaming and talking to other players while gaming. Cool! Read more about online gaming in Chapter 11.

- ✔ **Wireless network cameras:** The D-Link DCS-5300G (www.dlink.com/ products/?sec=1&pid=342) lets you not only view your home when you're away but also pan, tilt, scan, and zoom your way around the home. *That's* a nanny-cam.

- ✔ **Entertainment systems:** NETGEAR's EVA8000 Digital Entertainer HD enables you to use wireless technology to stream music, video, movies, photos, and Internet radio stations from your computer or file server to your home stereo system. The system uses a computer on your home network as a source, which stores your CDs in the MP3 (or other) electronic format, and attaches just like a CD or DVD player to your home entertainment system.

Most consumer manufacturers are trying to network-enable their devices, so expect to see everything from your washer and dryer to your vacuum cleaner network-enabled at some point. Why? Because after such appliances are on a network, they can be monitored for breakdowns, software upgrades, and so on without your having to manually monitor them.

Network infrastructure

Workstations must be electronically interconnected to communicate. The equipment over which the *network traffic* (electronic signals) travels between computers on the network is the *network infrastructure*.

Network hubs

In a typical office network, a strand of wiring similar to phone cable is run from each computer to a central location, such as a phone closet, where each wire is connected to a network hub. The *network hub,* similar conceptually to the hub of a wheel, receives signals transmitted by each computer on the network and sends the signals out to all other computers on the network.

Figure 2-1 illustrates a network with a star-shaped *topology* (the physical design of a network). Other network topologies include *ring* and *bus.* Home networks typically use a star topology because it's the simplest to install and troubleshoot.

Bridges

A network *bridge* provides a pathway for network traffic between networks or segments of networks. A device that connects a wireless network segment to a wired network segment is a type of network bridge. In larger networks, network bridges are sometimes used to connect networks on different floors in the same building or in different buildings. In a wireless home network, the device that manages the wireless network, the *access point,* often acts as a bridge between a wireless segment of the network and a wired segment.

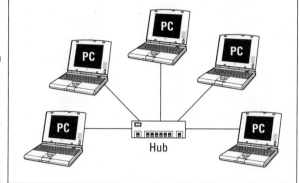

Figure 2-1:
It's all in the
stars —
a typical
network
star-shaped
topology.

Hub

Hubs and switches

Networks transmit data in bundles called *packets*. Along with the raw information being transmitted, each packet also contains the network address of the computer that sent it and the network address of the recipient computer. Network hubs send packets indiscriminately to all ports of all computers connected to the hub — which is why you don't see them much any longer.

A special type of hub called a *switched hub* examines each packet, determines the addressee and port, and forwards the packet only to the computer and port to which it is addressed. Most often, switched hubs are just called *switches*. A *switch* reads the addressee information in each packet and sends the packet directly to the segment of the network to which the addressee is connected. Packets that aren't addressed to a particular network segment are never transmitted over that segment, and the switch acts as a filter to eliminate unnecessary network traffic. Switches make more efficient use of the available transmission bandwidth than standard hubs, and therefore offer higher aggregate throughput to the devices on the switched network.

Routers

Over a large network and on the Internet, a *router* is analogous to a supereffi-cient postal service — it reads the addressee information in each data packet and communicates with other routers over the network or Internet to determine the best route for each packet to take. In the home, a *home* or *broadband router* uses a capability called *Network Address Translation* (NAT) to enable all the computers on a home network to share a single Internet address on the cable or DSL network. The home router sits between your broadband modem and all the computers and networked devices in your house, and directs traffic to and from devices both within the network and out on the Internet.

So, the local area network in your home connects to the wide area network, which takes signals out of the home and on to the Internet.

Transmission Control Protocol/Internet Protocol (TCP/IP) is the most common protocol for transmitting packets around a network. Every computer on a TCP/IP network must have its own *IP address,* which is a 32-bit numeric address that's written as four groups of numbers separated by periods (for example, 192.168.1.100). Each number of these four sets of numbers is known as an *octet,* which can have a value from 0 to 255. The Internet transmits packets by using the TCP/IP protocol. When you use the Internet, the Internet service provider (ISP) — such as AOL, EarthLink, or your cable or DSL provider — assigns a unique TCP/IP number to your computer. For the period that your computer is connected, your computer "leases" this unique address and uses it like a postal address to send and receive information over the Internet to and from other computers.

A router with the Network Address Translation (NAT) feature also helps to protect the data on your computers from intruders. The NAT feature acts as a protection because it hides the real network addresses of networked computers from computers outside the network. Many WAN routers also have additional security features that more actively prevent intruders from gaining unauthorized access to your network through the Internet. This type of protection is sometimes described generically as a *firewall.* Good firewall software usually offers a suite of tools that not only block unauthorized access but also help you to detect and monitor suspicious computer activity. In addition, these tools provide you with ways to safely permit computers on your network to access the Internet.

Internet gateways

These days, you can get a device that really does it all: a *wireless Internet gateway.* These devices combine all the features of an access point, a router, and a broadband modem (typically, cable or DSL, but this could also be a fiber-optic connection such as Verizon's FiOS or even another wireless connection). Some wireless Internet gateways even include a print server (which enables you to connect a printer directly to the gateway and use it from any networked PC), a dial-up modem, and even some Ethernet ports for computers and devices that connect to your network with wires.

For example, the Motorola Netopia MiAVo Series Gateways (www.netopia.com) include a built-in DSL modem, a router, a wireless access point, and other networking features such as a firewall and an easy-to-use graphical user interface (GUI) for configuring and setting up the gateway.

Not many of these devices are on the market; you can't buy many of them off-the-shelf, but you can get them directly from your broadband service provider.

The term *gateway* gets used a lot by different folks with different ideas about what such a device is. Although our definition is the most common (and, in our opinion, correct), you may see some vendors selling devices that they call Internet gateways that don't have all the functions we describe. For example, some access points and routers that don't have built-in broadband modems are also called gateways. We don't consider them to be Internet gateways because they link to the broadband modem. They're more of a modem gateway, but no one uses that term — it just isn't as catchy as an Internet gateway. We call them *wireless gateways* to keep everyone honest. Keep these subtle differences in mind when you're shopping.

Network interface adapters

Wireless networking is based on radio signals. Each computer, or *station,* on a wireless network has its own radio that sends and receives data over the network. As in wired networks, a station can be a *client* or a *server.* Most stations on a wireless home network are personal computers with a wireless network adapter, but increasingly non-PC devices such as phones, entertainment systems, gaming consoles, and cameras have wireless networking capabilities too.

Each workstation on the network has a network interface card or adapter that links the workstation to the network (we discuss these in Chapter 1). This is true for wireless and *wireline* (wired) networks. In many instances the wireless functionality is embedded in the device, meaning the network interface adapter is internal and preinstalled in the machine. In other instances, these internal and external adapters are either ordered with your workstation or device or you add them during the installation process. We describe these options in the following subsections.

Figure 2-2 shows an external wireless networking adapter designed for attachment to a computer's Universal Serial Bus (USB) port, and Figure 2-3 shows an internal wireless networking adapter designed for installation in a desktop computer.

Figure 2-2:
A wireless network adapter that attaches to a computer's USB port.

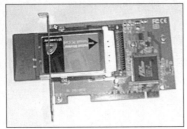

Figure 2-3:
A wireless network adapter for installation inside a desktop computer.

PC and Express Cards

When you want to add wireless networking capability to a laptop computer, your first choice for a wireless network interface should probably be a PC Card (see Figure 2-4), also called a PCMCIA (Personal Computer Memory Card International Association) Card. Nearly all Windows and some Mac laptops have PCMCIA ports that are compatible with these cards. (An AirPort card is a special type of PC Card. In Chapter 8, we tell you more about the AirPort card and how to set up a wireless Mac network.)

Figure 2-4:
A PC Card wireless network adapter.

A newer type of card called the *Express card* has been slowly taking over the role of the PC Card. The Express card (www.expresscard.org/web/site/) is a slightly smaller and more capable version of the PC Card. The Express card uses less power, takes up less space, and provides faster connections to the internal circuitry of the device in which it is installed.

All wireless PC Cards must have an antenna so that the built-in radio can communicate with an access point. Most have a built-in patch antenna enclosed in a plastic casing that protrudes from the PC while the card is fully inserted. You should always take care with this type of card because it's likely to get damaged if it's not stored properly when not in use (or if your dog knocks your laptop off the coffee table — don't ask!).

Many laptop computers use an internal Express card for wireless networking functionality. These cards don't slide into a slot on the side of the computer, but rather are installed at the factory and use an antenna built into the case of the computer.

PCI adapters

Nearly all desktop PCs have at least one Peripheral Component Interconnect (PCI) slot. This PCI slot is used to install all sorts of add-in cards, including network connectivity. Most wireless NIC manufacturers offer a wireless PCI adapter — a version of their product that can be installed in a PCI slot (see Figure 2-5).

Some wireless PCI adapters are cards that adapt a PC Card for use in a PCI slot. The newest designs, however, mount the electronics from the PC Card on a full-size PCI card with a removable dipole antenna attached to the back of the card.

USB adapters

The USB standard has, over the past several years, become the most widely used method of connecting peripherals to a personal computer. First popularized in the Apple iMac, USB supports a data transfer rate many times faster than a typical network connection, and is therefore a good candidate for connecting an external wireless network adapter to either a laptop or a desktop computer. Several wireless networking hardware vendors offer USB wireless network adapters. They're easy to connect, transport, and reposition for better reception.

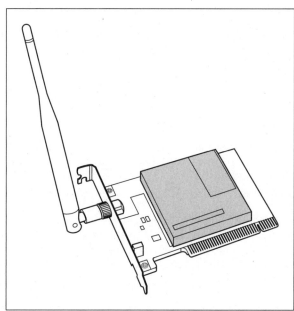

Figure 2-5:
A wireless
PCI adapter.

Most computers built in the past two or three years have at least two (and some have as many as eight) USB ports. If your computer has a USB port and you purchased a wireless USB network interface adapter, see Chapter 7 for more on setting up that adapter.

USB wireless NICs are sometimes a better choice than PC Cards or PCI cards because you can more easily move the device around to get a better signal, kinda like adjusting the rabbit ears on an old TV. If a desktop computer doesn't have a PC Card slot — most don't — but does have a USB port, you need to either install a PCI adapter or select a USB wireless network adapter.

Memory card wireless adapters

Most popular handheld personal digital assistant (PDA) computers and smartphones now come with wireless built right into them. If you still have an older PDA, you may be able to get it on your wireless network with a flash memory card wireless adapter. Many different kinds of flash memory cards are on the market (ask anyone who's shopping for a digital camera, and you'll be told more about SD, Micro SD, CF, Memory Stick, and the like than you'd ever want to hear). Most PDAs or smartphones use Compact Flash (CF) or Secure Digital (SD) cards, and you may be able to use that memory card slot to add wireless networking to your device.

Because wireless networking is being built into many of these devices, the market for memory card–style wireless adapters has shrunk, and many of the big manufacturers (such as Linksys) no longer make these products. You can still find CF or SD card wireless adapters from smaller specialty manufacturers, but they're typically a lot more expensive than the mainstream PC Card or USB adapters that you buy for a PC.

Get the (Access) Point?

Let's talk some more about the central pivot point in your wireless network: the access point. Somewhat similar in function to a network hub, an *access point* in a wireless network is a special type of wireless station that receives radio transmissions from other stations on the wireless LAN and forwards them to the rest of the network. An access point can be a stand-alone device or a computer that contains a wireless network adapter along with special access-point management software. Most home networks use a stand-alone AP, such as shown in Figure 2-6.

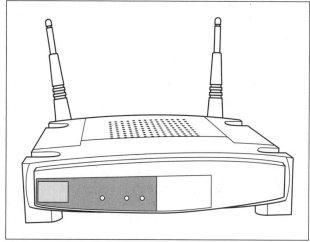

Figure 2-6:
A stand-
alone
access
point.

Because many homes and businesses use wireless networking, a method is needed to distinguish one wireless network from another. Otherwise, your neighbor may accidentally send a page to the printer on your network. (That could be fun or that could be a little scary.) Three parameters can be used to uniquely identify each segment of a wireless network:

✔ **Network name:** When you set up your wireless network, you should assign a unique name to the network. Some manufacturers refer to the network name by one of its technical monikers — *service set identifier* (SSID) or perhaps *extended service set identifier* (ESSID). This can be confusing and comes up most often if you're using equipment from different manufacturers. Rest assured, however, that network name, SSID, and ESSID all mean the same thing.

If the AP manufacturer assigns a network name at the factory, it assigns the same name to every AP it manufactures. Consequently, you should assign a different network name to avoid confusion with other APs that may be nearby (like your neighbor's). *Note:* All stations and the AP on a given wireless network must have the same network name to ensure that they can communicate.

Assigning a unique network name is good practice, but don't think of the network name as a security feature. Most APs broadcast their network name, so it's easy for a hacker to change the network name on his or her computer to match yours. Changing the network name from the factory setting to a new name just reduces the chance that you and your neighbor accidentally have wireless networks with the same network name.

✔ **Channel:** When you set up your wireless network, you have the option of selecting a radio channel. All stations and the access point must broadcast on the same radio channel to communicate. Multiple radio channels are available for use by wireless networks, and some of the newer wireless APs use multiple channels to increase the speed of the network. The number of channels available varies according to the type of wireless network you're using and the country in which you install the wireless network. Wireless stations normally scan all available channels to look for a signal from an AP. When a station detects an AP signal, the station negotiates a connection to the AP.

✔ **Encryption key:** Because it's relatively easy for a hacker to determine a wireless network's name and the channel on which it's broadcasting, every wireless network should be protected by a secret encryption key unless the network is intended for use by the general public. Only someone who knows the secret key code can connect to the wireless network.

The most popular wireless network technology, *Wi-Fi*, comes with two types of security: Wired Equivalent Privacy (WEP) and *Wi-Fi Protected Access* (WPA). WEP uses the RC4 encryption algorithm and a private key phrase or series of characters to encrypt all data transmitted over the wireless network. For this type of security to work, all stations must have the private key. Any station without this key cannot get on the network. WPA, which is now built into all new Wi-Fi equipment and is a free upgrade on most older Wi-Fi equipment, is far more secure than WEP, and we recommend that you use it. WPA uses either Temporal Key Integrity Protocol (TKIP) or Advanced Encryption System (AES) encryption, which dynamically changes the security key as the connection is used. We talk about using both types of systems in Chapter 9, with our primary emphasis on WPA, and we promise we won't test you on these acronyms at all!

In the home, you'll most likely get your access point functionality through a *wireless home router* or a *wireless Internet gateway.* These devices combine the access point with a router, a wired Ethernet network switch, and (in the case of the gateway) a broadband modem. Similar devices may even throw in a print server. This Swiss army knife–like approach is often a real bargain for use in a wireless home network. A stand-alone access point may be part of your network when you're adding a second wireless network to the mix (it would attach to one of the wired Ethernet ports on your router), or if you have some kind of fancy wired router in place (this isn't common, but some folks who work from home may have a special router supplied by their company for accessing the corporate network).

We use the term *AP* throughout this chapter to mean either a stand-alone AP or the AP built into a wireless home router or gateway.

Wireless networking devices can operate in one of two modes: infrastructure mode or ad hoc mode. The next two subsections describe the differences between these two modes.

Infrastructure mode

When a wireless station (such as a PC or a Mac) communicates with other computers or devices through an AP, the wireless station is operating in *infrastructure mode.* The station uses the network infrastructure to reach another computer or device rather than communicate directly with the other computer or device. Figure 2-7 shows a network that consists of a wireless network segment with two wireless personal computers, and a wired network segment with three computers. These five computers communicate through the AP and the network infrastructure. The wireless computers in this network are communicating in infrastructure mode.

Ad hoc mode

Whenever two wireless stations are close enough to communicate with each other, they're capable of establishing an *ad hoc network:* that is, a wireless network that doesn't use an AP. Theoretically, you could create a home network out of wireless stations without the need for an AP. It's more practical, however, to use an AP because it facilitates communication between many stations at once (as many as hundreds of stations simultaneously in a single wireless network segment). In addition, an AP can create a connection, or *bridge,* between a wireless network segment and a wired segment.

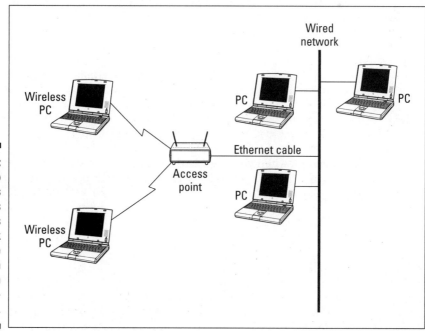

Figure 2-7:
The two wireless computers in this network communicate through the AP in infrastructure mode.

Ad hoc mode isn't often used in wireless home networks, but it could be used on occasion to connect two computers to transfer files where no AP is in the vicinity to create a wireless infrastructure.

We don't see any real advantage to using an ad hoc network in your home just to save a few bucks. You can buy a perfectly good wireless home router for under $50 (and even less when the sales are on!); the capabilities and ease-of-use you gain from this approach are well worth the minimal cost.

Your Wireless Network's Power Station: The Antenna

The main interface between your access point or network interface card and the network is the antenna. Signals generated and received by your wireless gear are dependent on a high-quality antenna interface. To be smart in wireless networking, you need to know the basics about antennas. If you know how they work, you can better optimize your network.

The newest APs, which use the 802.11n standard (discussed in the section titled "Industry Standards"), use a special technology called MIMO that uses advanced signal processing to "shape" the beam coming out of your antennas. These systems have a special antenna configuration optimized for this MIMO system; MIMO systems are not designed to be modified with different antennas.

Access point antennas vary from manufacturer to manufacturer. Many APs have a single external antenna about five inches long. This type of antenna is a *dipole* antenna. Some APs have two external dipole antennas. Dual external antenna models should provide better signal coverage throughout the house. APs with dual antennas may transmit from only one of the antennas but receive through both antennas by sampling the signal and using whichever antenna is getting the strongest signal — a *diversity antenna system*.

Typical omnidirectional dipole antennas attach to the AP with a connector that enables you to position the antenna at many different angles; however, omnidirectional dipole radio antennas send and receive best in the vertical position.

The range and coverage of a Wi-Fi wireless AP used indoors is determined by these factors:

✔ **AP transmission output power:** This is the power output of the AP's radio, usually referred to as *transmission power,* or *TX power.* Higher power output produces a longer range. Wi-Fi APs transmit at a power output of less than 30 dBm (one watt). Government agencies around the world regulate the maximum power output allowed. APs for home use generally have power outputs in the range of 13 dBm (20 mW) to 15 dBm (31.6 mW). The higher the power rating, the stronger the signal and the better range your wireless network will have. Some wireless networking equipment manufacturers offer add-on amplifiers that boost the standard signal of the AP to achieve a longer range. We talk about boosters in Chapter 18.

✔ **Antenna gain:** The AP's antenna and the antennas on the other devices on the network improve the capability of the devices to send and receive radio signals. This type of signal improvement is *gain.* Antenna specifications vary depending on vendor, type, and materials. Adding a higher-gain antenna at either end of the connection can increase the effective range.

✔ **Antenna type:** Radio antennas both send and receive signals. Different types of antennas transmit signals in different patterns or shapes. The most common type of antenna used in wireless home networks, the dipole antenna, is described as *omnidirectional* because it transmits its signal in all directions equally. In fact, the signal from a dipole antenna radiates 360° in the horizontal plane and 75° in the vertical plane, to create a doughnut-shaped pattern. Consequently, the area directly above or below the antenna gets a very weak signal.

Some types of antenna focus the signal in a particular direction and are referred to as *directional antennas.* In special applications where you want an AP to send its signal only in a specific direction, you could replace the omnidirectional antenna with a directional antenna. In a home, omnidirectional is usually the best choice, but that also depends on the shape of the home; some antennas are better for brownstones and multifloor buildings because they have a more spherical signal footprint rather than the standard flatish one.

✔ **Receive sensitivity:** The *receive sensitivity* of an AP or other wireless networking device is a measurement of how strong a signal is required from another radio before the device can make a reliable connection and receive data.

✔ **Signal attenuation:** A radio signal can get weaker as a result of interference caused by other radio signals because of objects that lie in the radio wave path between radios and because of the distance between the radios. The reduction in signal is *attenuation.* Read through Chapter 4 for a discussion of how to plan the installation of your wireless network to deal with signal attenuation.

To replace or add an antenna to an AP or other wireless device, you need to have a place to plug it in — as obvious a statement as that is, many antennas aren't detachable, and you can't add another antenna. Some access points use reverse TNC connectors that let optional antennas be used in 802.11b/g products, but there's a minor trend away from using detachable antennas in 802.11a products because of a potential conflict in the frequency channels allocated to 802.11a. This situation potentially thwarts misuse but also robs those deploying access points of their ability to choose optimal antennas.

Industry Standards

One of the most significant factors that has led to the explosive growth of personal computers and their effect on our daily lives has been the emergence of industry standards. Although many millions of personal computers are in use now around the world, only three families of operating system software run virtually all these computers: Windows, Mac OS, and Unix (including Linux). Most personal computers used in the home employ one of the Microsoft Windows or Apple Macintosh operating systems. The existence of this huge installed base of potential customers has enabled hundreds of hardware and software companies to thrive by producing products that interoperate with one or more of these industry-standard operating systems.

Computer hardware manufacturers recognize the benefits of building their products to industry standards. To encourage the adoption and growth of wireless networking, many companies that are otherwise competitors have worked together to develop a family of wireless networking industry standards that build on and interoperate with existing networking standards. As a result, reasonably priced wireless networking equipment is widely available from many manufacturers. Feel safe buying equipment from any of these manufacturers because they're all designed to work together, with one important caveat: You need to make sure your gear can all "speak" using the same version of Wi-Fi. The four major flavors of this wireless networking technology for LAN applications are IEEE 802.11a, 802.11b, 802.11g, and 802.11n — two of these, 802.11g and n are the current (and future) versions. You just have to

Understanding antenna gain

Antenna gain is usually expressed in dBi units (which indicate, in decibels, the amount of gain an antenna has). An antenna with a 4 dBi gain increases the output power (the effective isotropic radiated power, or EIRP) of the radio by 4 dBm. The FCC permits IEEE 802.11 radios to have a maximum EIRP of 36 dBm when the device is using an omnidirectional antenna.

The antennas included with wireless home networking equipment are typically omnidirectional detachable dipole antennas with gains of 2 dBi to 5 dBi. Some manufacturers offer optional high-gain antennas. (*Note:* The maximum EIRP output permitted in Japan is 100 mW; and the maximum output in Europe is only 10 mW.)

choose the flavor that best fits your needs and budget. (*Note:* There are other wireless standards, such as Bluetooth for short-range communications, for other applications in the home. We talk about these standards in Chapter 3 and elsewhere wherever their discussion is appropriate.)

The Institute for Electrical and Electronics Engineers

The *Institute for Electrical and Electronics Engineers* (IEEE) is a standards-making industry group that has for many years been developing industry standards that affect the electrical products we use in our homes and businesses. At present, the IEEE 802.11g standard is the overwhelming market leader in terms of deployed wireless networking products. Products that comply with this standard weren't the first wireless networking technology on the market — but they are now, by far, the dominant market-installed base. As you will soon see, however, the new generation of 802.11n products are entering the market and will eventually replace 802.11g.

The Wi-Fi Alliance

In 1999, several leading wireless networking companies formed the Wireless Ethernet Compatibility Alliance (WECA), a nonprofit organization (www. weca.net). This group has recently renamed itself the Wi-Fi Alliance and is now a voluntary organization of more than 200 companies that make or support wireless networking products. The primary purpose of the Wi-Fi Alliance is to certify that IEEE 802.11 products from different vendors *interoperate* (work together). These companies recognize the value of building a high level of consumer confidence in the interoperability of wireless networking products.

The Wi-Fi Alliance organization has established a test suite that defines how member products will be tested by an independent test lab. Products that pass these tests are entitled to display the Wi-Fi trademark, which is a seal of interoperability. Although no technical requirement in the IEEE specifications states that a product must pass these tests, Wi-Fi certification encourages consumer confidence that products from different vendors will work together.

The Wi-Fi interoperability tests are designed to ensure that hardware from different vendors can successfully establish a communication session with an acceptable level of functionality. The test plan includes a list of necessary features. The features themselves are defined in detail in the IEEE 802.11 standards, but the test plan specifies an expected implementation.

Understanding Wi-Fi channels

Now for a little talk about frequency bands used by the various Wi-Fi standards. In 1985, the FCC made changes to the radio spectrum regulation and assigned three bands designated as the industrial, scientific, and medical (ISM) bands. These frequency bands are

- **902 MHz–928 MHz:** A 26 MHz bandwidth

- **2.4 GHz–2.4835 GHz:** An 83.5 MHz bandwidth

- **5.15–5.35 GHz and 5.725 GHz–5.825 GHz:** A 300 MHz bandwidth

The FCC also opened some additional frequencies, known as Unlicensed National Information Infrastructure (U-NII), in the lower reaches of the five GHz frequencies.

The purpose of the FCC change was to encourage the development and use of wireless networking technology. The new regulation permits a user to operate, within certain guidelines, radio equipment that transmits a signal within each of these three ISM bands without obtaining an FCC license.

Wireless networks use radio waves to send data around the network. 802.11a uses part of the U-NII frequencies, and IEEE 802.11b and g use the ISM 2.4 GHz band. 802.11n can use either band, though not all 802.11n systems do (many use only the 2.4 GHz band).

An important concept when talking about frequencies is the idea of overlapping and nonoverlapping channels. As we discuss in Chapter 18, signals from other APs can cause interference and poor performance of your wireless network. This happens specifically when the APs' signals are transmitting on the same (or sometimes nearby) channels. Recall that the standards call for a number of channels within a specified frequency range.

The frequency range of 802.11g, for example, is between 2.4 GHz and 2.4835 GHz, and it's broken up into fourteen equal-sized channels. (Only eleven can be used in the United States — any equipment sold for use here allows you to access only these eleven channels.) The problem is that these channels are defined in such a way that many of the channels overlap with one another — and with 802.11g, there are only three nonoverlapping channels. Thus, you wouldn't want to have channels 10 and 11 operating side by side because you would get signal degradation. You want noninterfering, nonoverlapping channels. So you find that people tend to use Channels 1, 6, and 11, or something similar. 802.11a doesn't have this problem because its eight channels, in the 5 GHz frequency band, don't overlap; therefore, you can use contiguous channels. As with 802.11b and g, however, you don't want to be on the same channel.

Wi-Fi history: 802.11b and 802.11a

In 1990, the IEEE adopted the document "IEEE Standards for Local and Metropolitan Area Networks," which provides an overview of the networking technology standards used in virtually all computer networks now in prevalent use. The great majority of computer networks use one or more of the standards included in IEEE 802; the most widely adopted is IEEE 802.3, which covers Ethernet.

IEEE 802.11 is the section that defines wireless networking standards and is often called *wireless Ethernet.* The first edition of the IEEE 802.11 standard, adopted in 1997, specified two wireless networking protocols that can transmit at either 1 or 2 megabits per second (Mbps) using the 2.4 GHz radio frequency band, broken into fourteen 5 MHz channels (eleven in the United States). IEEE 802.11b-1999 is a supplement to IEEE 802.11 that added subsections to IEEE 802.11 that specify the protocol used by Wi-Fi certified wireless networking devices.

The 802.11b protocol is backward compatible with the IEEE 802.11 protocols adopted in 1997, using the same 2.4 GHz band and channels as the slower protocol. The primary improvement of the IEEE 802.11b protocol was a technique that enabled data transmission at either 5.5 Mbps or 11 Mbps.

802.11b is an *old* standard. Most vendors no longer sell 802.11b equipment (or they sell one single line of products for customers who want to replace old gear). 802.11g, which we discuss in a moment, is compatible with 802.11b, but is much faster and not a penny more expensive. It has pretty much replaced 802.11b, particularly in the home networking market.

IEEE adopted 802.11a at the same time it adopted 802.11b. 802.11a specifies a wireless protocol that operates at higher frequencies than the 802.11b protocol and uses a variety of techniques to provide data transmission rates of 6, 9, 12, 18, 24, 36, 48, and 54 Mbps. 802.11a has twelve nonoverlapping channels in the United States and Canada, but most deployed products use only eight of these channels.

Because it uses a different set of frequencies, 802.11a offers the following advantages over IEEE 802.11b:

- ✔ **Capacity:** 802.11a has about four times as many available channels, resulting in about eight times the network capacity: that is, the number of wireless stations that can be connected to the AP at one time and still be able to communicate. This isn't a significant advantage for a wireless home network because you almost certainly will never use all the network capacity available with a single access point (approximately 30 stations simultaneously).

- ✔ **Less competition:** Portable phones, Bluetooth, and residential microwave ovens use portions of the same 2.4 GHz radio frequency band used by 802.11b, which sometimes results in interference. By contrast, few devices other than IEEE 802.11a devices use the 5 GHz radio frequency band. *Note:* A growing number of cordless phones are starting to use this same frequency range, so the relative uncrowdedness of the 5 GHz spectrum isn't likely to last forever.

- ✔ **Improved throughput:** Tests show as much as four to five times the data link rate and throughput of 802.11b in a typical office environment. *Throughput* is the amount of data that can be transferred over the connection in a given period. (See the nearby sidebar, "Gauging your network's throughput.")

Like 802.11b, 802.11a has pretty much been superseded by newer technologies (802.11n is significantly faster and can also use those higher frequencies used by 802.11a). It's hard to find 802.11a wireless home routers or 802.11a network adapters on the market these days, with one exception. Some manufacturers carry *dual-band, dual-mode* networking gear that supports 802.11a *and* 802.11g in a single device — this equipment is often labeled *802.11a/b/g* because it also supports 802.11b equipment on the network. The idea behind this dual-band gear is that you can use the 802.11a frequencies for a "fast channel" for a specific purpose (such as sending audio and video from your PC to home theater) while using the 802.11g frequencies for all the normal Internet traffic in your network. 802.11n will support the same usage, with higher speeds, so many manufacturers have discontinued their a/b/g equipment. As we write in late 2007, several manufacturers (such as NETGEAR) still offer such wireless equipment.

The current standard: 802.11g

The most recent of the IEEE standards-based products to hit the street is 802.11g, which has become the standard wireless gear found in new computers and other devices. The g standard was finalized in June 2003. The appeal of 802.11g is so great that many vendors didn't wait for the final standard to be adopted before they released their first products based on this technology.

802.11g is backward compatible with 802.11b wireless networking technology, but delivers the same transmission speeds as 802.11a — up to 54 Mbps — thus effectively combining the best of both worlds.

802.11g equipment offers a nice upgrade path for people who have already invested in IEEE 802.11b equipment. When the first products were released, they carried prices that were only marginally more expensive than plain-old IEEE 802.11b, but today the prices for 802.11g equipment are considerably lower than 802.11b ever was.

Although 802.11g works great, if you're considering doing more than just share Internet connections on your wireless network, you should consider investing in the newer 802.11n technology discussed in the next section. This newer standard (well it's *almost* a standard, as we discuss) provides speeds up to five times as fast as 802.11g or 802.11a, and can support both frequency ranges (the 2.4 GHz frequency supported by 802.11g as well as the 5 GHz frequency supported by 802.11a) — opening up more channels and decreasing the possibility that your neighbor's network will interfere with yours (a potential problem in urban and even suburban areas).

The next big thing: 802.11n

The IEEE has been at work for several years defining a newer wireless networking standard, 802.11n. As we write in late 2007, 802.11n is a *draft standard,* meaning there's still work to be done before the final IEEE standard is ratified (which won't happen, by all accounts, until *2009!*). But even though 802.11n isn't a finalized standard, it is very close to the final standard, close enough that the folks who make 802.11 chips have begun mass producing 802.11n chips, and the folks who make networking gear have begun putting these chips into products that they are labeling "802.11n." Even more importantly, the Wi-Fi Alliance has begun certifying 802.11n products — meaning that you can buy equipment that has been certified to interoperate with other manufacturers' products. So you can buy an 802.11n router from company X and an 802.11n network adapter from company Y and have full confidence that they'll work together. Figure 2-8 shows the Wi-Fi Alliance certification logo you'll find on 802.11n draft-compliant gear (in this case, this gear is also compliant with 802.11b, a, and g).

Figure 2-8:
Look for this logo on the box of your new 802.11n gear.

Keep these few things in mind about 802.11n:

- **Speed:** The theoretical maximum speed of 802.11n is 248 Mbps — five times faster than 802.11g. Real-world speeds have been measured in test centers at about 100 Mbps (five times faster than 802.11g). With 802.11n, wireless can be a real alternative to wired networks, even for high-performance applications such as sending video around the home.

- **Distance:** 802.11n uses a special technology called *MIMO* (multiple inputs, multiple outputs) that modifies how signals are sent and received across your system's antennas. A MIMO system can send and receive data across more than one antenna at a time, and can use special signal processing to actually *beam form* the signal to extend its range and power in a certain direction. Although no one wants to quantify it exactly (or, to be more exact, everyone has a different figure), you can expect MIMO to extend the range of your wireless network by a factor of 2 or more.

Gauging your network's throughput

Wi-Fi standards call for different speeds, up to 11 Mbps for 802.11b and up to 54 Mbps for 802.11a and g — newer devices try to communicate at up to 110 Mbps. Radios attempt to communicate at the highest speed. If they encounter too many errors (dropped bits), the radio steps down to the next fastest speed and repeats the process until a strong connection is achieved. So, although we talk about 802.11g, for example, being 54–110 Mbps in speed, the reality is that unless you're very close to the AP, you're not likely to get that maximum rate. Signal fade and interference cut into your speeds, and the negotiated rate between the two devices drops.

That discussion represents just the speed. The actual throughput is another, related, matter. *Throughput* represents the rate at which the validated data flows from one point to another. It may take some retransmissions for that to occur, so your throughput is less than the negotiated speed of the connection. It may not be unusual for you to get only 40 to 50 percent of your maximum connection speed. In fact, that's rather normal.

✔ **Channels:** 802.11n gear can use either the 2.4 or the 5 GHz channels, providing it with a considerably larger number of channels to choose from when looking for the best connection between stations on your wireless network (something 802.11n gear does automatically). The highest speeds of 802.11n also use something called *channel bonding,* where more than one channel is used at the same time, to increase the amount of data sent across the network.

As a cost-saving measure, some 802.11n gear uses *only* 2.4 GHz frequencies. This equipment won't be able to use those relatively wide open 5 GHz channels but can still use the channel bonding feature for faster connections. Note that 802.11n gear that uses only the 2.4 GHz frequencies is *not* backward compatible with 802.11a (see the next bullet for more on this).

✔ **Backward compatibility:** 802.11n gear is backward compatible with any 802.11b or 802.11g gear, so your older network adapters will still work on a new 802.11n network. If your 802.11n router or access point works on the 5 GHz frequency range, it will also be backward compatible with 802.11a gear.

Adding 802.11a/b/g gear to an 802.11n network will *slow down* the whole network to a degree, but your network will still be faster than an 802.11a, b, or g network.

✔ **Cost:** Because it's a new technology, 802.11n equipment is about two to three times more expensive than 802.11g equipment. For example, the most popular 802.11n router on the market (Apple's AirPort Extreme with Gigabit Ethernet) is about $175, while the average 802.11g router costs $50 to $75. The least expensive 802.11n gear available as we write is about $100 for a router. You can expect these prices to drop rapidly as 802.11n becomes more mainstream, but 802.11n will still have a price premium for the next year or so.

As you shop for new wireless networking equipment, you'll have to make a decision between 802.11g and 802.11n. In general, we recommend that you strongly consider the 802.11n gear (the speed improvements are well worth the additional expense, in our minds), but also keep in mind that 802.11n *is* a *draft* standard. It's unlikely, but not impossible, that some changes in the final standard will make equipment you buy today not entirely compliant with the final standard in 2009. If you can find a manufacturer who guarantees that your equipment will be final-standard compliant (by means of a *firmware upgrade,* for example), that (in the words of Martha Stewart) is a good thing.

Regardless of the choice you make between 802.11g and n for your wireless *infrastructure* (routers and access points), we highly recommend that you select the 802.11n option when you're buying new computers (particularly laptops). There's not a big price difference here, and changing the internal networking cards on many computers (especially many laptops) isn't always a walk in the park — if you can get 802.11n put inside at the factory, so much the better.

Chapter 3

Bluetooth and Other Wireless Networks

In This Chapter

▶ Finding out about Bluetooth

▶ Understanding the difference between Bluetooth and Wi-Fi

▶ Integrating Bluetooth into your home network

▶ Extending your wireless home network with "no new wires" networking products

▶ Using your phone and powerlines to extend your network

▶ Wirelessly controlling your home

*G*etting the most from computer technology is all about selecting the best and most dominant technology standards. The most dominant technology for wireless home networks is clearly the 802.11 (Wi-Fi) family of technologies defined by the 802.11a, 802.11b, 802.11g, and 802.11n standards (which we describe in Chapter 2). Wi-Fi is, simply, the reason why you're reading this book. It's the technology that has made wireless networks such a huge hit.

But, Wi-Fi isn't the only game in town. You run into other home networking standards when you buy and install your Wi-Fi gear — standards that make it easier to get Wi-Fi where you want it.

Another popular wireless technology is Bluetooth (a short-range wireless networking system that's built into many cellular phones). Even if you intend to purchase and use only Wi-Fi wireless networking equipment, you should still be aware of Bluetooth. Who knows? It may come in handy.

We also talk about a few other key wired home networking standards (oops, did we say a dreaded word: *wired?*) such as HomePlug, the standard for networking over your electrical power cables in your home. As surprising as it may seem, you can actually connect your computers, access points, and other devices over these in-wall cables. What's more, many APs come with these interfaces onboard to make it easier for you to install that AP wherever you want it. Isn't that nice? You betcha.

Finally, we talk about a few wireless networking standards that are designed not for *data* networking in the home, but rather for *control networks*. These standards, lead by ZigBee and Z-Wave, send signals around your home that let you automate and remotely control devices in the home. For example, you could use a ZigBee or Z-Wave system to turn on lights in remote locations, raise or lower drapes, or adjust your central heat or air conditioning. These are things that adventurous homeowners have been able to do for a long time by using wired solutions or unreliable powerline solutions such as X10; with these new wireless systems, anyone can get into home control and automation without a big wiring job and without the headaches of dealing with the AC powerlines.

Who or What Is Bluetooth?

One of the most often talked about wireless standards, besides Wi-Fi, is *Bluetooth*. The Bluetooth wireless technology, named for the tenth-century Danish King Harald Blatand "Bluetooth," was invented by the L. M. Ericsson company of Sweden in 1994. King Harald helped unite his part of the world during a conflict around A.D. 960. Ericsson intended for Bluetooth technology to unite the mobile world. In 1998, Ericsson, IBM, Intel, Nokia, and Toshiba founded Bluetooth Special Interest Group (SIG), Inc., to develop an open specification for always-on, short-range wireless connectivity based on the Ericsson Bluetooth technology. Its specification was publicly released on July 26, 1999. The Bluetooth SIG now includes 3Com, Agere, Ericsson, IBM, Intel, Microsoft, Motorola, Nokia, Toshiba, and nearly 2,000 other companies. Thousands of Bluetooth-enabled products are already on the market, with many more on the way, and over *800 million* Bluetooth-enabled devices have been shipped worldwide (that's a not-so-insignificant number!).

Sometimes a network of devices communicating via Bluetooth is described as a *personal area network* (PAN) to distinguish it from a network of computers often called a local area network (LAN).

The most common use of Bluetooth these days is in the world of mobile phones (and the geeky or cool — we'll leave the distinction up to you — Bluetooth hands-free headsets hanging off millions of ears out there). But there's more to Bluetooth than just phones. The following is a small sampling of existing Bluetooth products:

- ✔ Microsoft Wireless IntelliMouse Explorer for Bluetooth (a wireless mouse)
- ✔ Apple wireless keyboard and mouse
- ✔ IOGEAR Bluetooth wireless stereo headphone kit
- ✔ HP Deskjet 460 printer
- ✔ Motorola V3 RAZR mobile phone

- Motorola Bluetooth hands-free car kit
- Jabra BT800 Bluetooth headset
- Belkin Bluetooth Universal Serial Bus (USB) adapter

Although intended as a wireless replacement for cables, Bluetooth is being applied to make it possible for a wide range of devices to communicate with each other wirelessly with minimal user intervention. The technology is designed to be low-cost and low-power to appeal to a broad audience and to conserve a device's battery life.

Wi-Fi versus Bluetooth

Wi-Fi and Bluetooth are designed to coexist in the network, and although they certainly have overlapping applications, each has its distinct zones of advantage.

The biggest differences between Wi-Fi and Bluetooth are

- **Distance:** Bluetooth is lower powered, which means that its signal can go only short distances (up to 10 meters, or a bit more than 30 feet). 802.11 technologies can cover your home, and in some cases more, depending on the antenna you use. Some Bluetooth devices operate under a high-powered scheme (called Class 1 Bluetooth devices), which can reach up to 100 meters. Most home Bluetooth devices don't have this kind of range, mainly because they're designed to be battery powered, and the shorter *Class 2* range of 10 meters provides a better trade-off between battery life and range.

- **Speed:** The latest versions of Wi-Fi can carry data at rates in the *hundreds* of megabits per second; the fastest existing Bluetooth implementations have a maximum data rate of 3 Mbps. So think of Wi-Fi as a networking technology that can handle high-speed transfers of the biggest files, and Bluetooth as something designed for lower speed connections (such as carrying voice or audio signals) or for the transfer or synchronization of smaller chunks of data (such as transferring pictures from a camera phone to a PC).

- **Application:** Bluetooth is designed as a replacement for cables: that is, to get rid of that huge tangle of cables that link your mouse, printer, monitor, scanner, and other devices on your desk and around your home. In fact, the first Bluetooth device was a Bluetooth headset, which eliminated that annoying cable to the telephone that got in the way of typing. Many new cars are also outfitted with Bluetooth so that you can use your cell phone in your car, with your car's stereo speakers and an onboard microphone serving as your hands-free capability. Pretty neat, huh?

Wi-Fi (802.11a/b/g/n) and Bluetooth are similar in certain respects: They both enable wireless communication between electronic devices, but they are more complementary than direct competitors. Wi-Fi technology is most often used to create a wireless network of personal computers that can be located anywhere in a home or business. Bluetooth devices usually communicate with other Bluetooth devices in relatively close proximity.

The easiest way to distinguish Wi-Fi from Bluetooth is to focus on what each one replaces:

- **Wi-Fi is wireless Ethernet:** Wi-Fi is a wireless version of the Ethernet communication protocol and is intended to replace networking cable that would otherwise be run through walls and ceilings to connect computers in multiple rooms or even on multiple floors of a building.

- **Bluetooth replaces peripheral cables:** Bluetooth wireless technology operates at short distances — usually about 10 meters — and most often replaces cables that connect peripheral devices such as a printer, keyboard, mouse, or personal digital assistant (PDA) to your computer.

- **Bluetooth replaces IrDA:** Bluetooth can also be used to replace another wireless technology — Infrared Data Association (IrDA) wireless technology — that's already found in most laptop computers, PDAs, and even many printers. Although IR signals are secure and aren't bothered with radio frequency (RF) interference, IrDA's usefulness is hindered by infrared's requirement for line-of-sight proximity of devices. Just like the way your TV's remote control must be pointed directly at your TV to work, the infrared ports on two PDAs must be lined up to trade data, and your laptop has to be "pointing" at the printer to print over the infrared connection. Because Bluetooth uses radio waves rather than light waves, line-of-sight proximity isn't required.

Like Wi-Fi, Bluetooth can offer wireless access to LANs, including Internet access. Bluetooth devices can potentially access the Public Switched Telephone Network (PSTN: you know, the phone system) and mobile telephone networks. Bluetooth is able to thrive alongside Wi-Fi by making possible such innovative solutions as a hands-free mobile phone headset, print-to-fax, and automatic PDA, laptop, and cell phone/address book synchronization.

Piconets, Masters, and Slaves

Communication between Bluetooth devices is similar in concept to the ad hoc mode of Wi-Fi wireless networks (which we describe in Chapter 2). A Bluetooth device automatically and spontaneously forms informal WPANs, called *piconets*, with one to seven other Bluetooth devices that have the same Bluetooth profile. (A Bluetooth profile is simply a specific Bluetooth application — like a headset profile for attaching a wireless headset to a phone, or an audio profile for playing music over a wireless Bluetooth connection.) Piconets get their name from merging the prefix *pico* (probably from the Italian word *piccolo* [small]) and *net*work. A capability called *unconscious connectivity* enables these devices to connect and disconnect almost without any user intervention.

A particular Bluetooth device can be a member of any number of piconets at any moment in time (see Figure 3-1). Each piconet has one *master,* the device that first initiates the connection. Other participants in a piconet are *slaves.*

The three types of Bluetooth connections are

- ✔ **Data only:** When communicating data, a master can manage connections with as many as seven slaves.

- ✔ **Voice only:** When the Bluetooth piconet is used for voice communication (for example, a wireless phone connection), the master can handle no more than three slaves.

- ✔ **Data and voice:** A piconet transmitting both data and voice can exist between only two Bluetooth devices at a time.

Each Bluetooth device can join more than one piconet at a time. A group of more than one piconet with one or more devices in common is a *scatternet.* Figure 3-2 depicts a scatternet made up of several piconets.

The amount of information sent in each packet over a Bluetooth connection, and the type of error correction that is used, determine the data rate a connection can deliver. Bluetooth devices can send data over a piconet by using 16 types of packets. Sending more information in each packet (that is, sending longer packets) causes a faster data rate. Conversely, more robust error correction causes a slower data rate. Any application that uses a Bluetooth connection determines the type of packet used and, therefore, the data rate.

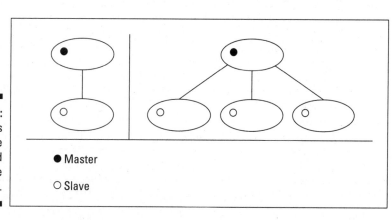

Figure 3-1:
Piconets
have one
master and
at least one
slave.

● Master

○ Slave

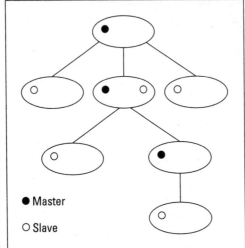

● Master

○ Slave

Figure 3-2:
A Bluetooth
scatternet
is composed
of several
piconets.

As mentioned, Bluetooth isn't nearly as fast as Wi-Fi — many Bluetooth devices reach a maximum data rate of 723 Kbps (compare that to 248 Mbps for 802.11n), but that's not usually important because Bluetooth is typically not used for transferring huge files and the like. The newest version of Bluetooth (Bluetooth 2.1) includes something called *EDR* (Enhanced Data Rate) that allows data transfers at speeds of up to 2.1 Mbps. (The raw speed is 3 Mbps; 2.1 is the actual data throughput rate.)

To maintain the security of the data you send over a Bluetooth link, the Bluetooth standard includes several layers of security. First, the two Bluetooth devices that are connecting use *authentication* to identify each other. After the authentication process (sometimes called *pairing* in the Bluetooth world), the devices can begin sharing information. The data being sent across the radio link is *encrypted* (scrambled) so that only other authenticated devices have the key that can *decrypt* (unscramble) the data.

Both Wi-Fi (the 802.11b, g, and n versions) and Bluetooth use the 2.4 GHz frequency radio band, but note the significant differences in how these technologies use the band. Bluetooth radios transmit a signal strength that complies with transmission regulations in most countries and is designed to connect at distances from 10 centimeters to 10 meters through walls and other obstacles — although like any radio wave, Bluetooth transmissions c an be weakened by certain kinds of construction material, such as steel or heavy concrete. Although Bluetooth devices can employ a transmission power that produces a range in excess of 100 meters, you can assume that most Bluetooth devices are designed for use within 10 meters of other compatible devices, which is fine for the applications for which Bluetooth is intended, such as replacing short-run cables.

To make full use of the 2.4 GHz frequency radio band and to reduce the likelihood of interference, Bluetooth uses a transmission protocol that hops 1,600 times per second between 79 discrete 1 MHz-wide channels from 2.402 GHz to 2.484 GHz. Each piconet establishes its own random hopping pattern so that you can have many piconets in the same vicinity without mutual interference. If interference does occur, each piconet switches to a different channel and tries again. Even though Wi-Fi (802.11b, g, and n) and Bluetooth both use the 2.4 GHz band, both protocols use hopping schemes that should result in little, if any, mutual interference.

Understanding Bluetooth versions

Bluetooth has been around for a few years now and, like most technologies, has undergone some growing pains and revisions. In fact, multiple versions of Bluetooth-certified equipment are available, as newer and more capable variants of Bluetooth arrive on the market.

The most common variant of Bluetooth is known as Bluetooth 1.2. This is basically a version of Bluetooth with all the bugs removed. Bluetooth 1.2 devices (most currently available devices, in other words) are *backward compatible* with earlier Bluetooth 1.0 and 1.1 devices. So, they work the same way, at the same speeds — just better. (Some technical advances in 1.2 allow most devices to have better real-world speeds.)

A growing number of Bluetooth devices support the *Bluetooth 2.0 + EDR* (extended data rate) standard. You can think of Bluetooth 2.0 + EDR versus the 1.x variants as being similar to 802.11g versus 802.11b. It is faster (with a maximum speed three times as high — 2.1 Mbps versus around 700 Kbps for the EDR, or enhanced data rate), is better at resisting interference, and just basically works better all around. If you're shopping for something that may be sending larger files or requiring faster data transfers, such as a Bluetooth-equipped laptop (or a Bluetooth-enabled smartphone that can be used as a modem for your laptop), consider insisting on Bluetooth 2.0 and EDR.

In mid-2007, Bluetooth 2.1 was released. This version of Bluetooth isn't any faster than 2.0 + EDR, but it includes some performance and battery life improvements. The biggest change in Bluetooth 2.1 (there are only a handful of 2.1 devices on the market as we write) is the support for something called *NFC* (Near Field Communications). With NFC, a special low-power radio system lets two devices in very close proximity (a few centimeters) "talk" to each other — two Bluetooth systems with NFC could be *paired* (we talk about pairing in Chapter 15) by simply holding them very close to each other. This NFC pairing (when it hits the market) will make using Bluetooth even easier by significantly reducing the steps needed to get two devices connected.

Coming down the pike is the Bluetooth 3.0 standard — and the Bluetooth folks have adopted a new technology called UWB (see the sidebar "Ultracool ultra wideband (UWB) is coming" for more on this technology) to make Bluetooth even faster in the future. Additionally, Bluetooth will also incorporate a technology from Nokia called *Wibree,* which allows ultra-low-power implementations of Bluetooth for devices with limited battery or power supplies.

Integrating Bluetooth into Your Wireless Network

Products that are the first to take advantage of Bluetooth technology include the following:

- ✔ Mobile phones
- ✔ Cordless phones
- ✔ PDAs
- ✔ Bluetooth adapters for PCs
- ✔ Bluetooth hands-free car kits
- ✔ Videocameras
- ✔ Videogaming consoles and controllers (the Nintendo Wii, for example)
- ✔ Digital still cameras
- ✔ Data projectors
- ✔ Scanners
- ✔ Printers

You can get a great idea of all the various ways that Bluetooth can be used in your network by going to the official Bluetooth products Web site at www. bluetooth.com/products/, which lists over *2,700* products. We also go into great detail in Chapter 15 about some of the more common ways you use Bluetooth.

One of the more interesting and most widely used applications of Bluetooth technology is for cell phones. Bring your Bluetooth-enabled phone home, dock it in a power station near your PC, and it instantly logs on to your wireless home network via a Bluetooth connection to a nearby PC or Bluetooth access point. Phones that function as PDAs can update their address books and sync data from the PC. All your events, to-do lists, grocery lists, and birthday reminders can be kept current just by bringing your Bluetooth-enabled product in range. You can even get Bluetooth headsets for your Bluetooth phones — getting rid of that wireless headset hassle.

Bluetooth technology is advancing into the arena of autos, too. In response to interest by the automotive industry, the Bluetooth SIG formed the Car Profile Working Group in December 1999. This working group has defined how Bluetooth wireless technology will enable hands-free use of mobile phones in automobiles. Car manufacturers have begun to embrace Bluetooth in a big way over the past few years. Acura was perhaps the first car maker to offer Bluetooth (at least in the U.S. market) with the Acura TL. Using the Bluetooth in this car, you can "pair" your mobile phone and then use the steering wheel controls, navigation system screen and controller, and the car's audio system to control and make phone calls. Very cool. Other manufacturers such as BMW, MINI, Ford, Mercedes Benz, Toyota, and Lexus have followed suit — those that haven't will soon, you can be sure. We talk about this topic more in Chapter 15.

The current versions of Microsoft Windows Mobile, Windows XP (Service Pack 2), and Windows Vista offer built-in support for Bluetooth devices. All versions of Mac OS (from 10.2 Jaguar on) also have integrated support for Bluetooth.

Bluetoothing your phones

As we write in late 2007, 75 percent of all new mobile phones ship with built-in Bluetooth capabilities. That's a lot of phones — and a lot of Bluetooth chips. The most common use of Bluetooth in phones is providing hands-free operation, either using a Bluetooth headset or a hands-free Bluetooth system inside a car. Hands-free operation of mobile phones can be handy (pun intended) whenever you're talking on your phone, but when you're in a car it can be not only convenient but legally mandated. A number of cities and states in the U.S. (and beyond) ban cell phone use in a car unless a hands-free system is in place.

If your car doesn't have built-in Bluetooth capabilities and you just can't imagine seeing yourself in the rear-view mirror with a Bluetooth headset jutting off your ear, you can install a hands-free kit in most cars without too much work. An even easier option is to consider a GPS navigation system; many aftermarket GPS systems now include Bluetooth and can use the speaker built into the GPS or connect to your car's stereo system for hands-free calling.

There's more to Bluetooth and your phone than just hands-free operation. Bluetooth can also be used to synchronize your phone with your PC or Mac. Most smartphones and many regular mobile phones (those in the industry call these feature phones) can use their Bluetooth connections to synchronize your phone book, calendar, photos, music, and more with a Bluetooth PC — no cables required. All you need is a Bluetooth adapter, like the one shown in Figure 3-3, for your PC (if it doesn't have Bluetooth built in already), some software from your phone manufacturer, and a few minutes of configuration (we talk about this in Chapter 15).

A final use of Bluetooth and mobile phones comes into play when your mobile phone includes a fast data plan (usually called *3G* networking, such as EV-DO, EDGE, or HSDPA, discussed in Chapter 16). Most of these services can be used on your laptop computer when it is *tethered* to your mobile phone using

Bluetooth. The specifics on how this works vary from phone to phone and from mobile phone carrier to carrier, so we can't tell you exactly how to set this up for your particular situation, but your mobile phone carrier will provide instructions.

Many mobile phone providers charge an extra monthly fee (on top of your probably already high mobile data service fee) for this use. Check your carrier's Web page for details before you do this.

Figure 3-3:
Use a USB adapter to add Bluetooth capability to a desktop or laptop PC.

Wireless printing and data transfer

Hewlett-Packard and other companies manufacture printers that have built-in Bluetooth wireless capability, which enables a computer that also has Bluetooth wireless capability to print sans printer cables. Bluetooth is used in other PC applications, such as wireless keyboards and wireless computer mice.

Another great use of Bluetooth wireless technology is to wirelessly transfer your digital photographs from your Bluetooth-enabled digital camera to your Bluetooth-enabled PC or Bluetooth-enabled printer — or even directly to your Bluetooth-enabled PDA. The newest wave of smartphones from several manufacturers includes wireless-enhanced models that include both Bluetooth and Wi-Fi built in. Wouldn't it be cool to carry your family photo album around on your Treo or iPhone to show off at the office?

Extending Your Wireless Home Network with "No New Wires" Solutions

Wireless networking is great — so great that we wrote a book about it. But in many instances, wireless is just one way to do what you want; and often,

---

Ultracool ultra wideband (UWB) is coming

With all the innovation happening in the Wi-Fi and Bluetooth areas, more neat stuff is on its way. *Ultra wideband* (UWB) is a revolutionary wireless technology for transmitting digital data over a wide spectrum of frequency bands with very low power. It can transmit data at very high rates (for wireless LAN applications in the home). Within the power limit allowed under current FCC regulations, ultra wideband also has the ability to carry signals through doors and other obstacles that tend to reflect signals at more limited bandwidths and higher power. At higher power levels, UWB signals can travel to significantly greater ranges.

Ultra wideband radio broadcasts digital pulses (rather than traditional sine waves) that simultaneously transmit a signal across a very wide spectrum. The transmitter and receiver are coordinated to send and receive pulses with an accuracy of trillionths of a second! Not only does UWB enable high data rates, but it also does so without suffering the effects of multipath interference. (*Multipath* is the propagation phenomenon that results in signals reaching the receiving antenna by two or more paths, usually because of reflections of the transmitted signal off walls or mirrors or the like.) Because UWB has the ability to *time-gate* (that is, prescribe the precise time when it's supposed to receive the data), the receiver allows it to ignore signals arriving outside a prescribed time interval, such as signals caused by multipath reflections.

UWB is still in the early stages, but it's coming on strong. UWB is simpler, cheaper, less power-hungry, and 100 times faster than Bluetooth. What more could you want? UWB communication devices could be used to wirelessly distribute services such as phone, cable, and computer networking throughout a building or home.

Many companies and groups of companies have been promoting UWB for a variety of uses. One of them, the WiMedia Alliance, made (another!) alliance with the Bluetooth SIG to develop a new 3.0 version of Bluetooth that will eventually allow speeds of up to 480 Mbps for Bluetooth devices.

You may be thinking, well won't that make Wi-Fi obsolete? Well it will be as fast as or faster than Wi-Fi, but it will still be a relatively short-range technology — this high-speed version of Bluetooth won't cover your entire home like Wi-Fi will, so it will still be best suited for cable replacement rather than whole-home networking.

---

wireless solutions need a hand from *wireline* (that is, wired) solutions to give you a solid, reliable connection into your home network.

A common application of wireline and wireless networking is a remote access point that you want to link back into your home network. Suppose that your cable modem is in your office in the basement, and that's where you have your main wireless router or access point. Now suppose that you want wireless access to your PC for your TV, stereo, and laptop surfing in the master bedroom on the third floor. Chances are that your AP's signal isn't strong enough for that application up there. How do you link one AP to the other?

You could install a wired Ethernet solution, which would entail running new CAT-5e/6 cables through your walls up to your bedroom. It's pretty messy if you ask us, but this approach certainly provides as much as 1,000 Mbps if you need it.

If you *can* run CAT-5e/6 cable and create an Ethernet network in your walls, you should, so by all means *do so!* But most folks can't do this, so these other solutions are the way to go.

A more practical way to get your cable modem up to the third floor is to run a *powerline* link between the two points. Think of this as one long extension cord between your router or AP in the basement and your AP in your bedroom. Although not all of these powerline technology links can carry data as fast as an 802.11n Wi-Fi connection, they will likely exceed the speed of your Internet connection. If that's your primary goal, these are great, clean, and easy options for you.

The powerline networking concept takes a little getting used to. Most of us are used to plugging an AC adapter or electrical cable into the wall and then another Ethernet cable into some other networking outlet for the power and data connections. With powerline networking, those two cables are reduced to one — the power cable! That electrical cord *is* your LAN connection — along with all the rest of the electrical cabling in your house. Cool, huh? To connect to your computer, you run an Ethernet cable from the powerline networking device (router, AP, and so on) to your computer, hub, or switch.

Networking on powerlines is no easy task. Powerlines are noisy, electrically speaking, with surges in voltage level and electrical interferences introduced by all sorts of devices both inside and outside the home. The state of the electrical network in a home is constantly changing, as well, when devices are plugged in and turned on. Because of this, powerline networking systems adopt a sophisticated and adaptive *signal processing algorithm,* which is a technique used to convert data into electrical signals on the power wiring.

When it comes to powerline networking, you have the following options:

- ✓ **HomePlug Networking:** This is the granddaddy of powerline networks, having been on the market for about ten years. Most equipment available today, such as NETGEAR's WGX102 Wireless Range Extender (www.netgear.com), uses the original HomePlug standard (HomePlug 1.0), which offers speeds of 14 Mbps. (The WGX102 actually uses a proprietary version of HomePlug that is faster.) The HomePlug folks have developed a newer version, called HomePlug A/V, which will, when it hits the market, support speeds of over 200 Mbps.

- ✓ **DS2 Powerline Networking:** A Spanish company called DS2 (www.ds2.es) has created their own powerline networking system that supports speeds of up to 200 Mbps over home powerlines. This system is mainly used in equipment provided to customers by phone companies in Europe, but in North America, D-Link (www.dlink.com) offers a set of powerline Ethernet adapters that are built around DS2's chips. Unlike the NETGEAR system, mentioned in the preceding paragraph, which has an 802.11g AP built into the adapter, the D-Link system simply extends your Ethernet network to the remote location. You'll need to add an additional access point to make this a wireless solution.

The most common application for powerline networking is as an Ethernet bridge. These devices look and act much like the external USB Wi-Fi NICs that we discuss in Chapter 2. You need two of them: one to connect to an Ethernet port on your router (or any LAN jack in your home) and another to plug into the wall outlet wherever you need LAN access.

The bridge typically has a power cord on one side of the box and an Ethernet or USB connector on the other. Plug the power cord into any wall outlet and plug the Ethernet or USB into the computer or other networked devices, and you have a connection. Figure 3-4 shows a typical use of HomePlug bridges.

Some manufacturers, such as NETGEAR, offer powerline networking adapters with a built-in Wi-Fi access point. Plug one of these into your wall, along with a stand-alone powerline Ethernet bridge back at your main router location, and you have an instant remote AP!

Using your TV cables to extend your Wi-Fi network

An interesting approach to expanding your 802.11b or g wireless network's reach has recently been launched by AuraOne Systems. The AuraGrid Wireless Extension system (which costs $89 for a four-room kit) uses your home's coaxial cable wiring — the wires used to connect your TVs to the cable TV network — as an antenna extension system that brings your wireless network signal to all the nooks and crannies in your home.

To use the system, you simply need to install the AuraGrid duplexer in your garage (or wherever your cable TV lines enter the house), and then simply connect antenna devices to each outlet where you want to improve your wireless signal. Finally, connect the antenna port on your access point to an AuraGrid splitter. That's it! If you can hook up your DVD and TV, you can handle this process. The AuraGrid works only with cable TV systems and interferes with a satellite TV signal, so if you have DirecTV or DISH Network, you can't use those wires for this purpose.

It's important to note that the AuraGrid system won't work with 802.11n systems, but for most folks that's not an issue, simply because 802.11n's greater range makes the system unnecessary.

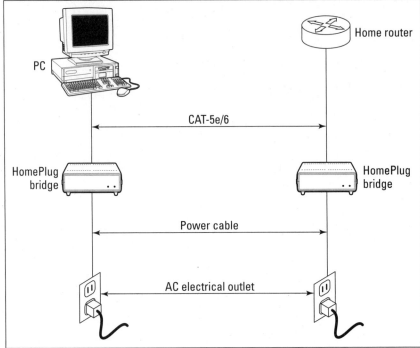

PC

Home router

CAT-5e/6

HomePlug
bridge

HomePlug
bridge

Power cable

Figure 3-4:
Plug your
computer
into the
wall — and
that's all.

AC electrical outlet

Controlling Your Home without Wires

Throughout this book, we talk about using wireless networks to send *data* around your home. This data could be what you traditionally think of as data (Web pages, e-mail, Word documents, and so on), or it could be different kinds of data (such as music MP3 files, digital photos, or video), but in the end it's all about getting one hunk of bits and bytes from one place in your home to another. The bits and the bytes — the *payload* of your networked communications — are the key here.

A completely different kind of wireless networking is control networking. In a *control network,* you aren't setting out to move data around the house; instead you are using a wireless network to send *commands* to devices in your home. In this instance you aren't sharing a data file with someone (or some device in your home) so much as telling it what to do (you bossy person you!).

Home control has been around a long time (we've been writing about it for over a decade, and it existed for decades before that), but traditional home control systems used complicated (and expensive) proprietary wiring systems or an old powerline networking system called X10.

Using other existing wires

Besides powerlines, your home will probably also have a number of phone lines and coaxial (cable TV) cables running through your walls. These wires can also potentially be used to extend the reach of your wireless network without installing new Ethernet cables in your home. We say *potentially* because although these wires definitely *can* do this job, no companies are currently shipping products to consumers that would let you use the wires this way.

In the past, a system called *HomePNA* (for Home Phoneline Networking Alliance) was widely available and did much the same thing that HomePlug and other powerline networking systems did, only leveraging the phone lines in your walls. Since the last edition of this book, HomePNA networking solutions have become unavailable in the consumer marketplace. That's too bad, because the technology has been greatly improved and works well. The companies behind the technology have, however, focused on the phone company market, rather than the consumer home networking market. HomePNA gear is found in many of the TV set-top boxes provided where phone companies offer television services — the technology is used to carry TV programming from a master set-top box to satellite set-top boxes throughout the home.

A similar technology, called *MoCA* (Multimedia over Coax) is used to carry TV programming and other data over the coaxial cables used for cable and satellite TV distribution. Again, like the current version of HomePNA, MoCA is a telephone (or cable) company technology — it's installed inside set-top boxes and not sold in the form of consumer equipment that can be purchased at the local Best Buy.

We think that this will change over time, and we hope that it does because phone lines and coaxial cables are better suited for carrying data than are powerlines. Keep your eyes peeled on these group's Web sites (www.homepna.org and www.mocalliance.org) to see when consumer products become available.

The big news in home control, however, is the introduction of wireless networking into the mix. Wireless home control networks are designed around extremely low-power and low-cost chips that can (eventually) be built right into all sorts of appliances and electrical devices in the home.

Home control networks are *low-speed* networks. Because home control networks don't need to be concerned with carrying a big fat stream of high-definition data or the 80 megabyte Windows update du jour, they can get away with relatively puny data rates in the name of cost savings (it doesn't take a lot of bandwidth to say "dim the lights in the hall").

In another effort to trim expenses, home control networks are short range (the chips can be smaller and cheaper if they don't transmit as much power as, for example, an 802.11n chip). This may seem a bit counterintuitive — after all, home control systems won't work well if you can't reach the devices in your home that you want to control — but these networks overcome the issue of short range by using a *mesh topology*. Mesh means that each radio in the system can talk to every other radio, and in doing so they can retransmit the commands you send throughout the home. The most common metaphor here is the frog in the lily pond — the frog can't jump all the way across the pond in one fell swoop, but he can bounce from pad to pad until he finds his way across. A wireless home control network does the same thing, "organizing" itself and providing a route throughout the home for your control signals.

The network effect is in full effect in mesh networks like this. In case you're not familiar with it, the *network effect* states that the value of networked devices is exponentially related to the number of those devices. (For example, if only one fax machine existed in the world, it would be useless; if millions exist, they can be *very* useful.) A similar thing is true for mesh networked home control devices (called *modules*). One or two would work okay, if they were near each other, but when a home has dozens (or even hundreds), all sorts of devices can communicate with each other and the whole network will perform significantly better.

The two main technology competitors for this (still new) marketplace are

- **ZigBee:** ZigBee is a wireless automation networking standard based on an international standard (called IEEE 802.15.4 — similar to the 802.11 standards used for Wi-Fi networks). As we mention earlier, ZigBee systems use a peer-to-peer networking infrastructure, called *mesh networking,* to reach throughout the home. ZigBee provides a data rate of 250 Kbps, while using chips that are inexpensive to manufacture. A group called the ZigBee Alliance (www.zigbee.org) — similar to the Wi-Fi Alliance — is helping manufacturers bring ZigBee products to market and helping ensure that the products work well together. As we write, only a few dozen ZigBee products are on the market, but dozens of manufacturers have joined the alliance.

- **Z-Wave:** A Danish semiconductor company called Zensys (www.zen-sys. com) has developed a competitor to ZigBee called Z-Wave. Z-Wave is a wireless, mesh, peer-to-peer automation networking protocol that's similar to ZigBee. Z-Wave systems operate at speeds of up to 9.6 Kbps (slower than ZigBee but still more than fast enough for home automation and control). Z-Wave products are still new to the market, but several major manufacturers, such as Leviton (www.leviton.com) and Wayne Dalton (www.waynedalton.com), are shipping products using Z-Wave.

ZigBee and Z-Wave are similar systems that *do not work together.* That is to say, a ZigBee chip and a Z-Wave chip can't talk to each other and work together in a home control network. But they can both be installed in the same home without causing interference nightmares. So while your ZigBee and Z-Wave networks can't directly interoperate, there's no problem with having both in your home (if you choose to do so) — for example, you could have a Z-Wave lighting control system and use ZigBee to control your heating and air-conditioning systems.

ZigBee and Z-Wave chips can be integrated directly into an appliance or electrical device (this will be more common in the future), or they can be integrated into a *control module* (a device that sits between your control network and the thing you want to control, and translates network commands into commands that the end device understands, such as on or off). In Chapter 14 we talk about some common ZigBee and Z-Wave devices, how they work, and how you can integrate them into your home.

Part II
Making Plans

The 5th Wave   By Rich Tennant

"You the guy having trouble staying connected to the network?"

In this part . . .

This part of the book helps you plan for installing your wireless home network — from deciding what you will connect to the network to making buying decisions and planning the installation of wireless networking equipment in your home. It used to be easy when there were only a few products on the market and only a few ways to get wireless into your house. Now, you can outfit your home in a myriad of ways, from devices that attach to your TV to Wi-Fi–denabled cell phones to trusty old access points. We'll help you figure out a good solid plan based on what you need — not what happens to be on sale at your local electronics store.

Chapter 4

Planning a Wireless Home Network

In This Chapter

▶ Determining what to connect to your network and where to put it

▶ Getting connected to the Internet

▶ Putting together a wireless home network budget

▶ Planning for security

*W*e're sure that you have heard this sage advice: "He who fails to plan, plans to fail." On the other hand, management guru and author Peter Drucker says, "Plans are only good intentions unless they immediately degenerate into hard work." Because you're going to be spending your hard-earned money to buy the equipment necessary for your wireless network, we assume that you want to do a little planning before you start building your network. But, if you prefer to shoot first and aim later, feel free to skip this chapter and move on to Chapter 5.

In this chapter, we show you how to plan a wireless home network — from selecting the right wireless technology (there are several variants), to deciding what things to connect and where to connect them, to the all-important act of budgeting. You also find out about other issues you should consider when planning your home network, including connecting to the Internet; sharing printers, other peripherals, and fun, noncomputer devices; and security. When you're ready to begin buying the wireless home networking parts (if you haven't done so already), head to Chapter 5, where we give detailed advice about buying exactly the equipment you need. In Part III, we show you how to set up and install your wireless home network.

Deciding What to Connect to the Network

Believe it or not, some technogeeks have a computer in every room of their house. We have some close friends who fit into that category (including, well, ourselves). You may not own as many computers as we do (Danny has more than 10 in his house and Ed is already past 15 — Pat comes in last with only 5, but for three people, how many do you really need?), but you probably own more than one, and we're guessing that you have at least one printer and some other peripherals. You're wirelessly networking your home for a reason, no matter whether it's to share that cool, new color inkjet printer (or scanner or digital video recorder), to play your computer-based video files on your new widescreen TV, or to give every computer in the house always-on access to the Internet. Whatever your reason, the first thing you must do when planning a wireless home network is to determine what you want connected to the network.

Counting network devices

The first step to take in planning a network is to count the number of devices you want to attach to the network — that means any computer or device that you want attached to your broadband Internet connection, to your file servers, or to shared resources, such as printers. You almost certainly will connect to your network each of the computers you use regularly.

Next, consider devices that aren't necessarily computers in the traditional sense but that can benefit from a network connection — for example, the printers we mention in the preceding paragraph. You don't need to connect a printer directly to a single PC in a networked environment — you can connect it to a device known as a *print server* and let all your networked PCs access it. Similarly, you can connect devices such as *NAS* (Network Attached Storage), which let you store big files in a centralized location (or even do PC backups over the network). In Chapter 14, we talk about a whole big bunch of networkable devices that can go on your wireless LAN.

If you're an audiophile or just enjoy digital media, you should consider adding your home entertainment system to your network so that you can share MP3 files, play video games, and watch DVDs from anywhere in your house, wirelessly! (These cool gadgets are covered in Chapters 11 and 12.) You can even make your phone calls over your wireless network with one of the Wi-Fi phones we talk about in Chapter 13.

As you plan out your network and count devices, consider that some devices already have all the wireless network capabilities they need built in. For example, most laptop computers and some printers support at least 802.11g wireless networking — so you should put them on your list, but you don't need to spend any money to add them to your network.

Choosing wired or wireless

After you know *what* you're networking, you need to choose *how* to network it. By that, we mean that you have to decide what to connect to your home's network with wires and what you should use wireless networking for. At first glance, this decision may seem obvious. You would expect us to always recommend using wireless because this book talks about wireless networks; however, using both wired and wireless connections can sometimes make the most sense.

Wireless network devices and wired network devices can be used on the same network. Both talk to the network and to each other by using a protocol known as Ethernet. (You should be getting used to that term by now if you have been reading from the beginning of the book. If not, read through Chapters 1 and 2 for more information about networking technology.)

The obvious and primary benefit of connecting to a network wirelessly is that you eliminate wires running all over the place. But, if two devices are sitting on the same desk or table — or are within a few feet of each other — connecting them wirelessly may be pointless. You can get Ethernet cables for $5 or less; an equivalent wireless capability for two devices may top $100 when everything is said and done. Keep in mind, however, that your computer must have a wired network adapter installed to be able to make a wired connection to the network. Fortunately, wired network adapters are dirt cheap these days. Virtually all new computers come with one installed as a standard feature (at no additional charge).

Figure 4-1 shows a simple drawing of a network that connects a wireless PC to a wired PC through two network devices: an access point (AP) and a hub. (Recall that your *AP* connects wireless devices to the rest of the wired network. A network *hub* or *switch* is often used to connect PCs to the network by a wired connection. In Chapter 1, we describe the purpose of, and differences between, APs and hubs and switches.) If you think that it seems absurd to need two network devices to connect two computers, you're not alone. Hardware manufacturers have addressed this issue by creating APs that have a built-in switch — in fact, it's hard to buy an AP that doesn't have a switch (as well as a broadband *router*) built into it. See the section "Choosing an access point," later in this chapter, for more information about these multifunction APs.

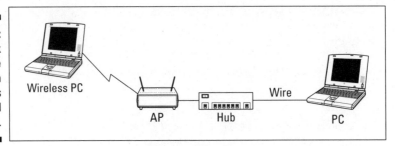

Figure 4-1:
A network
can use
both
wireless
and wired
connections.

Wireless PC

AP   Hub   Wire   PC

Choosing a wireless technology

After you know what you're networking *and* what will be on your wireless network, you have to decide how to network wirelessly. As we discuss extensively in Chapter 2, four main variants of wireless networking technologies exist: 802.11a, 802.11b, 802.11g and 802.11n (draft standard).

Collectively, all these technologies are usually referred to as *Wi-Fi*, which isn't a generic term, but, rather, refers to a certification of *interoperability*. The folks at the Wi-Fi Alliance (www.wi-fi.org) do extensive testing of new wireless gear to make sure that it works seamlessly with wireless equipment from different manufacturers. When it works, it gets the Wi-Fi logo on the box, so you can rest assured that it works in your network.

Wi-Fi certified gear works together — as long as it's of a *compatible* type. That means that any 802.11b, 802.11g, or 802.11n Wi-Fi certified gear works with any other equipment of that type; similarly, any 802.11a Wi-Fi certified gear works with any other 802.11a and 5 GHz capable 802.11n gear that has been certified. (Note that not all 802.11n gear is 5 GHz capable — if a particular piece of equipment supports this, it will say so and will also be 802.11a certified.) 802.11b and g gear *does not* work with 802.11a gear, even if it has all been certified because they work on different radio frequencies and cannot communicate with each other.

The discussion of wireless technology quickly degenerates into a sea of acronyms and technospeak. If you need a refresher on this alphabet soup — or to begin from square one — Chapter 2 is a primer on jargon, abbreviations, and other nuts-and-bolts issues.

For home users, the three most important practical differences between 802.11a, 802.11b, 802.11g, and 802.11n networks are speed, price, and compatibility:

- **802.11b** is an older standard that is no longer used these days. You would be hard pressed to find any 802.11b in your network, and only if you have been buying *legacy* equipment at flea markets or electronic junk yards.

- **802.11g** equipment has been the standard in use for a few years. Thanks to its proliferation, it's inexpensive but at least four times faster than 802.11b.

- **802.11a** can still be found in some special-use corporate environments, but it's no longer used in the home. It is as fast as 802.11g, costs much more, and has a shorter range.

- **802.11n** is five times faster than 802.11a and 802.11g and is 22 times faster than 802.11b.

- **802.11a and 802.11b** are *not* compatible.

- **802.11a and 802.11g** are *not* compatible.

- **802.11b and 802.11g** *are* compatible.

- **802.11n** is compatible with all other standards but at the cost of its higher speed — when you add 802.11a, b, or g gear to an 802.11n network, you slow down the ultimate *throughput* or speed of that network.

The 802.11n standard is compatible with all other standards, but not all 802.11n equipment supports both the 2.4 GHz (802.11b and g) and 5 GHz (802.11a) frequencies — many support only 2.4 GHz. An AP that includes 802.11n should work with any other device as well (though not always at the higher 248 Mbps speed of 802.11n). Thus, you don't have to look for a multimode AP.

If your primary reason for networking the computers in your house is to enable Internet sharing, 802.11g is more than fast enough because your Internet connection probably won't exceed the 54 Mbps of the 802.11g connection any time soon — unless you're one of the lucky few who lives where fiber-optic Internet services (such as Verizon's FiOS service) are installed.

Despite the fact that most Internet services are slower than 802.11g, we don't recommend that you buy only 802.11g gear. 802.11g is being superseded by 802.11n with full 802.11g compatibility. In fact, you would save only a few bucks by buying 802.11g gear new. The speed, range, and compatibility of 802.11n are more than worth the increased price tag.

802.11g is the minimum standard around which you should build your network.

If you want to hedge your bets, look for an 802.11n AP that can handle all Wi-Fi technology standards. Apple, Belkin, NETGEAR, D-Link, and several other leading manufacturers of wireless home networking equipment already offer 802.11n wireless devices.

Choosing an access point

The most important and typically most expensive device in a wireless network is the access point (AP; also sometimes called a base station). An AP acts like a wireless switchboard that connects wireless devices on the network to each other and to the rest of the wired network; it's required to create a wireless home network. Figure 4-2 depicts three PCs connected wirelessly to each other through an AP.

The vast majority of APs now available aren't just access points. Instead, most incorporate the functionality of a *broadband router* (which connects multiple computers to an Internet connection), a *network switch* (which connects multiple wired computers together), and even a *firewall* (which helps keep "bad guys" off your network).

The most popular APs for use in home networks are those that can do one or more of the following:

- **Connect wired PCs:** A *switch* is an enhanced version of a network hub that operates more efficiently and quickly than a simple hub. By building a switch inside the AP, you can use the one device to connect PCs to your network by using either wired network adapters or wireless adapters. We cover hubs and switches in more detail in Chapter 1.

- **Assign network addresses:** Every computer on a network or on the Internet has its own address: its Internet Protocol (IP) address. Computers on the Internet communicate — they forward e-mail, Web pages, and the like — by sending data back and forth from IP address to IP address. A Dynamic Host Configuration Protocol (DHCP) server dynamically assigns private IP addresses to the computers on your home network so that they can communicate. You could use a software utility in Windows (or Mac OS) to manually assign an IP address to each computer, but that process is tedious and much less flexible than automatic address assignment.

Figure 4-2:
Three PCs connected wirelessly to each other through an AP.

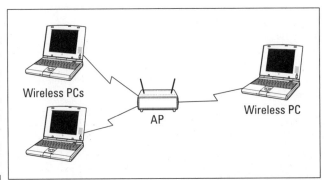

Wireless PCs

AP

Wireless PC

✔ **Connect to the Internet:** With a *cable/digital subscriber line (DSL) router* between a broadband modem and your home network, all computers on the network can access the Internet directly. An AP combined with a DHCP and a cable or DSL router is sometimes called a *wireless Internet gateway.* (See the "Connecting to the Internet" section, later in this chapter, for more about the Network Address Translation feature that makes Internet sharing possible and for more on Internet connectivity.)

✔ **Add a print server:** A *print server* enables you to connect a printer directly to the network rather than connect it to one of the computers on the network. See the "Adding printers" section, later in this chapter.

✔ **Connect in many ways:** The most common method of connecting an AP to your computer or to the wired portion of your network is through an Ethernet port, but other options may be much easier to install if your house isn't wired with Ethernet cable. If you have set up a HomePlug wired network using the powerlines in your home, shop for an AP with HomePlug connectivity. (For more on HomePlug, see Chapter 3.)

You need to have two HomePlug devices, one in — or near — your main AP or router and one in the location you want to extend the network to.

✔ **Provide firewall security:** A *firewall* is a device that basically keeps the bad guys off your network and out of your computers. We talk much more about firewalls in Chapters 9 and 10, but basically, a firewall is typically included in your access point to provide network security.

✔ **Be combined with a modem:** If you're a cable Internet or DSL subscriber, you may be able to use your own modem rather than lease one from your Internet service provider (ISP). In that case, consider purchasing a modem that's also a wireless AP. A cable or DSL modem combined with a wireless Internet gateway is the ultimate solution in terms of installation convenience and equipment cost savings.

You typically can't buy a modem/AP/router combination off the shelf (or at most Internet retailers) like you can buy a nonmodem AP/router. You get these all-in-one devices directly from your broadband service provider in almost all cases.

Deciding where to install the access point

If you have ever experienced that dreaded dead zone while talking on a cellular phone, you know how frustrating poor wireless coverage can be. To avoid this situation within your wireless home network, you should strive to install your wireless network equipment in a way that eliminates dead wireless network zones in your house. Ideally, you determine the best placement of your AP so that no spot in your house is left uncovered. If that isn't possible, you should at least find any dead zones in your house to optimize your signal coverage.

To achieve optimum signal coverage, the best place to install an AP is near the center of your home. Think about where you will place the AP when you make your buying decision. All APs can sit on a shelf or table, but some APs can also be mounted to a wall or ceiling. When making your AP selection, ensure that it can be installed where it works best for the configuration of your house as well as stays out of reach of your little ones or curious pets.

The position of the access point is critical because your entire signal footprint emanates from the AP in a known way, centered from the AP's antennas. Sometimes, not enough consideration is given to the positioning of the access point because it so often works well out of the box, just sitting on a table.

Other people install the AP wrong in the first place. For example, probably one of the worst manufacturing decisions was to put mounting brackets on access points. People get the impression that you should then — duh — mount them on the wall. That's great except for the fact that, depending on the antenna, you may just kill most of your throughput. You see, when an antenna is flush up against a wall, as is typical in a wall-mount situation, the signals of the antenna reflect off the wall back at the antenna, causing interference and driving down throughput precipitously. Yech. (But you see, customers *want* a wall-mount bracket, so product managers at wireless LAN companies decided that they had to give it to them.) The best mounting is six or more inches off the wall.

The vertical positioning of the mounting point is important as well. Generally, you have more interference lower to the ground. If you did a cross section of your house in 1-foot intervals, when you get higher and higher, you would see less on your map. Thus, signals from an access point located on a shelf low to the ground will find more to run into than the ones that are mounted higher. Although this may sound like common sense, consider that most DSL and cable modems are installed by technicians who are used to installing phone and cable TV lines. How many of these are generally located 5 feet off the floor? They're not; they tend to be along the floorboards and low to the ground or in the basement. It's not surprising that a combined DSL access point router would be plugged in low to the ground, too.

See where we're going with this? You don't care where your cable modem is, but you should care where your AP is located. And, if you have an integrated product, you're probably tempted to swap out the cable modem for the cable modem access point. Simply moving that unit higher almost always does a world of good.

Moving an AP out of the line of sight of microwaves, cordless phones, refrigerators, and other devices is a good idea, too. Mounting the AP in the laundry room off the kitchen doesn't make a great deal of sense if you plan to use the AP primarily in rooms on the other side of the kitchen. Passing through commonly used interferers (all those metal appliances and especially that microwave oven when it's in use) generally isn't a smart move.

Factors that affect signal strength

Many variables affect whether you get an adequate signal at any given point in your house, including these factors:

- **The distance from the AP:** The farther away from the AP, the weaker the signal. Wi-Fi 802.11g networks, for example, promise a maximum operating range of 100 feet at 54 Mbps to 300 feet at 1 Mbps. Indoors, a realistic range at 54 Mbps is about 60 feet. 802.11n networks have a significantly longer range outdoors of up to 750 feet and an indoor range up to 210 feet at 248 Mbps. The range differs from vendor to vendor as well.

- **The power of the transmitter:** Wi-Fi APs transmit at a power output of less than 30 dBm (one watt).

- **The directivity or gain of the antennas attached to the AP and to wireless network adapters:** Different antennas are designed to provide different radiation patterns. That's a fancy way of saying that some are designed to send radio waves in all directions equally, but others concentrate their strength in certain directions. We talk more about this in Chapter 6, but the thing to keep in mind here is that different brands and models of access points have different kinds of antennas designed for different applications. Check out the specifications of the ones you're looking at before you buy them.

- **The construction materials used in the walls, floors, and ceilings:** Some construction materials are relatively transparent to radio signals, but other materials — such as marble, brick, water, paper, bulletproof glass, concrete, and especially metal — tend to reflect some of the signal, thus reducing signal strength.

- **Your house plan:** The physical layout of your house may not only determine where it's practical to position an AP but also affect signal strength, because the position of walls and the number of floors, brick fireplaces, basements, and so on can partially or even completely block the wireless network's radio signal.

- **Client locations:** Reception is affected by the distance from the AP to the rooms in your house where someone will need wireless network access.

- **Stationary physical objects:** Objects permanently installed in your home — such as metal doors, heating ducts, and brick fireplaces — can block some, or all, of the signal to particular spots in your house.

- **Movable physical objects:** Other types of objects, including furniture, appliances, plants, and even people, can also block enough of the signal to cause the network to slow down or even to lose a good connection.

- **APs:** Interference can also be caused by the presence of other APs. In other words, if you have a big house (too big for a single AP to cover), you have to keep in mind that in parts of the house — like in the area that's pretty much directly between the two APs — you find that the radio waves from each AP can interfere with the other. The same is true if you live in a close packed neighborhood in which a lot of people have APs for their home networks. Check out the following subsection for more information regarding this phenomenon.

Wireless interference in the home

Probably the single biggest performance killer in your wireless home network is interference in the home. The Federal Communications Commission (FCC) set aside certain unlicensed frequencies that could be used for low-power wireless applications. In specific frequency bands, manufacturers can make (and you can use) equipment that doesn't require a license from the FCC for the user to operate. This is different from, for example, buying a 50,000-watt radio transmitter and blasting it over your favorite FM radio frequency band, which would be a major no-no because those bands are licensed for certain power levels.

As a result, all sorts of companies have created products (including cordless phones, wireless radio frequency [RF] remote controls, wireless speakers, TV set extenders, and walkie-talkies) that make use of these frequency bands. If you have lots of wireless devices already in your home, they may use some of the same frequency bands as your wireless home network.

Another form of wireless interference comes from devices that emit energy in the same bands, such as microwave ovens. If you have a cordless phone with its base station near a microwave and you notice that the voice quality degrades every time you use the microwave, that's because the micro (radio) waves are in the same radiation band as your cordless phone. Motors, refrigerators, and other home consumer devices do the same thing.

What's the answer? The good news is that you can deal with almost all these by knowing what to look for and being smart about where you place your equipment. If your access point is in the back office and you want to frequently work in the living room with your laptop — but your kitchen is in the middle — you may want to look at adding a second access point in the living room and linking it with the office via any of a number of alternative connections options (which we talk about in Chapter 3) that are immune to the problems we mention here.

Remember these specific things to look for when shopping. You see cordless phones operating primarily in the 900 MHz, 2.4 GHz, and 5 GHz frequencies. The 900 MHz phones pose no problems — but are also almost impossible to find these days — and the 2.4 GHz and 5 GHz phones interfere with your wireless network signals (in the 802.11b/g and 802.11a frequency ranges, respectively). Just know that cordless phones and wireless home networks really don't like each other much. You can find cordless phones that are designed not to interfere with your wireless network. These phones are usually labeled clearly that they are designed to work within and around wireless networks. We have tested a few, and while they do work much better — your network connection does not drop out when you answer the phone — they still cause enough interference that your connection will slow down a noticeable amount. In Chapter 13, we talk about cordless phones that carry your voice *over* your wireless network and are part of the network instead of interfering with it.

You should attempt to keep a direct line between APs, residential gateways, and the wireless devices on your network. A wall that is 1.5 feet thick, at a 45° angle, appears to be almost 3 feet thick. At a 2° angle, it looks more than 42 feet thick. Try to make sure that the AP and wireless adapters are positioned so that the signal travels straight through a wall or ceiling for better reception.

RF interference

Nowadays, many devices that once required wires are now wireless, and this situation is becoming more prevalent all the time. Some wireless devices use infrared technology, but many wireless devices, including your wireless network, communicate by using radio frequency (RF) waves. As a consequence, the network can be disrupted by RF interference from other devices sharing the same frequencies used by your wireless network.

Among the devices most likely to interfere with 802.11g and 802.11n networks are microwave ovens and cordless telephones that use the 2.4 GHz or 5 GHz band. The best way to avoid this interference is to place APs and computers with wireless adapters at least 6 feet away from the microwave and the base station of any portable phone that uses either band.

Bluetooth devices also use the 2.4 GHz band, but the hop pattern of the Bluetooth modulation protocol all but ensures that any interference is short enough in duration to be negligible.

Because relatively few devices are trying to share the 5 GHz frequencies used by some 802.11n devices, your network is less likely to experience RF interference if it's using 802.11n. If the 5 GHz frequency is the only clear band, 802.11n will work but at the cost of absolute distance.

You should also try to keep all electric motors and electrical devices that generate RF noise through their normal operation, such as monitors, refrigerators, electric motors, and universal power supply (UPS) units, at least 3 and preferably 6 feet away from a wireless network device.

Signal obstacles

Wireless technologies are susceptible to physical obstacles. When deciding where best to place your APs, look at Table 4-1, which lists obstacles that can affect the strength of your wireless signals. The table lists common household obstacles (although often overlooked) as well as the degree to which the obstacle is a hindrance to your wireless network signals.

Table 4-1	How Common Household Items Affect a Wi-Fi Signal	
Obstruction	**Degree of Attenuation**	**Example**
Open space	Low	Backyard
Wood	Low	Inner wall; door; floor
Plaster	Low	Inner wall (older plaster has a lower degree of attenuation than newer plaster)
Synthetic materials	Low	Partitions; home theater treatments
Cinder block	Low	Inner wall; outer wall
Asbestos	Low	Ceiling (older buildings)
Glass	Low	Nontinted window
Wire mesh in glass	Medium	Door; window
Metal tinted glass	Medium	Tinted window
Body	Medium	Groupings of people (dinner table)
Water	Medium	Damp wood; aquarium; in-home water treatments
Bricks	Medium	Inner wall; outer wall; floor
Marble	Medium	Inner wall; outer wall; floor
Ceramic (metal content or backing)	High	Ceramic tile; ceiling; floor
Paper	High	Stack of paper stock, such as newspaper piles
Concrete	High	Floor; outer wall; support pillar
Bulletproof glass	High	Windows; door
Silvering	Very high	Mirror
Metal	Very high	Inner wall; air conditioning; filing cabinets; reinforced concrete walls and floors

You may want to consider reading Chapter 18 on troubleshooting before you finish your planning. Some good tips in that chapter talk about setting up and tweaking your network.

Adding printers

In addition to connecting your computers, you may want to connect your printers to the network. Next to sharing an Internet connection, printer sharing is perhaps the biggest cost-saving reason for building a network of home computers. Rather than buy a printer for every PC, everyone in the house can share one printer. Or maybe you have one color inkjet printer and one black-and-white laser printer. If both printers are connected to the network,

---

The RF doughnut

The shape of the radio signal transmitted to the rooms in your home is determined by the type of antenna you have attached to the AP. The standard antenna on any AP is an *omnidirectional* antenna, which broadcasts its signal in a spherical shape. The signal pattern that radiates from a typical omnidirectional dipole antenna is shaped like a fat doughnut with a tiny hole in the middle. The hole is directly above and below the antenna.

The signal goes from the antenna to the floor above and the floor below, as well as to the floor on which the AP is located. If your house has multiple floors, try putting your AP on the second floor first. Most AP manufacturers claim a range of 200 feet indoors (at 74 Mbps for 802.11n and 54 Mbps for 802.11g). To be conservative, assume a range of 80 feet laterally and one floor above and below the AP. Keep in mind that the signal at the edges of the "doughnut" and on the floors below or above the AP are weaker than the signal nearer the center and on the same floor as the AP.

Because of this signal pattern, you should try to place the AP as close to the center of your house as is practically possible. Use a drawing of your house plan to locate the center of the house. This spot is your first trial AP location.

Draw a circle with an 80-foot radius on your house plan, with the trial AP location as the center of the circle. If your entire house falls inside the circle, one AP will probably do the job. Conversely, if some portion of the house is outside the circle, coverage may be weaker in that area. You need to experiment to determine whether you get an adequate signal there.

If you determine that one AP will not cover your house, you need to decide how best to place two APs (or even three, if necessary). The design of your house determines the best placement. For a one-level design, start at one end of the house and determine the best location for an 80-foot radius circle that covers all the way to the walls. The center of this circle is the location of the first AP. Then move toward the other end of the house, drawing 80-foot radius circles until the house is covered. The center of each circle is a trial location of an AP. If possible, don't leave any area in the house uncovered.

all computers on the network can potentially print to either printer. Or perhaps you just want to sit by the pool with your wireless laptop and still be able to print to the printer up in your bedroom; it's easy with a network-attached printer.

You can also share other peripherals, such as network-aware scanners and fax machines. Leading manufacturers of digital imaging equipment (such as Hewlett-Packard) offer feature-rich, multiple-function peripherals that combine an inkjet or laser printer with a scanner, copier, telephone, answering machine, and fax machine. HP and Brother both offer wireless printers that make adding a shared printer to your network simple and quick. If you already have a printer, you can find wireless print servers such as the HP Jetdirect ew2400 802.11g Wireless Print Server to convert your wired printer to a wireless printer.

Here are two ways to share printers over a wired or wireless network:

- **Connect to a computer:** The easiest and cheapest way to connect a printer to the network is to connect a printer to one of the computers on the network. Windows enables you to share any printer connected to any Windows computer on the network. (For more on this topic, read Chapter 10.) The computer to which the printer is connected has to be running for any other computers on the network to use the printer. Similarly, if you're using Apple computers, any computer connected to the network can print to a printer that's connected to one of the computers on the network.

- **Use a print server:** Another way to add a printer is through a print server. As we mention earlier, several hardware manufacturers produce print server devices that enable you to connect one or more printers directly to the network. Some of these devices connect via a network cable, and others are wireless. Many high-end printers even have print server options installed inside the printer cabinet. The cost for a home use, stand-alone network print server has come down a lot in the past few years, but printers with Wi-Fi built in tend to be at the high end of the price range. Surprisingly, some manufacturers bundle a print server with their wireless router at little or no additional cost. If you shop around, you can easily find a wireless AP, cable, or DSL router and print server bundled in one device.

You should be able to get your home network printer connections for free. Obviously, it doesn't cost anything to connect a printer to a computer that's already connected to the network. Several manufacturers also include a print server for free with other network devices. If you don't need one of those devices, just connect the printer you want to share to one of the computers on your home network.

Figure 4-3 depicts a home network with one printer connected to one of the PCs on the network and another printer connected to a wireless Internet *gateway,* which is a device that bundles a wireless AP and an Ethernet/cable/DSL router into a single unit. In this case, the wireless Internet gateway also has a connection for a printer and acts as a print server. Read through Chapters 1 and 5 for more information about these devices, what they do, and how to choose between them.

Connecting your printer to the wireless Internet gateway device is advantageous because a print server permits the printer to stand alone on the network, untethered from any specific computer. When you want to print to a printer that's connected directly to a computer on the network, that computer must be present and turned on; and, in many cases, you must have a user account and appropriate permission to access the shared printer. A print server makes its printers always available to any computer on the network — even from poolside.

Most folks don't mind having their printer connected to a computer or to a gateway device in their home — meaning that the computer is connected via peripheral cables to one of these devices. You may, however, want to make your printer *itself* wireless — so you can stick it *anywhere* in your house, even if that means that it's far away from any PCs or gateway devices. In this case, consider buying a *wireless print server* that can either be an internal part of your printer (in some cases this is an optional module from the printer manufacturer) or sit next to your printer. In this case, your printer is completely decoupled from your wired network — the server is a wireless network *client* — as well as the hardware and software to run the printer itself.

Why would you spring for the extra money (about $80 to $100)? Here's an example. Pat had a spot (a closet) right in the middle of his house (literally!) where he wanted to hide a printer — but no wires and no PCs nearby. A wireless print server solved the problem and got his printer out of the way (and still in a convenient location).

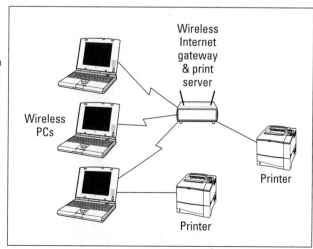

Figure 4-3:
A wireless home network with a wireless Internet gateway and a bundled print server.

Wireless Internet gateway & print server

Wireless PCs

Printer

Printer

Adding entertainment and more

When you're planning your wireless network, don't forget to include a few gadgets for fun and relaxation. The wildly popular videogame consoles from Sony, Microsoft, and Nintendo all offer network connectivity and Internet connectivity. Don't forget to consult with the gamers in your household when planning where you need network coverage in your home. And don't forget to take a look at Chapter 11 for the skinny about connecting your favorite console to your wireless network, as well as info on network-based, multiuser PC gaming.

An increasing number of consumer electronics devices, such as digital home entertainment systems, are network aware. Feature-packed home media servers can store thousands of your favorite MP3s and digital videos and make them available over the network to all the computers in your house. Several even include optional wireless networking connectivity. Connecting the sound and video from your PC to your home theater is even possible — really. Imagine surfing the Internet on a wide-screen TV! Jump to Chapter 12 for the details about connecting your A/V gear to your wireless home network.

Some of the coolest home electronic technology in recent years enables you to control the lights, heating, cooling, security system, home entertainment system, and pool right from your computer. Equally exciting technology enables you to use a home network to set up a highly affordable home video monitoring system. By hooking these systems to your wireless network and hooking the network to the Internet, you can make it possible to monitor and control your home's utilities and systems, even while away from home. Check out Chapter 14 for more about these smart home technologies as well as additional cool things you can network, such as connecting to your car or using your network to connect to the world.

Connecting to the Internet

When you get right down to it, the reason why most people build wireless networks in their homes is to share their Internet connection with multiple computers or devices that they have around the house. That's why we did it — and we bet that's why you're doing it. We have reached the point in our lives where a computer that's not constantly connected to a network and to the Internet is seriously handicapped. We're not really even exaggerating much here. Even things you do locally (use a spreadsheet program, for example) can be enhanced by an Internet connection; for example, in that spreadsheet program, you can link to the Internet to do real-time currency conversions. These days it's not uncommon to be using an online application such as Google Docs and Spreadsheets, working simultaneously with a handful of other people on a spreadsheet through your browser and Internet connection.

What a wireless network brings to the table is true whole-home Internet access. Particularly when combined with an always-on Internet connection (which we discuss in just a second) — but even with a regular dial-up modem connection (yes, some people still use modems) — a wireless network lets you access the Internet from just about every nook and cranny of the house. Take the laptop out to the back patio, let a visitor connect from the guest room, or do some work in bed. Whatever you want to do and wherever you want to do it, a wireless network can support you.

A wireless home network — or any home network, for that matter — provides one key element. It uses a NAT router (we describe this item later in this section) to provide Internet access to multiple devices over a single Internet connection coming into the home. With a NAT router (which typically is built into your access point or a separate home network router), you can not only connect more than one computer to the Internet but also simultaneously connect multiple computers (and other devices, such as game consoles) to the Internet over a single connection. The NAT router has the brains to figure out which Web page or e-mail or online gaming information is going to which *client* (PC or device) on the network.

Not surprisingly, to take advantage of this Internet-from-anywhere access in your home, you need some sort of Internet service and modem. We don't get into great detail about this topic, but we do want to make sure that you keep it in mind when you plan your network.

Most people access the Internet from a home computer in one of these ways:

- Dial-up telephone connection
- Digital subscriber line (DSL)
- Cable Internet
- Fiber-optic service (such as Verizon's FiOS service)
- Satellite broadband

DSL, cable, fiber-optic, and satellite Internet services are often called *broadband* Internet services, which is a term that gets defined differently by just about everyone in the industry. For our purposes, we define it as a connection that is faster than a dial-up modem connection (sometimes called *narrowband*) and is always on. That is, you don't have to use a dialer to get connected, but instead you have a persistent connection available immediately without any setup steps necessary for the users (at least after the first time you set up your connection).

Broadband Internet service providers are busily wiring neighborhoods all over the United States, but none of the services are available everywhere. (Satellite is available almost everywhere. But, as with satellite TV, you need to meet certain criteria, such as having a view to the south, that is, facing the satellites, which orbit over the equator.) Where it's available, however, growing numbers of families are experiencing the benefits of always-on and very fast Internet connectivity.

In some areas of the country, wireless systems are beginning to become available as a means of connecting to the Internet. Most of these systems use special radio systems that are proprietary to their manufacturers. That is, you buy a transceiver and an antenna and hook it up on your roof or in a window. But a few are using modified versions of Wi-Fi to provide Internet access to people's homes. In either case, you have some sort of modem device that connects to your AP via a standard Ethernet cable, just like you would use for a DSL, fiber-optic, cable modem, or satellite connection.

For the purpose of this discussion of wireless home networks, DSL, fiber-optic, and cable Internet are equivalent. If you can get more than one of these connections at your house, shop around for the best price and talk to your neighbors about their experiences. You might also want to check out www.broadbandreports.com, which is a Web site where customers of a variety of broadband services discuss and compare their experiences. As soon as you splurge for a broadband Internet connection, the PC that happens to be situated nearest the spot where the installer places the DSL, fiber-optic, or cable modem is at a distinct advantage because it is the easiest computer to connect to the modem — and therefore to the Internet. Most DSL and cable modems connect to the PC through a wired network adapter card. FiOS uses a device called a router to connect to the PC via the same wired network adapter card. The best way, therefore, to connect any computer in the home to the Internet is through a home network.

You have two ways to share an Internet connection over a home network:

- **Software-based Internet connection sharing:** Windows XP, Windows Vista, and Mac OS X enable sharing of an Internet connection. Each computer in the network must be set up to connect to the Internet through the computer connected to the broadband modem. The disadvantage with this system is that you can't turn off or remove the computer connected to the modem without disconnecting all computers from the Internet. In other words, the computer connected to the modem must be on for other networked computers to access the Internet through it. This connected computer also needs to have two network cards installed — one card to connect to the cable/DSL modem or FiOS router and one to connect to the rest of the computer on your network via an AP or switch.

- **Cable, DSL, or FiOS router:** When you connect to one of these services, the router used between the broadband modem and your home network allows all the computers on the network to access the Internet without going through another computer. The Internet connection no longer depends on any computer on the network. These routers are also

DHCP — and in most cases NAT — servers and typically include switches. In fact, the AP and the modem can also include a built-in router that provides instant Internet sharing all in one device.

As we mention earlier in the chapter, nearly all APs now available for home networks have a built-in broadband router.

Read through Chapter 10 for details on how to set up Internet sharing.

Given the fact that you can buy a router (either as part of an access point or a separate router) for well under $60 these days (and prices continue to plummet), we think it's false economy to skip the router and use a software-based, Internet connection sharing setup. In our minds, at least, the advantage of the software-based approach (*very* slightly less money up front) is outweighed by the disadvantages (requiring the PC to always be on, lower reliability, lower performance, and a much bigger electric bill each month).

Both software-based, Internet connection sharing and cable or DSL routers enable all the computers in your home network to share the same network (IP) address on the Internet. This capability uses *network address translation* (NAT). A device that uses the NAT feature is often called a *NAT router.* The NAT feature communicates with each computer on the network by using a private IP address assigned to that local computer, but the router uses a single public IP address in data it sends to computers on the Internet. In other words, no matter how many computers you have in your house sharing the Internet, they look like only one computer to all the other computers on the Internet.

Whenever your computer is connected to the Internet, beware the potential that some malicious hacker may try to attack your computer with a virus or try to break into your computer to trash your hard drive or steal your personal information. Because NAT technology hides your computer behind the NAT server, it adds a measure of protection against hackers, but you shouldn't rely on it solely for protection against malicious users. You should also consider purchasing full-featured firewall software that actively looks for and blocks hacking attempts, unless the AP or router you purchase provides that added protection. We talk about these items in more detail in Chapter 9.

As we recommend in the "Choosing an access point," section earlier in this section, try to choose an AP that also performs several other network-oriented services. Figure 4-4 depicts a wireless home network using an AP that also provides DHCP, NAT, a print server, and switched hub functions in a single stand-alone unit. This wireless Internet gateway device then connects to the DSL or cable modem, which in turn connects to the Internet. Such a configuration provides you with connectivity, sharing, and a little peace of mind, too.

If you already have a wired network and have purchased a cable or DSL router Internet gateway device without the AP function, you don't have to replace the existing device. Just purchase a wireless access point. Figure 4-5 depicts

the network design of a typical wired home network with an AP and wireless
stations added. Each PC in the wired network is connected to the cable or
DSL router, which is also a switch. By connecting the AP to the router, the AP
acts as a bridge between the wireless network segment and the existing wired
network.

Figure 4-4:
Go for a
wireless
gateway
that
combines
AP, DHCP,
NAT, print
server, and
switched hub
functions
in one unit.

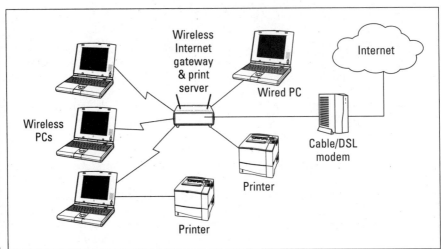

Figure 4-5:
A wired
home
network
with an
AP and
wireless
stations
added.

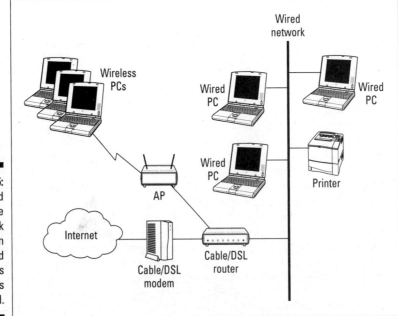

Budgeting for Your Wireless Network

Assuming that you already own at least one computer (and probably more) and one or more printers that you intend to add to the network, we don't include the cost of computers and printers in this section. In addition, the cost of subscribing to an ISP isn't included in the following networking cost estimates.

Wireless networking hardware — essentially APs and wireless network adapters — is available at a wide range of prices. With a little planning, you won't be tempted to bite on the first product you see. You can use the following guidelines when budgeting for an AP and wireless network adapters. Keep in mind, however, that the prices for this equipment will certainly change over time, perhaps rapidly. Don't use this information as a substitute for due diligence and market research on your part.

Pricing access points

At the time this chapter was written, wireless access points for home use ranged in price from about $35 (street price) to around $100.

Street price is the price at which you can purchase the product from a retail outlet, such as a computer-electronics retail store or an online retailer. The dreaded *suggested retail price* is often higher.

Multifunction access points that facilitate connecting multiple computers to the Internet — *wireless Internet gateways* if they contain modem functionality and *wireless gateways* or *routers* if they don't — range in price from about $50 to $150.

You need to budget roughly $60 for an 802.11g AP and about $160 for an 802.11n AP. If you have some older wireless equipment that you still want to use, you can find a combination a/b/g/n AP for about $350. Keep in mind that these combination APs, while great for leveraging your existing equipment, force your entire network to work at the slowest device speed on that network. (Frankly, if you still have any a or b equipment, it's time to retire it and just plan on purchasing new n equipment. It's more than worth it for the increased range and speed your wireless network will gain.)

The differences in price between the cheapest APs and the more expensive models generally correspond to differences in features. For example, APs that support multiple wireless standards are more expensive than similar APs that support only one standard. Similarly, an AP that is also a cable or DSL router costs more than an AP from the same manufacturer that doesn't include the router feature.

You may run across APs from well-known companies, such as Cisco (not from Cisco's Linksys brand, but labeled as "Cisco" APs) and 3COM, that are significantly more expensive than the devices typically purchased for home use. These "industrial-strength" products include advanced features and come with management software that enables corporate IT departments to efficiently and securely deploy enterprise-level wireless networks. The underlying technology, including the speed and the range of the wireless radios used, are essentially the same as those used in the economically priced APs in most wireless home networks. But the additional features and capabilities of these enterprise-level products save IT personnel countless hours and headaches rolling out dozens of APs in a large wireless network.

Pricing wireless network adapters

Wireless network adapters range from $25 to $125, depending on whether you purchase 802.11a, b, g, or n technology and whether you purchase a PC Card, USB, or internal variety of adapter.

Like APs, wireless network adapters that support multiple standards are somewhat more expensive than their counterparts. An 802.11a/b/g/n card costs between $45 and $100. Most notebook computers sold are equipped with at least b/g wireless built into them, and you can order them with a/b/g/n internal cards for about the same price as buying a quad standard card. You can find the Linksys WLAN-WPC4400N quad-standard card at a street price of $105 as we went to press. Wow!

Looking at a sample budget

Table 4-2 shows a reasonable hardware budget to connect a laptop computer, and a home desktop computer, and a cable Internet connection to an 802.11n wireless home network.

Table 4-2 An 802.11n or g Wireless Home Network Budget

Item	Price Range	Quantity Needed
Access point	$35–$125	1
Wireless network adapters	$25–$100	2
Network cable	$10–$20	1
Cable or DSL modem (optional)	$75–$100	1

Planning Security

Any network can be attacked by a persistent hacker, but a well-defended network discourages most hackers sufficiently to keep your data safe. However, it's easier for a hacker to gain access through the air to a wireless network than to gain physical access to a wired network, making wireless networks, and even home networks, more vulnerable to attack. Because a Wi-Fi signal is a radio signal, it keeps going and going and going, like ripples in a pond, in a weaker and weaker form until it hits something solid enough to stop it. Anyone with a portable PC, wireless network adapter, and an external antenna in a van driving by your house, or even a neighbor with this equipment, has a reasonable chance of accessing your wireless network. (Such skullduggery is known as *war driving.*) So, you must plan for security. We give you all the down-and-dirty details in Chapter 9, but here are some key things to keep in mind:

✔ **Internet security:** Any Internet connection — especially always-on broadband connections, but dial-up connections, too — can be vulnerable to attacks arriving from the Internet. To keep your PCs safe from the bad folks (who may be thousands of miles away), you should turn on any firewall features available in your AP or router. Some fancier APs or routers include a highly effective kind of firewall (a stateful packet inspection [SPI] firewall), but even just the basic firewall provided by any NAT router can be quite effective. You should also consider installing antivirus software as well as personal firewall software on each PC or Mac on your network for an extra level of protection.

✔ **Airlink security:** This is a special need of a wireless home network. Wired networks can be made secure by what's known as *physical security.* That is, you literally lock your doors and windows, and no one can plug into your wired network. In the wireless world, physical security is impossible (you can't wrangle those radio waves and keep them in the house), so you need to implement airlink security. You can't keep the radio waves from getting out of the house, but you can make it hard for someone to do anything with them (like read the data they contain). Similarly, you can use airlink security to keep others from getting onto your access point and freeloading on your Internet connection. The primary means of providing airlink security — and advances are on the way — is called WPA2 (Wi-Fi Protected Access). You absolutely should use WPA2 (and do a few other tricks that we discuss in Chapter 9) to preserve the integrity of your wireless home network.

Chapter 5

Choosing Wireless Home Networking Equipment

....

....

*W*hen you're building something — in this case, a wireless home network — the time comes when you have to decide which building supplies to buy. To set up a wireless home network, you need, at minimum, an access point (AP) and a wireless networking adapter for each computer or other network-enabled device you want to have on the network. Getting this network online means you also need a router, which is typically part of a combined AP/router device (the wireless router). This chapter helps you evaluate and choose from among the growing number of APs and wireless networking adapters on the market.

The advice in this chapter applies equally to PCs and Macs. You can use any access point for a Mac as long as it has a Web interface (that is, it doesn't require a Windows program to configure it). Despite that statement, if you have a Mac, you may want to consider using the Apple AirPort Extreme with Gigabit Ethernet system because it's easier to set up and use. On the network adapter/client side of the link, AirPort Extreme cards are definitely the easier choice for a Mac owner (as we discuss in Chapter 8) — it's somewhere between difficult and impossible to get many third-party Wi-Fi cards to work with a Mac.

In this chapter, we use the term *AP* (access point) generically to refer to the base station of your wireless network. In most cases it will be a part of a wireless router, but in some cases it will be a stand-alone AP. When it doesn't matter whether the AP is stand-alone or part of the router, we use the term *AP* or *access point.* When we're specifically talking about an AP that's integrated with a router, we use the term *wireless router.*

Access Point Selection

At the heart of each wireless home network is the access point (AP), also known as a base station. Depending on an AP's manufacturer and included features, the price of an AP suitable for home use ranges from about $35 to $175. Differences exist from model to model, but even the lowest-price units are surprisingly capable.

For most wireless home networks, the most important requirements for a wireless access point are as follows (sort of in order of importance):

- ✔ Certification and standards support (Wi-Fi certification)
- ✔ Compatibility and form factor
- ✔ Bundled server and router functionality
- ✔ Operational features
- ✔ Security
- ✔ Performance (range and coverage) issues
- ✔ Manageability
- ✔ Price
- ✔ Warranties
- ✔ Customer and technical support

With the exception of pricing (which we cover in Chapter 4), we explore the selection of access point products in depth in terms of these requirements throughout the following sections.

In Chapter 4, we describe how to plan the installation of a wireless home network, including how to use your AP to determine the best location in your house as well as the number of APs you need. If you can determine a location that gives an adequate signal throughout your entire house, a single AP obviously is adequate. If some areas of your home aren't covered, you need one or more additional APs or a more powerful AP (and we tell you how to extend your network coverage in Chapter 18). Fortunately, most residences can be covered by the signal from a single AP, particularly when that AP uses the further-reaching 802.11n standard (discussed in Chapter 3).

Certification and Standards Support

We talk in Chapter 2 about the Wi-Fi Alliance and its certification process for devices. At a minimum, you should ensure that your devices are Wi-Fi certified. This certification provides you with the assurance that your wireless LAN equipment has been through the wringer of interoperability and compliance testing and meets all the standards of 802.11b, g, or a, and the draft standard for 802.11n.

In fact, there's even more to Wi-Fi certification than just meeting the 802.11b, g, a, and n standards. Wi-Fi certification means that a piece of equipment has been thoroughly tested to work with other similar Wi-Fi equipment, regardless of brand. This is the interoperability part of the certification, and it means that you can plug a D-Link adapter into your desktop computer, use a built-in Intel Centrino adapter in your notebook, and install a NETGEAR AP as the hub of your network, and everything will work.

Back in the early days of wireless networking, this interoperability was *not* assured, and you needed to buy all your equipment from the same vendor — and then you were locked in to that vendor. Wi-Fi certification frees you from this concern.

The Wi-Fi Alliance certifies the following:

- **General Wi-Fi certification:** For 802.11a, b, g, and n equipment (as well as *multimode* equipment that supports more than one standard at a time — such as 802.11n gear that also supports 802.11a, b, and g), this certification simply lets you know that a given piece of Wi-Fi certified gear will connect to another piece of gear using the same standard.

This certification is the bottom-line "must have" that you should look for when you buy a wireless LAN system. We recommend that you choose products certified 802.11n unless your budget is very tight (in which case you should feel just fine about choosing an older 802.11g system).

- **Security certification:** Equipment that has been certified to work with the WPA (Wi-Fi Protected Access) and WPA2 security systems (see Chapter 9 for more on this topic). WPA certified equipment can be certified by the Wi-Fi Alliance for any of these types of WPA:

  - **WPA and WPA2 Personal:** This is the minimum you should look for — equipment that has been certified to work with the WPA Personal (or WPA-PSK) system described in Chapter 9.

    If you can help it, don't buy any Wi-Fi gear that isn't certified for at least WPA2 Personal. We think that this is the minimum level of security you should insist on with a Wi-Fi network.

- **WPA/WPA2 Enterprise:** This business-oriented variant of WPA provides the ability to use a special 802.1x or RADIUS server (explained in Chapter 9) to manage users on the network. For the vast majority of wireless home networkers, this capability is overkill, but it doesn't hurt to have it (any WPA/WPA2 Enterprise certified system also supports WPA/WPA2 Personal).

✔ **Other certifications:** The Wi-Fi Alliance provides a number of other specialized certifications that not all Wi-Fi certified gear will have earned, like the following:

- **WMM:** *Wi-Fi Multimedia* certification can be found on a growing number of audio/video and voice Wi-Fi equipment (these items are discussed in Chapters 12 and 13, respectively). WMM certified equipment can provide on your wireless LAN some *Quality of Service* (QoS), which can give your voice, video, or audio data priority over other data being sent across your network. We talk about WMM where appropriate in Chapters 12 and 13.

- **WPS:** *Wi-Fi Protected Setup* certification is increasingly common on new equipment, but still rather new as we write this. WPS, which we discuss in detail in Chapter 9, is a user-friendly front end to WPA2 Personal, and allows you to set up network security simply by pushing buttons (or entering preassigned PIN codes) on your AP/router and network clients.

- **EAP:** *Extensible Authentication Protocol* is part of the WPA Enterprise/802.1x system used in business wireless LANs — EAP provides the mechanism for authenticating users (or confirming that they are who they say they are). A number of different EAP types can be used with WPA Enterprise — each type can be certified by the Wi-Fi Alliance. You don't need to worry about this unless you're building a WPA Enterprise security system for your network.

The underlying IEEE standard for 802.11n (see Chapter 2 for more on this) is still in draft format — it won't be ratified until as late as 2009. Most of the items still up in the air in the final standard relate not to the core networking functionality of the 802.11n standard, but rather to some specialized aspects of 802.11n (such as how it will work in new generations of home entertainment devices). So the manufacturers and the Wi-Fi Alliance itself (which is made up of manufacturers of Wi-Fi gear) have reached a point where they're confident that 802.11n gear sold today is ready to go and they've been certifying equipment since early 2007. What this means to you is that even though it says *draft* on the certification, you shouldn't have anxiety about buying this gear. For more details on choosing 802.11n equipment, read the sidebar titled "What to look for in 802.11n gear."

What you *might* have some anxiety about buying is some of the older "pre-N" gear that some manufacturers are still offering. The time interval between the completion of 802.11g (the *last* Wi-Fi standard) and the completion of 802.11n has been relatively long (and still counting!). Because of this, a lot of manufacturers launched pre-N gear in 2004 and 2005 to offer customers a taste of what was coming. This gear is still on the market, and it works just fine — providing faster speeds with other gear from the same manufacturer and working as fully compliant 802.11g gear with equipment from other manufacturers. But it won't ever be 802.11n compliant despite the *pre-N* in the name. The manufacturers we know tell us they're still selling this gear because they have stock on hand and because some folks have invested in it and want to expand their networks. If you're starting a new network, we don't see *any reason* to not just step up to 802.11n.

Some of this pre-N gear goes by other names such as MIMO or Super-G or Turbo-G. Whatever the name, it's souped-up 802.11g, and *not* 802.11n.

Compatibility and Form Factor

When choosing an AP, make sure that it and its setup program are compatible with your existing components, check its form factor, and determine whether wall-mountability and outdoor use are important to you:

- ✔ **Hardware and software platform:** Make sure that the device you're buying supports the hardware and software platform you have. Certain wireless devices support only Macs or only PCs. And some devices support only certain versions of system software. Luckily, most APs use a Web browser for configuration, so they can work with any PC type and any operating system that supports 802.11 and Web browsing.

- ✔ **Setup program and your operating system:** Make sure that the setup program for the AP you plan to buy runs on your computer's operating system and on the next version of that operating system (if it's available — meaning if you're using XP, look for Vista support too, should you ever decide to upgrade). Setup programs run only on the type of computer for which they were written. A setup program designed to run on Windows doesn't run on the Mac OS, and vice versa. Again, most vendors are moving toward browser-based configuration programs, which are much easier to support than stand-alone configuration utilities.

- ✔ **Form factor:** Make sure you are buying the correct *form factor* (that is, the shape and form of the device, such as whether it's external or a card). For example, don't assume that if you have a tower PC, you should install a PCI card. It's nice to have the more external and portable form factors, such as a Universal Serial Bus (USB) adapter, because you can take it off if you need to borrow it for something or someone else, or if you just want to reposition it for better reception.

What to look for in 802.11n gear

The 802.11n draft standard has a bit more variation in its specifications than previous 802.11 standards such as 802.11g. What this means is that while all 802.11n gear will work at a certain (very high) baseline of performance, some gear may be more capable than others.

The biggest variation in the category of 802.11n gear revolves around the frequencies used. All 802.11n gear works within the 2.4 GHz band that was also used by 802.11b and 802.11g. Some — but far from all — 802.11n equipment also works in the 5 GHz frequency range that was previously the sole domain of the 802.11a standard. This higher frequency range is less crowded with other wireless gear (such as cordless phones and Bluetooth devices), so you're less likely to face interference. Additionally, the 5 GHz band has more channels (the frequency band is divided into a number of channels), making it even easier to find an uncrowded frequency.

Most of this *dual-band* (2.4 and 5 GHz) 802.11n gear today works in either one or another of the frequency bands at a time. What this means is that if you have any legacy 802.11b or g equipment on your network, the 5 GHz capability of your AP or router will not come into play. A few

APs and routers on the market (or soon to be on the market as we write in late 2007) have the capability to operate in both bands *simultaneously*. This is a great capability to have in a mixed 802.11g/802.11n network, because your old gear can happily hum along at 802.11g speeds by using the 2.4 GHz radio in your router, while your fancy new 802.11n gear can reach maximum 802.11n speeds in the 5 GHz band.

The final thing to look for when choosing 802.11n systems is the capability of the equipment to perform *channel bonding*. All Wi-Fi systems use 20 MHz wide channels to transmit and receive data across the network airlink; many 802.11n systems can *bond* two adjacent channels together to form one bigger 40 MHz channel. (For this reason, channel bonding is sometimes referred to as *40 MHz channel width*.) This bigger, bonded channel can carry more data and allow your system to reach the higher (200+ Mbps) speeds promised by 802.11n.

By the way, significantly more channels are available for bonding in the 5 GHz frequency range, which is another reason to choose a dual-band system.

USB comes in two versions: USB 1.1 and USB 2.0. If your computer has a USB 1.1 port, it has a maximum data-transfer speed of 12 Mbps. USB 2.0 ports can transfer data at 480 Mbps, which is 40 times faster than USB 1.1. If you plan to connect an 802.11g or n device to a USB port, it must be USB 2.0.

Many brands of PC Cards include antennas enclosed in a casing that is thicker than the rest of the card. The card still fits in the PC Card slot, but the antenna can block the other slot. For most users, this shouldn't pose a serious problem; however, several manufacturers offer wireless PC Cards that have antenna casings no thicker than the rest of the card. If you actively use both PC Card slots (perhaps you use one for a FireWire or USB 2.0 card), make sure that the form of the PC Card you're buying doesn't impede the use of your other card slot.

> ✔ **Wall-mountability:** If you plan to mount the device on the wall or ceiling, make sure that the unit is wall mountable, because many are not.
>
> ✔ **Outdoor versus indoor use:** Finally, some devices are designed for outdoor — not indoor — use. If you're thinking about installing it outside, look for devices hardened for environmental extremes.

Bundled Functionality: Servers, Gateways, Routers, and Switches

Wireless APs are readily available that perform only the AP function; but for home use, APs that bundle additional features are much more popular, for good reason. In most cases, you should shop for an AP that's also a network router and a network switch — a wireless home router like the one we define in Chapter 2. To efficiently connect multiple computers and to easily share an Internet connection, you need devices to perform all these functions, and purchasing one multipurpose device is the most economical way to accomplish that.

DHCP servers

To create an easy-to-use home network, your network should have a Dynamic Host Configuration Protocol (DHCP) server. A *DHCP server* dynamically assigns an IP address to each computer or other device on your network. This function relieves you from having to keep track of all the devices on the network and assign addresses to each one manually.

Network addresses are necessary for the computers and other devices on your network to communicate. Because most networks now use a set of protocols (Transmission Control Protocol/Internet Protocol, or TCP/IP) with network addresses (Internet Protocol, or IP, addresses), we refer to network addresses as *IP addresses* in this book. In fact, the Internet uses the TCP/IP protocols, and every computer connected to the Internet must be identified by an IP address.

When your computer is connected to the Internet, your Internet service provider (ISP), such as Time Warner Road Runner or Verizon FiOS, assigns your computer an IP address. However, even when your computer isn't connected to the Internet, it needs an IP address to communicate with other computers on your home network.

The DHCP server can be a stand-alone device, but it's typically a service provided by either a computer on the network or a network router. The DHCP server maintains a database of all the current DHCP clients — the computers

and other devices to which it has assigned IP addresses — issuing new
addresses as each device's software requests an address.

NAT and broadband routers

A *wireless router* is a wireless AP that enables multiple computers to share
the same IP address on the Internet. This fact would seem to be a contra-
diction because every computer on the Internet needs its own IP address.
The magic that makes an Internet gateway possible is Network Address
Translation (NAT). Most access points you buy now are wireless gateways.

Vendors sometimes call these wireless routers *wireless broadband routers* or
perhaps *wireless cable/DSL routers*. What you're looking for is the word *router*
somewhere in the name or description of the device itself. Stand-alone access
points (without the router functionality) usually are called just an access
point, so sometimes it's easier to look for something *not* called that!

In addition to providing NAT services, the wireless routers used in home
networks also provide the DHCP service. The router communicates with
each computer or other device on your home network via private IP
addresses — the IP addresses assigned by the DHCP server. (See the section
"DHCP servers," earlier in this chapter.) However, the router uses a single IP
address — the one assigned by your ISP's DHCP server — in packets of data
intended for the Internet.

In addition to providing a method for sharing an Internet connection, the NAT
service provided by a broadband router also adds a measure of security
because the computers on your network aren't directly exposed to the
Internet. The only computer visible to the Internet is the broadband router.
This protection can also be a disadvantage for certain types of Internet
gaming and computer-to-computer file transfer applications. If you find that
you need to use one of these applications, look for a router with *DMZ* (for
demilitarized zone) and *port forwarding* features, which expose just enough of
your system to the Internet to play Internet games and transfer files. (Read
more about this topic in Chapter 11.)

A *wireless Internet gateway* is an AP that's bundled with a cable, fiber-optic, or
DSL modem or router. By hooking this single device to a cable connection or
DSL line (or to the termination of your fiber-optic connection), you can share
an Internet connection with all the computers connected to the network,
wirelessly. By definition, all wireless Internet gateway devices also include
one (and typically, several) wired Ethernet port that enables you to add
wired devices to your network as well as wireless devices.

When your wireless network needs some order

Your home network is comprised of many parts. If you're smart, you've consolidated them as much as possible, because having fewer devices means easier installation and troubleshooting. But suppose that you have a cable modem, a router, a switch, and an access point — not an unusual situation if you grew your network over time. Now suppose that the power goes out. Each of these devices resets at different rates. The switch will probably come back fairly quickly because it's a simple device. The cable modem will probably take the longest to resync with the network, and the AP and router will come back up probably somewhere in-between.

The problem that you, as a client of the DHCP server (which is likely in the router in this instance), have is that not all the elements are in place for a clean IP assignment to flow back to your system. For example, the router needs to know the WAN IP address for you to have a good connection to the Internet. If the cable modem hasn't renegotiated its connection, it cannot provide that to the router. If the AP comes back online before the router, it cannot get its DHCP from the router to provide connectivity to the client. Different devices react differently when something isn't as it should be on startup.

Our advice: If you have a problem with your connectivity that you didn't have before the electricity went out and came back on, follow these simple steps. Turn everything off, start at the farthest point from the client (usually this is your broadband modem), and work back toward the client, to let each device get its full start-up cycle complete before moving to the next device in line — ending with rebooting your PC or other wirelessly enabled device.

Switches

Wireless routers, available from nearly any manufacturer, include from one to eight Ethernet ports with which you can connect computers or other devices via Ethernet cables. These routers are not only wireless APs but are also wired switches that efficiently enable all the computers on your network to communicate either wirelessly or over Ethernet cables.

Make sure that the switch ports support at least *100BaseT* Ethernet — this is the 100 Mbps variant of Ethernet. You should also ensure that the switch supports the *full-duplex* variant of 100BaseT — meaning that it supports 100 Mbps of data in both directions at the same time. If you're looking for the ultimate in performance, you should strongly consider paying a bit more for a router that supports *Gigabit Ethernet* (1000BaseT).

Even though you may intend to create a wireless home network, sometimes you may want to attach a device to the network through a more traditional network cable. For example, we highly recommend that when you configure a router for the first time, you attach the router to your computer by a network cable (rather than via a wireless connection).

Print servers

A few multifunction wireless routers have a feature that enables you to add a printer to the network: a print server. Next to sharing an Internet connection, printer sharing is one of the most convenient (and cost-effective) reasons to network home computers because everyone in the house can share one printer. Wireless print servers have become much more economical in the past few years. However, when the print server is included with the wireless router, it's suddenly very cost effective.

The disadvantage of using the print server bundled with the AP, however, is apparent if you locate your AP in a room or location other than where you would like to place your printer. Consider a stand-alone print server device (discussed in Chapter 10) if you want to have your printer wirelessly enabled but not near your AP.

When you choose an AP with a print server, make sure that you have the right interface to your printer — most printers these days use USB connections, but a few still use the parallel port connection. We recommend that you choose an AP print server that supports USB 2.0 for faster printing of big, graphically intensive files.

Operational Features

Most APs share a common list of features, and most of them don't vary from one device to the next. Here are some unique, onboard features that we look for when buying wireless devices — and you should, too:

- **Wired Ethernet port:** Okay, this one seems basic, but having a port like this saves you time. We tell you time and again to first install your AP on your wired network (as opposed to trying to configure the AP via a wireless client card connection) and then add the wireless layer (like the aforementioned client card). You can save yourself lots of grief if you can get your AP configured on a direct connection to your PC because you reduce the things that can go wrong when you add the wireless clients.

- **Auto channel select:** Some access points, typically more expensive models designed for office use, offer an automatic channel-selection feature. That's nice because, as you can read in Chapter 6 and in the troubleshooting areas of Chapter 18, channel selection can try your patience. (You may wonder why professional users pay more for more business-class access points — this feature, which adds to the expense of an AP, is a good reason.)

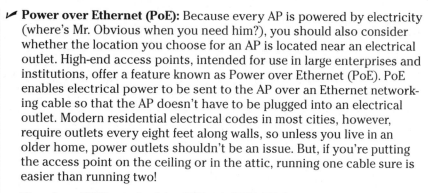

✔ **Power over Ethernet (PoE):** Because every AP is powered by electricity (where's Mr. Obvious when you need him?), you should also consider whether the location you choose for an AP is located near an electrical outlet. High-end access points, intended for use in large enterprises and institutions, offer a feature known as Power over Ethernet (PoE). PoE enables electrical power to be sent to the AP over an Ethernet networking cable so that the AP doesn't have to be plugged into an electrical outlet. Modern residential electrical codes in most cities, however, require outlets every eight feet along walls, so unless you live in an older home, power outlets shouldn't be an issue. But, if you're putting the access point on the ceiling or in the attic, running one cable sure is easier than running two!

There's an IEEE standard for POE; it's IEEE 802.3af.

✔ **Detachable antennas:** In most cases, the antenna or antennas that come installed on an AP are adequate for good signal coverage throughout your house. However, your house may be large enough or may be configured in such a way that signal coverage of a particular AP could be significantly improved by replacing a stock antenna with an upgraded version. Also, if your AP has an internal antenna and you decide that the signal strength and coverage in your house are inadequate, an external antenna jack allows you to add one or two external antennas. Several manufacturers sell optional antennas that extend the range of the standard antennae; they attach to the AP to supplement or replace the existing antennae.

The FCC requires that antennas and radios be certified as a system. Adding a third-party, non-FCC-certified antenna to your AP violates FCC regulations and runs the risk of causing interference with other radio devices, such as certain portable telephones.

Detachable antennas are a potentially big benefit for 802.11g (and earlier 802.11a and b) systems, but not so much for 802.11n. Because of the very tight integration between hardware and antenna in a MIMO 802.11n system, most 802.11n routers don't offer detachable antennas and wouldn't benefit from them if they did. We expect that eventually this will be an option, but as we write (during the early days of 802.11n), detachable antennas aren't really an option.

✔ **Uplink port:** APs equipped with internal three- and four-port hub and switch devices are also coming with a built-in, extra uplink port. The *uplink port* — also called the crossover port — adds even more wired ports to your network by uplinking the AP with another hub or switch. This special port is normally an extra connection next to the last available wired port on the device, but it can look like a regular Ethernet jack (with a little toggle switch next to it). You want an uplink port — especially if you have an integral router or DSL or cable modem — so that you can add more ports to your network while it grows. (And it will grow.)

Security

Unless you work for the government or handle sensitive data on your computer, you probably aren't overly concerned about the privacy of the information stored on your home network. Usually it's not an issue anyway because someone would have to break into your house to access your network. But if you have a wireless network, the radio signals transmitted by your network don't automatically stop at the outside walls of your house. In fact, a neighbor or even someone driving by on the street in front of your house can use a computer and a wireless networking adapter to grab information right off your computer, including deleting your files, inserting viruses, and using your computer to send spam — unless you take steps to protect your network.

The original security technology for Wi-Fi equipment was Wired Equivalent Privacy (WEP). Perhaps the most well-publicized aspect of Wi-Fi wireless networking is the fact that the WEP security feature of Wi-Fi networks can be *hacked* (broken into electronically). Hackers have successfully retrieved secret WEP keys used to encrypt data on Wi-Fi networks. With these keys, the hacker can decrypt the packets of data transmitted over a wireless network. Since 2003, the Wi-Fi Alliance has been certifying and promoting a replacement security technology for WEP: Wi-Fi Protected Access (WPA and the newer but closely related WPA2). WPA/WPA2 is based on an IEEE standard effort known as 802.11i (so many 802.11s huh?). This technology, which makes cracking a network's encryption key much more difficult, is standard in most Wi-Fi access points and network adapters available now. As discussed earlier in this chapter, in the section "Certification and Standards Support," look for Wi-Fi Alliance certifications for WPA equipment.

Any Wi-Fi gear that you buy should support the latest security certification — WPA2. Don't accept any less and don't forget to turn on your network's security.

See Chapter 9 for a full discussion of how to set up basic security for your wireless home network.

Other useful security features to look for when buying an AP include

- ✔ **Network Address Translation** (NAT), which we discuss earlier in this chapter

- ✔ **Virtual Private Network** (VPN) pass-through that allows wireless network users secure access to corporate networks

- ✔ **Monitoring software** that logs and alerts you to computers from the Internet attempting to access your network

- ✔ **Logging and blocking utilities** that enable you to log content transmitted over the network as well as to block access to given Web sites

We talk much more about security in Chapter 9. We encourage you to read that chapter so that you can be well prepared when you're ready to install your equipment.

Range and Coverage Issues

An AP's functional *range* (the maximum distance from the access point at which a device on the wireless network can receive a useable signal) and *coverage* (the breadth of areas in your home where you have an adequate radio signal) are important criteria when selecting an AP. Wi-Fi equipment is designed to have a range of hundreds of meters when used outdoors without any obstructions between the two radios. Coverage depends on the type of antenna used.

Just like it's hard to know how good a book is until you read it, it's hard to know how good an AP is until you install it. Do your research before buying an AP, and then hope that you make the right choice. Buying ten APs and returning the nine you don't want is simply impractical. (Well, maybe not impractical, but rather rude.) The key range and coverage issues, such as power output, antenna gain, or receive sensitivity (which we cover in Chapter 2) aren't well labeled on retail boxes. Nor are these issues truly comparable among devices because of the same lack of consistent information. Because many of these devices are manufactured using the same chipsets, performance usually doesn't vary extensively from one AP to another. However, that is a broad generalization and some APs do perform badly. Our advice: Read the reviews and be forewarned! Most reviews of APs and wireless routers do extensive range and throughput (speed) testing — look at sites such as CNET (www.cnet.com) or ZDNet (www.zdnet.com).

In Chapter 2, we talk about the differences between the 2.4 and 5 GHz frequency bands that different Wi-Fi systems use (802.11b and g use 2.4 GHz, 802.11a uses 5 GHz, and 802.11n can use either). In that chapter we also talk about the fact that higher frequencies (that is, 5 GHz compared to 2.4 GHz) tend to have shorter ranges than lower frequencies (all things equal — which they're not in the case of 802.11n, more on that in a moment). In general, 2.4 GHz systems have a longer reach, but they also operate in a more crowded set of frequencies and are therefore more prone to interference from other systems (other Wi-Fi networks *and* other devices such as phones and microwaves). In an urban environment, you may very well find that a 5 GHz system has a better range simply due to this lack of interference.

The 802.11n systems on the market use multiple antennas and special techniques to boost, or focus, the antenna power and greatly increase the range of the AP versus a standard 802.11g model. Even when operating in the 5 GHz frequency range, you should find that an 802.11n system has a range several times greater than that of an 802.11g system.

Manageability

When it comes to installing, setting up, and maintaining your wireless network, you rely a great deal on your device's user interface, so check reviews for this aspect of the product. In this section, we discuss the many different ways to control and manage your devices.

Web-based configuration

APs, wireless clients, and other wireless devices from all vendors ship with several utility software programs that help you set up and configure the device. An important selling feature of any wireless device is its setup process. The ideal setup procedure can be accomplished quickly and efficiently. Most available APs and devices can be configured through either the wired Ethernet port or a USB port.

The best setup programs enable you to configure the device by connecting through the Ethernet port and accessing an embedded set of Web (HTML) pages. Look for an AP with one of these. This type of setup program — often described as *Web-based* — can be run from any computer that is connected to the device's Ethernet port and has a Web browser. Whether you're using Windows, the Mac OS, or Linux, you can access any device that uses a Web-based configuration program.

Configuration software

When shopping for an AP, look for one with an automated setup process. Several AP manufacturers provide setup software that walks you step by step through the entire process of setting up the AP and connecting to your network. Windows automated setup programs are typically called *wizards*. If you're new to wireless technology, a setup wizard or other variety of automated setup program can help you get up and running with minimum effort.

Versions of Windows starting with Windows XP and versions of the Mac OS starting with Mac OS 9 are more wireless-aware than earlier versions of these operating systems. Automated setup programs are typically quick and easy to use when written to run on either Windows XP or Mac OS 9 or later.

Even if an AP comes with a setup wizard, it also ships with configuration software that permits you to manually configure all the available AP settings. For maximum flexibility, this configuration software should be Web based (refer to the preceding section).

Upgradeable firmware

Wireless networking technology is constantly evolving. As a result, many features of Wi-Fi access points are implemented in updateable software programs known as *firmware*. Before you decide which AP to buy, determine whether you can get feature updates and fixes from the vendor and whether you can perform the updates by upgrading the firmware (see the nearby sidebar, "Performing firmware updates," for some pointers). Check also for updated management software to match up with the new or improved features included in the updated firmware.

You may feel that frequent firmware updates are evidence of faulty product design. However, acknowledging that wireless technology will continue to be improved, buying a product that can be upgraded to keep pace with these changes without the need to purchase new equipment can save you money in the long run.

Price

Although we can't say much directly about price (except that the least expensive item is rarely the one you want), we should mention other things that can add to the price of an item. Check out which cables are provided. (Yes, wireless devices need cables, too!) In an effort to trim costs, some companies don't provide the Ethernet cable for your AP that you need for initial setup.

Also, before you buy, check out some of the online price comparison sites, such as CNET (shopper.cnet.com), Retrevo (www.retrevo.com), and Yahoo! Shopping (shopping.yahoo.com). Internet specials pop up all the time.

Performing firmware updates

Most firmware updates come in the form of a downloadable program you run on a computer connected to the AP (or other device) by a cable (usually Ethernet, but sometimes USB). Make sure that you carefully read and follow the instructions that accompany the downloadable file. Updating the firmware incorrectly can lead to real headaches. Here are a few tips:

- Make sure that you make a backup of your current firmware before performing the update.

- Never turn off the computer or the AP while the firmware update is in progress.

- If something goes wrong, look through the AP documentation for instructions on how to reset the modem to its factory settings.

Warranties

There's nothing worse than a device that dies one day after the warranty expires. The good news is that because most of these devices are solid state, they work for a long time unless you abuse them by dropping them on the floor or something drastic. In our experience, if your device is going to fail because of some manufacturing defect, it does so within the first 30 days or so.

You encounter a rather large variance of warranty schedules among vendors. Some vendors offer a one-year warranty; others offer a lifetime warranty. Most are limited in some fashion, such as covering parts and labor but not shipping.

When purchasing from a store, be sure to ask about its return policy for the first month or so. Many stores give you 14 days to return items, and after that, purchases have to be returned to the manufacturer directly, which is a huge pain in the hind end, as Pat would say. If you only have 14 days, get the device installed quickly so that you can find any problems right away.

Extended service warranties are also often available through computer retailers. (We never buy these because by the time the period of the extended warranty expires, they're simply not worth their price given the plummeting cost of the items.) If you purchase one of these warranties, however, make sure that you have a clear understanding of the types of problems covered as well as how and when you can contact the service provider if problems arise. As we mention earlier in this chapter, if you don't purchase a warranty, you probably need to contact the product manufacturer for support and warranty service rather than the store or online outlet where you purchased the product.

Customer and Technical Support

Good technical support is one of those things you don't appreciate until you can't get it. For support, check whether the manufacturer has toll-free or direct-dial numbers for support as well as its hours of availability. Ticklish technical problems seem to occur at the most inopportune times — nights, weekends, holidays. If you're like us, you usually install this stuff late at night and on weekends. (We refuse to buy anything from anyone with only 9 a.m.– 5 p.m., Monday–Friday hours for technical support.) Traditionally, only high-end (that is to say, expensive) hardware products came with 24/7 technical support. However, an increasing number of consumer-priced computer products, including wireless home networking products, offer toll-free, around-the-clock, technical phone support.

Part III
Installing a Wireless Network

The 5th Wave   By Rich Tennant

@RICHTENNANT

"...and Bobby here found a way to extend our data transmission an additional 3000 meters using coax cable. How did you do that, Bobby – repeaters?"

In this part . . .

*N*ow comes the work: installing a wireless network in your home and getting it up and running. Whether you're a Mac user or have PCs running a Windows operating system — or both — this part of the book explains how to install and configure your wireless networking equipment. No doubt you're also interested in sharing a single Internet connection and, of course, making your home network as secure as possible. (You don't want your nosy neighbors getting on your network, do you?) This part helps you get the most out of your home's wireless network — by getting it installed right, the first time.

Chapter 6

Installing Wireless Access Points in Windows

In This Chapter

▶ Doing your proper planning

▶ Installing a wireless network access point (AP)

▶ Modifying AP configuration

*I*n this chapter, we describe the installation and configuration of your wireless home network's access point. We explain how to set up and configure the access point so that it's ready to communicate with any and all wireless devices in your home network. In Chapter 7, we describe the process for installing and configuring wireless network adapters.

Chapters 6 and 7 deal solely with Windows-based PCs. For specifics on setting up and installing wireless home networking devices on a Mac, see Chapter 8.

Before Getting Started, Get Prepared

Setting up an AP does have some complicated steps where things can go wrong. You want to reduce the variables to as few as possible to make debugging any problems as easy as possible. Don't try to do lots of different things all at once, such as buying a new PC, installing Windows Vista, and adding a router, an AP, and wireless clients. (Go ahead and laugh, but lots of people try this.) We recommend that you follow these steps:

1. **Get your PC set up first on a stand-alone basis.**

   If you have a new computer system, it probably shouldn't need much setup because it should be preconfigured when you buy it. If you have an older system, make sure that no major software problems exist before you begin. If you have to install a new operating system (OS), do it now. Bottom line: Get the PC working fine on its own so that you have no problems when you add functionality.

2. **Add your dial-up or broadband Internet connection for that one PC.**

   Ensure that everything is working on your wired connection first. If you have a broadband modem, get it working on a direct connection to your PC first. If you're using a dial-up connection, again, get that tested from your PC so that you know the account is active and works. Make sure you can surf the Web (go to a number of sites that you know work) to ascertain that the information is current (as opposed to coming from cache memory from earlier visits to the site).

3. **Sharing a broadband or dial-up connection with a router, add your home network routing option.**

   This step entails shifting your connection from your PC to your router; your router will have instructions for doing that. After that's working, make sure you can add another PC or other device, if you have one, by using the same instructions for your router. Make sure that your PC can connect to the Internet and that the two devices can see each other on the local area network. This action establishes that your logical connectivity among all your devices and the Internet is working. Because you may be installing an AP on an existing broadband or dial-up network, we're covering the AP installation first; we cover the installation of the router and your Internet sharing in Chapter 10.

4. **Try adding wireless to the equation: Install your wireless AP and wireless NICs and disconnect the wired cable from each to see whether they work — one at a time is always simpler.**

   By now, any problems that occur can be isolated to your wireless connection. If you need to fall back on dialing into or logging on to your manufacturer's Web site, you can always plug the wired connection in and do so.

If your AP is in an all-in-one cable modem/router/AP combo, that's okay. Think about turning on the elements one at a time. If a wizard forces you to do it all at once, go ahead and follow the wizard's steps; just recognize that if all goes wrong, you can reset the device to the factory settings and start over (it's extreme, but usually saves time).

Setting Up the Access Point

Before you install and set up a wireless network interface adapter in one of your computers, you should first set up the wireless access point (also called a *base station*) that will facilitate communication between the various wireless devices on your network. In this section, we describe how to set up a typical AP.

Preparing to install a wireless AP

The procedure for installing and configuring most wireless APs is similar from one manufacturer to the next — but not exactly the same. You're most likely to be successful if you locate the documentation for the AP you have chosen and follow its installation and configuration instructions carefully.

As we discuss in Chapter 5, when deciding which AP to purchase, consider ease of setup. By far the easiest setup we have found is from Belkin. The Belkin N1 Vision has a simple CD-based installation. After its basic settings are in place, you can manage the router from the LCD screen on the front of it with little effort. Apple's AirPort Extreme wireless routers have a similarly simple setup for Mac users (and include software for Windows only users as well).

Because having a network makes it easy to share an Internet connection, the best time to set up the AP for that purpose is during initial setup. In terms of setting up a shared Internet connection, you will already have a wired computer on your broadband (cable or DSL) or dial-up Internet connection. This is very helpful as a starting place for most AP installations because most of the information you need to set up your AP is already available on your computer. If you don't have a wired computer on your Internet connection — that is, if this is the first computer you're connecting — first collect any information (special login information, such as username or password) that your Internet service provider (ISP) has given you regarding using its services.

Before you begin plugging things in, make sure that you've done your research:

✔ **Ensure that your computer has a standard wired Ethernet connection.** Most AP configurations require wired access for their initial setup. An Ethernet port is normally found on the back of your computer; this port looks like a typical telephone jack, only a little bit wider. If you don't have an Ethernet adapter, you should buy one and install it in your computer. Alternatively, if your computer has a Universal Serial Bus (USB) port (preferably USB 2.0, also known as USB High Speed), you can purchase an AP that connects to the USB port.

Very few APs have this USB interface, and almost all PCs now have an Ethernet port — so using USB to connect to your AP is extremely rare these days. We mention it just to cover all the bases.

✔ **Collect your ISP's network information.** You need to know the following information; if you don't already know this stuff, ask the tech support folks at your ISP or check the support pages of the ISP's Web site:

  • **Your Internet protocol (IP) address:** This is the equivalent of your network's phone number. Your IP address identifies your network on the Internet and enables communications. It's always four 1- to 3-digit numbers separated by periods (125.65.24.129, for example).

- **Your Domain Name System (DNS) or service, or server:** This special service within your ISP's network translates domain names into IP addresses. *Domain names* are the (relatively) plain English names for computers attached to the Internet. The Internet however, is based on IP addresses. For example, www.wiley.com is the domain name of the Web server computers of our publisher. When you type **www.wiley.com** into your Web browser address bar, the DNS system sends back the proper IP address for your browser to connect to.

- **Whether your ISP is delivering all this to you via Dynamic Host Configuration Protocol (DHCP):** In almost all cases, the Internet service you get at home uses DHCP, which means that a *server* (or computer) at your ISP's network center automatically provides all the information listed in the preceding bullet, without you needing to enter anything manually. It's a great thing!

In the vast majority of cases, your ISP *does* use DHCP, and you don't have to worry about any of this information. If your service is Verizon's FiOS, your ISP is delivering an Ethernet connection to a firewall box that may or may not have wireless already built in. Verizon gives you the access information to this box when it's installed, and you can find all the information about your network connection from this box.

✔ **Collect the physical address of the network card used in your computer** *only if you're already connected directly to a cable/DSL modem.* Many ISPs used to use the physical address as a security check to ensure that the computer connecting to its network was the one paying for the service. Because of this security check, many AP manufacturers have added a feature called *MAC address cloning* to their routers. MAC address cloning allows home users to pay for only one connection from their ISP while having many devices able to get to the Internet. Most AP and Internet access devices available today permit you to change their physical addresses (Media Access Control [MAC] addresses) to match the physical address of your computer's existing network card. How you do this varies from system to system, but typically you'll see a list of MAC addresses (in a pull-down menu) for all devices connected to your AP. Simply select the MAC address you're looking to clone and click the button labeled Clone MAC address (or something similar).

Because some providers still track individual machines by MAC address, it's best to be prepared by writing down the MAC address of your computer's NIC in case you need it. How will you know that your ISP is tracking MAC addresses? Well, unfortunately, it's not always obvious — you might not see a big banner on the ISP's Web site telling you that MAC address tracking is in effect. But if you switch from a direct connection to your PC to a Wi-Fi router connection and you can't get online, MAC address tracking may indeed be the issue. The first step in troubleshooting such a problem is to unplug *everything* from the power supply (router/AP, broadband modem, and PC), and then turn it back on starting with the modem and slowly working your way back to the PC(s). If you're still not getting online, call your ISP's technical support line. If MAC tracking is the issue, you can get around it by cloning your PC's MAC address in your router as discussed in the preceding paragraph.

Installing the AP

If you're connecting your first computer with your ISP, the ISP should have supplied you with all the information we list in the preceding section except for the physical address of the network card (which isn't needed if you aren't already connected).

Before you install your wireless gear, buy a 100-foot Ethernet cable. If you're installing your AP at a distance farther than that from your router or Internet-sharing PC, get a longer cable. Trust us: This advice comes with having done this a lot. You need a wired backup to your system to test devices and debug problems. To do that (unless you want to keep moving your gear around, which we don't recommend), you need a long cable. Or two. Anyone with a home network should have extra cables, just like you have electrical extension cords around the house. You can get good-quality 100-foot CAT-5e/6 patch cables online at places like Deep Surplus (www.deepsurplus.com) or a host of other online retailers for around $15.

When you're ready to do the AP installation, follow these steps:

1. **Gather the necessary information for installing the AP (see the preceding bulleted list) by following these steps:**

   In Windows XP:

   a. **Choose Start⇨Programs⇨Accessories⇨Command Prompt.**

   This step brings up the command prompt window, which is a DOS screen.

   b. **Type** IPCONFIG /ALL **and then press Enter.**

   The information scrolls down the screen. Use the scroll bar to slide up to the top and write down the networking information we list earlier in this chapter (physical address, IP address, default gateway, subnet mask, DNS servers) and whether DHCP is enabled. You use this information to configure the AP in Step 4.

   In Windows Vista:

   a. **Choose Start⇨Network⇨Network and Sharing Center.**

   The Network and Sharing Center appears, which gives you access to all network adapters and their properties.

b. From the Network and Sharing Center, click the View Status link.

A pop-up status window appears with all the information you need.

2. **Run the setup software that accompanies the AP or device containing your AP, like a wireless or Internet gateway.**

The software probably starts when you insert its CD-ROM into the CD drive. In many cases, this software detects your Internet settings, which makes it much easier to configure the AP for Internet sharing and to configure the first computer on the network. For example, Figure 6-1 shows the Linksys Wireless-G Setup Wizard that accompanies the Linksys WAP54G Wireless-G Access Point, which is a wireless gateway from Linksys, a division of Cisco Systems, Inc.

If your computer is using Windows Vista, you will see a lot of security dialog box pop-ups. The enhanced security in Vista asks for your permission every time the installation software tries to do anything. As long as you have administration rights on your user account, you can keep saying yes to these security pop-ups and move through your AP setup. Be sure to look at the top left of the pop-up window so you know when you are saying yes to a security warning and when you are saying yes to the install. Even though Vista dims the rest of the screen when a security warning pops up, it is confusing with the number of pop-ups you can run into. Just read the top left of the window and you will always know what you are working in.

3. **When you're prompted by the setup software to connect the AP (see Figure 6-2), unplug the network cable that connects the broadband modem to your computer's Ethernet port and plug this cable into the Ethernet port that's marked *WAN* or *Modem* on your network's cable or DSL router or Internet gateway.**

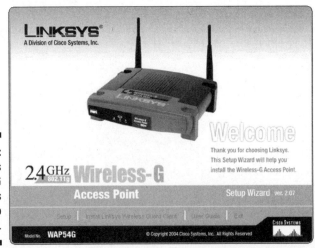

Figure 6-1:
The Linksys Wireless-G Access Point Setup Wizard.

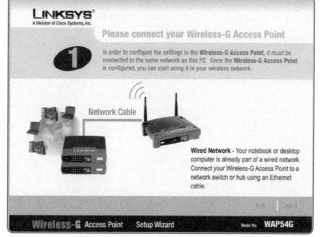

Figure 6-2:
It's time to
connect
the AP or
wireless
router.

If you're using an Internet or wireless gateway, run a CAT-5e/6 cable from one of its Ethernet ports to the computer on which you're running the setup software. (*CAT-5e/6 cable* is a standard Ethernet cable or patch cord with what look like oversized phone jacks on each end. You can pick one up at any computer store or Radio Shack.)

If you're using a separate AP and router (in other words, if your AP *is not* your router), you need to connect a CAT-5e/6 cable between the AP and one of the router's Ethernet ports. Then connect another cable from another one of the router's Ethernet ports to the computer on which you're running the setup software.

Most new APs try to obtain an IP address automatically and configure themselves for you by choosing the channel and setting default parameters for everything else (see Figure 6-3). In most cases, you need to manually configure the security and some of the other information you collected in Step 1 (so have that information handy).

4. **Record the following access point parameters:**

- Service set identifier (SSID)

- Channel — if you're using an 802.11n draft 2 AP, this should be set to Auto

- WEP key or WPA2 passphrase (see Chapter 9 for more details on this subject), if your system doesn't use WPS

- Router pin, if your system *does* use WPS (again, see Chapter 9 for more details on Wi-Fi Protected Setup)

- Admin username and password

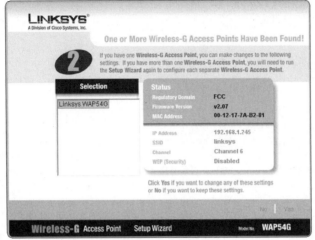

- MAC address

- Dynamic or static wide area network (WAN) IP address

- Local IP address

- Subnet mask

- PPPoE (Point-to-Point Protocol over Ethernet) — usually found on DSL connections, and rarely for cable modems

The preceding list covers the AP parameters you most often encounter and need to configure, but the list isn't comprehensive. (Read more about them in the "Configuring AP parameters" subsection.) You need this information if you plan to follow the steps for modifying AP configuration, which we cover in the later section "Changing the AP Configuration." (What did you expect that section to be called?) Other settings you probably don't need to change include the transmission rate (which normally adjusts automatically to give the best throughput), RTS/CTS protocol settings, the beacon interval, and the fragmentation threshold.

5. Complete the installation software, and you're finished.

After you complete the AP setup process, you should have a working access point ready to communicate with another wireless device.

Configuring AP parameters

Here's a little more meat on each of the access point parameters you captured in Step 4 of the preceding section.

✔ **Service set identifier (SSID):** The SSID (sometimes called the *network name, network ID,* or *service area*) can be any alphanumeric string, including upper- and lowercase letters, up to 30 characters long. The AP manufacturer may set a default SSID at the factory, but you should change this setting. Assigning a unique SSID doesn't add much security; nonetheless, establishing an identifier that's different from the factory-supplied SSID makes it a little more difficult for intruders to access your wireless network. And, if you have a nearby neighbor with a wireless AP of the same type, you won't get the two networks confused. When you configure wireless stations, you need to use the same SSID or network name that's assigned to the AP. It's also a good idea to turn off the SSID broadcast, a feature whereby the AP announces itself to the wireless world in general. Turning this off helps hide your AP from the bad guys who might want to hang off your network. However, hiding your SSID by no means absolutely hides your network (think of it as a mechanism for keeping out casual intruders to your network — dedicated intruders won't be stopped by a hidden SSID).

✔ **Router PIN:** This is the PIN number used for rapid implementation of network encryption and security using the WPS (Wi-Fi Protected Setup) system that many new APs include. See Chapter 9 for details.

✔ **Channel:** This is the radio channel over which the AP communicates. If you plan to use more than one AP in your home, you should assign a different channel (over which the AP communicates) for each AP to avoid signal interference. If your network uses the IEEE 802.11g protocols, eleven channels, which are set at 5 MHz intervals, are available in the United States. However, because the radio signals used by the IEEE 802.11g standard are spread across a 22 MHz-wide spectrum, you can only use as many as three channels (typically 1, 6, and 11) in a given wireless network. If you have an 802.11n draft 2.0 AP, you will want to have this set to Auto so that the AP and the wireless network card can switch between channels and use the ones with the least interference.

You can use other channels besides 1, 6, and 11 in an 802.11g network, but those three channels are the ones that are *noninterfering.* In other words, you could set up three APs near each other that use these channels and they wouldn't cause any interference with each other.

If you're setting up an 802.11a AP, or an 802.11n router that supports the 5 MHz frequency range, you have somewhere between 12 and 23 channels from which to choose (depending upon which country you live in). These channels don't overlap (like the 2.4 GHz channels do), so you can use them all without interference, while you can use only three without interference in the 2.4 GHz band. If you operate only one AP, all that matters is that all wireless devices on your network be set to the same channel. If you operate several APs, give them as much frequency separation as possible to reduce the likelihood of mutual interference.

Most 802.11g access points, such as some from Linksys, default to Channel 6 as a starting point and detect other access points in the area so that you can determine which channel to use. 802.11n access points will dynamically switch channels and choose the channels with the least interference automatically, which is cool.

Most 802.11n APs available today use only the 2.4 GHz frequency range. They can use multiple channels in this range, switching dynamically between channels if they find too much interference. The 2.4 GHz range is also the same frequency as Bluetooth devices. All new 802.11n draft 2 APs have the option to work in a default mode, using only 20 MHz of bandwidth inside the 2.4 GHz channel space (a single channel), or they can use a combined pair of channels (providing 40 MHz of bandwidth). Using combined (or *bonded*) channels allows your 802.11n gear to reach greater data speeds and has the fringe benefit of helping your network avoid interference with Bluetooth devices. If you use a lot of Bluetooth devices around your computer — such as a Bluetooth headset, mouse, keyboard, and camera — make sure you are in combined mode so that your 802.11n connection does not affect your Bluetooth devices and vice versa.

When you have multiple access points set to the same channel, sometimes roaming doesn't work when users move about the house, and the transmission of a single access point blocks all others that are within range. As a result, performance degrades significantly (you see this when your *throughput,* or speed of file and data transfers, decreases noticeably.) Use different, widely separated channels for 802.11g; because the 5 GHz 802.11a (and some 802.11n) channels are inherently not overlapping, you don't have to worry about choosing widely separated channels in this case.

✔ **WPA2:** Wi-Fi Protected Access (WPA2) is one of the best solutions in Wi-Fi security. Two versions of WPA are available:

• **WPA2 Personal, or Pre-Shared Key (PSK),** gives you a choice of two encryption methods: TKIP (Temporal Key Integrity Protocol), which utilizes a stronger encryption method and incorporates Message Integrity Code (MIC) to provide protection against hackers, and AES (Advanced Encryption System), which utilizes a symmetric 128-bit block data encryption. TKIP was the only system available in the first version of WPA; WPA2 added the ability to use AES, a stronger encryption system.

• **WPA2 Enterprise, or RADIUS** (Remote Authentication Dial-In User Service) utilizes a RADIUS server for authentication and the use of dynamic TKIP, AES, or WEP. RADIUS servers are specialized computer devices that do nothing but authenticate users and provide them with access to networks (or deny unauthorized users access). If you don't know what a RADIUS server is all about, chances are good that you don't have one.

We talk about both types of WPA2 in much greater detail in Chapter 9. WPA2 Enterprise is, frankly, overkill for the home environment and much more difficult to set up. We recommend that you use WPA2 Personal instead — it gets you 99 percent of the way there in terms of security and is much easier to set up and configure.

✔ **WEP keys:** You should always use some security on your wireless network, and if your network cannot support WPA, you should use, at minimum, Wired Equivalent Privacy (WEP) encryption. Only a determined hacker with the proper equipment and software can crack the key. If you don't use WEP or some other form of security, any nosy neighbor with a laptop, wireless PC Card, and range-extender antenna may be able to see and access your wireless home network. Whenever you use encryption, all wireless stations in your house attached to the wireless home network must use the same key. Sometimes the AP manufacturer assigns a default WEP key. Always assign a new key to avoid a security breach. Read Chapter 9 for great background info on WEP and WPA2.

✔ **WPS:** *Wi-Fi Protected Security* works with WPA2 and makes it considerably easier to set up WPA2 security on your network by automating the process. As we discuss in Chapter 9, you can implement WPS in two ways:

   • **PIN code:** You can turn on WPA2 by simply entering a PIN code printed on your Wi-Fi hardware (usually on a label).

   • **Pushbutton:** You can press a button on your Wi-Fi router (a physical button or a virtual button on a screen on the router). When the button is pushed, your devices can automatically connect to the router and automatically configure WPA2 in 2 minutes. Simply push the button(s) and let things set themselves up with no further intervention.

✔ **Username and password:** Configuration software may require that you enter a password to make changes to the AP setup. The manufacturer may provide a default username and password (see the user documentation). Use the default password when you first open the configuration pages, and then immediately change the password to avoid a security breach. (***Note:*** This isn't the same as the WPA2 shared key, which is also called a *password* by some user interfaces.) Make sure that you use a password you can remember and that you don't have to write down. Writing down a password is the same as putting a sign on the equipment that says "Here's how you hack into me." If you ever lose the password, you can always reset a device to its factory configuration and get back to the point where you took it out of the box.

✔ **MAC address:** The *Media Access Control (MAC) address* is the physical address of the radio in the AP. This number is printed on a label attached to the device. You may need to know this value for troubleshooting, so write it down. The AP's Ethernet (RJ-45) connection to the wired network also has a MAC address that's different from the MAC address of the AP's radio.

✔ **Dynamic or static wide area network (WAN) IP address:** If your network is connected to the Internet, it must have an IP address assigned by your ISP. Most often, your ISP dynamically assigns this address. Your router or Internet gateway should be configured to accept an IP address dynamically assigned by a DHCP server. It's possible, but unlikely, that your ISP will require a *set* (static) IP address.

✔ **Local IP address:** In addition to a physical address (the MAC address), the AP also has its own network (IP) address. You need to know this IP address to access the configuration pages by using a Web browser. Refer to the product documentation to determine this IP address. In most cases, the IP address is 192.168.*xxx.xxx*, where *xxx* is between 1 and 254. It's also possible that an AP could choose a default IP that's in use by your cable or DSL router (or a computer that got its IP from the cable or DSL router's DHCP server). Either way, if an IP conflict arises, you may have to keep the AP and cable or DSL routers on separate networks while configuring the AP.

✔ **Subnet mask:** In most cases, this value is set at the factory to 255.255.255.0. If you're using an IP addressing scheme of the type described in the preceding paragraph, 255.255.255.0 is the correct number to use. This number, together with the IP address, establishes the subnet on which this AP will reside. Network devices with addresses on the same subnet can communicate directly without the aid of a router. You really don't need to understand how the numbering scheme works except to know that the AP and all the wireless devices that will access your wireless network must have the same subnet mask.

✔ **PPPoE:** Many DSL ISPs still use Point-to-Point Protocol over Ethernet (PPPoE). The values you need to record are the username (or user ID) and password. The DSL provider uses PPPoE as a means of identifying and authorizing users.

Changing the AP Configuration

Each brand of AP has its own configuration software you can use to modify the AP's settings. Some products provide several methods of configuration. The most common types of configuration tools for home and small-office APs are

✔ **Software-based:** Some APs come with access point setup software you run on a workstation to set up the AP over a wireless connection, a USB cable, or an Ethernet cable. You don't see this much any longer except in professional high-end equipment that needs remote management not meant to work over the local network. One big exception here is Apple's AirPort Extreme (discussed in Chapter 8), which uses software built into Apple's OS X operating system (or a downloadable software client for Windows) instead of a Web-based configuration system.

✔ **Web-based:** Most APs intended for home and small-office use have a series of HTML forms stored in firmware. You can access these forms by using a Web browser over a wireless connection or over a network cable to configure each AP. In many cases when you are setting up your AP, you simply open the Web browser on the machine you have connected to the wired port on the AP; the browser automatically takes you to the AP setup wizard. This is so much simpler than the old days of having to load software on your machine just to set up your AP.

To access your AP's management pages with a Web browser, you need to know the local IP address for the AP. If you didn't note the IP address when you initially set up the AP, refer to the AP's user guide to find this address. It's a number similar to 192.168.2.1. If you're using an Internet gateway, you can also run `ipconfig` (Windows XP), or Network and Sharing Center (Windows Vista), as we describe in Chapter 7. The Internet gateway's IP address is the same as the default gateway.

Some APs and wireless routers have their administrative and configuration Web page IP addresses printed on labels on the back or bottom of the AP. If yours doesn't, we recommend that you get a label maker and print your own. There's nothing worse than looking for the user manual at an inopportune time when you need to be online now!

Most APs use the first address available on the network, such as 192.168.2.1. Note the last digit is almost always 1 to show the first of a possible 254 addresses in that last position. If you can't remember your AP's IP address, you can use the methods mentioned earlier in this chapter to get your computer's IP address. This will give you the first three numbers, and just putting a 1 at the end will work most of the time. When you know the AP's IP address, run your Web browser software, type the IP address on the Address line, and then press Enter or click the Go button. You will probably see a screen that requests a password. This password is the one you established during the initial setup for the purpose of preventing unauthorized individuals from making changes to your wireless AP's configuration. After you enter the password, the AP utility displays an AP management screen. If you're not using a Web-based tool, you need to open the application that you initially installed to make any changes.

You should also bookmark your AP's configuration page in your Web browser for easier access in the future.

Within the AP's management utility, you can modify all the AP's settings, such as the SSID, channel, and WEP encryption key. The details of how to make these changes vary from manufacturer to manufacturer. Typically, the AP management utility also enables you to perform other AP management operations, such as resetting the AP, upgrading its firmware, and configuring any built-in firewall settings.

AP manufacturers periodically post software on their Web sites that you can use to update the AP's firmware, which is stored in the circuitry inside the device. Many new APs have the ability to automatically update the firmware directly from the manufacturer's site. We don't recommend that you set this up because most of the time you are not going to need it, and upgrading firmware is serious business. If you decide to install a firmware upgrade, follow the provided instructions very carefully. ***Note:*** Do *not* turn off the AP or your computer while the update is taking place.

The best practice is to modify AP settings only from a computer that's directly connected to the network or the AP by a network cable. If you must make changes over a wireless connection, think through the order that you will make changes; otherwise, you could orphan the client computer. For example, if you want to change the wireless network's WPA2 key, change the key on the AP first and make sure that you write it down. As soon as you save the change to the AP, the wireless connection is effectively lost. No data passes between the client and the AP, so you can no longer access the AP over the wireless connection. To reestablish a useful connection, you must change the key on the client computer to the same key you entered on the AP.

Chapter 7

Setting Up a Wireless Windows Network

In This Chapter

▶ Installing wireless network interface adapters

▶ Modifying your adapter's settings

▶ Connecting with ease by using Windows XP's Wireless Zero Configuration

▶ Setting up your network with Windows Vista

▶ Keeping track of your network's performance

*I*n this chapter, we describe the installation and configuration of wireless devices on Windows computers. To that end, we explain how to set up and configure the wireless network interface adapter in each of your computers (and other wireless devices) so that they can communicate with the access point (AP) and with one another. We also include special coverage for installing and configuring wireless network adapters in computers running Windows XP and Vista (it's amazingly easy) and in handheld computers running one of the Microsoft mobile operating systems.

Read through Chapter 6 for information about physically installing APs, and see Chapter 8 for a discussion of setting up a Mac-based wireless network. If you find yourself lost in acronyms, check out Chapter 2 for the background on this equipment.

Setting Up Wireless Network Interface Adapters

After you have the AP successfully installed and configured (see Chapter 6), you're ready to install and set up a wireless network interface adapter in each client device. Wireless network adapters all require the same information to be installed, although the installation on different platforms may differ to some degree. From most manufacturers, the initial setup procedure differs somewhat depending on the operating system that's running your computer.

In this section, we walk you through installing device drivers and client software before addressing the typical setup procedure for various wireless network interface adapters.

The installation procedure for most types of PC devices consists of installing the hardware (the device) in your computer and then letting Windows detect the device and prompt you to supply a driver disc or CD. With most wireless network adapters, however, you should install the software provided with the wireless networking hardware *before* installing the hardware.

Installing device drivers and client software

Whenever you install an electronic device on your Windows PC, including a wireless network interface adapter, Windows needs to know certain information about how to communicate with the device. This information is a *device driver.* When you install a wireless network adapter, depending on which version of Windows you're using, you may be prompted to provide the necessary device driver. Device driver files typically accompany each wireless networking device on an accompanying CD-ROM. Most wireless device manufacturers also make the most up-to-date device driver files available for free download from their technical support Web sites.

When you install the wireless adapter into your computer, Windows uses the device driver files to add the adapter to your computer's hardware configuration. The new network adapter's driver also must be configured properly for it to communicate with other computers over the Windows network.

Even if you receive a driver CD with your wireless network interface adapter, we still recommend checking the manufacturer's Web site for the most recent software. Check the manufacturer's Web site and see if you need to download the newest driver software as well as the newest *firmware,* which is the special software that resides in the flash memory of your network adapter and enables it to do its job.

The exact procedure for installing the drivers and software for the wireless network adapters varies from manufacturer to manufacturer, so read the documentation that accompanies the product you're installing *before* you begin. Although the details may differ from the instructions that accompany your product, the general procedure is in the following set of steps.

Because some antivirus programs often mistake installation activity for virus activity, shut down any antivirus programs you may have running on your PC *before* you begin any installation of software or hardware. (Remember to turn it back on when you're done!) In Windows Vista, you must have an account with administrator access to install any software on the device. Normally this is the default account you set up for yourself when you first configured the computer.

To installing the software:

1. **Insert into the CD-ROM drive the CD that accompanies the wireless network adapter.**

   If the CD's startup program doesn't automatically begin, choose Start⇨ Run or use Windows Explorer to run the Setup.exe program on the CD.

2. **Install the software for configuring the network adapter by following the instructions on your screen.**

   Typically, you follow along with an installation wizard program.

Don't insert the network adapter until prompted to do so by the installation software (see Figure 7-1). In some cases, you may be prompted to restart the computer before inserting the adapter. For some older versions of Windows, you're prompted to insert your Windows CD in order for the setup program to copy needed networking files.

Because you installed the wireless network adapter's drivers and configuration software before inserting the adapter, the operating system should be able to automatically locate the driver and enable the new adapter.

Figure 7-1: Don't connect your wireless network adapter until prompted by the setup software.

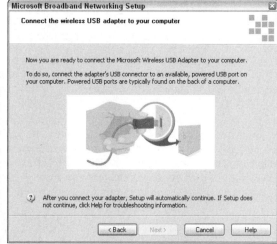

If Windows can't find the driver, it may start the Found New Hardware Wizard (or Add/Remove Hardware Wizard or even New Hardware Wizard — it depends on which OS you're using). If this does happen, don't panic. You can direct Windows to search the CD-ROM for the drivers it needs, and they should be installed without issues (although you may have to reboot again).

After you insert or install your wireless network adapter — and restart the computer, if prompted to do so — the OS might prompt you to configure the new adapter. In most cases the configuration is handled through the OS automatically, but if it's not, keep reading. If you just get a message that your hardware is installed and ready to use, you can skip Step 3 and move on.

3. **If the software prompts you to configure the new adapter, you need to make sure that the following settings, at minimum, match those of your network's wireless AP:**

  • **SSID (network name or network ID):** Most wireless network adapter configuration programs display a list of wireless networks that are in range of your adapter. In most instances, you see only one SSID listed. If you see more than one, it means that one (or more) of your neighbors also has a wireless network that's close enough for your wireless adapter to "see." Of course, it also means that your neighbor's wireless adapter can see your network too. This is one good reason to give your wireless network a unique SSID (network name), and it's also a compelling reason to use encryption.

  • **WPA2 passphrase (or WEP key):** Enter the same key or passphrase you entered in the AP's configuration. We discuss this concept in greater detail in Chapter 9.

  • **Device PIN:** If your Wi-Fi gear supports the new WPS security configuration system, you can skip entering the passphrase and just enter the PIN for connecting to your AP. Typically the PIN is located on a label attached to your network adapter. We discuss WPS in greater detail in Chapter 9.

After you configure the wireless network adapter, the setup program may announce that it needs to reboot the computer.

As a bonus, most wireless adapters — as part of their driver installation package — include a bandwidth monitor. This handy tool is used to debug problems and inform you of connection issues. Almost all these tools are graphical and can help you determine the strength of the signal to your AP device as well as the distance you can travel away from the device before the signal becomes too weak to maintain a connection.

PC Cards and mini-PCI cards

Nearly all Windows laptops and some Mac laptop computers have PC Card ports that are compatible with these cards. Belkin, Linksys, NETGEAR, D-Link, and others offer an 802.11n/g PC Card wireless network interface adapter. Most such devices already come preinstalled in portable computers and in some desktop computers. Many new laptops have DisplayPort adapters that are similar to PC Card slots. Don't confuse the two; even though they look the same, you don't want to jam a PC Card into a DisplayPort socket.

Most PC Card wireless network adapters require that you install the software drivers *before* inserting the PC Card for the first time. This is very important. Doing so ensures that the correct driver is present on the computer when the operating system recognizes that you have inserted a PC Card. Installing the drivers first also ensures that you can configure the wireless network connection when you install the device.

If you're installing a PC Card in a Windows-based computer with a PC Card slot, use the following general guidelines and don't forget to refer to the documentation that comes with the card for detailed instructions. (See Chapter 8 if you're a Mac user.)

Even if you received a CD with the PC Card, checking the manufacturer's Web site for the most recent drivers and client station software is a good idea. Wireless networking technology is continually evolving, so we recommend that you keep up with the changes.

To install a wireless PC Card in your computer, follow these steps:

1. **Insert the CD that accompanies the PC Card into the CD-ROM drive.**

   If the setup program doesn't automatically start, choose Start⇨Run (in Windows) or open Windows Explorer to run the Setup.exe program on the CD.

2. **Install the wireless client software.**

   During this installation, you may be asked to indicate the following:

   • Whether you want the PC Card set to infrastructure (AP) mode or to ad hoc (peer-to-peer) mode. Choose infrastructure mode to communicate through the AP. We talk about the difference between infrastructure and ad hoc modes in Chapter 2.

   • The SSID (network name).

   • Whether you will use a network password (which is the same as WPA2 encryption).

3. **After the wireless client software is installed, restart the computer if the install tells you to do so.**

4. **While the computer restarts, insert the PC Card wireless network adapter into the available PC Card slot.**

   Windows XP comes with generic drivers for many wireless PC Cards to make installation simpler than ever. Some PC Cards, which are made specifically for XP and certified by Microsoft, have no software included and rely on XP to take care of it. Even so, we recommend that you follow the directions that come with your PC Card and check whether your card is compatible with XP. Later in this chapter, we discuss the Windows XP Wireless Zero Configuration tools, which provide software for many Windows XP compliant and noncompliant cards.

   Windows Vista does not have many built-in generic drivers, and you will want to be sure that your PC Card has certified Vista drivers. At a minimum, the card should have a gray box on the package that says "Works with Windows Vista" and the Microsoft logo.

   When Windows finds the driver, it enables the driver for the card, and you're finished.

PCI and PCIx cards

If you purchase a wireless networking adapter that fits inside your PC, you must make sure that you have the right type for your computer. Most desktop computers built in the past five years contain PCI slots. The type of slot your computer has is most likely standard PCI. If you have a newer computer that uses PCIx, you're all set because PCIx is fully backward compatible. That means that you can use standard PCI cards in PCIx slots. The only difference you see is that the card doesn't fill the slot — the PCIx card slot is almost twice the length of the older standard PCI slot. Refer to your computer's documentation to determine which type of slot is inside your computer, and then purchase a wireless network interface adapter to match.

Most manufacturers choose to mount a PC Card on a standard PCI adapter. Some of the newest PCI adapters consist of a mini-PCI adapter mounted to a full-size PCI adapter. In either of these configurations, a black rubber dipole-type antenna, or another type of range-extender antenna, is attached to the back of the PCI adapter.

Most PCI cards come with specific software and instructions for installing and configuring the card. We can't tell you exactly what steps you need to take with the card you buy, but we can give you some generic steps. Don't forget to read the manual and follow the onscreen instructions on the CD that comes with your particular card.

Follow these general guidelines for installing a PCI adapter card:

1. **Insert into the CD-ROM drive the CD that accompanied the adapter.**

   If necessary, choose Start⇨Run (in Windows) or open Windows Explorer to run the Setup.exe program on the CD.

2. **Select the option for installing the PCI card driver software.**

   At this point, the driver is only copied to the computer's hard drive. The driver is added to the operating system in Step 4.

3. **If you're prompted to restart the computer, select No, I Will Restart My Computer Later, and then click the Next (or Finish) button.**

   In some cases, Steps 2 and 5 are accomplished in a single software-installation step. In other cases, you only install the wireless station software at this point.

   During the install process, many Windows-based computers prompt you to restart the computer by displaying a pop-up box with a question similar to "New drivers have been installed, do you want to restart for the changes to take effect?" The normal reaction may be to do what it asks and click the OK button — but *don't do it!* The software installation needs to be fully completed before the computer can be restarted. You know that it's completed because the installation wizard (not a Windows pop-up) prompts you for your next step. After the software has completed its installation process, *it* prompts you in its own software window to restart your computer, or it informs you that you need to restart to complete the installation.

4. **While the wireless station software is being installed, you may need to indicate whether you want the PC Card to be set to infrastructure (AP) mode or to ad hoc (peer-to-peer) mode. Choose infrastructure mode. You may also need to provide the SSID (network name) and indicate whether you will use WEP/WPA or WPA2 encryption.**

   We recommend WPA2 because it's the most secure encryption for your wireless network.

5. **After the PCI card driver is installed, shut down the computer.**

6. **Unplug the computer and install the PCI card in an available slot.**

7. **Plug in the computer and restart it.**

   Windows recognizes that you have installed new hardware and automatically searches the hard drive for the driver. When Windows finds the driver, it enables the driver for the adapter, and you're finished.

USB adapters

If you purchased a USB adapter, it's easy to install in your USB port. All new PCs and laptops come with at least one USB port (and usually more). Most USB adapters attach to the USB port via a USB cable. Many come with a base and an extension cable that allow you to move the USB adapter into a better position for its antenna. (See Chapter 8 if you're a Mac user.)

Here are the general guidelines for installing a USB wireless NIC:

1. **Insert into the CD-ROM drive the CD that accompanied the USB adapter.**

   If the CD's AutoRun feature doesn't cause the setup program to start, use the Run command from the Start button (in Windows) or open Windows Explorer to run the Setup.exe program on the CD.

2. **Install the driver software for the device.**

   In most cases the software will ask you to attach the USB device as soon as the drivers are installed. When finished, you see a confirmation in the lower-right task menu in Windows letting you know your USB network card has been installed and configured for use with Windows.

3. **After the wireless station software is installed, restart the computer if the installation software requires it.**

   You see the wireless adapter as a new network adapter in your system, and you have a new icon in your task tray indicating that the wireless is working correctly.

Wireless Zero Configuration with XP

Windows XP makes connecting to new wireless networks easier through a service that Microsoft has dubbed *Wireless Zero Configuration.* Although the Microsoft claim of zero configuration is a bit of an exaggeration, configuration is pretty easy. When you're installing or configuring a wireless adapter that's supported by Windows XP, you don't need to use software provided by the manufacturer. Instead, Windows XP itself recognizes the adapter and installs its own driver and configuration software. That does not mean you don't use the drivers that come from the manufacturer with the hardware you purchased. In most cases the manufacturer will have given to Microsoft the latest drivers for the device, or a pointer so the OS can download and install the drivers directly from the manufacturer's Web site.

Most 802.11n draft 2.0 adapters require specific hardware drivers to be able to take advantage of the advanced features of the standard.

Easy installation

As an alternative to the manufacturer's installation and configuration software, follow these steps to install and configure a supported wireless network adapter. (*Note:* We recommend that you check the documentation that accompanies your wireless adapter to determine whether it's supported by Windows XP Wireless Zero Configuration before continuing with these steps.)

1. **If you plan to use a wireless network interface adapter that you have to install inside the case of the computer, turn off the computer and install the PCI or ISA adapter.**

2. **Log on to Windows XP as a user with administrator rights.**

   If you installed Windows XP, you probably have administrator rights. To check, choose Start⇨Settings⇨Control Panel⇨User Accounts to display the User Accounts screen that shows the accounts on your computer. If you're not listed as Computer Administrator, you need to find out who the administrator is and get that person to change your account.

3. **Insert the PC Card or attach the USB adapter.**

   Windows XP displays a message that your new hardware is installed and ready to use. Because your computer is within range of your network's wireless AP (they have to be close enough to talk to each other), Windows XP announces that at least one wireless network is available and suggests that you click the Network icon to see a list of available networks.

4. **Click the Network icon in the notification area of the taskbar in the lower-right corner of the screen.**

   Windows XP displays the Wireless Network Connection dialog box, as shown in Figure 7-2.

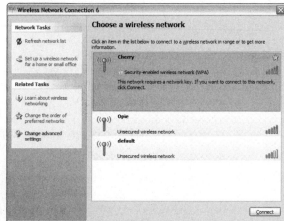

Figure 7-2:
The
Wireless
Network
Connection
dialog box.

5. **In the Network Key text box, type the WPA passphrase you used in the AP configuration, enter the key again in the Confirm Network Key text box, and then click the Connect button.**

The dialog box disappears, and Windows XP displays a balloon message that announces a wireless network connection and indicates the connection's speed and signal strength (poor, good, or excellent). The Network icon on the status bar occasionally flashes green to indicate network traffic on the wireless connection.

In a matter of minutes, you have installed and configured a wireless network connection. If you have trouble connecting, you can access more configuration information by clicking the Advanced button in the Wireless Network Connection dialog box (refer to Figure 7-2) to display the Wireless Network Connection Properties dialog box (Figure 7-3).

Figure 7-3:
The
Wireless
Network
Connection
Properties
dialog box.

Automatic network connections

Easy installation and configuration is only half the Windows XP wireless networking story. If you know that you will use your computer to connect to several different wireless networks — perhaps one at home and another at work — Windows XP enables you to configure the wireless adapter to automatically detect and connect to each network on-the-fly, without further configuration.

To configure one or more wireless networks for automatic connection, follow these steps:

1. **In the notification area of the status bar, at the bottom of the screen, click the Network icon to display the Wireless Network Connection dialog box, and then click the Properties button.**

2. **In the Wireless Network Connection Properties dialog box that appears, click the Wireless Networks tab (refer to Figure 7-3).**

   Notice that your wireless home network is already listed. If your computer is in range of the second wireless network, its SSID is also listed.

3. **To add another network to the list, click the Add button on the Wireless Networks tab.**

4. **In the Wireless Network Properties dialog box that appears, type the Network Name in the text box labeled Network Name (SSID).**

   This is the name of the wireless network AP to which you will connect your computer.

   You may want to enter the network name (SSID) for the wireless network at your office, for example.

5. **If you're connecting to a wireless network at your office, make sure that you have appropriate authorization and check with the network administrator for encryption keys and authorization procedures that he or she has implemented.**

   If the network administrator has implemented a system for automatically providing users with WEP/WPA2 keys, click OK.

   If the wireless network to which you plan to connect doesn't have an automatic key distribution system in place, do this:

   a. **Deselect the check box labeled The Key Is Provided for Me Automatically.**

   b. **Enter the WPA passphrase.**

   c. **Click OK to save this network SSID.**

6. **Move on to the next network (if any) that you want to configure.**

   Notice the Key Index scroll box near the bottom of the dialog box. By default, the key index is set to 1. Your office network administrator knows whether you need to use the key index. This feature is used if the system administrator has implemented a *rotating key system,* which is a security system used in some office settings. You don't need to mess with this feature unless you're setting up your computer to use at work — it's not something you use in your wireless home network.

7. **After adding all the necessary wireless networks, click OK on the Wireless Networks tab of the Wireless Network Connection Properties dialog box.**

   Windows XP now has the information it needs to automatically connect the computer to each wireless network whenever the wireless station comes into range.

Windows Vista Wireless Network Setup

Windows Vista has incorporated wireless networking into the standard networking built right into the OS. You no longer have a separate application and Windows to work in to manage your wireless network connection — though you still have a lot of windows to navigate through.

In Windows Vista, everything takes place in the Network and Sharing Center. From this one location, you can work with any of your network connections and get any information about those connections — from your IP address and your available bandwidth to troubleshooting connections with problems.

To get to the Network and Sharing Center, follow these steps:

1. **Click the Windows Start icon — the Start button of XP has been replaced with a round Windows icon button — in the lower-left corner of the screen. Select Network from the right column.**

   The Network dialog box appears.

2. **Select Network and Sharing Center from the links bar — this is just below the menu at the top of the screen.**

   Once inside the Network and Sharing Center (see Figure 7-4), the default network you see is your wired network. To connect to your wireless network, you need to use the link on the left menu, Manage Your Wireless Networks link on the left menu. The list is blank by default because you have not set up a wireless connection at this point.

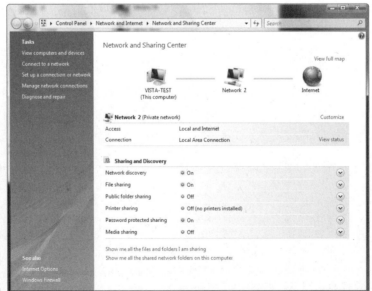

Figure 7-4:
The
Windows
Vista
Network
and Sharing
Center.

3. Click the Add button to have Windows search for wireless networks in range of your AP.

At this point you should have the SSID and the WEP/WPA2 passphrase you set up in your AP handy — or your AP's router PIN if your AP supports WPS. You have the option to have Windows search for any available wireless networks, manually set up a profile for your AP, or set up an ad hoc network. If you have turned off the broadcast of the SSID on your AP, you need to use the manual setup in Vista to add your AP to the list.

After the clicking the Add button, dialog boxes appear, asking you to fill in the appropriate information for any wireless network it can find. If you have to go through the manual process of setting up your AP, Vista's manual add wizard will walk you through the process to get you connected.

4. Enter the WEP/WPA2 key.

The New Connection Wizard tests the connection before it finishes. If your AP supports WPS, the wizard asks for your AP PIN number.

5. Configure the connection.

After your AP has been discovered, or set up, you are asked to configure the connection to the AP. In Vista, security has been tightened on all network connections, so you must choose whether this is a Public or Private network connection. If you want to share anything from your Vista machine, choose Private (see Figure 7-5). After you complete the selection, you return to the Manage Wireless Networks window, where you see your connection in the list.

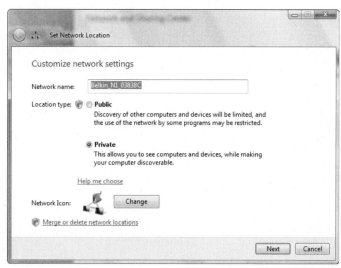

Figure 7-5:
Setting the network location.

TIP

If you're not sure you want to share anything from your Vista machine, you can gain a lot more security by choosing Public — you can always change it to Private later. When the connection is classified as Public, the Windows firewall is set with its strongest security, and many programs are restricted from using the connection — all programs to which you have not specifically granted access to an Internet connection are blocked from using this network connection. Vista security asks for permission to do everything, so any virus that's trying to use the connection will trigger the security to pop up and alert you.

6. **Close the Manage Wireless Networks window.**

   You return to the Network and Sharing Center.

7. **Now that you have added your wireless network to your system, you can disconnect your Ethernet connection and try out your network.**

You can discover and learn a lot more about your new wireless connection by using the tools in the Network and Sharing Center. In Figure 7-6, we have our Belkin AP set up as a Private network. From here we can use the View Status link to see all the details of our connection. Clicking the Details button will bring up all the information you might need about the speed, the amount of data that has been passed over the connection, the IP address, and pretty much everything else you may want to know about your connection. If you're having problems with your connection, the View Status pop-up also has a Diagnose button that can help determine the cause of your connection problem.

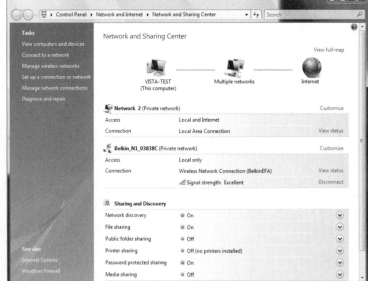

Figure 7-6:
The
Network
and Sharing
Center
showing
the new
wireless
network.

The Network and Sharing Center includes a helpful Signal Strength meter (which you can see from the View Status screen). We found in our tests that the Windows meter is not as fast to respond as some of the vendors' software that comes with your wireless network card. But if your vendor does not give you a signal meter, this one works fine to find weak coverage areas in your house.

Tracking Your Network's Performance

After you have your network adapters and APs installed and up and running, you may think that you have reached the end of the game — wireless network nirvana! And, in some ways you have, at least after you go through the steps in Chapter 9 and get your network and all its devices connected to the Internet. But part of the nature of wireless networks is the fact that they rely on the transmission of radio waves throughout your home. If you have ever tried to tune in a station on your radio or TV but had a hard time getting a signal (who hasn't had this problem — besides kids who have grown up on cable TV and Internet radio, we suppose), you probably realize that radio waves can run into interference or just plain peter out at longer distances.

The transmitters used in Wi-Fi systems use very low power levels — at least compared with commercial radio and television transmitters — so the issues of interference and range that are inherent to any radio-based system are even more important for a wireless home network.

Luckily, client software — usually in the form of a link test program — comes with some wireless network adapters, and signal meters are built into Windows XP and Vista. These tools enable you to look at the performance of your network. With most systems (and client software), you can view this performance-monitoring equipment in two places:

- ✔ **In your system tray:** Most wireless network adapters install a small signal-strength meter on the Windows system tray (usually found in the lower-right corner of your screen, although you may have moved it elsewhere on your screen). This signal-strength meter usually has a series of bars that light up in response to the strength of your wireless network's radio signal. It's different with each manufacturer, but most that we've seen light up the bars in green to indicate signal strength. The more bars that light up, the stronger your signal.

- ✔ **Within the client software itself:** The client software you installed along with your network adapter usually has a more elaborate signal-strength system that graphically (or using a numerical readout) displays several measures of the quality of your radio signal. This is often called a *link test* function, although different manufacturers call it different things. (Look in your manual or in the online help system to find it in your network adapter's client software.) The link test usually measures several things:

- **Signal strength:** Also called *signal level* in some systems, this is a measure of the signal's strength in dBm. The higher this number, the better, and the more likely that you can get a full-speed connection from your access point to your PC.

- **Noise level:** This is a measure of the interference that's affecting the wireless network in your home. Remember that electronics in your home (such as cordless phones and microwaves) can put out their own radio waves that interfere with the radio waves used by your home network. Noise level is also measured in dBm, but in this case, lower is better.

- **Signal to Noise Ratio (SNR):** This is the key determinant to the performance of your wireless network. This ratio is a comparison of the signal (the good radio waves) with the noise (the bad ones). SNR is measured in dB, and a higher number is better.

Many link test programs not only provide an instantaneous snapshot of your network performance but also give you a moving graph of your performance over time. This snapshot can be helpful in two ways. First, if you have a laptop PC, you can move it around the house to see how your network performance looks. Second, it can let you watch the performance while you turn various devices on and off. For example, if you suspect that a 2.4 GHz cordless phone is killing your wireless LAN, turn on your link test and keep an eye on it while you make a phone call.

When you grow more comfortable with your wireless LAN — and start using it more and more — you can leverage these tools to tweak your network. For example, you can have your spouse or a friend sit in the living room watching the link test results while you move the access point to different spots in the home office. Or you can use the link test with a laptop to find portions of your house that have weak signals and then use these results to decide where to install a second access point.

Chapter 8

Setting Up a Wireless Mac Network

In This Chapter

▶ Understanding the Apple AirPort System

▶ Using AirPort with OS X Macs

▶ Adding a non-Apple PC to your AirPort network

▶ Connecting to *non*-AirPort networks

*I*f you're an Apple Macintosh user and you've just decided to try wireless networking, this chapter is for you. We cover installing and setting up the AirPort Extreme card in an Apple computer as well as setting up an AirPort Extreme base station. We focus on Mac OS X versions 10.4 (Tiger) and 10.5 (Leopard) because they are the most current versions of the Mac operating system at the time of this writing (as we write, Leopard is brand spanking new!), but the advice we offer in this chapter gets you up and running with *any* version of OS X. Along the way, Apple has added a few new features to its wireless networking software (such as, in OS X 10.5, the ability to rapidly see which networks have encryption turned on), but by and large the Wi-Fi connectivity in OS X has been the same in all versions.

Note: Apple has phased out OS 9 support for its recent computers. If you have an older Mac that still runs only OS 9, you're not out of luck — OS 9 PCs can support and connect to AirPort and other Wi-Fi networks, but not all the features we are discussing here apply.

We're focusing on the Apple AirPort system in this chapter simply because Apple has its own (robust and easy to use) Wi-Fi home router hardware that is tightly integrated into the OS X system software — and many Mac users prefer sticking with an all-Apple network. However, this doesn't mean that Apple computers *must* use AirPort routers (they can connect to any standards-based Wi-Fi router using the 802.11b, g, or n standard), or conversely, that *other* computers and devices can't use an AirPort system as their Wi-Fi router (they can, again given a common Wi-Fi standard).

Understanding AirPort Hardware

Back in 1999, Apple Computer had a product launch for the iBook notebook (remember the multicolored curvy ones that looked like nothing in the world quite as much as they did a toilet seat?), and part of that big dog-and-pony show (*all* Apple product launches are extravaganzas!) was the introduction of the AirPort Wi-Fi wireless networking system. AirPort was the first mainstream, consumer-friendly, and consumer-focused wireless networking system. Over the years, AirPort (it's gone through a few name changes and design upgrades, as we discuss) has become an integral part of the Apple product lineup and is installed (or available) in *all* of Apple's desktop and notebook computers.

The AirPort product line includes both *client adapters* (known as AirPort cards), which are installed inside Apple computers, and *wireless routers* (known as AirPort base stations) that act as the base station for a Wi-Fi network.

Apple's current AirPort products use the newest Wi-Fi 802.11n draft 2.0 technology, which is (as we write) the state of the art in the wireless LAN world. Apple computers equipped with AirPort Extreme cards can connect to any Wi-Fi compatible 2.4 GHz 802.11b, g, or n wireless network, as well as 5 GHz 802.11a and 802.11n networks — regardless of whether the network uses Apple equipment or wireless equipment from any other Wi-Fi certified vendor.

The current generation of AirPort products (dubbed AirPort Extreme) is compatible with the 802.11n draft 2.0 standard. You may also run into some older generations of AirPort equipment (just plain *AirPort* by name, as well as earlier editions of the AirPort Extreme) that are compatible with the older 802.11b or g standards but that don't support 802.11n or a.

Getting to know the AirPort card

Apple computer models were the first on the market to feature a special wireless adapter — known as the AirPort card — as an option. The original AirPort card was similar in form to a PC Card (a Personal Computer Memory Card International Association [PCMCIA] Card) but was designed to be installed in a special AirPort slot inside an Apple computer. If you get your hands on one of the original AirPort cards, you should not try to use it in a PC Card slot found on most laptop computers. As we mention in the nearby sidebar, "The amazing disappearing AirPort card," the original 802.11b AirPort card is no longer being produced and supplies are limited — luckily, all Macs built in the past two years support the newer AirPort Extreme card, and all Macs built since late 2006 support the 802.11n version of AirPort Extreme.

The current AirPort Extreme card is a mini-PCI Card (well, it's the same size and shape but designed to fit *only* in AirPort slots in Macs). It fits inside an Apple computer, such as several recent PowerBook G4s, iBooks, and iMacs, but doesn't fit in the original AirPort slot in older Macs — and isn't required for any of Macs built since 2005 (all of which already have Wi-Fi built in). The AirPort Extreme card has a retail price of $49. The AirPort Extreme card is Wi-Fi certified to be compliant with 802.11g, so it connects to any Wi-Fi certified 802.11b or 802.11g access point, including (but not limited to) the Apple AirPort Extreme base stations.

Some recent Intel-based Macs were shipped with 802.11n capable AirPort Extreme cards installed but without the software that turned on the 802.11n functionality. In other words, these Macs were sold as 802.11a/b/g compatible, even though their hardware could support 802.11n as well. In order to turn on this functionality, Apple requires you to download a small software firmware patch for the card. You can get this file (called the AirPort Extreme 802.11n Enabler for Mac) in two ways:

✔ Pay Apple $1.99 and download it from the Apple Online Store (http://store.apple.com).

✔ Buy an AirPort Extreme base station with Gigabit Ethernet (Apple's 802.11n Wi-Fi router) — the software patch is included for free in the box.

If you have a MacBook Pro with Intel Core 2 Duo, Mac Pro with AirPort Extreme option, or iMac with Intel Core 2 Duo (except the 17-inch 1.83GHz iMac), you may want to upgrade to 802.11n. You can check if you already have the Enabler file by opening the Network Utility (found in the Utilities folder in your Mac's Applications folder) and viewing the Info tab: If the en1 Network Interface is described as 802.11a/b/g/n, you don't need the Enabler; if it just says 802.11a/b/g/, you do.

Apple AirPort Extreme–ready computers

Apple has been including Wi-Fi capability as a standard feature of all its computers for a few years — so any Mac laptop or desktop purchased since mid-to-late 2005 has at least 802.11g Wi-Fi capability built in. The only exceptions are the MacPro desktop machines, which are most often used in business environments (where wired Ethernet connections are common); these computers have the AirPort capability as an option in some configurations.

A number of Apple computers (since mid-to-late 2006) have been capable of supporting 802.11n as well, including the following:

✔ iMac with Intel Core 2 Duo (except the 17-inch 1.83 GHz iMac)
✔ MacBook with Intel Core 2 Duo

✔ MacBook Pro with Intel Core 2 Duo

✔ Mac Pro with AirPort Extreme card option

Some older Macintosh computers may not have an AirPort card installed but can be equipped with Apple's AirPort Extreme card (discussed in the preceding section).You can find a list of these computers at the following URL: http://docs.info.apple.com/article.html?artnum=107440. This Web page also includes a link to another Apple Web page that lists all Macintosh computers that can use the older AirPort card as well.

Apple computers that are equipped for installation of an AirPort Extreme card have an antenna built into the body of the computer. When you install the AirPort card, you attach the AirPort Extreme card to the built-in antenna. (All radios need an antenna to be able to send and receive radio signals, and wireless networking cards are no exception.)

If your older Mac doesn't support AirPort or AirPort Extreme, you can try using a standard Wi-Fi network adapter with the drivers found at www.ioxperts.com/devices/devices_80211b.html.

The amazing disappearing AirPort card

The original AirPort card — the one that fits into all the older G3 and Titanium G4 PowerBooks, original iBooks, and original iMacs — has been discontinued by Apple. Not because they aren't good guys and not because they don't want to sell such cards to their customers. The problem is that the 802.11b chips inside these cards are no longer available (the chip vendors are spending all their time building 802.11g chips like those found in the AirPort Extreme card).

The result is that cards for these Macs are extremely rare — the only real source of these cards is the small number that have been stockpiled by folks who repair Macs as service parts. Think back to Econ 101, and you can see how this situation may drive up prices. We've seen these older cards (which originally cost about $100) for more than $150 on eBay and on various reseller Web sites. (They're nowhere to be found on Apple's own site.)

The only other alternative is to find a third-party Wi-Fi adapter that can work with your older Mac. For notebook computers such as the PowerBook, it's a PC Card adapter (see Chapter 2 for more on this), and for desktop Macs (such as Power Macs), it's a PCI card. The AirPort software built into Mac OS X doesn't work with these devices (and almost none of them have a set of Mac *driver* software). The solution is to mate a card with some specialized software that works with a Macintosh.

The most popular solution here is to find an 802.11b PC or PCI card that works with the IOXpert 802.11b driver for Mac OS X ($19.95 after a free trial period). This software works with a large number of 802.11b cards and all versions of OS X (including the current Tiger version). Go to www.ioxperts.com/devices/devices_80211b.html to find out more, to see a list of compatible (and incompatible) cards, and to download the trial version.

"Come in, AirPort base station. Over."

Apple currently sells two wireless routers, which they call *base stations*. The current state-of-the-Apple-art is the AirPort Extreme base station with Gigabit Ethernet. This $179 base station is fully compatible with the 802.11n draft 2.0 standard (see Chapter 3) and includes the following features:

✔ **High-speed networking:** Using 802.11n on the wireless side of the house and full Gigabit (1000 Kbps) wired Ethernet connections for three devices, this router provides connections as fast as any on the market.

✔ **A USB port:** The USB port can be configured to provide

- A printer connection (using the built-in print server) that lets you share just about any USB printer over the network, so you can send print jobs from your Macs or Windows computers to a central printer.

- A shared storage device (called AirPort Disk), using a USB hard drive. You simply plug in any USB external hard drive and enable the AirPort Disk feature by using Apple's software, and Macs and Windows computers can share the hard drive space for backups, storage of media files (such as digital music), and more.

- A USB hub feature (you need to provide your own hub), with which you can "double up" your AirPort Extreme base station's USB port, attaching more than one printer and/or hard drive at once.

✔ **Up-to-date security support:** The AirPort Extreme base station with Gigabit Ethernet supports WPA and WPA2 encryption, as well as support for business-grade security standards such as RADIUS and 802.1x.

✔ **Dual-band support:** Like most 802.11n draft 2.0 devices, the AirPort Extreme base station with Gigabit Ethernet can be used on either the 2.4 GHz or 5 GHz bands, meaning you can move your wireless traffic to the less crowded 5 GHz band if that's an issue in your home, or keep it on the 2.4 GHz band for maximum range and compatibility with older 802.11b or g equipment.

Figure 8-1 shows the AirPort Extreme base station with Gigabit Ethernet.

Getting aboard the Express

The AirPort Extreme isn't the only Apple entry in the AP space (and, in fact, it's not even the most interesting!). Apple also has a small form factor (about the size of a deck of cards) access point known as the AirPort Express (see Figure 8-2).

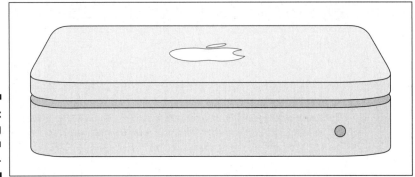

Figure 8-1:
Going
802.11n
Apple style.

Figure 8-2:
The AirPort
Express is
a jack of all
trades.

This $99 device can fulfill a bunch of different roles in your wireless life, including the following:

✔ **A full-fledged AP and router:** The AirPort Express can do pretty much everything any full-size AP can do — you can build your entire wireless LAN around an AirPort Express.

✔ **A *travel router:*** A cool new category of APs are those designed for use on the road — travel routers that you can pack up and plug into any broadband access (like that available in most hotels) and provide yourself with an instant Wi-Fi hot spot. The small size of the AirPort Express lets you stick it in your laptop bag and bring it wherever you go. Pat wrote this chapter in a hotel room in Vegas using his AirPort Express — a pretty sad commentary on his after-hours life these days!

✔ **A WDS repeater:** The Apple AirPort system supports the WDS (wireless distribution system) standard, which allows you to extend your network throughout even a *huge* house by having your wireless signals hop from AP to AP until they reach your distant clients.

✔ **A USB print server:** You can plug a USB printer into the AirPort Express and get printer access from the entire network.

✔ **An AirTunes player:** Perhaps our favorite feature of the AirPort Express is its support for AirTunes. AirTunes is the Apple software system that lets you listen to the music in your iTunes collection (and from your iPod) throughout your entire network. The AirPort Express has analog and digital audio connectors that you plug into a stereo or home theater. Although Apple's fancy AppleTV is an even better way of doing this, it costs four times as much as the AirPort Express, so if your focus is on music more than TV, you might consider choosing the AirPort Express.

Like the AirPort Extreme base station, the AirPort Express uses the 802.11g standard and can work with any type of Wi-Fi certified 802.11g or 802.11b client.

We haven't heard anything about this from Apple, but we certainly expect that Apple will come out with an 802.11n version of the AirPort Express in the not-so-distant future. If you are setting up a new network and don't need a router to fill the roles that the AirPort Express fills right away, you might want to hold off on the purchase of the device for a while.

Using AirPort with OS X Macs

Apple makes it exceptionally easy to configure an AirPort Extreme base station or an AirPort Express. All Mac OS X computers that are capable of working with an AirPort system have two bits of software installed in the Utilities folder (found in your Applications folder):

✔ AirPort Setup Assistant

✔ AirPort Admin Utility

The Setup Assistant is a "follow along with the steps" program (like the wizard programs often used on Windows computers) that guides you through the setup of an AirPort system by asking you simple questions. The Admin Utility is used for tweaking and updating your settings later, after you already have everything set up. Most people can just use the Setup Assistant for all their configuration needs — though we recommend that you occasionally run the Admin Utility program to upgrade the *firmware* (the underlying software inside your AirPort), as we discuss later in the "Upgrading AirPort base station firmware on OS X" section.

Configuring the AirPort base station on OS X

When you've purchased a new AirPort Extreme base station or AirPort Express (that you will use as a base station), the easiest way to set it up for use in your wireless home network is to use the AirPort Setup Assistant. The AirPort Setup Assistant reads the Internet settings from your computer and transfers them to the base station so that you can access the Internet over your wireless network. To use the AirPort Setup Assistant, follow these steps:

1. **Before running the AirPort Setup Assistant, set up your computer to connect to the Internet by dial-up modem or by broadband (cable or DSL) modem.**

   Check with your ISP for instructions on getting connected:

   • **If you connect to the Internet by dial-up modem:** Connect the telephone line to the phone line port on the base station.

   • **If you connect to the Internet by DSL or cable modem:** Use an Ethernet cable to connect the modem to the base station's WAN port.

2. **Click the Applications Folder on the dock.**

3. **When the Applications folder opens, double-click the Utilities folder icon.**

4. **In the Utilities folder, double-click the AirPort Setup Assistant icon to display the AirPort Setup Assistant window, as shown in Figure 8-3.**

5. **Select the Set Up a New AirPort Base Station option, and then click the Continue button.**

   If your computer is in range of your wireless network, the Setup Assistant automatically configures your AirPort card to select that network and proceeds to the America Online Access panel. However, if you happen to be in range of more than one wireless network, you see the Select an AirPort Network panel, which asks you to select your network from a pop-up list. Your network will have its name assigned at the factory, similar to *Apple*

Network xxxxxx, where *xxxxxx* is a six-digit hexadecimal number. After selecting your network, click the Continue button to go to the next panel.

6. **In the America Online Access panel:**

    • **If you connect to the Internet via AOL:** Select the I Am Using America Online option, and then click the Continue button.

    • **If you're not using AOL:** Select the I Am Using Another Internet Service Provider option, and then click the Continue button to display the Internet Access panel.

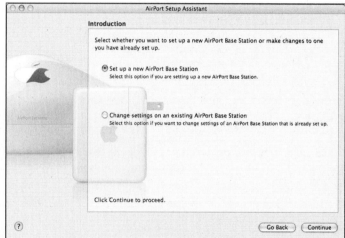

Figure 8-3:
The OS X
AirPort
Setup
Assistant
window.

7. **In the Internet Access panel, choose one of the following options, and then click the Continue button:**

    • **Local Area Network:** You should select this option if your computer is connected to a high-speed LAN.

    • **Cable Modem or DSL Using Static IP or DHCP:** Select this option if you connect to the Internet by cable modem or by DSL, but only if your ISP doesn't use the PPP over Ethernet (PPPoE) protocol.

    • **Cable Modem or DSL Using PPPoE:** If your ISP uses the PPPoE protocol, select this option. It's important that you make a successful connection to the Internet with your computer connected directly to the cable or DSL modem before attempting to configure the base station. The AirPort Setup Assistant can then copy the PPPoE settings from your computer to the base station so that the base station can log on to the Internet with your user ID and password. All the computers on your wireless network can then share the Internet connection without needing to log on.

8. **The next panel you see at this step depends on the choice you make in Step 7. After you enter the appropriate information, click the Continue button:**

   - **LAN, or Broadband Using Static IP or DHCP:** If you choose either a LAN or a broadband (cable modem or DSL) connection that doesn't use PPPoE, the Ethernet Access panel presents the option to use DHCP or to assign a static IP address. If your ISP has assigned you a static IP address — along with other values, such as subnet mask, router address, domain name, and DHCP client name — you have to enter this data if it isn't automatically copied from your computer.

   - **Broadband Using PPPoE:** If you select the Cable Modem or DSL Using PPPoE option, the PPPoE Access panel presents text boxes for entering an account name, password, and other account information sometimes required by PPPoE providers. Again, in most cases, this information is automatically copied from your computer.

9. **In the Network Name and Password panel that appears, enter the name and password you want to use for your wireless network, and then click the Continue button.**

10. **In the base station Password panel, use the network password or assign a different password for changing the settings on your base station.**

   If you're the only person who will configure the computers on the network, using the same one in both places is probably the easiest. However, if you plan to share the network password with other users, assign a different password to the base station so that only you can change the base station's settings.

11. **Click the Continue button.**

   You see a Conclusion panel, which informs you that the Setup Assistant is ready to set up your base station.

12. **Click the Continue button.**

   After the Setup Assistant downloads the new settings to the base station, it displays a message that it's waiting for the base station to reset. As soon as the base station resets, the Setup Assistant displays a panel announcing that it's finished and that it has been able to configure this computer to connect to the Internet.

13. **Click the Done button to close the AirPort Setup Assistant.**

Upgrading AirPort base station firmware on OS X

In this section, we explain how to upgrade the firmware of a new AirPort Extreme base station. Upgrading the firmware on your AirPort Extreme base station through a direct Ethernet cable connection is easiest. Use an Ethernet cable (either a straight-through cable or a crossover cable; the base station automatically detects the type of cable you're using) to connect your computer's Ethernet port to the base station's LAN port. You can also do the upgrade over a wireless connection.

To upgrade the firmware of a new AirPort base station that you're setting up for the first time, follow these steps:

1. **On the Dock, click the Applications folder.**

2. **When the Applications folder opens, double-click the Utilities folder.**

3. **Double-click the AirPort Admin Utility icon to display the Select Base Station window, shown in Figure 8-4.**

4. **Highlight the base station name and then click the Configure button.**

5. **After a message pops up requesting a password, enter** public **as the password and then click OK.**

   • If the firmware installed in the base station is older than the firmware supplied with your updated software, you see a message prompting you that a newer version of the base station software is available. Click the Upload button to install it.

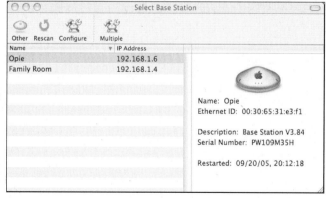

Figure 8-4:
The OS X
Select Base
Station
window.

• If a message pops up stating that uploading the software will cause the wireless network to be disconnected, click OK. The new firmware is copied to the base station.

If the Select Base Station window — rather than a message that a newer version of the base station software is available — is displayed when you click the Configure button, your base station already contains the most recent firmware. Close the Select Base Station window and then close the AirPort Admin utility.

6. **After a message says that the system is waiting for the base station to restart and that the base station has been successfully updated, click OK.**

7. **When the Select Base Station window returns, close it.**

8. **Disconnect the Ethernet cable between your computer and the base station, if you're using one.**

Connecting another computer to your AirPort network on OS X

When you set up your AirPort base station by following the directions in the preceding section, you also set up the AirPort card in the computer you used to configure the base station. However, you need to configure the AirPort cards in the other Mac computers in your house to enable them to connect to the AirPort network. Follow these steps:

1. **Click and hold the Applications folder on the Dock, and select the Internet Connect application.**

2. **When Internet Connect opens, select the AirPort tab, shown in Figure 8-5.**

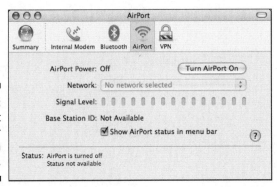

Figure 8-5:
Start making your connection here.

3. **Make sure that the AirPort Power is on — if it's not, click the button labeled Turn AirPort On.**

4. **In the Network pull-down menu, select the AirPort network you created.**

5. **Select the Show AirPort Status in Menu Bar check box while you're at it.**

   This step streamlines the process the next time you want to get connected to this network. If you've turned on Encryption for your AirPort network, you're prompted to enter a password.

6. **Select the appropriate type of encryption (see Chapter 9 for more on this topic; we recommend that you use WPA Personal), and then type your password in the Password text box, shown in Figure 8-6. Select the Remember Password in My Keychain check box to retain the password for future use.**

7. **Click the OK button.**

8. **When the Internet Connect window indicates that you're connected to the AirPort network, you can close the window.**

   Figure 8-7 shows Pat's PowerBook connected to his network, Cherry.

Figure 8-6:
Enter your
password
here.

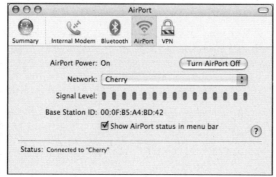

Figure 8-7:
All done!

After you've gone through these steps, you have an AirPort icon on your menu bar. The next time you want to connect to this AirPort network, simply go up to the menu bar, click the AirPort icon, and select the network name. That's it!

Adding a Non-Apple Computer to Your AirPort Network

One reason why wireless home networking has become so popular is the interoperability between wireless networking equipment from different vendors. Because it adheres to the standards and is Wi-Fi certified, Apple wireless networking equipment is no exception. You can even use a Windows or Linux computer to connect to an Apple AirPort base station.

The procedure for entering wireless network parameters in non-Apple wireless software when configuring a wireless network adapter varies by manufacturer. Follow these general steps to add your non-Apple computer (or even your Apple computer with non-Apple wireless hardware and software) to your AirPort Network:

1. **Select the network name of the AirPort base station.**

   The wireless network adapter configuration software usually presents a list of available wireless networks in range of the adapter. From the list, select the network name you assigned to the AirPort base station.

   For example, in Windows XP, right-click the Network icon in the notification area of the taskbar and select View Available Wireless Networks from the pop-up menu that appears. Then select the AirPort base station's network name from the list presented in the Wireless Network Connection dialog box.

2. **Enter the network password (your WEP key or WPA passphrase).**

   If you're using WEP, the password you entered in the AirPort base station setup probably doesn't work. Here's how to find the password — the WEP key — that works. Apple uses a different password naming convention than other wireless manufacturers. Fortunately, Apple has provided a function in the AirPort Admin Utility that does the conversion for you:

   a. **Using the computer you used to configure the AirPort, open the AirPort Admin utility.**

   b. **Select your base station from the list, and then click the Configure icon.**

   c. **When presented with a pop-up window, enter the password for configuring the base station, and then click OK to display the main AirPort Admin Utility window.**

  d. From the Base Station menu, choose Equivalent Network Password.

  If the toolbar isn't visible, click the View menu and choose Show Toolbar.

  The utility opens a drop-down window that displays the equivalent network password (WEP key) that you should enter in the configuration software for your non-Apple wireless network adapter.

3. **Make sure that you set the adapter to obtain an IP address automatically.**

  How you do this depends on what kind of PC and which PC operating system you're using.

4. **Close the configuration software, and you should be connected to the AirPort network.**

  If you're not connected, go through the steps again and pay particular attention when entering the equivalent network password.

If you're really having a hard time, try turning WEP off on your AirPort base station (deselect the Use Encryption check box in the Airport Setup program) and see whether you can connect without any encryption. If this works, double-check your equivalent network password and look in the manual for your network adapter. You may need to enter a special code before the Equivalent Network Password.

If you're using Windows XP and have Wireless Zero Configuration enabled, just follow the steps we discuss in Chapter 7 for that software — you can connect to an AirPort network simply and quickly that way.

Connecting to Non-Apple-based Wireless Networks

One scenario you may encounter in a home network is the need to connect a Macintosh computer to a non-Apple-based network. Follow the procedures outlined in this chapter for adding a computer to a wireless network — using the Internet Connect AirPort pane, the procedure should be identical. If you have any trouble, it almost certainly relates to the network password. Here are a few troubleshooting tips to resolve password issues:

 ✔ **Try turning off encryption on the wireless network:** If you can successfully connect your Mac to the network without the need of a password, you can be sure that the password was the problem. Don't leave the network unprotected, however. Read on.

✔ **Check the password configuration:** When you turn on the access point's encryption, determine whether the password is an alphanumeric value or a hexadecimal number. Some hardware vendors provide configuration software that has you enter a passphrase, but the software then generates a hexadecimal number. You have to enter the hexadecimal number, not the passphrase, in the AirPort software.

✔ **Watch for case sensitivity:** If the Windows-based access point configuration software enables you to enter an alphanumeric password, keep in mind that the password is case sensitive. For WEP, the password should be either exactly 5 characters (letters and numbers) for 64-bit encryption or 13 characters for 128-bit encryption. You should then enter exactly the same characters in the Password text box in the AirPort pane of Internet Connect.

✔ **Use current software:** Make sure that you're using the most current version of AirPort software. The most up-to-date software makes it easier to enter passwords connecting to a Windows-based wireless network. The new software automatically distinguishes between alphanumeric and hexadecimal passwords. With earlier versions of the software, to connect to a WEP-encrypted Windows-based network, you have to type quotation marks around alphanumeric values and type $ in front of hexadecimal numbers.

These guidelines should help you get your Mac connected to a Windows wireless network, including the capability to share the Internet. Keep in mind, however, that other factors determine whether you can also share files, printers, and other resources over the wireless network.

Chapter 9

Securing Your Wireless Home Network

*I*f you read the news — well, at least if you read the same networking news sources that we do — you've probably seen and heard a thing or two (or a hundred) about wireless local area network (LAN) security. In fact, you really don't need to read specialized industry news to hear about this topic. Many major newspapers and media outlets — *The New York Times,* the *San Jose Mercury News,* and *USA Today,* among others — have run feature articles documenting the insecurity of wireless LANs. Most of these stories have focused on *wardrivers,* folks who park in the lots in front of office buildings, pull out their laptops, and easily get onto corporate networks.

In this chapter, we talk a bit about these security threats and how they may affect you and your wireless home network. We also (helpful types that we are) give you some advice on how you can make your wireless home network more secure. We talk about a system called Wi-Fi Protected Access (WPA), which can make your network secure to most attacks, and also an older system called Wired Equivalent Privacy (WEP), which doesn't do such a good job but may be the best you can do in many cases.

The advice we give in this chapter applies to any 802.11 wireless network, whether it uses a, b, g, or n, because the steps you take to batten down the hatches on your network are virtually identical, regardless of which version of 802.11 you choose. (If you missed our discussion on 802.11 basics, jump over to Chapter 2.)

No network security system is absolutely secure and foolproof. And, as we discuss in this chapter, Wi-Fi networks have some inherent flaws in their security systems, which means that even if you fully implement the security system in Wi-Fi (WPA or especially WEP), a determined individual could still get into your network. We're not trying to scare you off here. In a typical residential setting, chances are good that your network won't be subjected to some sort of determined attacker like this. Follow our tips, and you should be just fine.

Assessing the Risks

The biggest advantage of wireless networks — the fact that you can connect to the network just about anywhere within range of the base station (up to 300 feet, or even longer with the new 802.11n technology) — is also the biggest potential liability. Because the signal is carried over the air via radio waves, anyone else within range can pick up your network's signals, too. It's sort of like putting an extra RJ-45 jack for a wired LAN out on the sidewalk in front of your house: You're no longer in control of who can access it.

One thing to keep in mind is that the bad guys who are trying to get into your network probably have bigger antennas than you do. Although you may not pick up a usable signal beyond a few hundred feet with that PC Card with a built-in antenna in your laptop PC, someone with a big directional antenna that has much more gain than your PC's antenna (*gain* is a measure of a circuit's ability to increase the power of a signal) may be able to pick up your signals — you would never know it was happening.

General Internet security

Before we get into the security of your wireless LAN, we need to talk for a moment about Internet security in general. Regardless of what type of LAN you have — wireless or wired or using powerlines or phone lines or even none — when you connect a computer to the Internet, some security risks are involved. Malicious *crackers* (the bad guys of the hacker community) can use all sorts of tools and techniques to get into your computers and wreak havoc.

For example, someone with malicious intent could get into your computer and steal personal files (such as your bank statements you've downloaded by using Quicken) or mess with your computer's settings — or even erase your hard drive. Your computer can even be hijacked (without your knowing it) as a jumping off point for other people's nefarious deeds; as a source of an attack on another computer (the bad guys can launch these attacks remotely using your computer, which makes them that much harder to track down); or even as source for spam e-mailing.

What we're getting at here is that you need to take a few steps to secure *any* computer attached to the Internet. If you have a broadband (DSL, satellite, fiber-optic, or cable modem) connection, you *really* need to secure your computers. The high-speed, always-on connections that these services offer make it easier for a cracker to get into your computer. We recommend that you take three steps to secure your computers from Internet-based security risks:

- ✔ **Use and maintain antivirus software.** Many attacks on computers don't come from someone sitting in a dark room, in front of a computer screen, actively cracking into your computer. They come from viruses (often scripts embedded in e-mails or other downloaded files) that take over parts of your computer's operating system and do things you don't want your computer doing (such as sending a copy of the virus to everyone in your e-mail address book and then deleting your hard drive). Choose your favorite antivirus program and use it. Keep the *virus definition files* (the data files that tell your antivirus software what's a virus and what's not) up to date. And for heaven's sake, use your antivirus program!

- ✔ **Use a personal firewall on each computer.** *Personal firewalls* are programs that basically look at every Internet connection entering or exiting your computer and check it against a set of rules to see whether the connection should be allowed. After you've installed a personal firewall program, wait about a day and then look at the log. You may be shocked and amazed at the sheer number of attempted connections to your computer that have been blocked. Most of these attempts are relatively innocuous, but not all are. If you have broadband, your firewall may block hundreds of these attempts every day.

  We like ZoneAlarm (www.zonealarm.com) for Windows computers as well as the firewall built into Windows XP Service Pack 2 and Windows Vista, and we use the built-in firewall on our Mac OS X computers.

- ✔ **Turn on the firewall functionality in your router.** Whether you use a separate router or one integrated into your wireless access point, it will have at least some level of firewall functionality built in. Turn this function on when you set up your router or access point. (It's an obvious option in the configuration program and may well be turned on by default.) We like to have both the router firewall and the personal firewall software running on our PCs. It's the belt-and-suspenders approach, but it makes our networks more secure.

  In Chapter 11, we talk about some situations (particularly when you're playing online games over your network) where you need to disable some of this firewall functionality. We suggest that you do this only when you must. Otherwise, turn on that firewall — and leave it on.

Some routers use a technology called *stateful packet inspection* (SPI) firewalls, which examine each packet (or individual chunk) of data coming into the router to make sure that it was truly something requested by a computer on the network. If your router has this function, we recommend that you try using it because it's a more thorough way of performing firewall functions. Others simply use Network Address Translation (NAT, which we introduce in Chapter 2) to perform firewall functions. This strategy isn't quite as effective as stateful packet inspection, but it works quite well.

Airlink security

The area we focus on in this chapter is the aspect of network security that's unique to wireless networks: the airlink security. These security concerns have to do with the radio frequencies beamed around your wireless home network and the data carried by those radio waves.

Traditionally, computer networks use wires that go from point to point in your home (or in an office). When you have a wired network, you have physical control over these wires. You install them, and you know where they go. The physical connections to a wired LAN are inside your house. You can lock the doors and windows and keep someone else from gaining access to the network. Of course, you have to keep people from accessing the network over the Internet, as we mention in the preceding section, but locally it would take an act of breaking and entering by a bad guy to get on your network. (It's sort of like it was on *Alias,* where they always seem to have to go deep into the enemy's facility to tap into anything.)

Wireless LANs turn this premise on its head because you have absolutely no way of physically securing your network. Of course, you can do things like go outside with a laptop computer and have someone move the access point around to reduce the amount of signal leaving the house. But that's really not 100 percent effective, and it can reduce your coverage within the house. Or you could join the tinfoil hat brigade ("The NSA is reading my mind!") and surround your entire house with a Faraday cage. (Remember those from physics class? We don't either, but they have something to do with attenuating electromagnetic fields.)

Some access points have controls that let you limit the amount of power used to send radio waves over the air. This solution isn't perfect (and it can dramatically reduce your reception in distant parts of the house), but if you live in a small apartment and are worried about beaming your Wi-Fi signals to the apartment next door, you may try this. It doesn't keep a determined cracker with a supersize antenna from grabbing your signal, but it may keep honest folks from accidentally picking up your signal and associating with your access point.

Basically, what we're saying here is that the radio waves sent by your wireless LAN gear will leave your house, and there's not a darned thing you can do about it. Nothing. What you can do, however, is make it difficult for other people to tune into those radio signals, thus (and more importantly) making it difficult for those who can tune into them to decode them and use them to get onto your network (without your authorization) or to scrutinize your e-mail, Web surfing habits, and so on.

You can take several steps to make your wireless network more secure and to provide some airlink security on your network. We talk about these topics in the following sections, where we discuss both easy and more complex methods of securing your network.

Getting into Encryption and Authentication

Two primary (and related) security functions enable you to secure your network: encryption and authentication.

- ✔ **Encryption:** Uses a cryptographic *cipher* to scramble your data before transmitting it across the network. Only users with the appropriate *key* can unscramble (or decipher) this data.

- ✔ **Authentication:** Simply the act of verifying that a person connecting to your wireless LAN is indeed someone you want to have on your network. With authentication in place, only authorized users can connect with your APs and gain access to your network and to your Internet connection.

No security!

The vast majority of wireless LAN gear (access points and network cards, for example) is shipped to customers with all the security features turned off. That's right: zip, nada, zilch, no security. A wide-open access point sits there waiting for anybody who passes by (with a Wi-Fi equipped computer, at least) to associate with the access point and get on your network.

This isn't a bad thing in and of itself; initially configuring your network with security features turned off and then enabling the security features after things are up and running is easier

than doing it the other way 'round. Unfortunately, many people never take that extra step and activate their security settings. So a huge number of access points out there are completely open to the public (when they're within range, at least).

We should add that some people *purposely* leave their access point security turned off to provide free access to their neighborhoods. (We talk about this topic in Chapter 16.) But we find that many people don't intend to do so.

With most wireless network systems, you take care of both functions with a single step — the assignment of a network *key* or *passphrase* (we explain later in this chapter, in the section "Enabling encryption," where each of these is used). This key or passphrase is a secret set of characters (or a word) that only you and those you share it with know.

The key or passphrase is often known as a *shared secret* — you keep it secret but share it with that select group of friends and family whom you want to allow access to your network. With a shared secret (key or passphrase), you perform both of these security functions:

✔ You authenticate users because only those who have been given your supersecret shared secret have the right code word to get into the network. Unauthenticated users (those who don't have the shared secret) cannot connect to your wireless network.

✔ Your shared secret provides the mechanism to encrypt (or scramble) all data being sent over your network so that anyone who picks up your radio transmissions sees nonsensical gibberish, not data that they can easily read.

The two primary methods of providing this authentication and encryption are

✔ Wired Equivalent Privacy (WEP)

✔ Wi-Fi Protected Access (WPA)

Note that there are two versions of WPA, WPA and WPA2, but we refer to them jointly as WPA except when discussing their differences.

We talk about the WEP and WPA security systems in more detail in the remaining parts of this chapter. WEP, an older system, provides only a limited amount of security because certain flaws in its encryption system make it easy for crackers to figure out your shared secret (the *WEP key*) and therefore gain access to your network and your data.

WPA is the current, up-to-date, security system for Wi-Fi networks (there are several variants, which we discuss later in this chapter), and it provides you with much greater security than does WEP. If you have the choice, *always* use WPA on your network rather than WEP.

The shared secret method of securing a network is by far the most common and the easiest method. But it doesn't really provide truly bulletproof user authentication, simply because having to share the same secret passphrase or key with multiple people makes it a bit more likely that somehow that secret will get into the wrong hands. (In fact, some experts would probably hesitate to even call it an authentication system.)

For most home users, this *isn't* a problem (we don't think that you have to worry about giving Nana the passphrase for your network when she's in town visiting her grandkids), but in a busy network (such as in an office), where people come and go (employees, clients, customers, and partners, for example), you can end up in a situation where just too many people have your shared secret.

When this happens, you're stuck with the onerous task of changing the shared secret and then making sure that everyone who needs to be on the network has been updated. It's a real pain.

These kinds of busy networks have authentication systems that control the encryption keys for your network and authorize users on an individual basis (so that you can allow or disallow anyone without having to start from scratch for *everyone,* like you do with a shared secret).

If you have this kind of busy network, you may want to consider securing your network with a system called *WPA Enterprise* and *802.1x.* See the sidebar "802.1x: The corporate solution" later in this chapter, for more information on this topic.

Introducing Wired Equivalent Privacy (WEP)

The original system for securing a wireless Wi-Fi network is known as *WEP,* or *Wired Equivalent Privacy.* The name comes from the admirable (but, as we discuss, not reached) goal of making a wireless network as secure as a wired one.

In a WEP security system, you enter a *key* in the Wi-Fi client software on each device connecting to your network. This key must match the key you establish when you do the initial setup of your access point or wireless router (which we describe in Chapter 7).

WEP uses an encryption protocol called *RC4* to secure your data. Although this protocol (or *cipher*) isn't inherently bad, the way that it's implemented in WEP makes it relatively easy for a person to snoop around on your network and figure out your key. And after the bad guys have your key, they can access your network (getting into PCs and other devices attached to the network or using your Internet connection for their own purposes) or stealthily intercept everything sent across the wireless portion of your network and decode it without your ever knowing!

It doesn't take superhacker skills to do this either — anyone with a Windows or Linux or Mac PC with wireless capabilities can download free and readily available software from the Web and, in a short time, figure out your key.

How about a bit more about WEP?

WEP encrypts your data so that no one can read it unless they have the key. That's the theory behind WEP, anyway. WEP has been a part of Wi-Fi networks from the beginning. (The developers of Wi-Fi were initially focused on the business market, where data security has always been a big priority.) The name itself belies the intentions of the system's developers; they wanted to make wireless networks as secure as wired networks.

To make WEP work, you must activate it on all the Wi-Fi devices on your network via the client software or configuration program that came with the hardware. And every device on your network must use the same WEP key to gain access to the network. (We talk a bit more about how to turn on WEP in the later section, "Clamping Down on Your Wireless Home Network's Security.")

For the most part, WEP is WEP is WEP. In other words, it doesn't matter which vendor made your access point or which vendor made your laptop's PC Card network adapter — the implementation of WEP is standardized across vendors. Keep this one difference in mind, however: WEP key length. Encryption keys are categorized by the number of bits (1s or 0s) used to create the key. Most Wi-Fi equipment these days uses *128-bit* WEP keys, but some early gear (such as the first generation of Apple AirPort equipment) supported only a 64-bit WEP key.

Many access points and network adapters on the market support even longer keys — for example, many vendors support a 256-bit key. The longest standard key, however, is 128 bits. Most equipment enables you to decide how long to make your WEP key; you can often choose between 64 and 128 bits. Generally, for security purposes, you should choose the longest key available. If, however, you have some older gear that can't support longer WEP key lengths, you can use a shorter key. If you have one network adapter that can handle only 64-bit keys but have an access point that can handle 128-bit keys, you need to set up the access point to use the shorter, 64-bit key length.

Should you use WEP?

WEP sounds like a pretty good deal, doesn't it? It keeps your data safe while it's floating through the ether by encrypting it, and it keeps others off your access point by not authenticating them. But, as we mention earlier in this chapter, WEP isn't all that secure because flaws in the protocol's design make it not all that hard for someone to crack your WEP code and gain access to your network and your data. For a typical home network, a bad guy with the right tools could capture enough data flowing across your network to crack WEP in a matter of hours.

Almost all APs, wireless routers or gateways, and network adapters now being sold support the newer (and much more secure) WPA protocol. And, almost any computer with Windows XP or Macintosh OS X will also have built-in support for WPA. So there are many good reasons to skip WEP entirely and just go with WPA.

But (there's often a *but* in these situations) at times you may need to consider using WEP encryption. You run into this situation with certain pieces of Wi-Fi gear because you can't have "mixed" encryption methods on the same network. In other words, you can't have laptop A connected to the Wi-Fi AP using WPA and laptop B connected using WEP. It's one security system or the other.

We say earlier in this chapter that almost all PCs support WPA, but the dirty little secret of the Wi-Fi business is that not all Wi-Fi peripheral devices — such as wireless print servers, media adapters, and other non-PC devices — support WPA yet. Before you buy any of these devices, check the product specs and make sure you see WPA (or even better, WPA2) listed on that long list of acronyms of supported protocols and features.

If any device on your network doesn't support WPA, you need to use WEP on that network. Similarly, if you have a device that doesn't even support WEP (an exceedingly rare situation that we've only rarely run across), you can't even use WEP on that network. We think that having WPA encryption on your network is darned important, so if you run into this situation, we highly recommend that you try to find devices that support WPA rather than weaken your overall network security.

A better way: WPA

If you can use WPA — meaning if your access point or wireless gateway and *all* the wireless clients on your network support it — you should enable and use WPA as the airlink security system on your network. WPA is significantly more secure than WEP and keeps the bad guys off your network much more effectively than any implementation of WEP.

Two variants of WPA are available: WPA and WPA2. The major difference between these two is the *cipher,* or *encryption,* system used to encode the data sent across the wireless network. WPA2 — which is the latest and most powerful wireless security system — uses a system called Advanced Encryption Standard (AES), which is pretty much uncrackable by mere mortals. But even the original WPA version (that's just WPA to you and us), with its Temporal Key Integrity Protocol (TKIP), is much more secure than WEP.

WPA2 is also known as 802.11i. 802.11i is simply the IEEE (the folks who make the standards for wireless LANs) standard for advanced Wi-Fi security. WPA was a step toward 802.11i set by the Wi-Fi Alliance. WPA2 incorporates all the security measures included in 802.11i.

What's better about WPA?

- **More random encryption techniques:** WPA has basically been designed as an answer for all the current weaknesses of WEP, with significantly increased encryption techniques. One of WEP's fatal flaws is that because its encryption isn't sufficiently random, an observer can more easily find patterns and break the encryption. WPA's encryption techniques are more random — and thus harder to break.

- **Automatic key changes:** WPA also has a huge security advantage in the fact that it automatically changes the key (although you, as a user, get to keep using the same password to access the system). So, by the time a bad guy has figured out your key, your system has already moved on to a new one.

It's possible to use an 802.1x system, as described in the sidebar "802.1x: The corporate solution," later in this chapter, to provide automatic key changes for WEP systems. This is *not* something you would find in anyone's home network, but some businesses use it, and it does indeed minimize the effect of WEP's fixed keys.

- **More user friendly:** WPA is easier for consumers to use because there's no hexadecimal stuff to deal with — just a plain text password. The idea is to make WPA much easier to deal with than WEP, which takes a bit of effort to get up and running (depending on how good your access point's configuration software is).

The type of WPA (and WPA2) we're talking about here is often called *WPA Personal* or *WPA PSK* (preshared key). The more complex (and not suitable for the home) version of WPA/WPA2 that is often used by businesses is *WPA Enterprise*. We talk about WPA Enterprise in the sidebar titled "802.1x: The corporate solution."

Clamping Down on Your Wireless Home Network's Security

Well, that's enough of the theory and background, if you've read from the beginning of this chapter. It's time to get down to business. In this section, we discuss some of the key steps you should take to secure your wireless network from intruders. None of these steps is difficult, will drive you crazy, or make your network hard to use. All that's required is the motivation to spend a few minutes (after you have everything up and working) battening down the hatches and getting ready for sea. (Can you tell that Pat used to be in the Navy?)

The key steps in securing your wireless network, as we see them, are the following:

1. Change all the default values on your network.

2. Enable WPA.

3. Close your network to outsiders (if your access point supports this).

In Chapter 16 we talk about using a *virtual private network* (VPN) to secure your wireless connection when you're away from home and when using public Wi-Fi hot spots. A virtual private network encrypts *all* the data that you send and receive through your computer's network connection by creating a secure and encrypted network *tunnel* that runs from your computer to an Internet gateway (which could be in your office's network or run by a service provider on the Internet). If you really wanted to be as secure as possible, you could use a VPN from a service provider such as Witopia (www.witopia.net) to encrypt your traffic at home too. The added benefit of a VPN, beyond security, is anonymity. To folks on the Internet, you will "look" like you're surfing the Internet from that Internet gateway and not your home — which makes it harder for folks to track your comings and goings on the Internet. A VPN isn't required to have a secure Wi-Fi network, but if you have one and your WEP or WPA security is broken by a bad guy, your communications will be secured by another layer of encryption.

Hundreds of different access points and network adapters are available. Each has its own unique configuration software. (At least each vendor does; and often different models from the same vendor have different configuration systems.) You need to RTFM (Read the Fine Manual!). We give you some generic advice on what to do here, but you really, really, really need to pick up the manual and read it before you enable security on your network. Every vendor has slightly different terminology and different ways of doing things. If you mess up, you may temporarily lose wireless access to your access point. (You should still be able to plug in a computer with an Ethernet cable to gain access to the configuration system.) You may even have to reset your access point and start over from scratch. Follow the vendor's directions (as painful at that may be). We tell you the main steps you need to take to secure your network; your manual gives you the exact line-by-line directions on how to implement these steps on your equipment.

Most access points also have some wired connections available — Ethernet ports you can use to connect your computer to the access point. You can almost always use this wired connection to run the access point configuration software. When you're setting up security, we recommend making a wired connection and doing all your access point configuration in this manner. That way, you can avoid accidentally blocking yourself from the access point when your settings begin to take effect.

Getting rid of the defaults

It's incredibly common to go to a Web site like Netstumbler.com, look at the results of someone's Wi-Fi reconnoitering trip around their neighborhood, and see dozens of access points with the same service set identifier (SSID, or network name; refer to Chapter 2). And it's usually Linksys because Linksys is the most popular vendor out there (though NETGEAR, D-Link, and others are also well represented). Many folks bring home an access point, plug it in, turn it on, and then do nothing. They leave everything as it was set up from the factory. They don't change any default settings.

Well, if you want people to be able to find your access point, there's nothing better (short of a sign on the front door) than leaving your default SSID broadcasting out there for the world to see. In some cities, you could proba-bly drive all the way across town with a laptop set to `Linksys` as an SSID and stay connected the entire time. (We don't mean to just pick on Linksys here. You could probably do the same thing with an SSID set to `default`, the D-Link default, or any of the top vendors' default settings.)

When you begin your security crusade, the first thing you should do is to change all the defaults on your access point. You should change, at minimum, the following:

- ✔ Your default SSID
- ✔ Your default administrative password

If you don't change the administrative password, someone who gains access to your network can guess at your password and end up changing all the set-tings in your access point without your knowing. Heck, if they want to teach you a security lesson — the tough love approach, we guess — they could even block you out of the network until you reset the access point. These default passwords are well known and well publicized. Just look on the Web page of your vendor, and we bet you can find a copy of the user's guide for your access point available for download. Anyone who wants to know them does know them.

When you change the default SSID on your access point to one of your own making, you also need to change the SSID setting of any computers (or other devices) that you want to connect to your LAN. To do this, follow the steps we discuss in this part's earlier chapters.

This tip really falls under the category of Internet security (rather than airlink security), but here goes: Make sure that you turn off the Allow/Enable Remote Management function (it may not be called this exactly) if you don't need it. This function is designed to allow people to connect to your access point over the Internet (if they know your IP address) and do configuration stuff from a distant location. If you need this turned on (perhaps you have a home office and your IT gal wants to be able to configure your access point remotely), you know it. Otherwise, it's just a security hole waiting to be opened, particularly if you haven't changed your default password. Luckily, most access points have this function set to Off by default, but take the time to make sure that yours is set to Off.

Enabling encryption

After you eliminate the security threats caused by leaving all the defaults in place (see the preceding section), it's time to get some encryption going. Get your WPA (or WEP) on, as the kids say.

We've already warned you once, but we'll do it again, just for kicks: Every access point has its own system for setting up WPA or WEP, and you need to follow those directions. We can give only generic advice because we have no idea which access point you're using.

To enable encryption on your wireless network, we suggest that you perform these generic steps:

1. **Open your access point's configuration screen.**

2. **Go to the Wireless, Security, or Encryption tab or section.**

   We're purposely being vague here; bear with us.

3. **Select the option labeled Enable WPA or WPA PSK (or, if you're using WEP, the one that says Enable WEP or Enable Encryption or Configure WEP).**

   You should see a menu similar to the one shown in Figure 9-1. (It's for a NETGEAR access point or router.)

4. **If you're using WEP, select the check box or pull-down menu option for the appropriate WPA key length for your network. If you're using WPA, skip this step.**

   We recommend 128-bit keys if all the gear on your network can support it. (See the earlier section "How about a bit more about WEP?" for the lowdown on WEP keys.)

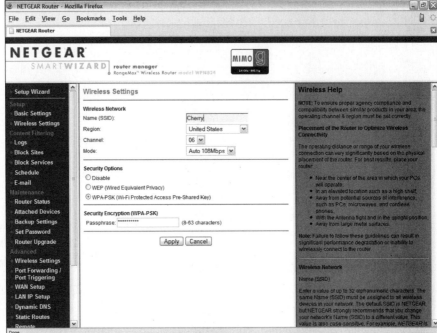

5. **For WPA, create a passphrase that will be your network's shared secret. For WEP, create your own key if you want (we prefer to let the program create one for us):**

   a. **Type a passphrase in the Passphrase text box.**

   b. **Click the Generate Keys (or Apply or something similar) button.**

Remember the passphrase. Write it down somewhere, and put it someplace where you won't accidentally throw it away or forget where you put it. Danny likes to tape his passphrase to the box that his Wi-Fi gear came in so that he can always track it down.

Whether you create your own key or let the program do it for you, a key should now have magically appeared in the key text box. *Note:* Some systems allow you to set more than one key (usually as many as four keys). In this case, use Key 1 and set it as your default key by using the pull-down menu.

Remember this key! Write it down. You'll need it again when you configure your computers to connect to this access point.

Some access points' configuration software doesn't necessarily show you the WEP key you've generated — just the passphrase you've used to generate it. You need to dig around in the manual and menus to find a command to display the WEP key itself. (For example, the Apple AirPort software shows just the passphrase; you need to find the *Network Equivalent Password* in the Airport Admin Utility to display the WEP key — in OS X, this is in the Base Station menu.)

For WEP, the built-in wireless LAN client software in Windows XP numbers its four keys from 0–3 rather than 1–4. So, if you're using Key 1 on your access point, select Key 0 in Windows XP.

6. **Click OK to close the WPA or WEP configuration window.**

You have finished turning on WPA or WEP. Congratulations.

Can we repeat ourselves again? Will you indulge us? The preceding steps are *very* generic. Yours may vary slightly (or, in rare cases, significantly). Read your user's guide. It tells you what to do.

After you configure WPA or WEP on the access point, you must go to each computer on your network, get into the network adapter's client software (as we describe in Chapters 7 and 8), turn on WEP, and enter the passphrase or the WEP key. Typically, you find an Enable Security dialog box containing a check box to turn on security and one to four text boxes for entering the key. Simply select the check box to enable WEP, enter your key in the appropriate text box, and then click OK. Figure 9-2 shows this process using Windows XP and its built-in Wireless Zero Configuration client.

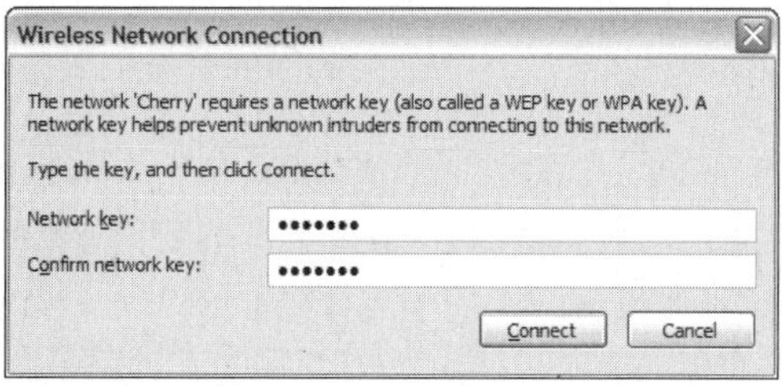

Figure 9-2:
Setting
up WPA
using the
Windows
XP Wireless
Zero
Configura-
tion.

> **Wireless Network Connection**
>
> The network 'Cherry' requires a network key (also called a WEP key or WPA key). A network key helps prevent unknown intruders from connecting to this network.
>
> Type the key, and then click Connect.
>
> Network key: ●●●●●●●
>
> Confirm network key: ●●●●●●●
>
> [Connect] [Cancel]

Closing your network

The last step we recommend that you take in the process of securing your wireless home network (if your access point allows it) is to create a *closed network* — a network that allows only specific, predesignated computers and devices onto it. You can do two things to close down your network, which makes it harder for strangers to find your network and gain access to it:

✓ **Turn off SSID broadcast:** By default, most access points broadcast their SSID out onto the airwaves. This makes it easier for users to find the network and associate with it. If the SSID is being broadcast and you're in range, you should see the SSID on your computer's network adapter client software and be able to select it and connect to it — that is, assuming you have the right WEP key, if WEP is configured on that access point. When you create a closed network, you turn off this broadcast so that only people who know the exact name of the access point can connect to it.

You can find access points even if they're not broadcasting their SSIDs (by observing other traffic on the network with a network *sniffer* program), so this security measure is an imperfect one — and no substitute for enabling WPA. But it's another layer of security for your network. Also, if you're in a situation where you will have lots of people coming into your home and wanting to share your connection, you may not want to close off the network, so you'll need to balance convenience for your friends against the small exposure of a more open network.

✔ **Set access control at the MAC layer:** Every network adapter in the world has assigned to it a unique number known as a Media Access Control (MAC) address. You can find the MAC address of your network adapter by looking at it (it's usually physically printed on the device) or using software on your computer:

- **Open a DOS window and use the `winipcfg` command in Windows 95, 98, or Me or the `ipconfig/all` command in Windows NT, 2000, or XP.**

- **Look in the Network Control Panel or System Preference on a Mac.**

Dealing with the WEP hex and ASCII issues

One area that is consistently confusing when setting up a WEP key — and often a real pain — is the tendency of different vendors to use different formats for the keys. The most common way to format a key is to use *hexadecimal* (hex) characters. This format represents numbers and letters by using combinations of the numbers 0–9 and the letters A–F. (For example, the name of Pat's dog, Opie, would be represented in hexadecimal as *4f 70 69 65*.) A few other vendors use *ASCII*, which is simply the letters and numbers on your keyboard.

Although ASCII is an easier-to-understand system for entering WEP codes (it's really just plain text), most systems make you use hexadecimal because it's the standard. The easiest way to enter hex keys on your computers connecting to your access point is to use the passphrase we discuss in the section "Enabling encryption." If your network adapter client software lets you do this, do it! If it doesn't, try entering the WEP key you wrote down when you generated it (it's probably hexadecimal). If that doesn't work either, you may have to dig into the user's manual and see whether you need to add any special codes before or after the WEP key to make it work. Some software requires you to put the WEP key inside quotation marks; other software may require you to put an *0h* or *0x* (that's a zero and an *h* or an *x* character) before the key or an *h* after it (both without quotation marks).

With some access points, you can type the MAC addresses of all the devices you want to connect to your access point and block connections from any other MAC addresses.

Again, if you support MAC layer filtering, you make it harder for friends to log on when visiting. If you have some buddies who like to come over and mooch off your broadband connection, you need to add their MAC addresses as well, or else they cannot get on your network. Luckily, you need to enter their MAC addresses only one time to get them "on the list," so to speak — at least until you have to reset the access point (which shouldn't be that often).

Neither of these "closed" network approaches is absolutely secure. MAC addresses can be *spoofed* (imitated by a device with a different MAC address, for example), and hidden SSIDs can be seen (with the right tools), but both are ways to add to your overall security strategy.

Taking the Easy Road

We hope that the preceding section has shown you that enabling security on your wireless network isn't all that hard. It's straightforward, as a matter of fact. But a percentage of folks are always going to want things to be even easier (count us in that group!). So the Wi-Fi Alliance and Wi-Fi equipment manufacturers have developed a new standard (yeah, another standard!) called *Wi-Fi Protected Setup,* or WPS.

WPS (in its early days of development WPS was called *Simple Config*) is an additional layer of hardware or software or both built into Wi-Fi APs, routers, and network adapters that makes it easier for users to set up WPA in their network and easier to add new client devices to the network.

WPS is still pretty new (the Wi-Fi Alliance specification for the system was approved in early 2007), and not all Wi-Fi equipment on the market supports the system. But based on what WPS brings to the table, it's an attractive system that we suspect will be made available more widely over time.

So what *does* WPS do? Well, it essentially automates the authentication and encryption setup process for WPA by using one of two methods:

✔ **A PIN:** All WPS certified equipment will have a PIN (personal information number) located on a sticker. When a WPS certified router or AP detects a new wireless client on the network, it will prompt the user to enter this PIN — either through the management software or Web page for the router, or directly on the router itself using an interface (such as an LCD screen) located on the router. If the correct PIN is entered, the network will automatically configure WPA and allow that device to join the network. That's all there is to it!

✓ **A button:** The other mechanism for using WPS is called *PBC* (or push button configuration). As the name implies, a button (either a physical button or a virtual one on a computer screen or LCD display) is used — there's a button on both the AP/router and the client hardware. When the router or AP detects a new Wi-Fi client wanting to join the network, the buttons are activated — if you want to grant the new client permission to join the network, you simply press the buttons on both the router/AP and the client; configuration is automatic at this point.

WPS takes the drudgery out of setting up WPA and makes the process pretty much foolproof. WPS *doesn't* change the actual level of security you're getting on your network — all it does is turn on WPA (WPA2, to be exact). One thing to keep in mind about WPS is that you need to have WPS capabilities on both ends of the connection — the AP/router and the network client — to use the system, but you can *still use* the old-fashioned manual configuration process described in the preceding section to add non-WPS capable gear to your network.

As WPS becomes more widespread, the Wi-Fi Alliance folks have a few more tricks up their sleeves to make things even easier. These tricks come in the form of two additional ways of using WPS:

✓ **NFC:** NFC (near field communications) is an extremely short-range (think centimeters, not feet) radio system (similar, and related, to the RFID tags now in use in warehouses and other logistics systems). With NFC, you would simply put the WPS client and AP/router in very close proximity and they'd automatically configure network access and security. Pretty cool.

✓ **USB:** The final method for using WPS involves USB flash drives (the little stick memory cards so many folks carry around these days. WPS can allow a user to simply "carry" the network credentials to a client on a flash drive — plug the flash drive into the AP/router and then into the network client, and configuration is automatic.

These final two methods are *optional* in the WPS standard — the first two are mandatory (found in all WPS certified devices).

As we mention at the outset, WPS is still pretty darned new, but you can see the growing list of WPA compliant products at the Wi-Fi Alliance Web site at www.wi-fi.org/wifi-protected-setup/ (just scroll down to the link titled Products Certified for Wi-Fi Protected Setup).

Going for the Ultimate in Security

Setting up your network with WPA security keeps all but the most determined and capable crackers out of your network and prevents them from doing anything with the data you sent across the airwaves (because this data is securely encrypted and appears to be just gibberish).

But WPA has a weakness, at least the way it's most often used in the home: the preshared key (your shared secret or passphrase) that allows users to connect to your network and that unlocks your WPA encryption.

Your preshared key can be vulnerable in two ways:

- ✔ **If it's not sufficiently difficult to guess (perhaps you used the same word for your passphrase as you used for your network's ESSID):** You would be shocked by how many people do that! Always try to use a passphrase that combines letters (upper- and lowercase is best) and numbers and doesn't use simple words from the dictionary.

- ✔ **If you've given it to someone to access your network and then they give it to someone else:** For most home users, this isn't a big deal, but if you're providing access to a large number of people (maybe you've set up a hot spot), it's hard to put the genie back in the bottle when you've given out the passphrase.

802.1x: The corporate solution

Another new standard that's become quite popular in the corporate Wi-Fi world is 802.1x. This isn't an encryption system but, rather, an authentication system. An 802.1x system, when built into an access point, allows users to connect to the access point and gives them only extremely limited access (at least initially). In an 802.1x system, the user could connect to only a single network port (or service). Specifically, the only traffic the user could send over the network is your login information, which is sent to an authentication server that would exchange information (such as passwords and encrypted keys) with the user to establish that he or she was allowed on the network. After this authentication process has been satisfactorily completed, the user is given full access (or partial access, depending on what policies the authentication server has recorded for the user) to the network.

Neither of these two circumstances is usually a problem for the typical home — WPA-PSK (WPA Home) is more than sufficient for most users. But if you want to go for the ultimate in security, you may consider using an AP (and wireless clients) that supports *WPA Enterprise.*

WPA Enterprise uses a special server, known as a *RADIUS* server, and a protocol called 802.1x (see the nearby sidebar, "802.1x: The corporate solution"), which provide authentication and authorization of users using special cryptographic keys. When a RADIUS server is involved in the picture, you get a more secure authorization process than the simple shared secret used in WPA Home. You also get a new encryption key created by the RADIUS server on an ongoing basis — which means that even if a bad guy figured out your key, it would change before any damage could be done.

Now you *can* create and operate your own RADIUS server on a spare computer in your home (see the commercial software available at www.lucidlink.com, or the free software at www.freeradius.org), but that topic is beyond the scope of this book. (We do tell you more about this subject in our *other* wireless book, *Wireless Hacks and Mods For Dummies,* also published by Wiley.)

You can use a hosted RADIUS service on the Internet. Such services charge a small monthly fee (about $5 per month) and let you use a RADIUS server that's hosted and maintained in someone's data center. All you need to do is pay your monthly bill and follow a few simple steps on your access point and PCs to set up RADIUS authentication and WPA Enterprise.

You need to have an AP that supports WPA Enterprise — check the documentation that came with yours because not all APs support it.

Several services provide WPA Enterprise RADIUS support. An example is the *SecureMyWiFi* service offered by Witopia (www.witopia.net). SecureMyWiFi provides security for one AP and as many as five users for free, and charges for additional users.

802.1x is *not* something we expect to see in any wireless home LAN any time soon. It's a business-class kind of thing that requires lots of fancy servers and professional installation and configuration. We just thought we would mention it because you no doubt will hear about it when you search the Web for wireless LAN security information.

Part IV
Using a Wireless Network

The 5th Wave   By Rich Tennant

"I guess you could say this is the hub of our network."

In this part . . .

After you get your wireless home network installed and running, you probably can't wait to use it, in both practical and fun ways. In this part, we cover the basics on what you can do with your network, such as share printers, files, folders, and even hard drives. But you can do many other cool things over a wireless network, too, such as play multiuser computer games, access your music collection, talk to your friend in Paris, and operate various types of smart-home conveniences. We help connect your car, your cameras, your cellphones, and even your iPod. How cool is that? Of particular interest to many is our full chapter on using Bluetooth-enabled devices such as printers, cameras, and phones. (Bluetooth and Wi-Fi are like chocolate and peanut butter — they go great together.)

Chapter 10

Putting Your Wireless Home Network to Work

Remember that old Cracker Jack commercial of the guy sitting in the bed when the kid comes home from school? "What did you learn in school today?" he asks. "Sharing," says the kid. And then, out of either guilt or good manners, the old guy shares his sole box of caramel popcorn with the kid.

You shouldn't hog your caramel popcorn, and you shouldn't hog your network resources, either. We're going to help you share your Cracker Jacks now! (After all, that's kinda the purpose of the network, right?) You have a wireless network installed. It's secure. It's connected. Now you can share all sorts of stuff with others in your family — not just your Internet connection but also printers, faxes, extra disk space, Telephony Application Programming Interface (TAPI) devices (telephone-to-computer interfaces and vice versa for everybody else), games, and A/V controls — oodles and oodles of devices.

In this chapter, we give you a taste of how you can put your wireless network to work. We talk about accessing shared network resources, setting up user profiles, accessing peripheral devices across the network (such as network printing), checking out network shares on other PCs, and other such goodies.

Entire books have been written about sharing your network. *Home Networking For Dummies,* 4th Edition (by Kathy Ivens), *Mac OS X All-in-One Desk Reference For Dummies* (by Mark L. Chambers, Erick Tejkowski, and Michael L. Williams), *Windows XP For Dummies,* 2nd Edition (by Andy

Rathbone), and *Windows Vista For Dummies* (also by Andy Rathbone), all from Wiley Publishing, Inc., include some details about networking. These books are all good. In fact, some smart bookstore should bundle them with *Wireless Home Networking For Dummies* because they're complementary. In this chapter, we expose you to the network and what's inside it (and there's probably a free prize among those Cracker Jacks somewhere, too!). That should get you started. But if you want to know more, we urge you to grab one of these more detailed books.

It's one thing to attach a device to the network — either directly or as an attachment — but it's another to share it with others. Sharing your computer and devices is a big step. You not only open yourself up to lots of potential unwanted visitors (such as bad folks sneaking in over your Internet connection), but you also make it easier for friendly folks (like your kids) to erase stuff and use things in unnatural ways. That's why you can (and should!) control access by using passwords or by allowing users to only read (open and copy) files on your devices rather than change them. In Windows XP, security is paramount, and you must plan how, what, and with whom you share. Windows Vista takes that security to the next level by securing who can allow sharing in the first place. Definitely take the extra time to configure your system for these extra security layers. We tell you in this chapter about some of these mechanisms (see the later sections "Setting permissions" and "Windows Vista and a New Way to Share"); the books we mention previously go into these topics in more detail.

A Networking Review

Before we get too far into the concept of file sharing, we review the basic networking concepts (which we touch on in earlier chapters of this book). In particular, we describe what a network is and how it works.

Basic networking terminology

Simply defined, a *network* is something that links computers, printers, and other devices. A *protocol* is the language that devices use to communicate with each other on a network. These days, the standard protocol used for most networking is Ethernet.

For one device to communicate with another under the Ethernet protocol, the transmitting device needs to accomplish a few things. First, it must announce itself on the network and declare which device it's trying to talk to. Then it must authenticate itself with that destination device — by confirming that the sending device is who it says it is. This is done by sending a proper name, such as a domain or workgroup name, and also a password that the receiving device accepts.

For our purposes, when we talk about networking, we're talking about sharing devices on a Windows-based network. Windows XP starts the network tour with My Network Places, where you see all the computers and other network devices on your network. Your computer knows the identity of other networked devices because it has been monitoring your home network and has seen each device announce itself and what it has to offer to the entire network when each one first powered up.

With the new Vista operating system, Microsoft has taken a simpler — and more intuitive — approach that looks surprisingly like Mac OS X when you use Vista's Details view. In Vista, you just have Network, and under Network you can see all the computers and resources that you can access shares on within your network. All the domain and workgroup information is in the Details view in the right-hand window pane. This spreadsheet type of view is easy to understand and work with.

With the release of Windows Vista, Microsoft introduced a new look and feel to the desktop. The differences are not as drastic as the upgrade from Windows 2000 to XP, but they're enough that Microsoft decided to maintain a choice about which look and feel a person wants by using *themes*. When we talk about the XP desktop in this chapter, we're referring to the *Windows Classic* theme in XP. When we talk about Vista, we're referring to the *Windows Vista* theme, which is the standard for Vista.

If you have trouble following any of our steps, do this if you're using Windows XP:

1. **Right-click the desktop and choose from the pop-up menu that appears.**

   The Windows XP Display Properties dialog box appears.

2. **Choose Windows Classic from the Themes pull-down menu.**

   You can always change the theme back without affecting any personal preferences you've set.

And if you're using Vista, follow these steps:

1. **Right-click the desktop and choose Personalize from the pop-up menu that appears.**

2. **Choose the Themes option to display the Themes Settings dialog box.**

3. **Select Windows Vista Classic.**

   You can always change the theme back without affecting any personal preferences.

Setting up a workgroup in Windows XP

To set up networking on any Windows-based computer, you need to decide on a few basic networking options. Many of these are decided for you, based on the equipment you happen to be using on your network. As an example, if you have a server on your wireless network, you have many more options concerning the type of network you may create. With a server on your network, you gain the ability to centralize your security policies and to use domains to control devices. In Windows, a *domain* is a set of network resources (applications, printers, and so on) for a group of users. The user only has to log on to the domain to gain access to the resources, which may be located on one or a number of different servers on the network.

If you don't have a server (which most of us don't on our home networks), you end up using the most common type of network: a *workgroup*.

The distinction between a workgroup and a domain can best be summed up in one word: security. Domains make managing, maintaining, and modifying security much simpler. In many cases, the *domain controller* — the server that controls the domain — can set up security on each device on the network remotely, and security can be managed in groups so that you don't have to add every family member to every machine or device on the network. Of course, all this great management comes at a price. Servers tend to be expensive and require a much higher skill level to maintain. The initial setup of a domain can take lots of planning and time to implement. We don't take you through setting up your own domain because you can find more detailed books already written on the subject. If you do happen to choose some type of domain for networking, keep in mind that the security of your domain is only as strong as the security on each individual piece of equipment attached to your network — and that includes *all* your wireless devices.

On the other hand, setting up a workgroup is relatively simple. All that's really required is to decide on the name of your workgroup. Many people use family names or something similar. Microsoft has a default of Workgroup for Windows XP Pro and MSHome for Windows XP Home, for example.

To set up a workgroup in Windows XP, start by right-clicking the My Computer icon (in the upper-left corner of your desktop) or by choosing Start⇨Settings⇨Control Panel and then double-clicking the System icon. On the Network Identification tab of the System Properties window that opens, you can click the Network ID button to have a wizard walk you through the process of setting up your networking options. A simpler method is to click the Properties button and just enter the computer name, description, and workgroup name. (This is also a handy way to quickly check — and rename if necessary — workgroup names on the computers on your network.)

Will You Be My Neighbor?

"Hello! I'm here!" When a computer attached to a network is turned on, it broadcasts its name to every other device on the network and asks every device to broadcast as well. If that computer is sharing something, such as a folder or a printer, the other devices can see it. By asking the other devices to broadcast, it can then see all of them. This process is repeated (on average) every 15 minutes in most networks with Windows computers attached to them.

The "Hello, I'm here" process is a great way to add devices to a network. Unfortunately, it's not too great at detecting whether a device falls off or is disconnected from that network. If a machine or shared device seems to be visible on your network but doesn't respond when you try to access it, the problem may not be on your computer. Devices that get disconnected from your network don't immediately appear to be disconnected on some of your other computers. They usually get removed from the list of available networked computers only if they fail to answer the every-15-minutes "Hello" calls from the other machines.

The My Network Places icon is your ticket to the network and seeing what shared resources are available, such as a printer. (The risk versus reward of sharing these types of items just makes sense. The chances of a bad guy getting into your printer and printing documents are rather low — there's not much reward for doing that.)

You can see what's shared on your network by checking out your PC's My Network Places. Double-click the My Network Places icon (also usually found on your desktop) to see options such as Entire Network and Computers Near Me. Microsoft consolidated the devices in the same workgroup or domain to the Computers Near Me folder. The Entire Network folder still shows all available devices on your physical network. The root of the My Network Places folder is reserved for shortcuts to network resources that you tend to use regularly.

My Network Places (see Figure 10-1) serves a similar (but enhanced) purpose. My Network Places gives you access to your entire network resources and also enables you to add shortcuts to your favorite places. To check out everything on your home network, click the Entire Network icon. This action shows you your workgroup.

Regardless of the operating system, devices that are set up to share are always represented by small computer icons. If you double-click one of these icons, you can see any shared printers, folders, or other devices represented by appropriate icons. Sometimes you have to *drill down* (continue to double-click icons) a little to find all the shared items on your network.

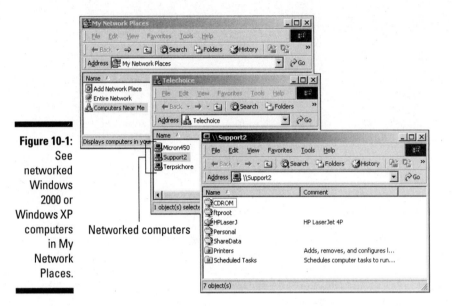

Figure 10-1:
See
networked
Windows
2000 or
Windows XP
computers
in My
Network
Places.

Networked computers

In general, you see two types of devices on your network:

- **Stand-alone network devices:** These are computers, storage devices, gaming devices, and so on that have a network port and are on the network in their own right.

- **Attached devices:** These are peripherals, drives, or other devices that are on the network because they're attached to something else, such as a PC.

Just double-click your workgroup to see all your home computers and other networked devices. Click any to see what you can share within them.

All this mouse clicking can be a pain. Save your wrist and create a shortcut to your shared resources by right-clicking the item and choosing Create Shortcut — creating shortcuts works the same in Vista as in XP. Shortcuts are especially handy for people who have networked devices that they visit often on the Internet, such as File Transfer Protocol (FTP) sites.

If you find a computer that you expect to be on the network but it's not, make sure that its workgroup name is the same as the other machines — this is a common mistake. (See the earlier section "Setting up a workgroup in Windows XP.")

We find using Windows Explorer to be the best way to visualize what's on your computer and your network. You can get to Windows Explorer in Windows XP in two ways. Either right-click the Start button and choose Explore, or choose Start➪Programs➪Windows Explorer. Figure 10-2 shows Windows Explorer looking at available network resources.

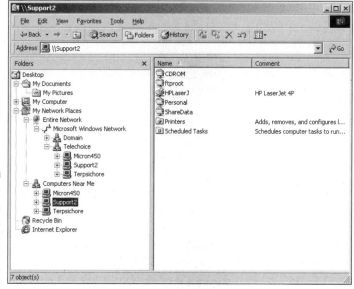

Figure 10-2:
Use
Windows
Explorer to
see network
resources.

Just because you see a device in My Network Places doesn't mean that you can *share* with that device — where *share* means that you can view, use, copy, and otherwise work on files and resources on that device. The devices need to be set up for sharing for that to happen. (Think of it like your regular neighborhood, where you can see many of the houses, but you can't go in some of them because they're locked.) To set up sharing, see the next section.

Sharing — I Can Do That!

File sharing is a basic feature of any home network. Whether sharing MP3 files on a computer with other devices (including your stereo, as we discuss in Chapter 12) or giving access to financial files for Mom and Dad to access on each other's computers, sharing files is a way to maintain one copy of something and not have a zillion versions all over the network.

You can share your whole computer, only certain things (documents or folders), or some stuff in only certain ways. Here's an idea of what you can share on your network:

- ✔ **The entire computer:** You can choose to make the entire computer or device accessible from the network. (We don't advise sharing your entire computer because it exposes your entire PC to anyone who accesses your network. In Windows Vista you no longer get this option.)

- ✔ **Specific internal drives:** You can share a specific hard drive, such as one where all your MP3s or computer games are stored.

✔ **Specific peripheral drives:** You can share PC-connected or network-enabled peripheral drives, such as an extra USB-attached hard drive, a Zip or Jaz backup drive, or an external CD/DVD read/write drive.

✔ **Files:** You can set up particular folders or just a specific file to share across your network. *Note:* File storage schemes on devices are *hierarchical:* If you share a folder, all files and folders within that folder will be shared. If you want to share only one file, share a folder with only the one file in it (but if you add an additional file to that folder, it too will be shared).

Enabling sharing on Windows XP

In Windows XP, sharing is enabled by default on each network connection on your machine. When Microsoft released Service Pack 2 for Windows XP, they still allowed sharing to be enabled, but they also enabled Windows Firewall to not allow any connections for file and printer sharing. If you have a wired network card and a wireless card, you can have sharing enabled on one card and not on the other. This is helpful if you only want to share files on one of the networks you connect to. For example, if you want to share files when connected to your wireless home network and turn off sharing when you plug your laptop in at work, turn sharing on for your wireless card and off for your wired Ethernet card. When you first install a new network card, or wireless network card for our purposes, the default is to have sharing turned on.

You can never be too protected

The number of ways that someone can get on your network multiplies with each new technology you add to your network. We note in Chapter 9 that wireless local area networks (LANs) seep out of your home and make it easy for others to log in and sniff around. If someone does manage to break into your network, the most obvious places to snoop around and do damage are the shared resources. Sharing your C: drive (which is usually your main hard drive), your Windows directory, or your My Documents directory makes it easier for people to get into your machine and do something you would rather they not.

You see, sharing broadcasts to the rest of the network the fact that something is shared, telling everyone who has access your computer's name on the network and how to find it. Sharing can broadcast that availability across firewalls, proxies, and servers. Certain types of viruses and less-than-friendly hackers look for these specific areas (such as your shared C: drive) in broadcast messages and follow them back to your machine.

If you're going to share these parts of your system on your network, run a personal firewall or the Windows Firewall on your machines for an added layer of security. Get virus software. Protect your machine, and limit your exposure. (And, by all means, be sure to follow our advice in Chapter 9 for securing your wireless network.)

To enable sharing on a Windows XP machine, follow these steps, which are similar to those in the preceding section:

1. **Choose Start➪Control Panel. When the Control Panel window opens, double-click Network Connections.**

2. **Right-click the icon of the network connection over which you want to enable File and Printer Sharing and then choose Properties from the pop-up menu that appears.**

3. **On the General tab, select the check box for File and Printer Sharing for Microsoft Networks. (If Service Pack 2 is installed, this will already be selected.) Click OK.**

   This step enables your PC to share files and also printers.

You can use Windows Explorer to control file sharing on a file-by-file or folder-by-folder basis. When you right-click any folder or file and then select Sharing, you can control the sharing of that file or folder — only if File and Printer Sharing has already been enabled as described in the steps above.

Setting permissions

In Windows XP, controlling the sharing of files is a bit more complex than previous versions because of the enhanced security that comes with those operating systems. To share folders and drives, you must be logged on as a member of the Server Operators, Administrators, Power Users, or Users groups. Throughout the rest of this section, we describe these user types and then show you how to add users to your Windows XP network. If Service Pack 2 is installed for Windows XP, you also need to deal with the adjustments to Windows Firewall that will allow connection to your machine so you can share.

Determining user types

The *Server Operators* group is used only on large networks that incorporate the Microsoft Active Directory technology; if you're trying to set up your office computer at home and it's configured using the Server Operators group, you may not be able to access your home network. This is not a common situation, but if you run into this, you'll need to talk to your office IT personnel to get your access settings configured — as long as your IT director isn't Ed, who probably won't help you (just kidding Ed!). The groups you need to concern yourself with are the Administrators, Power Users, and Users groups:

✔ The **Administrators group** contains the system gods. Anyone set up as an administrator can do anything he or she wants — no restrictions. In Windows XP, the first person you set up when installing the OS has administrator access to the machine.

✔ Those in the **Power Users group** can't do as much as administrators, but they can do a lot — as long as what they're doing doesn't change any of the files that make Windows operate. In other words, power users can add and remove software, users, hardware, and so on to a system as long as their actions don't affect any files keeping the system running the way it's running.

✔ The **Users group** is just that. Users simply use what the system has to offer and aren't able to do anything else. The Users group provides the most secure environment in which to run programs, and it's by far the best way to give access to your resources *without* compromising the security of your computer and network.

How do you know what kind of access you have? Unfortunately, that's not an easy thing to find out unless you're an administrator. If you know that you're not an administrator, the only way to find out what you *can* do is by trying to do it. If you don't have the proper access to do something, you see a warning message telling you exactly that — sometimes the message may tell you what access you need to have to do what you want.

Adding users

For others to get access to what you have shared, you need to give them permission. You do that by giving them a logon on your computer and assigning them to a group — essentially adding them to the network as a user. The group is then given certain rights within the folder you have shared; every user in the group has access only to what the group has access to. For more details on this process, we strongly recommend that you use the Windows Help file to discover how to set up new users and groups on your system.

In Windows XP, creating users and adding them to groups is best done by using the administrator logon. If you're using an office computer and you're not the administrator or a member of the Power Users group, you can't create users. Talk to your system administrator to get permission and help in setting up your machine.

We're guessing that you're the administrator of your home-networked computer (it's your network, right?), so you have access to the administrator logon. Thus, you can set up new users by logging on to the machine as administrator. As with the hierarchical folder permissions, user permissions are hierarchal as well. If you're a power user, you can only create users who have less access than yourself (members of the Users group in other words). By using the administrator logon, you can create any type of user account you may need — including other administrators.

Unless you're very comfortable with the security settings of Windows XP, you should never give new user accounts more access than the Users group provides. (For a description of user types, see the preceding section.) Keep in mind that by creating these accounts, you're also creating a logon that can be used to turn on and access your computer directly. For the purposes of sharing files and peripherals, the standard Users group provides all the access that any individual on the network would normally need.

To add users to your network, follow these steps:

1. **Choose Start⇨Settings⇨Control Panel and double-click the Users and Passwords icon.**

   This step displays the Users and Passwords dialog box.

2. **Click the Add button to launch the New User Wizard and add users to your machine.**

3. **Follow the wizard's onscreen prompts to enter a name, logon name, description, and password, and then select which group the user will be part of.**

   New users should always start as part of the Users group (also referred to as the Restricted Access group), which is the lowest possible access level. Starting users at the lowest possible access level is the best way for you to share your files without compromising your network's security.

Accessing shared files

Whether drives, folders, or single files are set up for sharing on your wireless home network, you access the shared thing in pretty much the same way. On any networked PC, you simply log on to the network, head for Network (or My Network Places, as the case may be), and navigate to the file (or folder or drive) you want to access. It's really as easy as that.

Just because you can *see* a drive, folder, or file on the network doesn't necessarily mean that you have *access* to that drive, folder, or file. It all depends on set permissions.

Be Economical: Share Those Peripherals

Outside of the fact that there's only so much space on your desk or your kitchen countertop, you simply don't need a complete set of peripherals at each device on your network. For example, digital cameras are quite popular, and you can view pictures on your PC, on your TV, and even in wireless picture frames around the house. But you probably need only one color printer geared toward printing high-quality photos for someone to take home (after admiring your wireless picture frames!).

The same is true about many peripherals: business card scanners, backup drives (such as USB hard drives and NAS — *network attached storage —* boxes), and even cameras. If you have one device and it's network enabled, anyone on the wireless network should be able to access that for the task at hand.

Setting up a print server

The most common shared peripheral is a printer. Setting up a printer for sharing is easy, and using it is even easier.

You may have several printers in your house, and different devices may have different printers — but they all can be shared. You may have the color laser printer on your machine, a less expensive one (with less expensive consumables such as printer cartridges, too) for the kid's computer, and a high-quality photo printer maybe near the TV set plugged into a USB port of a networkable A/V device. Each of these can be used by a local device — if it's properly set up.

Here are the steps you need to take to share a printer:

1. Enable printer sharing in the operating system of the computer to which the printer is attached.

2. Set up sharing for the installed printer. We say *installed* printer because we assume that you've already installed the printer locally on your computer or other device.

3. Remotely install the printer on every other computer on the network. We describe remote installation in the aptly named section "Remotely installing the printer on all network PCs," later in this chapter.

4. Access the printer from any PC on the network!

Throughout the rest of this section, we go through these four general steps in much more detail.

Sharing your printer in Windows XP

Windows Vista and Windows XP are more sophisticated than previous Windows operating systems and subsequently have a *server type* of print sharing. In other words, they offer all the features of a big network with servers on your local machine. These features include the ability to assign users to manage the print queue remotely, embed printer software for easier installation, and manage when the printer is available based on a schedule you define.

To share a printer on Windows XP, follow these steps:

1. **Choose Start➪Control Panel, and then double-click Printers and Faxes.**

   Or simply choose Start➪Printers and Faxes, depending on how your Start menu is configured.

2. **Right-click the printer in the Printers folder and choose Properties from the pop-up menu that appears.**

3. **On the Sharing tab of the dialog box that appears, click the Share this printer option. In the Share Name text box below this option, type a share name for your printer.**

   The share name can be any name you choose. We recommend something you'll remember, such as Danny's Super Duper Printer.

4. **If you have computers using different operating systems (for example, a mixture of Windows XP, Vista, and even Windows 98 machines on your network), you'll need to add additional printer drivers to support those machines. If this is the case, follow the additional steps below, otherwise click OK and you're done.**

5. **Click the Additional Drivers button. Select which operating systems you want to support to use this shared printer, and also select the other types of drivers needed for your other computer systems and devices. Then click OK.**

6. **When prompted, insert a floppy disk or CD-ROM and direct the subsequent dialog boxes to the right places on those devices to get the driver for each operating system you chose.**

   Windows finds those drivers and downloads them to the Windows XP hard drive. Then, when you go to install the printer on your other computers (see the next section), the Windows XP machine, which is sharing the printer, automatically transfers the proper printer drivers and finishes the installation for you. It's darned sweet, if you ask us!

Before you go out and start to put your newly shared printer on all your computers, you may want to create a shared folder on the computer you're using to host your printer. In the folder, copy the driver software that came with the printer. If, in the process of installing the printer on other workstations, you need a driver that isn't automatically available — such as an OS X driver for the printer — it's ready and available on your network so that you don't have to go looking for installation CDs to bring to the computer you're trying to set up. Trust us, this one can save you a *ton* of frustration.

Remotely installing the printer on all network PCs

You perform the third step at every other PC in the house. Basically, you install the printer on each of these computers, but in a logical way — *logically* as opposed to *physically* installing and connecting the printer to each computer. You install the printer just like any other printer except that you're installing a *network* printer, and the printer installation wizard searches the network for the printers you want to install.

The process you use will vary depending on the operating system you use and the type of printer you're trying to install. In every case, read the printer documentation before you start because some printers require their software to be partially installed before you try to add the printer. We've seen this a lot with multifunction printers that support scanning, copying, and faxing.

With Windows, the easiest way to start the installation of a printer is to look inside My Network Places, find the computer sharing the printer, and double-click the shared printer. This action starts the Add Printer Wizard, which takes you through the process of adding the printer. This wizard works like any good wizard — you make a few selections and click Next a lot. If you didn't add the drivers to the shared printer already, you may be asked for the printer drivers. Just use the Browse button to direct the wizard to look in the shared folder or CD-ROM drive where you put the printer software on the computer that the printer is attached to.

You have two options for installing a network printer:

- ✔ **From your Printers folder:** Choose Start➪Settings➪Printers and Faxes (or simply Start➪Printers and Faxes, depending on how your Start menu is configured).

- ✔ **From My Network Places:** Double-click the computer that has the printer attached. An icon appears, showing the shared printer. Right-click the icon and then choose Connect from the pop-up menu that appears.

Either route leads you to the Add Printer Wizard, which guides you through the process of adding the network printer.

Don't start the Add Printer Wizard unless you have installed the proper drivers to the shared printer or you have the installation CDs for your printer handy. The Add Printer Wizard installs the printer *drivers* (software files that contain the info required for Windows to talk to your printers and exchange data for printing). The wizard gets these from the CD that comes with your printer. If you don't have the CD, go to the Web site of your printer manufacturer and download the driver to your desktop and install from there. Don't forget to delete the downloaded files from your desktop when you've finished installing them on the computer.

Note also that the wizard allows you to browse your network to find the printer you want to install. Simply click the plus sign next to the computer that has the printer attached, and you should see the printer below the computer. (If not, recheck that printer sharing is enabled on that computer.)

At the end of the wizard screens, you have the option to print a test page. We recommend that you do this. You don't want to wait until your child has to have a color printout for her science experiment (naturally, she waits until 10 minutes before the bus arrives to tell you!) to find out that the printer doesn't work.

Accessing your shared printers

After you have the printers installed, how do you access them? Whenever your Print window comes up (by pressing Ctrl+P in most applications), you see a field labeled Name for the name of the printer accompanied by a pull-down menu of printer options. Use your mouse to select any printer — local or networked — and the rest of the printing process remains the same as though you had a printer directly plugged into your PC.

You can even make a networked printer the default printer by right-clicking the printer and then choosing Set As Default Printer from the pop-up menu that appears.

Sharing other peripherals

Sharing any other peripheral is similar to sharing printers. You need to make sure that you're sharing the device on the computer it's attached to. Then you need to install that device on another PC by using that device's installation procedures. Obviously, we can't be specific about such an installation because of the widely varying processes that companies use to install devices. Most of the time — like with a printer — you need to install the drivers for the device you're sharing on your other computers.

Note that some of the devices you attach to your network have integrated Web servers in them. This is getting more and more common. Danny's AudioReQuest (www.request.com) music server, for example, is visible on his home network and is addressable by any of his PCs. Thus, he can download music to and from the AudioReQuest server and sync it to other devices he wants music on. Anyone else in the home can do the same — even remotely, over the Internet. We talk more about the AudioReQuest system in Chapter 12.

Danny has also set up a virtual CD server in his home to manage all the CDs his kids have for their games. This server is shared on the home network. By using Virtual CD software from H+H Zentrum fuer Rechnerkommunikation

GmbH (www.virtualcd-online.com, $85 for a five-user license), Danny has loaded all his CDs and many of his DVDs onto a single machine so that his kids (he has four) can access those CDs from any of their individual PCs (he has four *spoiled* kids). Rather than look to the local hard drive for the CD, any of the kids' PCs looks to the server to find the CD — hence, the name *virtual CD*. Now those stacks of CDs (and moans over a scratched CD!) are gone.

Windows Vista and a New Way to Share

If you are familiar with file sharing using Windows XP, you already know most of what you need to share with Windows Vista.

All the action in Windows Vista takes place in the Network and Sharing Center. The hardest part of using the Network and Sharing Center is finding out where the options are located to set up your networked PCs and devices. Often you will have to work your way through several layers of menus to find the options you want.

Setting up your workgroup

We've mentioned that you want to have all your computers in the same work-group — unless you have a server and domain, but we don't expect a lot of you will because it's not common in home networks. If you do, you don't need to read the rest of this section.

The default workgroup name in Windows Vista is Workgroup. If you're mixing Windows XP Pro and Windows Vista and you have never made any changes to the default workgroup name, you don't need to change it now. However, if you're mixing Windows XP Home and Vista, make sure that all of your computers are in the same workgroup if for no other reason than it makes finding things that are shared much simpler for everyone.

Just like in Windows XP, you need to have the proper security permissions in Windows Vista to be able to make any changes to your system. The security levels are the same in XP and Vista, but you access them differently in Vista. Just as in Windows XP, if you initially set up the machine, the first account you set up will have Administrator access.

You have two ways to check and change the Workgroup name in Vista. The first and simplest is to use the main Vista Welcome Center screen:

1. **In the Welcome Center, choose the first option, View Computer Details, and then select Show More.**

   The Vista system information screen comes up.

2. **To change the Name of your PC, click the Change Settings link.**

   The System Properties dialog box appears.

3. **Click the Change button.**

   The Computer Name/Domain Change dialog box appears.

4. **At this point you can you can change the computer name and the Workgroup name if required. When you've made your changes, click OK.**

   Make sure to use the same Workgroup name on each PC that you want to enable file sharing with.

Windows Vista displays a User Account Security Control window after most changes to the system. This prompt is asking you to confirm that you really want to change what you said you want to change, or access what you said you want to access. You are going to see this prompt a lot in Windows Vista.

The second way to check and change the Workgroup name in Vista is to open Windows Explorer:

1. **Left-click the Windows Start orb.**

   Yes, it's called an orb now (we don't know why), and it replaces the Start Menu button.

2. **To the right of the pop-up menu, you see a menu option labeled Computer. Right-click Computer and choose Properties.**

   Your local machine used to be called My Computer but is now called simply Computer. Ed figures the programmers at Microsoft just got tired of typing, given all the changes they already made to Vista.

3. **At this point you are back at Step 2 and can follow the same steps to change the computer name and Workgroup name.**

Setting up sharing in Vista

Now that you have your workgroup set up correctly, you should be able to see other shared computers and resources on the network. If you were using a Windows XP machine, you could just start setting up shares right now. Not so in Vista. Microsoft took all the security complaints about XP to heart when they created Vista, adding a second layer of firewall security (beyond the standard Windows Firewall) onto the network adapter itself. This prevents the machine from announcing itself on the network. (See the previous section, "Will You Be My Neighbor?") Before you can share anything, you need to configure your network adapter so it will announce itself to the network:

1. **Left-click the Start orb, and from the menu in the right column choose Network.**

2. **In the Network browser, select Network and Sharing Center from the upper bar.**

The upper bar is like the familiar toolbar in most Microsoft applications. The difference is that the upper bar appears only in the Vista Explorer window. It's always located below the standard menu bar — the one that has menu options such a File and Edit — and it changes based on what you've selected in Vista Explorer. The Network and Sharing Center is where you'll see all your network adapters.

3. **If your wireless adapter is set up correctly, you'll see it in the list of adapters. Click the Customize link on your wireless network connection.**

4. **If you have Windows Vista Home Premium or above, you must choose the network location type the first time you connect your PC to the network. (The network location type determines your Microsoft Vista firewall settings.)**

   • **Public:** If you're connecting to a network in a public place, such as a coffee shop or an airport, choose a Public location type. Choosing Public will keep your computer from being visible to others on the network. Public offers the most security.

   • **Private:** Use this option for a home, small office, or work network. Choosing Private automatically configures the firewall settings to allow for communication

If you want to enable communication between your PCs and other network devices, such as a printer, you need to choose the Private location.

If you decide to use the Private location type, you're all set to start sharing resources from your Vista machine.

If you're running a mix of XP and Vista on your home network, you could run into problems as soon as you turn on your Vista computer and let it announce itself to the network. When Vista starts broadcasting across your network, it can hide the rest of the computers on the network from each other. You won't be able to see any computers in the Map view in Vista or My Network Places in XP — although you can still access the computers and devices. The reason for this is that Microsoft introduced a new protocol to Windows Vista that XP might not be set up to support. The Link Layer Topology Discovery (LLTD) protocol is a licensed data link layer protocol for network topology discovery and quality of service diagnostics, developed by Microsoft as part of their Windows Rally set of technologies. Windows Vista has this protocol installed by default, but Windows XP does not. If you are going to run both XP and Vista on your network and share between them, you need to install the LLTD responder for Windows XP. You can download this from the Microsoft site by searching (at search.microsoft.com) for KB922120. Or go to the following URL:

```
http://support.microsoft.com/kb/922120
```

After you install this update on your XP machine, if you still have issues with sharing your XP and Vista machines, the reason could be that the LLTD protocol is disabled on the network adapter of the XP machine or is not supported by the network adapter itself (a likely culprit).

In Windows Vista, Microsoft installed the IPv6 protocol as a default on all network adapters. If you find that you are still having issues sharing, you will need to remove the IPv6 protocol. From the Network and Sharing Center, choose Manage Network Connections and then select the View Details link of the connection. Click the Properties button to display the Properties dialog box for the connection. Deselect the IPv6 protocol to turn it off. For most home networks, you will be using only IPv4; having IPv6 on the network is just futureproofing your investments. We don't like to turn this off on our Vista machines, and we strongly recommend that you don't unless this is the absolute last thing to try to get things working correctly.

At this point, unless you have an oddly configured XP firewall or a highly secured PC, your Vista machine should be connected to your home network. If you have more than one workgroup in your home, you can also turn on Network Sharing and Discovery — located in the Network and Sharing Center. This will allow your computer to see other network computers and devices, and makes your computer visible to those other workgroups.

Sharing in Microsoft Windows Vista

Keep in mind that sharing opens up your machine to anyone and anything on your network. We strongly recommend that you turn on password-protected sharing, which is a feature you access through your Network and Sharing Center. Although Microsoft added a lot of extra windows and menu layers to every process, we have to admit that Vista has gone a long way in simplifying many operations, and lets you get things done in a more intuitive way. You can click an option to turn on and off password-protected sharing. With the password-protected sharing feature on, only users with a login and password can access shared files and folders.

To give access to users on your network, you need to create user accounts for them on your Vista machine. The process is the same as the one for Windows XP.

To create a user account:

1. **Click the Start orb, and select Control Panel.**

2. **Choose User Accounts.**

3. **If you have only one account, select the Manage Another Account link on the Manage Your Account screen.**

    The Add or Remove User Accounts screen appears.

4. **Click the Add or Remove User Accounts option.**

   Your accounts management screen appears, where you can add a new user and set the account type.

5. **Click the Create a New Account link to bring up the New Account window. When you create a new user account, you have two options for the account type:**

   - **Standard User:** This account can use most software and can change system settings that do not affect other users or the security of the computer.

   - **Administrator:** This account has complete access to the computer and can make any changes. You don't normally want to give Administrator access to an account you're setting up for sharing. Any accounts with Administrator access can manage the computer system remotely and change anything they want to on your computer.

6. **Follow the onscreen instructions to create the user.**

   After you create the new account, you are brought back to the New Account window.

7. **To set up a password for the new account, right-click the account icon and select Create Password. Enter the desired password and then select Accept Changes.**

   You need to do this for each new account you create.

You're now ready to share your folders, printers, and any other devices you have attached to your Vista machine.

Thankfully, sharing a folder or device in Vista is the same as in Windows XP. From Explorer, right-click the file, folder, or device and choose Properties. On the Sharing tab, choose Sharing and then choose Share. This displays a new window where you have the option to Stop Sharing or Change Sharing Permission. If you are using password-protected sharing — which you should be using — you need to select the users for whom you want to allow access. When you select Sharing Permission, you have the option to add a user. From the Add User drop-down list, you can choose a single user name or you can select Everyone in this list if you want all user accounts to have access to the folder or file. After you have added a user to the list for this share, you can also change his or her permission level to reader, co-owner, or contributor.

If you don't want to deal with setting up share properties on multiple folders, you can copy or move files to your Public folder and share from that location. This allows you to turn on sharing in the directory of folders named Public, and you simply put all files you want shared into those directories. In this case, anyone with a user account and password on your computer will be able to access those files. Also, anyone on your network will be able to see and read those files but not change them.

Sharing between Macs and Windows-based PCs

If you have an OS X Macintosh computer (using OS X versions 10.2 right on through to the current 10.5), you don't need to do anything special to get your Mac connected to a PC network for file sharing. All these versions of OS X support Windows networking protocols rights out of the box, with no add-ons or extra software required.

Getting on a Windows network

To connect to your Windows PCs or file servers, simply go the OS X Finder and then choose Go⇨Connect to Server (Command+K). In the dialog box that appears, you can type the IP address or host name of the server you're connecting to and then click the Connect button. Alternatively, click the Browse button in the dialog box to search your local network for available servers and shares.

Letting Windows users on your network

To let Windows users access your Mac, you simply turn on file sharing in your Mac's System Preferences. To do so in OS X versions 10.4 and earlier, follow these steps:

1. **Open System Preferences (click the System Preferences icon on your Mac's dock).**

2. **Click the Sharing tab to view your file-sharing options. Make sure that the Services tab is open.**

3. **Select Windows Sharing in the services listing, and then click the Start button to activate it.**

4. **Close the Sharing dialog box.**

If you're using the latest version of OS X (10.5 Leopard), just do the following:

1. **Open System Preferences and click the Sharing tab (as described above).**

2. **Select the File Sharing check box.**

3. **Click the Options button.**

4. **In the dialog box that appears, select the Share Files and Folders Using SMB check box.**

5. **Click the Done button.**

Bonjour, Madam!

One cool feature that Apple has added to its latest versions of Mac OS — Mac OS versions 10.2 and beyond — is a networking system named Bonjour. Bonjour, previously known as Rendezvous, is based on an open Internet standard (IETF, or Internet Engineering Task Force, Zeroconf) and is being adopted by a number of manufacturers outside of Apple.

Basically, Bonjour (and Zeroconf) is a lot like Bluetooth (which we discuss in Chapter 15) in that it allows devices on a network to discover each other without any user intervention or special configuration. Bonjour is slowly being incorporated into many products, such as printers, storage devices (basically, networkable hard drives), and even household electronics such as TiVo.

Here's one great feature about Bonjour: On Macs equipped with Apple AirPort network adapter cards, it lets two (or more) Macs in range of each other — in other words, within Wi-Fi range — *automatically* connect to each other for file sharing, instant messaging, and other tasks without going through any extra steps of setting up a peer-to-peer network.

Bonjour is enabled automatically in Mac OS version 10.2/3/4/5 computers if you enable Personal File Sharing (found in System Preferences; look for the Sharing icon) or use Apple's iChat Instant Messaging program, Apple's Safari Web browsers, or any Bonjour-capable printer connected to your AirPort network.

That's it! Your Mac automatically turns on Windows sharing and opens the appropriate holes (ports) in your firewall. If you haven't already enabled accounts on your Mac for sharing, you're prompted by OS X to do so now. Simply click the Enable Accounts button, and in the dialog box that opens, select the accounts (or users) of your Mac that you want to allow access to. To do this, just select the check box next to each name you want to enable, and then click Done. That's all there is to it. If you want to connect to your LAN from a Windows computer, simply browse your Neighborhood Network in Windows XP or Vista or enter your network's address on an Explorer address bar. It's something like the following:

```
\192.168.1.3\username
```

(Substitute your Mac OS X username for *username,* of course!)

Chapter 11

Gaming Over a Wireless Home Network

*I*n case you missed it, gaming is huge. We mean *huge.* The videogaming industry is, believe it or not, bigger than the entertainment industry generated by Hollywood. Billions of dollars per year are spent on PC game software and hardware and on gaming consoles such as PlayStation and Xbox. You probably know a bit about gaming — we bet that you at least played Minesweeper on your PC or Pong on an Atari when you were a kid. What you may not know is that videogaming has moved online in a big way. For that, you need a network.

All three of the big gaming console vendors — Sony (www.us.playstation. com), Microsoft (www.xbox.com), and Nintendo (www.gamecube.com) — have made it easy for you to connect your console to a broadband Internet connection (such as a cable or DSL) to play against people anywhere in the world. Online PC gaming has also become a huge phenomenon, with games such as EverQuest II attracting millions of users.

A big challenge for anyone getting into online gaming is finding a way to get consoles and PCs in different parts of the house connected to your Internet connection. For example, if you have an Xbox 360, it's probably in your living room or home theater, and we're willing to bet that your cable or DSL modem is in the home office. Lots of folks string a CAT-5e/6 Ethernet cable down the hall and hook it into their game machine — a great approach if you don't mind tripping over that cable at 2 a.m. when you let the dogs out.

Enter your wireless home network, a much better approach to getting these gaming devices online.

In this chapter, we talk about some of the hardware requirements for getting a gaming PC or game console online. In the case of gaming consoles, you may need to pick up some extra gear. However, Nintendo's and Sony's current consoles have Wi-Fi built in — in fact, Nintendo's Wii is so wireless friendly that you have to pay extra for a *wired* network connection, as opposed to the tradition of wireless being the option! We also talk about some steps you need to take to configure your router (or the router in your access point, if they're the same box in your wireless local area network) to get your online gaming up and running.

Our focus here is on wireless *networking* connections. Keep in mind that gaming consoles have also become unwired in terms of the connections that their controllers use. All three of the current consoles (the Wii, the PlayStation 3, and the Xbox 360) use wireless technologies such as Bluetooth (see Chapter 3 for more on Bluetooth) to connect their controllers to the console. The Xbox 360 can even work with wireless headsets, so you can wirelessly yell "I'm ripping your head off right now" to the gamer on the far end of the connection (you Seth Rogen fans out there know what we're talking about here!).

We're approaching this chapter with the assumption that your wireless gaming network will be connected to the Internet using an always-on, broadband connection, such as DSL, fiber-optic, or a cable modem, using a home router (either the one built into your access point or a separate one). We have two reasons for this assumption: First, we think that online gaming works much, much better on a broadband connection; second, because with some console systems (particularly the Xbox), you're *required* to have a broadband connection to use online gaming. And, even if the console (like the PS2) doesn't *require* broadband, many of the games *do*.

PC Gaming Hardware Requirements

We should preface this section of the book by saying that this book isn't entitled *Gaming PCs For Dummies*. Thus, we don't spend any time talking about PC gaming hardware requirements in any kind of detail. Our gamer pals will probably be aghast at our brief coverage here, but we really just want to give you a taste of what you may want to think about if you decide to outfit a PC for online gaming. In fact, if you're buying a PC for this purpose, check out the class of computers called *gaming PCs,* optimized for this application. Throughout this chapter, we use the term *gaming PC* generically to mean any PC in your home that you're using for gaming — not just special-purpose gaming PCs.

Your best resource, we think, is to check out an online gaming Web site that has a team of experts who review and torture-test all the latest hardware for a living. We like CNET's www.gamespot.com and www.gamespy.com.

At the most basic level, you need any modern multimedia PC (or Màcintosh, for that matter) to get started with PC gaming. Just about any PC or Mac purchased since 2002 or so will have a fast processor and a decent graphics or video card. (You hear both terms used.) If you start getting into online gaming, think about upgrading your PC with high-end gaming hardware or building a dedicated gaming machine. Some key hardware components to keep in mind are the following:

- ✔ **Fast processor:** Much of the hard work in gaming is done by the video card, but a fast Intel Core Duo (or the AMD equivalent) central processing unit (CPU) is always nice to have.

- ✔ **Powerful video card:** The latest cards from ATI and nVIDIA (www.nvidia. com) contain incredibly sophisticated computer chips dedicated to cranking out the video part of your games. If you get to the point where you know what frames per second (fps) is all about and you start worrying that yours are too low, it's time to start investigating faster video cards.

  We're big fans of the ATI (www.ati.com) Radeon HD 3850 card, but then we're suckers for fast hardware that can crank out the polygons (the building blocks of your game video) at mind-boggling speeds.

- ✔ **Fancy gaming controllers:** Many games can be played by using a standard mouse and keyboard, but you may want to look into some cool specialized game controllers that connect through your PC's Universal Serial Bus (USB). For example, you can get a joystick for flying games or a steering wheel for driving games. Check out Creative Technologies (www.creative.com) and Mad Catz (www.madcatz.com) for some cool options.

- ✔ **Quality sound card:** Many games include a *surround sound* soundtrack, just like DVDs provide in your home theater. If you have the appropriate number of speakers and the right sound card, you hear the bad guys creeping up behind you before you see them on the screen. Très fun.

Networking Requirements for PC Gaming

Gaming PCs may (but don't have to) have some different innards than regular PCs, but their networking requirements don't differ in any appreciable way from the PC you use for Web browsing, e-mail, or anything else. You shouldn't be surprised to hear that connecting a gaming PC to your wireless network is no different from connecting any PC.

You need some sort of wireless network adapter connected to your gaming PC to get it up and running on your home network (just like you need a wireless network adapter connected to *any* PC running on your network, as we discuss in Chapter 5). These adapters are often built right into your PC. If your PC doesn't have a network adapter, you can fit one in the PC Card slot (of a laptop computer, for example), add one internally (in your desktop PC) using a PCI card, or connect the adapter to a USB or Ethernet port of a desktop computer. If you have a Mac that you're using for gaming, you'll probably use one of the Apple AirPort or AirPort Extreme cards (which we discuss in Chapter 8). There's nothing special you need to do, hardware-wise, with a gaming PC.

When it comes to *playing* online games, you may need to do some tweaking to your home network's router — which may be a stand-alone device or part of your access point. In the upcoming sections "Dealing with Router Configurations" and "Setting Up a Demilitarized Zone (DMZ)," we discuss these steps in further detail.

 Depending on which games you're playing, you may not need to do any special configuring. Some games play just fine without any special router configurations — particularly if your PC isn't acting as the *server* (which means that other people aren't connecting to your PC from remote locations on the Internet).

Getting Your Gaming Console on Your Wireless Home Network

Although PC gaming can be really cool, we find that many people prefer to use a dedicated game console device — such as a PlayStation 2 (PS2) or an Xbox — to do their gaming. And, although hard-core gamers may lean toward PC platforms for their gaming (often spending thousands of dollars on ultra-high-end gaming PCs with the latest video cards, fastest processor and memory, and the like), we think that for regular gamers, consoles offer some compelling advantages:

✔ **They're (relatively) inexpensive.** Although they are more expensive than the previous generation of consoles, today's current consoles are cheaper than a PC — the Wii (if you can find one) starts at about $250, the Xbox 360 starts at $350, and the PS3 starts at about $400. Even if you dedicate an inexpensive PC for gaming, you'll probably spend closer to $800 — and even more if you buy the fancy video cards and other equipment that gives the PC the same gaming performance as a console.

✔ **They're simple to set up.** Although it's not all that hard to get games running on a PC, you're dealing with a more complicated operating system on a PC. You have to install games and get them up and running. On a game console, you simply shove a disc into the drawer and you're playing.

✔ **They're in the right room.** Most folks don't want PCs in their living rooms or home theaters, although some really cool models are designed just for that purpose. A game console, on the other hand, is relatively small and inconspicuous and can fit neatly on a shelf next to your TV.

✔ **They work with your biggest screen.** Of course, you can connect a PC to a big-screen TV system (using a special video card). But consoles are designed to plug right into your TV or home theater system, using the same cables you use to hook up a VCR or DVD player.

✔ **They can replace your DVD player.** The PS3 and Xbox 360 (as well as the previous Xbox and PlayStation 2) can play DVD videos on your big screen. The PS3 even includes a built-in Blu-ray disc player for high-definition movies (which makes it a great deal, because stand-alone Blu-ray players cost as much as the PS3), and the Xbox 360 can be accessorized with a $199 external HD-DVD player. (The HD-DVD and Blu-ray systems are two new disc formats aiming to replace the DVD with a new high-definition format for HDTVs.)

Today's game consoles offer some awesome gaming experiences. Try playing the Xbox 360 game Halo 3 on a big-screen TV with a surround sound system in place — it's amazing. You can even get a full HDTV picture on the Xbox 360 and PlayStation 3. And, because these gaming consoles are really nothing more than specialized computers, they can offer the same kind of networking capabilities that a PC does; in other words, they can fit right into your wireless home network.

Getting your console onto your wireless network is possible (and easy) with almost all current or recent gaming consoles. The steps you need to take depend on which console you have.

People who own the most current generation of consoles are pretty much all set. Nintendo Wii and Sony PlayStation 3 have built-in Wi-Fi capabilities. If you're using an Xbox 360, you need to pick up the Xbox 360 Wireless Networking Adapter ($99, www.xbox.com/en-US/hardware/x/xbox360 wirelessnetadapter/default.htm).

Owners of the older PlayStation 2 or original Xbox need to add some hardware to their systems to get online via a wireless network. Both of these consoles include a built-in Ethernet port.

Early PS2 units (before the "slim" case design was introduced in 2004) do *not* have built-in Ethernet. Sony used to offer a *PlayStation Network Adapter* that provided this feature, but it is no longer available. If you have one of these older PS2s and don't have the adapter, search sites like eBay and Craigslist for a used adapter.

To connect one of these Ethernet-only consoles to your wireless network, you need a special Wi-Fi adapter known as a *Wi-Fi Ethernet bridge* (discussed in the upcoming section titled "Console wireless networking equipment").

Console wireless networking equipment

As we mention earlier, the current consoles all have inherent Wi-Fi networking capabilities (though this is optional with the Xbox 360). For older Ethernet consoles, you simply need to add an inexpensive Wi-Fi Ethernet bridge. The deeper you get into the networking world, the more likely you are to run into the concept of a *bridge,* which is simply a device that connects two segments of a network. Unlike hubs or switches or routers or most other network equipment (we talk about much of this stuff in Chapters 2 and 5), a bridge doesn't do anything with the data flowing through it. A bridge basically passes the data straight through without manipulating it, rerouting it, or even caring what it is. A wireless Ethernet bridge's sole purpose is to send data back and forth between two points. (It's not too tough to see where the name came from, huh?)

While we're discussing these wireless Ethernet bridges in terms of game console networks in this chapter, they're handy devices that can be used for lots of different applications in your wireless LAN. Basically, any device that has an Ethernet port — such as a personal video recorder (PVR), an MP3 server (such as the AudioReQuest), and even an Internet refrigerator (such as the Samsung Internet Refrigerator) — can hook into your wireless home network by using a wireless Ethernet bridge.

The great thing about wireless Ethernet bridges, besides the fact that they solve the problem of getting noncomputer devices onto the wireless network, is that they're the essence of plug and play. You may have to spend three or four minutes setting up the bridge itself (to get it connected to your wireless network), but you don't need to do anything special to your game console other than plug in the bridge. All the game consoles we discuss in this chapter (at least when equipped with the appropriate network adapters and software) "see" your wireless Ethernet bridge as just a regular Ethernet cable. You don't need any drivers or other special software on the console. The console doesn't know (nor does it care in its not-so-little console brain) that there's a wireless link in the middle of the connection. It just works!

If you have encryption (such as WPA) set up on the network, you need to complete one step before plugging your wireless bridge into your gaming console's Ethernet port. Plug the bridge into one of the wired Ethernet ports on your router and access the bridge's built-in Web configuration screens; there, you enter your WPA passphrase (or WEP key if you're using WEP) and network name (or ESSID). After you've made these settings, you're ready to plug the bridge into your console and get online. It's that simple!

Not all the wireless Ethernet bridges support the (much more secure) WPA encryption technology that we discuss in Chapter 9 (and which we highly recommend you use on your wireless network). If you're using WPA, make sure that you choose a wireless Ethernet bridge that supports this encryption method: You can't mix and match WPA with lesser encryption systems like WEP, so you would have to make your whole network less secure if you mixed in a less secure wireless Ethernet bridge.

D-Link DGL-3420 wireless 108AG gaming adapter

D-Link (www.dlink.com) has developed the DGL-3420 wireless 108AG ($99 list price) with gaming consoles in mind. D-Link even has its own online Gamer-Lounge site with lots of great gaming information (games.dlink.com). The DGL-3420 (see Figure 11-1) doesn't need any special drivers or configuration. It does include a Web-browser-based configuration program that enables you to do things like enter your Wi-Fi Protected Access (WPA) passphrase. (Check out Chapter 9 for more information on this topic.)

The DGL-3420 is a loaded Ethernet bridge that supports both 802.11a and 802.11g (most folks use 802.11g) and even supports the higher-speed Super G 108 Mbps variant of 802.11g — if your router also supports it.

There's even some special "secret sauce" for making gaming faster — the D-Link GameFuel prioritization technology, as discussed in the nearby sidebar, "Getting your router optimized for gaming."

SMC SMCWEBT-G EZ Connect g wireless Ethernet bridge

The SMC Network SMCWEBT-G wireless Ethernet bridge is an inexpensive Swiss army knife of an Ethernet bridge. First, it's an 802.11g wireless Ethernet bridge with a theoretical 108 Mbps maximum speed (you need a router that also supports the Super G protocol). Like the D-Link bridge we discuss in the preceding section, the SMCWEBT-G supports WPA encryption, which means that it plays nicely on your secured wireless network.

Figure 11-1:
The D-Link DGL-3420 gaming adapter.

There's more to it, though: The SMCWEBT-G can be configured to work as an access point all on its own (so that you can plug it into a stand-alone router to provide wireless access) and even as a *WDS repeater* that can extend the range of your network if your primary router is one of the SMC wireless routers. For only $79.99, it's a relative bargain and well worth checking out.

 As we write, no manufacturers offer 802.11n versions of these adapters. We expect that such adapters will hit the market by mid- to late-2008. If you're installing an 802.11n network *and* if all your other network clients use 802.11n, you might consider holding off on buying an 802.11g bridge until the 802.11n models arrive — simply because having 802.11g clients on your 802.11n network will slow down the overall speed of the network. If you can't wait (and we don't blame you — who wants to wait), you might consider searching online classifieds and auctions for a used 802.11g bridge as a stop-gap measure.

Console online gaming services

Having the hardware to bring your console online is only half the battle — you also need to sign up for an online gaming service. Each of the big console manufacturers offers an online gaming service, providing head-to-head network game play as well as fun stuff like game downloads (both demos and full-blown games), text and voice chat, shopping, and Web browsing.

 Not all console games are designed for online play. Each service has dozens (if not hundreds) of online-capable games, but just as many games are not network-enabled.

 In this chapter, we're talking about the network gaming services offered by the three major console manufacturers. For the most part, these services are the way you will access most online games for each of the consoles. Some games, however, might use their own network, or are accessed via the console manufacturer's network but require an additional subscription to use.

Living large with Xbox Live

The Microsoft online gaming service Xbox Live (www.xboxlive.com; in the U.S., this URL will take you directly to the home page: www.xbox.com/en-US/live/?WT.svl=nav) is the longest running of the three console online gaming networks, launched right after the original Xbox was put on market in late 2001–early 2002. Xbox Live has over 8 million subscribers worldwide, as we write in late 2007, so it should always be easy to find someone to play with!

Xbox Live isn't just about playing against someone else; it's almost a new lifestyle. With Xbox Live, you can

✔ Communicate in real time during games.

✔ Set up chats with your friends.

✔ Meet gamers from all over the world and put together a posse of your favorite teammates to go after others.

✔ Set up your own clans and start competitions with Xbox Live features.

✔ Join Xbox Live tournaments.

✔ Download cool new stuff for your favorite games that's available only online — new maps, missions, songs, skins, vehicles, characters, quests, and more. You can even download entertainment content (such as movies and music) for your Xbox 360.

✔ Play games against hot celebs that Microsoft courts online.

With the discontinuation of the original Xbox and the focus on the Xbox 360, Xbox Live has been mainly focused on users of the new console. There *is* still service available for the original Xbox, but we devote most of our discussion here to the Xbox 360.

There are two levels of service for Xbox Live:

✔ **Silver:** This is a free service; anyone with an Xbox 360 can sign up for it and access game content (like additional levels), and get the ability to create a *gamertag* (online identity) and participate in online chats with friends. What you can't do with the free silver service is participate in multiplayer online games; to do that, you need to be a gold member (read on!).

✔ **Gold:** This is the subscription (in other words, pay) service in Xbox Live. You get to play online games against friends (and strangers) and get additional features such as access to an online marketplace and enhanced friends list functionality. There are a number of different plans for signing up for Xbox Live Gold; the most common is a $59.99 plan, which provides a year's worth of service and includes a headset for live voice chat during gaming.

Microsoft doesn't provide the broadband service for Xbox Live (none of the gaming companies do) — just the gaming service itself. Thus, you need to already have a cable, fiber-optic, or DSL modem set up in your home.

If you're going to play Xbox Live, you need to make sure that your router is Xbox Live compatible. Go to www.xbox.com/en-US/support/connecttolive/xbox360/homenetworking/equipment.htm. On this page, Microsoft lists routers that don't work with its Live service, so be sure to check the list before you buy. If your router isn't on the Works or Does Not Work list, it's in a huge gray area of "we have no clue, but don't blame us if it doesn't work." Microsoft always loves a scapegoat!

If your current router isn't on this list, don't despair. Check the router manufacturer's Web site. Often, it has specific steps, such as installing a *firmware* update (updating the router's software), that make the router work just fine. Some routers work just as they are, but they simply haven't been certified for some reason.

Playing online with PlayStation Network

Sony's previous game console, the PlayStation 2 (PS2), was the most successful console ever, with over 120 million (say that really slowly in a Dr. Evil voice for full effect) consoles sold by 2007. This older console, as we mentioned, had some networking capabilities, and indeed over 200 network-capable games have been released over the years, with millions of users taking advantage of them. But Sony never put together an integrated competitor to Microsoft's Xbox Live with the PS2 — essentially the gaming software companies themselves set up online portals for their individual games.

With the new PS3 console, however, Sony has pulled out all the stops and launched the PlayStation Network. The *PlayStation Network,* a free service for PS3 and PSP (PlayStation Portable) owners, provides the following services:

- **PlayStation Store:** You can shop online for downloadable games (they get stored on your PS3's hard drive), demos of new games, and high-definition trailers of new games and movies.

- **Online game play:** Registered users can participate in free online head-to-head gaming. PlayStation Network also supports online gaming for some specific titles that require additional subscriptions (typically directly with the game software company itself) — so while the PlayStation service is free, you may have to pay a subscription fee for certain games.

- **Online community:** As is the case with Xbox Live, when you register with PlayStation Network, you can establish an online identity and participate in message boards and live text or voice chats with your gaming buddies over your wireless network.

- **Web browsing:** Not actually part of the PlayStation Network (in other words, you don't need to register to do this) but neat nonetheless. The PS3 has a built-in Web browser so you can surf the Web on your big-screen TV.

You can find more information about PlayStation Network online gaming at the Sony site (www.us.playstation.com/PS3/Network).

Wii? No, wheeeeeee!

The best selling of the three new-generation gaming consoles is Nintendo's Wii — fueled by a lower price and especially by the absolutely cool Wiimote, which uses motion control instead of buttons to control game action. The Wii

---

PSP: Your passport to Wi-Fi gaming

If you're into handheld gaming devices, the Sony PSP (PlayStation Portable) may be just the ticket. For about $200 (for a Value Pack including a couple of games and accessories), this slick little handheld lets you take your gaming with you. But there's more to the PSP than just gaming. The PSP is an all-purpose media player, with a Memory Stick DUO slot designed to let you carry photos, music, and even video along with you.

That's all cool, but what's cooler is that the PSP has a built-in Wi-Fi (802.11b) adapter that lets you connect to any 802.11b or 802.11g Wi-Fi network. The initial PSPs shipped with support for only WEP encryption, but a firmware upgrade in 2005 lets you connect even the older models to a properly secured WPA network. When connected via Wi-Fi, you can play online games against others on your network or over the Internet. There's even a built-in Web browser, so that when your thumbs need a break from all that hot gaming action, you can surf your favorite Web sites.

---

has been essentially "sold out" for over a year. (It's just as hard to get one as we write this as it was in 2006.)

With the Wii, Nintendo has pulled out all the online stops — the Wii includes built-in Wi-Fi, a Web browser, loads of online games, and an online ecosystem for you to enjoy using your motion-controlled gaming controllers.

Nintendo's Wi-Fi Connection service provides free online gaming for the Wii and also for Nintendo's DS handheld gaming device (both have built-in Wi-Fi). As is the case with the PS3, most networked Wii games can be played online for free, but some titles require you to purchase a subscription with the game's software vendor.

The Wii also includes an Internet Channel — which is Wiispeak for a Web browser (specifically the Opera Web browser) that allows you to surf the Web on your TV. Additionally, like the other gaming consoles, the Wii includes an online store for buying games, downloading game demos, and more.

In previous editions of this book we talked about the online gaming hardware and service available for Nintendo's older console, the (very cute little) GameCube. Online gaming never took off with the GameCube (most likely because the target audience for that console was younger kids), and in the end only three games were available for online play. As of April 2007 there were none, as online play for those games has been suspended. So get a Wii!

Going Wi-Fi and portable with Nintendo DS

Nintendo has a nifty handheld gaming console called the Nintendo DS (it's Nintendo's competitor to the Sony PSP) that features, among many things, *two screens*. (Imagine driving in a race while looking simultaneously out your windshield and at a bird's-eye view of your car on the track.)

Like the PSP, the DS has built-in support for Wi-Fi network connectivity. This connectivity is now used for hooking up with other nearby DS users — using a feature of the DS called *PictoChat*, which allows you to share drawings and have text chats.

To make it even easier to get your DS online, Nintendo has its *free* Nintendo Wi-Fi Connection service. This service allows you to connect the DS to your home Wi-Fi network to play a number of online games being launched with the service

(just as you can connect your Wii to your home Wi-Fi network).

The coolest part of this service is that Nintendo is in the midst of launching thousands of free Nintendo DS-accessible hot spots around the United States to connect to online gaming when you're on the road. The biggest issue you'll face with the DS on the road (and this is true for a lot of portable devices, as we discuss in Chapter 16), is that you can't log into Wi-Fi hot spots that require you to sign in on a Web page for full access. Nintendo's own hot spots (they aren't actually building their own, but rather have partnered with some hot spot providers) won't have this limitation (you'll be able to log in automatically). Go to www.nintendowifi.com/ to find out where Nintendo has hot spots near you.

Dealing with Router Configurations

So far in this chapter, we talk a bit about the services and hardware you need to get into online gaming using your wireless network. What we haven't covered yet — getting online and playing a game — is either the easiest or the hardest part of the equation. The difficulty of this task depends on two things:

- ✔ **The platform you're using:** If you're trying to get online with a PC (whether it's Windows-based or a Mac), well, basically there's nothing special to worry about. You just need to get it connected to the Internet as we describe in Chapter 9. For certain games, you may have to do a few fancy things with your router, which we discuss later in this chapter. If you're using a gaming console, you may have to adjust a few things in your router to get your online connection working, but when you're using a game console with many routers, you can just plug in your wireless equipment and go.

- ✔ **What you're trying to do:** For many games, after you establish an Internet connection, you're ready to start playing. Some games, however, require you to make some adjustments to your router's configuration. If you're planning to host the games on your PC (which means that your online friends will be remotely connecting to your PC), you definitely have to do a bit of configuration.

Don't sweat it, though. It's usually not all that hard to get gaming set up, and it's getting easier every day because the companies that make wireless LAN equipment and home routers realize that gaming is a growth industry for them. They know that they can sell more equipment if they can help people get devices such as game consoles online.

You need to accomplish two things to get your online gaming — well, we can't think of a better term — online:

1. **Get an Internet Protocol (IP) address.**

   Your access point needs to recognize your gaming PC's or console's network adapter and your console's wireless Ethernet bridge, if you have one in your network configuration. If you have WEP or, better yet, WPA configured (refer to Chapter 9), your game machine needs to provide the proper passphrase or key. Your router (whether it's in the access point or separate) needs to provide an IP address to your gaming machine.

2. **Get through your router's firewall.**

   The part that takes some time is configuring the firewall feature of your router to allow gaming programs to function properly.

Getting your router optimized for gaming

A few vendors have begun to sell wireless routers (or gateways, depending on their terminology) tweaked to support gaming. A wireless router manufacturer can do two things to ensure that gaming works well:

✔ **Make it easier to support online game play:** Routers can be designed to work specifically with online gaming applications. For example, a router may include more built-in game application support in its Web configuration, so you can easily "turn on" game support in the firewall and NAT routing functionality, without having to go through lots of trouble setting up port forwarding and DMZs (discussed in the final two sections of this chapter). Many gaming-specific routers support Universal Plug and Play (UPNP), also discussed in those sections, which makes the configuration of game applications automatic.

✔ **Provide *prioritization* to game applications:** For the ultimate in gaming experience,

some routers prioritize gaming applications over other traffic flowing through the router. Therefore, if two (or more) different applications are trying to send traffic through your router at the same time (such as your game and your spouse's e-mail application sending a work document to the server), the router makes sure that the gaming data gets through to the Internet first. This concept can reduce the *latency* (or delay) you experience in playing online games and make the experience better (you can blow up the other guy faster!).

An example of this kind of wireless router is the D-Link DGL-4500 Wireless Gaming Router (http://games.dlink.com/products/?pid=643, $199.99). This router includes the D-Link *GameFuel* prioritization technology, an 802.11n draft AP (promising raw speeds, when used with D-Link's own adapters, of up to 300 Mbps), and a wired switch supporting Gigabit (1000BaseT) connections for your wired PCs and consoles.

Getting an IP address

For the most part, if you've set up your router to provide IP addresses within your network using DHCP (as we discuss in Chapters 5 and 6), your gaming PC or gaming console automatically connects to the router when the device is turned on and sends a Dynamic Host Configuration Protocol (DHCP) request to the router, asking for an IP address. If you've configured your gaming PC, as we discuss in Chapters 7 and 8, your computer should get its IP address and be online automatically. Or, as we like to say about this kind of neat stuff, auto*magically.* You may need to go into a program to select an access point and enter your WEP password, but otherwise it should just work without any intervention.

If you have a game console with a wireless Ethernet bridge, the process should be almost as smooth. The first time you use the bridge, you may need to use a Web browser interface on one of your PCs to set up WEP keys or WPA passphrases; otherwise, your router should automatically assign an IP address to your console.

Before you get all wrapped around the axle trying to get your game console connected to your router, check out the Web site of your console maker *and* your router manufacturer. We have no doubt that you can find lots of information about how to make this connection. In many cases, if you're having trouble getting your router to assign an IP address to your console, you need to download a firmware upgrade for your router. *Firmware* is the software that lives inside your router and tells your router how to behave. Most router vendors have released updated firmware to help their older router models work with gaming consoles.

Some older router models simply don't work with gaming consoles. If online gaming is an important part of your plans, check the Web sites we mention earlier in this chapter *before* you choose a router.

In most cases, if your console doesn't get assigned an IP address automatically, you need to go into your router's setup program — most use a Web browser on a networked PC to adjust the configuration — and manually assign a fixed IP address to the console. Unlike DHCP-assigned IP addresses (which can change every time a computer logs on to the network), this fixed IP address is always assigned to your console.

Every router has a slightly different system for doing this, but typically you simply select an IP address that isn't in the range of DHCP addresses that your router automatically assigns to devices connected to your network.

You need to assign an IP address that isn't in the range of your router's IP address pool but is within the *same subnet.* In other words, if your router assigns IP addresses in the 192.168.0.*xxx* range, you need to use an IP address beginning with 192.168.0 for your game console. For example, if your router uses the range of 192.168.0.0 to 192.168.0.32 for computers connected to the network, you want to choose an IP address such as 192.168.0.34 for your console. Every router's configuration program is different, but you typically see a box that reads something like DHCP Server Start IP Address (with an IP address next to it) and another box that reads something like DHCP Server Finish IP Address with another box containing an IP address. (Some routers may just list the start address, followed by a *count,* which means that the finish address is the last number in the start address plus the count number.)

The key thing to remember is that you have to come up with only the last number in the IP address, the number after the third period in the IP address. The first three (which are usually 192.168.0) don't change. All you need to do to assign this IP address is to choose a number between 1 and 254 that is *not* in the range your router uses for DHCP. (Most routers use the .1 address, so you should use a number between 2 and 254.)

Dealing with port forwarding

After you have assigned an IP address to your gaming PC or game console. and are connected to the Internet, you may well be ready to start playing games. Our advice: Give it a try and see what happens. Depending on the games you play, any additional steps may not be needed.

The steps we're about to discuss shouldn't be required for a game console. And, although we haven't checked out every single game out there, we haven't run into any incidences where you need to get involved with the port forwarding, which we're about to discuss, with a game console. If you have an older router that doesn't work well with console games, you may consider putting your console on the router's DMZ, as we discuss in the upcoming section "Setting Up a Demilitarized Zone (DMZ)."

If, however, your games don't work, you may need to get involved in configuring the firewall and Network Address Translation (NAT). As we discuss in Chapter 5, home network routers use a system called NAT to connect multiple devices to a single Internet connection. Basically, NAT translates between public Internet IP addresses and internal IP addresses on your home's network. When a computer or other device is connected to your home network (wirelessly or even a wired network), the router assigns it an internal IP address. Similarly, when your router connects to the Internet, it's assigned its own public IP address: that is, its own identifying location on the Internet. Traffic flowing to and from your house uses this public IP address to find its way. After the traffic (which can be gaming data, an e-mail, a Web page, whatever) gets to the router, the NAT function of the router figures out to which PC (or other device) in the house to send that data.

One important feature of NAT is that it provides firewall functionality for your network. NAT knows which computer to send data to on your network because that computer has typically sent a request over the Internet for that bit of data. For example, when a computer requests a Web page, your NAT router knows which computer made the request so that when the Web page is downloaded, it gets sent to the right PC. If no device on the network has made a request — meaning that an unrequested bit of data shows up at your public IP address — NAT doesn't know where to send it. This process provides a security firewall function for your network because it keeps this unrequested data (which could be some sort of security risk) off your network.

NAT is a cool thing because it lets multiple computers share a single public IP address and Internet connection and helps keep the bad guys off your network. NAT can, however, cause problems with some applications that may require this unrequested data to work properly. For example, if you have a Web server on your network, you would rightly expect that people would try to download and view Web pages without your PC sending them any kind of initial request. After all, your Web server isn't clairvoyant. (At least ours isn't!)

Gaming can also rely on unrequested connections to work properly. For example, you may want to host a game on your PC with your friends, which means that their PCs will try to get through your router and connect directly with your PC. Even if you're not hosting the game, some games send chunks of unrequested data to your computer as part of the game play. Other applications that may do this include audio- and videoconferencing programs (such as Windows Messenger) and remote control programs (such as pcAnywhere).

To get these games (or other programs) to work properly over your wireless home network and through your router, you need to get into your router's configuration program and punch some holes in your firewall by setting up NAT port forwarding.

Of the many routers out there, they don't all call this process *port forwarding*. Read your manual. (Really, we mean it. Read the darn thing. We know it's boring, but it can be your friend.) Look for terms such as *special applications support* or *virtual servers*.

Port forwarding effectively opens a hole in your firewall that not only allows legitimate game or other application data through but may also let the bad guys in. Set up port forwarding only when you have to, and keep an eye on the logs. (Your router should keep a log of whom it lets in — check the manual to see how to find and read this log.) We also recommend that you consider using personal firewall software on your networked PCs (we like ZoneAlarm, www.zonelabs.com) and keep your antivirus software up to date.

Some routers let you set up *application-triggered* port forwarding (sometimes just called *port triggering*), which basically allows your router to look for certain signals coming from an application on your computer (the triggers) and then enable port forwarding. This option is more secure because when the program that requires port forwarding (your game, in this case) isn't running, your ports are closed. They open only when the game (or other application) requires them to be open.

When you set up port forwarding on your router, you're selecting specific ports (ports are subsegments of an IP address — a computer with a specific IP address uses different numbered ports to connect different applications to the network) and sending all incoming requests using those ports to a specific computer or device on your network. When you get involved in setting up port forwarding, you notice two kinds of ports: TCP (Transmission Control Protocol) and UDP (User Datagram Protocol). These names relate to the two primary ways in which data is carried on the Internet, and you may have to set up port forwarding for both TCP and UDP ports, depending on the application.

Every router or access point will have its own unique system for configuring port forwarding. Generally speaking, you find the port forwarding section of the configuration program and simply type into a text box on the screen the port numbers you want to open. For example, Figure 11-2 shows port forwarding being configured on a NETGEAR WPN824 router/access point.

As we mention earlier in this chapter, ports are assigned specific numbers. To get some gaming applications to work properly, you need to open (assign) port forwarding for a big range of port numbers. The best way to find out which ports need to be opened is to read the manual or search the Web page of the game software vendor. You can also find a relatively comprehensive list online at practicallynetworked.com/sharing/app_port_list.htm.

If your router is UPnP enabled (Universal Plug and Play, a system developed by Microsoft and others that, among other things, automatically configures port forwarding for you) and the PC game you're using uses Microsoft DirectX gaming, the router and the game should be able to talk to each other and automatically set up the appropriate port forwarding. Just make sure that you enable UPnP in your router's configuration system. Usually you simply click a check box in the router's configuration program.

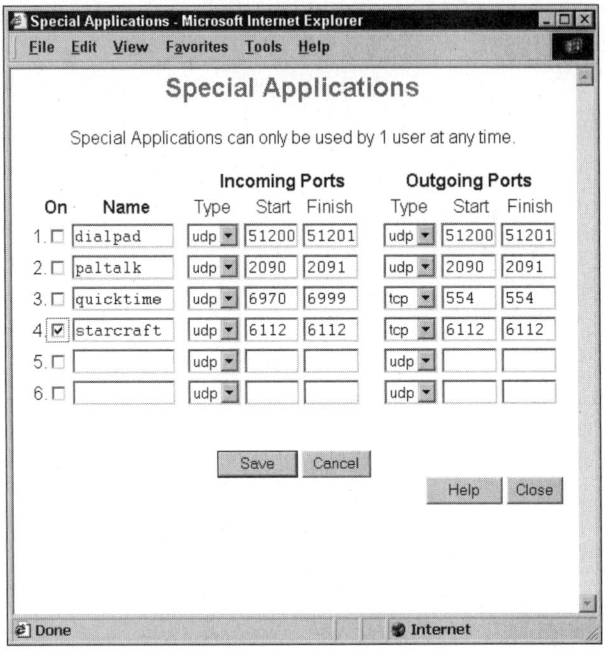

Special Applications - Microsoft Internet Explorer

File   Edit   View   Favorites   Tools   Help

Special Applications

Special Applications can only be used by 1 user at any time.

		Incoming Ports			Outgoing Ports		
On	Name	Type	Start	Finish	Type	Start	Finish
1. ☐	dialpad	udp ▾	51200	51201	udp ▾	51200	51201
2. ☐	paltalk	udp ▾	2090	2091	udp ▾	2090	2091
3. ☐	quicktime	udp ▾	6970	6999	tcp ▾	554	554
4. ☑	starcraft	udp ▾	6112	6112	tcp ▾	6112	6112
5. ☐		udp ▾			udp ▾		
6. ☐		udp ▾			udp ▾		

[Save]   [Cancel]

[Help]   [Close]

Done   Internet

Figure 11-2:
Setting
up port
forwarding.

Setting Up a Demilitarized Zone (DMZ)

If you need to do some special port forwarding and router tweaking to get
your games working, you may find that you're spending entirely too much
time getting it all up and running. Or you may find that you open what *should*
be the right ports — according to the game developer — and that things still
just don't seem to be working correctly. It happens; not all routers are equally
good at implementing port forwarding.

Here's another approach you can take: Set up a *demilitarized zone* (DMZ).
This term has been appropriated from the military (think the North and
South Korean borders) by way of the business networking world, where
DMZs are used for devices such as Web servers in corporate networks. In a
home network, a DMZ is a virtual portion of your network that's completely
outside your firewall. In other words, a computer or device connected to
your DMZ accepts all incoming connections — your NAT router forwards all
incoming connections (on any port) to the computer connected to the DMZ.
You don't need to configure special ports for specific games because everything is forwarded to the computer or device you have placed on the DMZ.

Most home routers we know of set up a DMZ for only one of your networked
devices, so this approach may not work if you have two gaming PCs connected to the Internet. However, for most people, a DMZ does the trick.

Although setting up a DMZ is perhaps easier to do than configuring port forwarding, it comes with bigger security risks. If you set up port forwarding, you lessen the security of the computer that the ports are being forwarded to — but if you put that computer on the DMZ, you've basically removed all the firewall features of your router from that computer. Be judicious when using a DMZ. If you have a computer dedicated only to gaming, a game console, or a kid's computer that doesn't have any important personal files configured to be on your DMZ, you're probably okay — but you run a risk that even that computer can be used to attack the others on your network. DMZs are perfectly safe for a console, but they should be used for PCs and Macs only if you can't make port forwarding work.

Depending on the individual router configuration program that comes with your preferred brand of router, setting up a DMZ is typically simple. Figure 11-3 shows a DMZ being set up on a Siemens SpeedStream router/access point. It's a dead-simple process. In most cases, you need only mark a check box in the router configuration program to turn on the DMZ and then use a pull-down menu to select the computer you want on the DMZ.

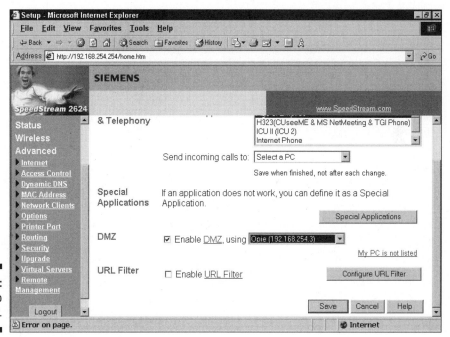

Figure 11-3:
Setting up
a DMZ.

Chapter 12

Networking Your Entertainment Center

. . . .

. . . .

*W*ithout doubt, the most significant news in wireless home networking — aside from the general price drops that are driving growth in the industry — is the movement of the 802.11-based networking outside the realm of computers and into the realm of entertainment.

The linkage of the two environments yields the best of both possible worlds. You can use your hard drive on your PC to store audio and video tracks for playback on your TV and through your stereo. You can stream movies from the Internet and play them on your TV. You can take pictures with your digital camera, load them on your PC, and view them on your TV. You get the picture (oops, pun).

You will simply not believe how much the ability to link the home entertainment center with the PC will affect your computing and entertainment experiences. It could affect which PC you buy. For example, if you're buying a Windows PC, you may choose one that supports Microsoft's Window's *Media Center* functionality (part of the Windows Vista Home Premium and Vista Ultimate variants), designed to power your home entertainment system (it's too irresistible). It could affect how you rent movies: Why go all the way to Blockbuster when you can just download a movie over the Internet from Movielink (www.movielink.com) with a single click? It could even affect how you watch your favorite shows because with computer-based personal video recorders (PVRs), you can record the shows you want to watch but always miss because you could never figure out how to record on the VCR. Whew. That's *some* change.

In this chapter, we expose you to some of the ways wireless home networking is enabling this revolution toward a linked TV/PC world. You will find that much of what we talk about throughout this book serves as the perfect foundation for linking PCs and audio/video systems.

You may be thinking, "Whoa, wait a minute, I thought wireless was just for data. Are you telling me that I need to move my PC to my living room and put it next to my TV?" Rest assured: We're not suggesting that, although you may find yourself putting a PC near your TV sometime soon. You could indeed put your PC next to your TV, link it with a video cable, and run your Internet interconnection to the living room. But, if that's your only PC and your spouse wants to watch the latest basketball game, you may find it hard to do your work!

The revolution we're talking about — and are just getting started with in this chapter and the ones that follow — is the whole-home wireless revolution, where that powerful data network you install for your PCs to talk to one another and the Internet can also talk to lots of other things in your home. You hear us talk a great deal about your *whole-home audio network* or a *whole-home video network*. That's our code for "you can hear (view) it throughout the house." You built that wireless network (in Part III), and now other devices will come and use it. And coming they are, indeed — by the boxful. Be prepared to hear about all these great devices — things you use every day, such as your stereo, refrigerator, and car — that want to hop onboard your wireless home highway.

Wirelessly Enabling Your Home Entertainment System

If you're like most of us, your home entertainment system probably consists of a TV, a stereo receiver, some components (such as a record player, tape deck, or CD/DVD player), and a few speakers. For most parties, this setup is enough to make for a memorable evening!

And, if you're like most of us, you have a jumble of wires linking all this audio/visual (A/V) gear together. The mere thought of adding more wiring to the system — especially to link, for example, your receiver to your computer to play some MP3s — is a bit much.

We have some good news for you. Regardless of whether you have a $250 television set or a $25,000 home theater, you can wirelessly enable almost any type of A/V gear you have. Before we get into the specific options now on the market, we need to discuss at a high level the wireless bandwidth requirements for the two major applications for your entertainment system: audio and video.

Here are the two predominant ways that audio and video files are handled with your entertainment/PC combo:

- ✔ **Streaming:** The file is accessed from your PC's hard drive (or over the Internet) and sent via a continuous signal to your entertainment hardware for live playback. This is the way most media content is handled in home networks today.

- ✔ **File transfer:** The file is sent from your PC to your stereo system components, where it's stored for later playback.

These two applications have different effects on your wireless home network. Streaming applications are *real-time* applications (meaning that what you are hearing or seeing, or both, is what's being streamed over the network *right now*), and any problems with the network, such as not having enough bandwidth to support the media you're playing, has a noticeable effect in your playback experience (for example, dropped audio or blocky video). File transfers, on the other hand, can pretty much work over *any* network connection.

With file transfer, lots of transmissions take place in the background. For example, many audio programs allow for automatic synchronization between file repositories, which can be scheduled during off hours to minimize the effect on your network traffic when you're using your home network. And, in these cases, you're not as concerned with how long it takes as you would be if you were watching or listening to it live while it plays.

A streaming application is sensitive to network delays and lost data packets. You tend to notice a bad picture pretty quickly. Also, with a file transfer, any lost data can be retransmitted when its loss is detected. But with streaming video and audio, you need to get the packets right the first time because most of the transmission protocols don't even allow for retransmission, even if you want to. You just get clipped and delayed sound, which sounds bad.

A good-quality 802.11g signal is fine in most instances for audio or video file transfers and is also more than adequate for audio streaming. Whether it's okay for *video streaming* depends a great deal on how the video was encoded and the size of the file. The larger the file size for the same amount of running time, the larger the bandwidth that's required to transmit it for steady video performance. Video is a bandwidth hog; whereas audio streaming might require a few hundred Kbps of bandwidth (or maybe one or two Mbps for uncompressed audio), video can require much more. Low-resolution Internet video (for example, YouTube videos) doesn't require a lot of bandwidth; it also doesn't look all that great on your TV. If you want to send DVD-quality video across your wireless network, you need several Mbps's worth of wireless bandwidth to do so — HDTV can require as much as 20 Mbps.

The high bandwidth requirements of video were one of the driving forces behind the development of 802.11n. 802.11g may have a nominal bandwidth of 54 Mbps, but in the real world users can expect less than 20 Mbps of real throughput across the whole network. A single channel of HDTV would stop the entire network dead.

If you're considering streaming high-quality video across your wireless network, you should definitely build an 802.11n network. Most wireless audio and video gear now available on the market is shipping with 802.11g on board, but a few vendors have begun selling 802.11n equipment. Again, remember, if you're just doing audio streaming, 802.11g is more than adequate.

You can choose from a number of different options when you build a wireless entertainment network, including the following:

✔ **Media adapters:** The most basic (but by no means unsophisticated) wireless media systems are known as *media adapters*. These devices have no storage themselves, so they are strictly for streaming media. A media adapter does exactly what its name says it does — it converts (or adapts) a streaming audio or video file coming from your computer (such as an MP3 music file) to an analog or digital audio (or video) format that your TV or audio equipment understands. A media adapter connects to your wireless network on the computer side using Wi-Fi, and connects to your home entertainment gear using standard audio and video cables. Examples of such gear include Logitech's Squeezebox (www.slimdevices.com, shown in Figure 12-1) and Apple's AirPort Express (www.apple.com).

Figure 12-1:
The Squeeze-Box digital media adapter is one of our favorites.

✔ **Media players/servers:** Media players or servers add storage to the mix. Typically, these devices have a built-in hard drive that lets you locally store entertainment content for playback, so you don't have to rely as much on the performance of your wireless network. Most media players also will stream content from your computer network (and the Internet), so you can think of them as a media adapter with a hard drive. Examples include Apple's AppleTV (www.apple.com/appletv), and D-Link's Media-Lounge players (such as the DSM-510, www.dlink.com/products/?sec= 0&pid=542).

There's not a Ministry of Naming Esoteric Wireless Entertainment Gear out there (if there was, we think it would be right next door to the Ministry of Banning Common Household Items from Airplanes, but that's another story entirely!). What we mean by this statement is that not all vendors use exactly the same terms we are using here to delineate the difference between an *adapter* and a *player/server.* The bottom line is that an adapter has no local storage and is a streaming-only device, whereas a player/server has a hard drive and can work independently of your PC's hard drive (syncing the content and then playing it back whenever, even when your spouse has the laptop at work).

✔ **Media center extenders:** A specialized category of media adapters/players, *media center extenders* work specifically with Windows XP or Vista computers running Microsoft's Windows Media Center software. A media center extender essentially replicates the Media Center user interface on your TV and lets you access all the content stored on your Media Center PC remotely. A media center extender may have a hard drive for local content storage, but it is primarily a streaming solution, with the content you're accessing all coming from your Media Center PC. Examples here include Microsoft's Xbox 360 gaming console (discussed in Chapter 11), and the Linksys DMA 2100 Media Center Extender (www.linksys.com).

✔ **Networked audio/video gear:** Some audio/video gear has the networking built right in. This could be a home theater receiver with networking capabilities that let you stream audio from your computer directly into the receiver (without requiring a stand-alone media adapter), or it could be a purpose-built wireless entertainment system that uses Wi-Fi to distribute audio (and to a lesser degree, video) around your home. A good example of the former is Denon's AVR-4308CI home theater receiver, with built-in Wi-Fi (http://usa.denon.com/ProductDetails/3494.asp); an example of the latter is the Sonos Digital Music System (www.sonos.com), which uses Wi-Fi to create a multiroom, whole-home audio distribution system.

Most networked home theater receivers do *not* have built-in Wi-Fi but instead provide only a wired Ethernet connection. You can use a *Wi-Fi Ethernet bridge,* discussed later in the chapter, to connect these devices to your wireless network.

✔ **Home theater PCs:** Finally, you can bring the content right to your home theater or media room by installing a home theater PC. These are purpose-built PCs designed to function as your home theater's DVR (digital video recorder), DVD player, and general jack-of-all-trades content source.

In the following sections we take a deeper dive into these product categories and talk about how you can get audio and video onto your wireless network.

Almost all the entertainment networking equipment we discuss in this chapter includes wired Ethernet connections in addition to Wi-Fi networking. So if your whole-home network consists of both wired and wireless network infrastructure, and the wired part of your network reaches your entertainment system, you can use Ethernet instead of Wi-Fi to connect your audio/video gear — we recommend that you do so if the cables are there!

When you shop for a wireless entertainment device of any sort, it's important to make sure it's certified not only for the variant of 802.11 you're using (g or n), but also for the level of wireless networking security you're using (see Chapter 9 for more on this). Most new devices support all current Wi-Fi security standards (up to and including WPA2 Personal), but traditionally this category of product lagged behind computer networking products in terms of security. Remember that you can't have a mix of WEP and WPA/WPA2 on the same network — we recommend walking away from a product that supports only WEP unless you're comfortable reducing the security on your entire network.

Getting Media from Computers to A/V Equipment

The most common question we're asked in the realm of wireless entertainment is, "How do I play the thousands of digital songs stored on my computer on the high-quality audio system in my family room?" The *second* most common question we're asked is, "How do I take all of those videos on my computer and play them on my big-screen TV?"

Well these are questions we can answer. In fact, this entire chapter is designed to answer those questions and variants thereof. But let's start off with the simplest answer to these simple questions: get a digital media adapter (or player)!

If audio is your biggest concern (and for most folks it is), a digital media adapter can be an easy-to-configure and inexpensive route between point A (your computer) and point B (your A/V system). Adding video to the equation means you'll have to spend a bit more money (and will probably benefit from the *local storage* contained in a digital media player instead of an adapter).

Cutting the cord in your home theater

This chapter focuses on the wireless equipment used to distribute audio (or video) from one part of your home to another — for example, taking music from your PC to a stereo in another room. Another place where we are starting to see wireless systems become an option is in the home theater. Home theaters are great (we wrote *Home Theaters For Dummies* because we love them so much), but they're also a lot of work — getting the wires around the room for five to seven surround-sound speakers and a flat panel TV on the wall is not always easy. To date, wireless speakers have not always been as good (in terms of sound performance) as wired speakers, and most systems required a mix of wired (in front) and wireless speakers (in the back of the room). At the 2008 Consumer Electronics Show, a company called Neosonik

(www.neosonik.com) announced a new wireless home theater solution that provides wireless connections for all five speakers *and* a wireless video connection for an HDTV.

A number of other companies announced *wireless HDMI* (high definition multimedia interface) solutions that replace the digital video cables used to connect HDTVs to source components such as cable or satellite TV set-top boxes. If you have a flat-panel TV (plasma or LCD) on the wall, or a projection system mounted to your ceiling, the last thing you want to do is deal with hiding the cables that bring the picture into your TV system. With these wireless HDMI systems — from vendors such as Belkin (www.belkin.com) and Gefen (www.gefen.com) — you can go wire free and still enjoy a full-quality HDTV picture!

What should you look for when choosing a media adapter or player? We think the following things are important:

- **Network compatibility and performance:** Any media adapter or player you choose should be Wi-Fi certified and support at least 802.11g. If you're choosing a system that supports video as well, we strongly recommend that you choose an 802.11n system. You may also consider choosing a system certified by the Wi-Fi Alliance to support the WMM quality of service standard. See the sidebar titled "Understanding Wi-Fi Multimedia (WMM)" for more on this. Finally, you should ensure that your adapter or player supports the Wi-Fi security system you're using on your network. (We recommend that you use WPA2.)

  Even if your requirements are for audio only, if your AP or wireless router uses 802.11n, you should choose an 802.11n media player or adapter simply because mixing 802.11g and 802.11n on the same network decreases the overall speed of the network. Keep your network all n to maximize throughput for any use of the network.

- **Software requirements:** Most media adapters and players require the installation of software on your PC or Mac. This software acts like Windows Media Player or iTunes does on your computer, and indexes all the media on your computer and streams (or forwards) it to your adapter or player. Some media adapters or players actually use iTunes and Windows Media Player (which you probably already have installed on your PC), which simplifies matters greatly.

✔ **User interface:** The user interface is simply the mechanism that you use to control your media player. For some simple media adapters (such as Apple's multipurpose AirPort Express — which can also be used as a router or as a print server), the interface is back on your computer (so you have to use the software on the computer to control the media adapter, which isn't convenient). Other adapters and players have a simple remote control that lets you skip forward and back through songs or video programs, pause, and stop and start the program.

✔ **Display:** Your media player or adapter's display is part of its user interface, but we're mentioning it separately simply because not all media adapters and players even have a display — which is inconvenient to say the least. For media adapters and players that do have a display, you'll find two distinct mechanisms:

   • **LCD/LED screens on the device itself:** Many media players or adapters have a small text display on the device, which can display your playlists, the title or song name currently playing, and more. Keep in mind that you don't want this display to be too small, because you're likely to be trying to read it from across the room.

   • **TV onscreen displays:** These are typical for media players and adapters that can handle video content. An onscreen menu (similar to the one that your cable or satellite set-top box offers) lets you view (and browse through) all your PC-based media on the big screen. An onscreen display is sexy and a lot easier to use from across the room than a smaller screen on the device itself, but an onscreen display does require you to have your TV turned on, even when you're only listening to music — so you might consider a player/adapter that offers *both* an onscreen display and a built-in display.

An adapter without a screen isn't necessarily completely inconvenient. For example, Pat uses Apple's AirPort Express for playing music on his home theater system — because he always has at least one of his Apple laptop computers in that room, he can simply open iTunes and choose music. With Apple's FrontRow software (included on all current Macs), he can even use a remote control to control his music playback.

✔ **File format support:** You can use a number of file formats for storing audio and video on a computer. Examples in the audio world include MP3, WMA (Windows Media Audio), and AAC (used by iTunes). The video world includes formats such as WMV (Windows Media Video), MPEG-2, and MPEG-4. Most media adapters and players support the most common file formats (particularly widely used standards such as MP3 and MPEG), but you should pay close attention to the formats you actually use to make sure that your adapter or player matches up with them.

✔ **DRM support:** DRM (or *digital rights management*) is a blanket term to describe various copy protection and usage restriction systems used by online music and video stores to control how customers use music and videos that they download or purchase. DRM is, at its essence, an effort to keep digital music and video downloads off the Internet and off file-sharing services (such as peer-to-peer networks). Unfortunately for consumers, most DRM is overly restrictive and makes it hard to distribute your purchased music and video not only to strangers over the Internet but also to *yourself* over your home network. If a lot of the music and video that you have on your computers is from an online store, check carefully to see whether your media adapter or player can support the variant of DRM that the store uses — oftentimes the answer is no. We talk more about this in the section titled "Internet Content for Your Media Adapters, Players, and HTPCs" at the end of this chapter.

✔ **Support for Internet Services:** Although most music and video obtained online is downloaded to a PC and stored there for future playback, some online services support a streaming model (often called a subscription service). With these services (an example is Rhapsody, www.rhapsody. com), you don't actually own a song or album, but you can access any of millions of songs on demand (as long as your subscription is current). Some media adapters and players allow you to *directly* access these services, so you can completely bypass your computer and listen to (or watch) this online content through your wireless network and broadband Internet connection.

In addition to subscription services such as Rhapsody, hundreds of Internet *radio stations* play their own chosen music playlists (like traditional radio stations). You can't choose which songs to listen to with Internet radio (like you can with a subscription service), but you don't have to pay anything either. Many media adapters and players can tune into Internet radio stations — without requiring you to use your computer to tune in.

✔ **Outputs:** Remember again that media adapters and players are designed to sit in between your computer(s) and your audio/video gear and to covert digital music and video files into a format that your A/V gear can understand. To connect your adapter or player to that A/V gear, you'll need to use some standard audio/video cables. As a baseline, you should expect your adapter/player to have a stereo pair of analog audio outputs (RCA cables, just like the ones that connect DVD players, tape decks, and the like). More advanced models have digital audio outputs (TOSLINK or coaxial) for connecting to a home theater receiver. On the video side, at a minimum you should have a composite video connection (the yellow video cable found on VCRs). If you want to get a high-definition picture from your adapter or player, you should expect to find either a set of analog *component video* outputs (three cables, like the ones found on many DVD players) or an HDMI (High Definition Multimedia Interface) digital video connector. (HDMI can actually carry both video *and* digital audio on one cable.)

Understanding Wi-Fi Multimedia (WMM)

Another 802.11 standard (man, there sure are a lot of them) that you might occasionally hear about (if you're reading up on 802.11 technologies online) is called _802.11e_. 802.11e is a _quality of service_ (or QoS) enhancement to other 802.11 technologies (a, b, g, or n) — 802.11e can determine when bandwidth- or delay-sensitive traffic is moving across your network (like voice conversations over a Wi-Fi phone — see Chapter 13 — or audio/video signals), and it can then _prioritize_ that traffic over things such as e-mail to keep your e-mail download from making your video signal break up on your TV.

The Wi-Fi Alliance folks have created, as they did with just about all the other 802.11 standards, a certification program for 802.11e-capable equipment called _WMM_ (or Wi-Fi Multimedia). WMM-certified equipment incorporates the QoS mechanisms defined in 802.11e

and additionally has been certified to work across vendors. If you want WMM to work for your Wi-Fi entertainment gear, you need to be sure that both the entertainment device itself (for example, a digital media adapter) _and_ your access point or wireless router are certified for WMM. (The box will have the WMM logo.)

Overall, WMM can help improve your multimedia experience within your wireless network; one thing that it can't do, however, is control the QoS of your Internet connection. So if your audio or video network is being affected by traffic inside your home network, WMM can help — if the bottleneck is in your Internet connection (for example, someone downloading a big file while you're trying to watch streaming video from the Internet), WMM won't be of any assistance.

Choosing Networked Entertainment Gear

The digital media adapters and players we discuss in the preceding section make a connection between your computer network and traditional (non-networked) A/V gear. Not all A/V gear is incapable of being networked though. In fact, a growing number of home theater receivers and even televisions are being outfitted with network capabilities. Most networked A/V gear (be it a receiver or a TV) simply incorporates a digital media adapter (or the functionality of one) into the device itself — providing you with the ability to access digital media files across your home network. Almost all these network-enabled receivers and TVs are Ethernet devices and _not_ Wi-Fi enabled. Later in this section, we tell you how to connect Ethernet entertainment gear to your wireless network.

You can also find whole-home wireless audio distribution systems that can connect to your computers, but that also can be self-contained wireless entertainment systems. We talk about both types of systems in this section.

Adding Wi-Fi to Ethernet A/V gear

In the future, we expect that most networked entertainment gear will have built-in Wi-Fi. And in fact, several high-end receivers and TVs do have built-in Wi-Fi today. (An example of this is Denon's AVR-4308CI receiver, which costs $2,500 and includes built-in 802.11g networking.) Manufacturers have been reluctant to incorporate Wi-Fi due to the rapid pace of technological change (802.11b being replaced by 802.11g, which is now being replaced by 802.11n). Rather than be caught with outdated wireless technology, many manufacturers have skipped wireless entirely.

Unfortunately for us as consumers, nothing is worse than having a great piece of entertainment gear that you want to get onto your home network, but the nearest outlet is yards away and you don't have a cable long enough to plug it in. So, you can imagine Danny's face when he had his brand-new, networking-capable AudioReQuest system (www.request.com) with no Ethernet connection near to plug it into. Argh!

To get this gear on your net, you need a wireless *bridge.* A popular model is the D-Link (www.d-link.com, $89) DWL-G820 Wireless Ethernet Bridge (802.11g) that comes with Wi-Fi Protected Access (WPA2) and 128-bit WEP security. On the back is a simple Ethernet port that enables you to bring any networkable device onto your wireless backbone. Another popular product is the 802.11g Apple Airport Express (www.apple.com, $99), which is a great little multi-purpose device that is a media adapter, a wireless Ethernet bridge, a travel router, an access point, and a print server all in one slick white package. (It can't do all these things at once, but it can be configured for any of these uses.) Oh, and it can play music purchased at the iTunes store (and it supports WPA2).

Other Ethernet bridge products include the Linksys WET-54G Wireless-G Ethernet Bridge (www.linksys.com, $89.99) and the Belkin F5D7330 802.11g Wireless Ethernet Bridge and Game Adapter (www.belkin.com, $100).

All the wireless bridges we mention here are 802.11g and *not* 802.11n. That's the case simply because, as we write, 802.11n is still a new technology and most vendors have only gotten around to releasing 802.11n access points, wireless routers, and network adapter cards. We fully expect to see 802.11n variants of the wireless bridges discussed in the two previous chapters to be released in early 2008 — likely by the time you read this.

Here are a couple of tips for buying wireless bridges:

✔ **Buy at least 802.11g for this application.** You need the bandwidth, and 802.11n will be an even better choice, when it becomes available. Video doesn't work well at 802.11b speeds, so if you see an older 802.11b product of this sort on eBay, resist the urge to buy it.

✔ **Make sure the security matches your network security needs.** All the wireless bridges we've mentioned in this chapter support WPA/WPA2 security on the network, but other products on the market don't. Remember that security in a wireless network is a least-common-denominator concept — if even one of your devices supports only WEP and not WPA, your entire network will run using the (not-so-secure) WEP security system.

Equipment with built-in Wi-Fi

Some manufacturers are building whole-home wireless entertainment systems (typically focused on music-only applications) that let you set up a centralized, remotely controlled multiroom audio system without wires or complicated installations. Essentially, you can use Wi-Fi to get a whole-home audio system like the really rich folks have in their mansions with $200,000 custom-installed wiring systems. (Wireless) power to the people!

We focus on a leading-edge wireless media server product, the Sonos Music System (www.sonos.com, about $900 for a two-room system), as shown in Figure 12-2. This technogeek's dream system consists of a controller (the brains of the system), a "zone" player (the endpoints of the system where all the speaker and system interfaces are housed, as well as a four-port switch so that you can network other items in the vicinity — nice!), and matching speakers you can use if you want everything to match.

Figure 12-2:
The Sonos
Music
System is
advanced
stuff!

Most buyers of the Sonos also buy a local Network Attached Storage (NAS) hard drive because the Sonos itself doesn't have one — a non-NAS system just plays music found elsewhere, such as on your PC. You can also have more than one Sonos zone player; the players talk to each other and the controller in a meshlike fashion, so if you have a really long house, you can still use the Sonos system. In such instances, the Sonos system synchronizes the music so that it all plays at the same time, avoiding any weird echo-type sounds around the house. Sonos uses 802.11g for its wireless protocol — and creates its own mesh network hopping from Sonos to Sonos throughout your home.

If you want to connect your Sonos system to your existing wireless network (and to your Internet connection, for playing back Internet radio stations), you can add in the $99 Sonos Zonebridge, which plugs into an Ethernet port on your home router and automatically bridges your PC and Sonos wireless networks.

Putting a Networked PC in Your Home Theater

When you talk about your home entertainment center, you often talk about *sources:* that is, devices such as tape decks, AM/FM receivers, phono players, CD units, DVD players, and other consumer electronics devices that provide the inputs of the content you listen to and watch through your entertainment system.

When you think about adding your networked PC or PCs to your entertainment mix, the PC becomes just another high-quality source device attached to your A/V system — albeit wirelessly. To connect your PC to your entertainment system, you must have some special audio/video cards and corresponding software to enable your PC to "speak stereo." When the PC is configured like this, you effectively have a *home theater PC* (or *HTPC,* as the cool kids refer to them). In fact, if you do it right, you can create an HTPC that funnels audio and video into your system at a higher-quality level than many moderately priced, stand-alone source components. HTPC can be that good.

You can either buy a ready-to-go HTPC right off the shelf or build one yourself. We don't recommend that you build an HTPC unless you have a fair amount of knowledge about PCs. If that's the case, have at it. Another obvious point: It's much easier to buy a ready-to-go version of an HTPC off the shelf. You can find out more about HTPCs in *Home Theater For Dummies* (Pat and Danny wrote that one, too) by Wiley. What we include here is the short and sweet version of HTPC.

What you expect from your home theater PC is quite different from what David Bowie might expect from his HTPC. Regardless of your needs, however, a home theater PC should be able to store music and video files, play CDs and DVDs, let you play video games on the big screen, and tune in to online music and video content. Thus, it needs ample hard drive space and the appropriate software (see the following section). Also, your HTPC acts as a DVR (see the nearby sidebar, "Checking out PC DVRs," for the lowdown on PC-based DVRs). In addition, an HTPC can

- ✔ **Store audio (music) files:** Now you can easily play your MP3s anywhere on your wireless network.

- ✔ **Store video clips:** Keeping your digital home video tapes handy is quite the crowd pleaser — you can have your own *America's Funniest Home Videos* show.

- ✔ **Play CDs and DVDs:** The ability to play DVDs is essential in a home theater environment.

- ✔ **Act as a DVR (digital video recorder):** This optional (but almost essential, we think) function uses the HTPC's hard drive to record television shows like a TiVo (www.tivo.com).

- ✔ **Let you play video games on the big screen:** With the right hardware, PCs are sometimes even better than gaming consoles (which we cover in Chapter 11).

- ✔ **Tune in to online music and video content:** Grab the good stuff off the Internet (yes, and pay for it), and then enjoy it on the big screen with good audio equipment.

- ✔ **Provide a high-quality, progressive video signal to your TV video display:** This is behind-the-curtain stuff. Simply, an HTPC uses special hardware to display your PC's video content on a TV. Sure, PCs have built-in video systems, but most are designed to be displayed only on PC monitors, not on TVs. To get the highest possible video quality on your big-screen HDTV, you need a special video card that can produce a high-definition, progressive-scan video signal. (This investment also gives you better performance on your PC's monitor, which is never bad.)

- ✔ **Decode and send HDTV content to your high-definition TV display:** HTPCs can provide a cheap way to decode over-the-air HDTV signals and send them to your home entertainment center's display. You just need the right hardware (an HDTV-capable video card and a TV tuner card). If you have HDTV, this is a cool optional feature of HTPC.

For example, the HP z560 Digital Entertainment Center (www.hp.com, $1,799) is a full-fledged digital media center PC with onboard 802.11g functionality and includes Microsoft's Windows XP Media Center Edition or Windows Vista

Home Premium (which also includes Media Center software). From regular and high-definition TV broadcasts to movies, music, games, and digital photos, this baby has it all, and you can connect to it wirelessly. What more could you want? Note that this current model does not have built-in 802.11n networking — we expect that by the time you read this, HP will have updated the networking to include 802.11n.

The term *Media Center PC* is often used generically, but it can mean two different things: a PC configured to be a repository and driver for media applications or a PC sold with the Microsoft Windows XP Media Center Edition or Windows Vista Home Premium software on board. You can get this software only by buying a new, specially configured Media Center PC. Not all Media Center PCs have the Windows Media Center Edition software, so read the fine print.

If you have a Windows XP or Vista Media Center PC, you will probably want to link it to other TVs, using a Media Center Extender. An example is Linksys DMA 2200 Media Center Extender with DVD player (price unknown as we write). This sleek device works like a media adapter for a Media Center PC and allows you to view any media on the Media Center PC on a remote TV, including recorded (DVR) shows and even live TV programming being picked up by the TV tuner in the PC. The DMA 2200 uses 802.11n networking (so it will work with video wirelessly, unlike previous generations of these products), and comes with a built-in DVD player. Figure 12-3 shows the DMA 2200.

Checking out PC DVRs

Using the HTPC's hard drive to record television shows like the way a TiVo does is an optional (but almost essential, we think) function. And using an HTPC as a DVR is a standard feature in a Windows XP/Vista Media Center PC — and something that we think you should consider adding to your home-built HTPC. Even if this were the only thing you wanted to do with your HTPC, it would be worth it. You can simply install a PC DVR kit and skip much of the other stuff (such as the DVD player, decoder, and software).

Tip: Because the biggest limitation to any DVR system is the amount of space on your hard drive for storing video, consider a hard drive upgrade regardless of your other HTPC intentions.

PC DVR kits on the market include the ATI TV Wonder 650 or 600 Series (http://ati.amd.com/products/atitvwonder.html), SnapStream Beyond TV (www.snapstream.com), and Pinnacle PCTV (www.pinnaclesys.com).

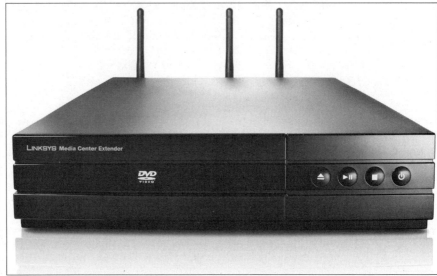

Figure 12-3:
The DMA 2200 from Linksys will hook your Media Center PC to remote TVs.

Internet Content for Your Media Adapters, Players, and HTPCs

If you're really into this HTPC thing, think about whether setting up an HTPC is worth the trouble just to play back DVDs (although the quality would be way high). Probably not, huh? "So," you may ask yourself, "what else is in it for me?" What makes an HTPC useful is its ability to provide a portal to all sorts of great Internet-based content — that is, music and video content. A *portal* is simply a one-stop shop for movies, songs, animation clips, and video voice mail. Think of it as a kind of Yahoo! for your audio and video needs. (In fact, Yahoo!, a portal itself, is trying to position itself to be just that! You can play great music videos from its Web site, at launch.yahoo.com.)

You're not getting much Internet content if your HTPC isn't connected to the Internet. And, don't forget that a connection to your high-speed Internet access (DSL, fiber-optic, or cable modem) is part of the overall equation. (Yup, a regular ol' vanilla dial-up connection works, but — we can't stress this enough — not nearly as well. If you're one of the 90 to 95 percent of the population who can get broadband, get it! If you're out of range, we're sorry, and recommend that you check out the satellite broadband services offered by folks such as DirecTV.)

Other wireless ways (where there's a will . . .)

We are obviously biased toward the 802.11 technologies because we believe in a wireless home network backbone. We think that with all the focus on standards, costs will decrease, new features will evolve, and the overall capability will continue to get better. Collectively, it simply gives you more options for the home.

That doesn't mean, however, that standards are the only way to go. Plenty of proprietary 900 MHz, 2.4 GHz, and 5 GHz approaches — as well as other frequency bands — are popular because they're cheap to manufacture and cheap to implement. For example, check out the Audiovox Terk (www.audiovox.com, $99) Leapfrog Series Wireless A/V System (Model LF-30S, for example), which uses the same 2.4 GHz frequency spectrum as 802.11b and 802.11g to carry audio and video around the house. The gear we've tested in this space, like the X10 Entertainment Anywhere and various Radio Shack 900 MHz models, has been somewhat of a disappointment, but it does work.

So, 802.11 isn't the only way, but we prefer it based on experience. Just remember: The more signals you put in the 2.4 GHz and 5 GHz ranges to compete with your 802.11 signals, the more problems you have. The 802.11 products are building in new quality-of-service capabilities designed to deal with multiple simultaneous audio and video transmissions, and over time will be more robust, accessible, and reliable, we think. Look for the Wi-Fi icon when you buy.

You've undoubtedly read about Hollywood's drive to rid the Internet of peer-to-peer file-sharing programs, to halt the *ripping* (copying) of DVDs from rented DVD discs, and so on. For the rest of us, who have better things to focus on, a slew of great online music stores and services are legal, economical, and easy to use — you just have to try them.

You find three types of online music offerings:

- ✔ Online music and video stores, such as Apple's iTunes Store, where you download music to your PC or network-capable device. There are limits to what you can do with these songs after they're downloaded, but generally you can play them anywhere on your network.

- ✔ Online music subscription services, such as Rhapsody and Yahoo! Music, where you can play any songs available in their catalogs. These are streaming audio songs that you play as often as you like, wherever you want, as long as you have Internet access. For many of these services, if you want to play them *off* your PC, you need a media adapter or player designed for that service.

- ✔ A combination of the preceding two items where you can play any songs you want during your subscription period and optionally download (and keep) songs for an extra fee.

Some of the most popular online music hangouts include

- ✔ Apple iTunes Music Store (www.itunes.com)
- ✔ Real Network's Rhapsody (www.rhapsody.com)
- ✔ Napster (newly relaunched at www.napster.com)
- ✔ eMusic (www.emusic.com)
- ✔ Yahoo! Music (music.yahoo.com)

Some sites require monthly fees to join, typically around $5 to $10 per month; others have their business model driven by download fees on a per song or per video basis.

You don't have to pay to get some music from the Internet — lots of Internet radio stations are out there. You can find Internet-only stations (Pat's favorite is Radio Paradise, at www.radioparadise.com) and simulcasts from traditional broadcasters, such as National Public Radio (www.npr.org). To find online radio stations, check out SHOUTcast (www.shoutcast.com), Live365 (www.live365.com), or Radio-Locator (www.radio-locator.com), or just do a Web search on Yahoo! or Google.

Remember that most online services incorporate DRM (digital rights management) technologies in their downloaded files. If you want to play these files across your network, you need to ensure that your media adapter or player supports the DRM system of the content you've downloaded (or of the service you are subscribed to). Unfortunately, this can limit your choices, but it's a sad fact of how the entertainment industry treats their customers these days. There are some (happy) exceptions, however. Apple's iTunes Store offers a number of DRM-free song downloads, and eMusic and Amazon.com's online music stores are free of DRM.

Chapter 13

Using Your Wireless Network for Phone Calls

. . . .

In This Chapter

▶ Understanding Voice over IP (VoIP)

▶ Using VoIP Wi-Fi phones

▶ DECTing your VoIP

▶ Using Skype without wires

▶ Understanding fixed mobile convergence

. . . .

*P*hones have been around for over a hundred years. In developed countries such as the U.S., the European Union, and many parts of Asia, there are more phones (several times more in some cases) than people. In the intervening century, the phone hasn't stood still. Two big trends have affected the phone business: the advent of digital technologies and the rise of wireless technologies.

Digital technologies have been in use within phone networks for decades. Phone companies use digital (and Internet protocol — IP) technologies within their networks to carry and route calls from place to place. Even if your home phone line is still an old-fashioned analog *POTS* (plain old telephone service) line, chances are nearly 100 percent that some major part of your phone call is carried over digital lines. And if you're using a broadband *VoIP* (Voice over IP) service (for example, Vonage or Skype) in your home, your calls are 100 percent digital.

Similarly, wireless technologies have been around for decades as well. We suspect that a lot of readers of *Home Wireless Networking For Dummies* have never known a time without a cordless phone in the home. And cell phones are beyond ubiquitous. There are over 3 billion (with a *b*) cell phone subscriptions in the world (a bit less than that number of users, because many people have more than one), and over 80 percent of the world's population lives in an area covered by cell phone systems. These are big, big numbers.

Now you may be wondering what all of this has to do with wireless networks (of course, you could argue that even an old-fashioned cordless phone system is a wireless network, but we're mainly talking about computer-based networks in this book). Well the answer is this: These technological trends are bringing about a convergence of digital (and VoIP) phone technologies and wireless technologies and are turning your phones (both in-home phones and mobile phones) into full-fledged members of your home wireless network.

In this chapter, we talk about what VoIP is all about, including a discussion of some of the biggest providers of VoIP service. We then talk about wireless (mainly Wi-Fi) phones that can let you use your wireless network to make VoIP calls. Finally, we talk about how cell phones are beginning to join into the Wi-Fi fun, allowing you to use your Wi-Fi network to get better coverage inside your home while saving money on calls. It's going to be fun, so read on!

Understanding VoIP

Voice over IP (VoIP) is exactly what its name implies it is. Voice calls (phone calls) are made using a broadband Internet connection (such as a cable or DSL modem), and instead of being routed through the Public Switched Telephone Network (PSTN) — the phone network run by companies such as AT&T and Verizon — they are routed across the Internet (or across private networks, perhaps run by those same phone companies that run on the Internet Protocol, IP).

Chances are good that you've already made a VoIP phone call — even if you don't know that you did. For example, many discount phone card companies, alternative long-distance providers, and even the biggest of phone companies use VoIP in part or all of their network. They do this because it's cheaper and more efficient to route phone calls this way than it is using the old-fashioned phone network. So many phone companies will use traditional phone lines on the ends of calls (from the local phone company office to your home) but use VoIP in the *core* of the network.

You've also made a VoIP phone call if you've ever used the voice functionality in an *instant messenger* program. For example, Yahoo! Messenger, AOL IM (AIM), Google Talk, and Microsoft's Windows Live Messenger all let you make VoIP calls from computer to computer over the Internet. Many of these services also let you make calls to standard phone numbers (for a fee).

And, of course, there are services that aren't just instant messaging services (such as AOL IM) but are explicitly built around the concept of providing individuals with VoIP calling capabilities. Skype (www.skype.com), for example, offers both computer-to-computer and computer-to-phone calling, and companies such as Vonage (www.vonage.com) incorporate special hardware in your home that lets you plug regular phones (wired or cordless) into your broadband connection for making VoIP calls.

Understanding VoIP terminology

Like any self-respecting Internet technology, VoIP is laden with acronyms and jargon. Heck, even the name (VoIP) is an acronym! For the most part, you don't need to understand all these acronyms, but you may run across them as you shop for VoIP equipment for your wireless network (or just plain old wired VoIP equipment). So here are a few we think you should know:

- ✔ **SIP:** SIP, or *Session Initiation Protocol,* is the predominant *signaling and control* mechanism for VoIP calls. SIP is a standardized way for Internet clients (such as VoIP phones and networks) to create a *session* (or call) and to control that call (for example, to hang up). The other signaling and control mechanism for VoIP phone calls is called *H.323.*

  Some VoIP systems, such as Skype, use their own proprietary protocols to control VoIP calls.

- ✔ **RTP:** RTP, or *Real-time Transport Protocol,* is the underlying IP protocol used for carrying voice calls over IP networks. RTP is used with another protocol called *RTCP* (Real-time Transport Control Protocol) to provide Quality of Service *(QoS)* support to help prioritize real-time applications (such as voice calls) over other traffic on the network which isn't time or delay sensitive (such as e-mail).

- ✔ **Codec:** VoIP calls digitize and compress the analog signal created by the microphone in your phone. The specific encoder/decoder used to do this is known as the *codec.* The amount (and type) of compression used in a VoIP codec affects the sound quality of the call — many VoIP systems use codecs that offer a higher quality of sound than the analog phone calls you're used to!

- ✔ **Telephone adapter:** Most VoIP implementations use standard analog POTS telephones. The device that sits between these phones and the broadband Internet connection is known as a *telephone adapter* (or sometimes an *analog telephone adapter,* or *ATA*). The telephone adapter digitizes the analog phone signal and handles the SIP (or other protocol) signaling.

- ✔ **VoIP phone:** You can also find phones that handle all the telephone adapter's functionality internally; these are called *VoIP phones* (or, commonly, *SIP phones* if they support the SIP protocol). *Dual-mode* VoIP phones can work as both VoIP phones and as standard POTS phones (which can be handy when you're making local phone calls).

- ✔ **Softphone:** You don't need a phone to make VoIP calls — your PC or Mac (when equipped with speakers and microphones or a headset) can be a full-fledged VoIP phone as well. In fact, that's how the whole VoIP phenomenon started back in the late 1990s, with people making free PC-to-PC phone calls over the Internet. The software program used on computers for VoIP calls is called a *softphone client* (*software phone*). You can even find softphones on phones — smartphones may have softphone software to allow users to place international calls, for instance, over the cellular broadband data connection.

Understanding VoIP services

Like traditional telephony services (POTS and cell phone service), VoIP requires you to have a *service provider.* The service provider provides two main functions:

- ✔ A *gateway* **between the VoIP network and the PSTN:** Your VoIP service provider provides the software and hardware (within their network) to move calls between the VoIP network and the PSTN (POTS phones and cell phones). This functionality gives your VoIP phone the capability to make calls anywhere in the world, to any phone. This gateway service is part of a paid subscription service, but typically the monthly and/or per-call costs are lower than they are for POTS or cell phone service.

- ✔ *Directory* **services:** Your VoIP service provider also provides directory services, which gives your VoIP phone a "phone number" and lets people find and call you. Traditional phone services use a global standard for numbering, but VoIP doesn't (yet), so your service provider runs a service that associates your broadband connection's IP address to your identity. This service can be part of a for-pay monthly service, or it can be free for PC-to-PC VoIP services. Note that many leading VoIP providers, such as Vonage, let you transfer your landline phone number to their directory service; this essentially tells all other service providers that when that number is dialed, they should send the call to the Vonage network for call completion.

VoIP and 911

The 911 emergency services used in standard landline (POTS) phone systems are well-honed, well-oiled machines that have been developed over decades and decades. POTS phone systems have extensive directory records in place that know exactly where each phone is located (the name of the subscriber, the address, and so on). So when you make a 911 call, emergency officials pretty much know instantaneously where you are calling from and can react accordingly.

Mobile (cell) phone systems now have similar capabilities, due to the adoption of a technology called *Enhanced 911* (or E911). Mobile phone operators use either a specialized radio triangulation technology in their networks (which determines where you are based on how long it takes your signal to reach several cell towers in your area) or a GPS chip embedded in your cell phone to determine your location and pass it on to authorities in case of emergency.

VoIP and 911, however, have a more tenuous relationship. The nature of VoIP gear (even wired VoIP gear) means that it can be plugged into a broadband connection anywhere — so there's no one-to-one relationship between your VoIP phone number and your current location. Your IP address doesn't provide the kind of location information that a traditional phone line does — in fact, your IP address could frequently change as your ISP rotates IP addresses among its customers.

It's hard for a VoIP 911 system not only to tell authorities where you are, but also to route your 911 call to the right 911 call center. If, for example, you take your VoIP phone to work, you might be in the coverage area of an entirely different 911 call center than you are at home — currently there's no way for VoIP systems to know this.

So VoIP providers are required to give you more than ample notice that they are not as good at handling 911 calls as are landline or even mobile phones. Some providers give you the opportunity to register your VoIP phone equipment with your current address information — this can then be used to route your 911 call and to provide the 911 folks with your address. If you're using a VoIP system as your primary home phone system, we think you should *absolutely take this step* and register for your VoIP provider's 911 system. (If they had bothered asking us, we would have simply told them to put GPS chips into all VoIP phones and the problem would have been solved!)

One last fact to keep in mind about VoIP and 911 and other emergency calls: Unlike POTS phones (which get their power from the telephone line itself), VoIP phone systems need external AC power to work. If your power goes out, it's likely that both your broadband connection and your VoIP phone or telephone adapter will also go out. If you move entirely to VoIP in your home, we recommend that you purchase an *uninterruptible power supply* (UPS) and make sure that your broadband modem, wireless router, and telephone adapter are all connected to it. This won't keep you up and running for days at a time, but it can keep the phones working during brief power outages.

All sorts of VoIP services are on the market today, ranging from simple IM client-based voice chat services right on up to sophisticated multiline services designed to replace all landline phones in a business. For the purposes of a home user, we can divide VoIP service providers into two (not so distinct) buckets. We say *not so distinct* because many VoIP service providers can fit into either of these two categories, depending on which individual elements of their service you choose. Without further adieu, let's talk about what these two categories are:

- ✔ **Home phone replacement services:** These services are primarily *telephone adapter based* (or hardware based). They are designed to completely replace your existing POTS landline voice service and to work with all existing phones in your home. These services provide you with a traditional phone number (that anyone can call). Vonage is the biggest example here.

- ✔ **PC-based supplementary voice services:** These services are primarily built around PC usage (though, as we discuss later in this chapter, they can work with phones) and are primarily marketed as (and used as) supplements to existing landline services — in other words, you use them for specific calls (such as overseas calls) but keep your POTS phone for local calls, inbound calls, and so on. These services typically provide you with a username (like the username you might have for AOL IM) — other users of the service can call you by clicking your username in their VoIP software program. The primary example here is Skype, which began as a PC-to-PC-only service but has since branched out to include PC-to-phone, phone-to-PC, and now phone-to-phone calling.

As we mention earlier, these two categories have a lot of overlap. For example, most hardware-based VoIP providers offer a softphone client that allows PC-to-PC or PC-to-phone calling (and can be used on your laptop when you travel), and many of the primarily PC-to-PC providers now offer phone devices that let you connect your home phones to the service and can assign you a traditional phone number (for example, Skype's SkypeIN service). In this chapter we talk about wireless hardware that fits into both types of VoIP service.

Some of the leading providers of VoIP services follow:

- ✔ Home phone replacement services:
  - Vonage (www.vonage.com)
  - Verizon VoiceWing (www.verizon.com/voicewing)
  - AT&T CallVantage (www.callvantage.att.com/)
  - Lingo (www.lingo.com)
  - BroadVoice (www.broadvoice.com)
  - TelTel (www.teltel.com)

- VoipYourLife (www.voipyourlife.com)

- Packet8 (www.packet8.com)

✔ Supplementary VoIP services (these services include both PC-to-PC voice chat and inbound or outbound calling to regular phones):

- Skype (www.skype.com)

- Yahoo! Voice (voice.yahoo.com)

- AOL AIM Call Out (call.aim.com)

- Google Talk (talk.google.com)

- Gizmo Project (www.gizmoproject.com)

This is only a partial list — hundreds of VoIP providers are out there these days. We chose the largest and most well-known providers, but you can find a great list of providers at www.voipproviderslist.com. You can also find reviews of VoIP providers and an online bandwidth/latency testing program that will let you know how well your broadband connection can handle VoIP at the following URL: www.voipreview.org.

Going Wireless with Your VoIP Service

Most VoIP services available today are focused on either conventional phones (through a telephone adapter) or the PC (using a softphone client). Nothing is wrong with these approaches — both have their place — but what excites us is the ability to leverage the Wi-Fi network you've installed in your home to carry your phone calls. With a Wi-Fi VoIP phone, you can make calls from anywhere in your house, and you can also take your Wi-Fi phone with you to work, to a friend's house, on a business trip (using the Wi-Fi in your hotel room), or even to a Wi-Fi hot spot (bring it along on your midday caffeine refueling trip to the local café). With VoIP, it doesn't matter *where* you are. As long as you have a broadband connection, you can make and receive calls as if you were home. (Even when you're overseas, you can receive calls on your home phone number, saving your friends and family expensive long-distance charges.)

We know what you're thinking: "Heck, I can bring my cell phone to any of those places and make and receive calls, with or without a Wi-Fi access point and broadband connection!" Well you sure can (and we never leave home without our cell phones, of course), but VoIP can provide you with some significant money savings (depending on your location). VoIP phone calls are usually a fraction of the cost (per minute) of mobile phone calls, particularly when you're in a roaming environment with your mobile phone (for example, when you're out of the country). A big trend is to incorporate both a VoIP and cell phone into a single phone, so you can use the cellular network when you need to and also make cheaper calls using VoIP when you're in range of a Wi-Fi network. We talk about this *fixed mobile convergence* in the section titled "Understanding FMC (Fixed Mobile Convergence)."

In this section, we talk about Wi-Fi VoIP phones. These phones, which look just like a cell or cordless phone, connect to Wi-Fi networks (typically they use 802.11g technology) and provide you with a full VoIP experience without the need to use a telephone adapter or a softphone client on a PC. They're truly stand-alone phones that can make and receive calls with only a broadband-connected Wi-Fi access point required.

We also talk about wireless VoIP phones that use the *DECT* technology standard. You can use them only in your home, but they tend to be a bit cheaper and have better battery life than Wi-Fi phones.

Wi-Fi VoIP phones can operate on your own network, on a friend's network, over the network at work, or in a public hot spot. The only thing you'll need to worry about is gaining access to that network through its security and authentication system. Luckily, most current Wi-Fi VoIP phones support the latest WPA2 Personal security system (described in Chapter 9), so you'll be able to enter a WPA passphrase on the phone and gain access to the network. Where things can get a bit dicey is in the realm of corporate and hot spot networks. There are two issues here:

✔ In corporate networks, it's common to find WPA2 Enterprise security, which uses the 802.1x authentication system (see Chapter 9). Most Wi-Fi VoIP phones support only the Personal version of WPA2, which uses a passphrase, and not the Enterprise version, which uses a RADIUS server to authenticate users (and allow them on the network). If you're planning on using your Wi-Fi VoIP phone on one of these networks, you'll need to do some research when looking for a phone.

✔ In public hot spots, it's common to find a system called a *captive portal* that provides the authentication for users to get on the network. A captive portal uses a Web browser — a page pops up for you to make a payment or enter a code or simply agree to terms of usage before you can get on the network. These Wi-Fi VoIP phones typically don't have a Web browser built in, so they can't get onto these types of networks. An example of a phone that *does* have a built-in Web browser is SMCWSP-100 (www.smc.com, $200) from SMC Networks.

Some Wi-Fi VoIP phones let you get around this hot spot conundrum by incorporating client software or a special internal configuration in their phones that enables hot spots to recognize the phones and allow them access. For example, Wi-Fi VoIP phones for Skype (discussed in the "Choosing Skype phones" section) work at any Boingo hot spot right out of the box. Many

Wi-Fi VoIP phone manufacturers have (or are working on) similar partnerships with hot spot providers to provide browserless access, so check the documentation or Web site of your phone to see if yours does too.

A company to keep an eye on is Devicescape (www.devicescape.com). This software company, based in the Silicon Valley area, is built around the premise that non-PC devices need an easy way to get logged onto Wi-Fi networks. The company currently offers beta versions of its *supplicant* software (essentially security client software) for a number of non-PC platforms, including Apple's iPhone, some Nokia mobile phones, and (most appropriately for this discussion) the Linksys WIP 300 Wi-Fi VoIP phone. Devicescape is a startup, but they have plans to spread broadly throughout this market, so keep an eye on their Web site if you need help getting online at hot spots with your VoIP phone.

Choosing VoIP Wi-Fi phones

As mentioned, most VoIP services use SIP as the underlying technology for their service. SIP is an international standard, which means it is widely used and also relatively *interoperable* — a SIP phone is a SIP phone, no matter who makes it and whether it's wired, wireless, or embedded in your skull (which doesn't sound all that pleasant, but folks in labs are working on embedded phones that will be with us always).

Because SIP is so standardized and widely used, manufacturers of Wi-Fi gear (companies such as NETGEAR, Linksys, D-Link, Belkin, and SMC) are making and selling *SIP Wi-Fi phones* that you can use with most major VoIP providers.

Skype does not use SIP (at least not in an interoperable way — Skype's VoIP protocols are their "secret sauce" and they're not telling!). So the phones we're talking about here won't work with your Skype account.

Consider the following when choosing a Wi-Fi VoIP phone:

- **Wi-Fi standards supported:** You'll want a phone that supports at least 802.11g. As we write, no 802.11n Wi-Fi VoIP phones are on the market, but we expect that eventually these will trickle onto the market and replace the 802.11g models.

- **Battery life:** Battery life is a crucial issue with any cordless (or cellular) phone. Unfortunately, Wi-Fi was not designed to be a low-power technology suitable for use with small phone batteries. (It uses much more power than, for example, a mobile phone radio system.) So battery life is the Achilles' heel of many Wi-Fi VoIP phones. Check the different manufacturers' rated battery life, see how easy it is to recharge (many phones come with a cradle you can drop them in, just as you do with a home cordless phone), and see how easy it is to replace the battery should it wear out.

✔ **Security support:** As mentioned, most of these Wi-Fi phones will *not* work in a WPA2 Enterprise/802.1X network. Most *do* support WPA and WPA2 Personal, the minimum level of security you should shoot for.

✔ **Web browser support:** If you plan on using the Wi-Fi phone in a lot of hot spot environments, consider a model that includes a built-in Web browser to provide a mechanism for logging into hot spots that require use of a captive portal log-in page.

✔ **Codec support:** The codec is the voice compression algorithm used by a VoIP system. A number of different codecs are used by VoIP service providers. A Wi-Fi VoIP phone must support the codecs (such as G.711) used by your service provider. (The best way to determine these codecs is to look in the support section of your VoIP provider's Web site or to call tech support.)

✔ **Form factor:** *Form factor* (the shape and look and feel of the phone) is unimportant to some folks and vitally important to others. VoIP Wi-Fi phones can be big and bulky (the early ones were) or small and sleek. The biggest distinction you'll find is between flip phones (similar in size and shape to flip mobile phones) and *candy bar*–style phones. Which you prefer is, of course, up to you.

✔ **Everything else:** Finally, a lot of little things may or may not be important to you as you examine Wi-Fi VoIP phones. Examples here could include the size and quality of the screen, support for additional applications on the phone (such as e-mail or IM), button and keypad quality, and the user interface and menus.

The most important criteria of a Wi-Fi VoIP phone is whether or not it will work with *your* VoIP service. SIP VoIP services are based on standards, and any SIP-compliant phone *should* work with any SIP-compliant VoIP service (which is most services). Many VoIP service providers, however — in an attempt to keep their support overhead to a minimum — don't explicitly support phones and devices on their network beyond the phones they sell or provide to their customers. Some providers may even make it hard for you to find the information about their service's servers and IP addresses needed to configure your phone.

There are a number of manufacturers of Wi-Fi VoIP phones, ranging from big networking companies down to small specialist companies you've never heard of. Some of the more popular include

✔ Linksys (www.linksys.com)

✔ SMC Networks (www.smc.com)

✔ Zyxel (www.zyxel.com)

✔ D-Link (www.dlink.com)

An alternative to Wi-Fi phones

Wi-Fi, in its current form of 802.11g and draft 802.11n, is a wireless system that has not been designed for small, battery-powered devices. The problem is simply that Wi-Fi was never designed with power saving features that can extend battery life on these portable devices (though some manufacturers have created their own battery saving schemes, and we expect that the final 802.11n standard will include more advanced power management as well).

What this means is that many Wi-Fi VoIP phones are limited to just a few hours of talk time and less than a day of standby time, so you'll have to charge your phone daily, if not more often.

An alternative to Wi-Fi VoIP phone systems is a new (to North America) cordless phone system called *DECT* 6.0. DECT (Digital Enhanced Cordless Telecommunications) has been around in Europe and other parts of the world for about a decade but was not available in the U.S. until the FCC approved its use in late 2005. (The phones became available in the U.S. the following year.) DECT uses the 1900 MHz frequency range, which keeps it out of the way of both 2.4 and 5 GHz Wi-Fi frequencies. DECT phones are known for their long range (compared to traditional cordless phones), their high-quality voice reproduction, and the fact that you can have repeaters to daisy chain DECT calls over distances (such as from one side of your home to the other).

For the most part, DECT phones are just regular old cordless phones, using the DECT system for transmission between the handset and the base station (the base station is then plugged directly into a POTS jack). Using an analog telephone adapter in lieu of a POTS jack is a great way to wirelessly expand a VoIP system, and is the fastest and cheapest way to take your VoIP wireless.

You can use any cordless phone — even that ancient one you have out in the garage with the 4-foot-long shiny retractable antenna — with your analog telephone adapter (ATA). That's the point of an ATA — any analog phone can plug into it. We're focusing on the new (to the U.S. at least) DECT phones because, frankly, we think they work better than old-fashioned cordless phones and also because several models have VoIP built right into the phone and don't need an ATA. How good is DECT? Well in Danny's home in Maine (with its 3-foot-thick brick and masonry walls that kill just about any wireless signal), he can reach every point from the basement to the third floor with his DECT phone. All of Danny's other wireless systems require repeaters and signal boosters and secondary base stations to reach through his wireless worst-case-scenario house!

Several manufacturers of DECT phones have begun selling phones that have both POTS and VoIP phone capabilities built into a single device. These phones have two connectors on the handset's base station. One plugs into a regular phone jack (just like any other cordless phone in the world), and the other plugs into an Ethernet jack connected to your wireless or wired broadband router. Calls then can be made (and received) over your standard landline phone service or over a VoIP connection.

Most of these dual-mode DECT phones are designed to work with Skype (discussed in the next section), but some manufacturers are also offering SIP dual-mode DECT phones as well. (For our readers in North America, these SIP dual-mode phones are not yet widely available, but we expect as DECT becomes more popular here they will be on the shelf at your favorite electronics store.)

One feature that a few dual-mode phones have is the ability to conference between a Skype or VoIP call and a second call on the landline. This is a great way to get distant family or co-workers on the phone without paying excessive toll charges. One phone that supports this functionality is DualPhone's 3088 (dualphone.net/DUALphone_3088_for_Skype-789.aspx).

If you have a big family or a big house, look for a DECT system that supports multiple handsets. You'll need to plug only one base station into your router and phone jack. The remaining phones can connect to that base station and need only remote charging stations. This makes it easy to extend your wireless VoIP network throughout the house without extra wires.

Choosing Skype phones

A special category of Wi-Fi VoIP phones are those designed to work with the Skype network. These phones are similar in size, shape, and functionality to the Wi-Fi VoIP phones we just described, but instead of being built around the SIP protocol, they work specifically with the Skype VoIP service.

There are two types of Skype wireless phones:

✔ **Phones that work with your computer:** The simplest (and cheapest) wireless Skype phones are those that connect to your PC (typically with a dongle that plugs into one of your computer's USB ports). These phones work with the Skype client software installed on your computer, and calls are actually placed and received *through* your computer. When the computer is turned off, the phone no longer works.

✔ **Phones that work independently:** Other Skype phones are full-fledged Skype clients in their own right and don't need a running PC (though a PC may be used to set them up in the first place. These phones can use Wi-Fi, or they may be DECT phones as discussed in the preceding section.

Skype keeps a current list of certified Skype wireless phones in the Phones section of its online store at www.skype.com/go/shop.accessories.

Wireless Skype phones are capable of supporting free calls worldwide to other Skype users, as well as inexpensive inbound (to your number) and outbound (to other people) calls using Skype's SkypeIn and SkypeOut services. (We talk more about Skype's different services in the sidebar titled "Why Skype is different.")

Following are some manufacturers of Skype wireless phones:

- DualPhone (www.dualphone.net)
- Philips (www.philips.com)
- GE (www.home-electronics.net)
- NETGEAR (www.netgear.com)
- Belkin (www.belkin.com)
- Linksys (www.linksys.com)
- SMC (www.smc.com)

Why Skype is different

Skype is a peer-to-peer VoIP network, which means that rather than having a centralized control point for routing calls around the network (and around the world), each individual Skype *client* (the software on your PC or on a Skype phone) contributes to the effort and assists in call routing.

At its most basic level, Skype is a client-to-client VoIP system. This means that with a Skype client installed on your PC (or phone), you can make calls to anyone else in the world who has installed the (free) Skype client. This level of Skype is free for anyone (beyond what you pay for your broadband Internet connection). Even this free level is handy because there are often as many as *ten million* Skype users online at any given time, and hundreds of millions of registered accounts.

The next level of Skype is called *SkypeOut*. SkypeOut enables outbound calls from your Skype client to regular landline or mobile phones. You can buy SkypeOut service plans (which, for example, offer unlimited calling within certain geographies — in North America you can subscribe to a $3/month plan that allows unlimited calling to anywhere in the U.S. or Canada). You can also buy Skype credits (in $10 increments), which allow you to make calls to anywhere in the world, with rates starting at $0.021 per minute.

The final level of Skypedom is to subscribe to a *SkypeIn* account. This provides you with a Skype phone number (in your local area code) that anyone can call. SkypeIn also includes free voicemail, so you can pick up calls that you've missed after the fact.

Skype has a lot of different calling plans, and rates to different countries vary, so check out www.Skype.com for all the current details.

A (future) alternative to FMC

Cell phone service providers and equipment makers have more tricks than just FMC up their sleeves when it comes to improving your in-home service coverage. Another technology being developed and seriously considered by the cell phone industry is known as the femtocell. Simply put, a *femtocell* is a small (the size of a cable modem) cellular base station that can sit inside a home or a small business — an even tinier version of the *picocells* that many cell phone companies use to improve their coverage inside shopping malls and convention centers.

A femtocell will connect to your broadband Ethernet connection (just as a Wi-Fi FMC solution uses that connection), and your mobile phone will switch over to the femtocell whenever it is in range. Where FMC solutions and femtocells differ is in how your cell phone connection is transmitted wirelessly in the home. With FMC, your *phone* switches over Wi-Fi and then sends the calls over your broadband connection. With a femtocell, your phone doesn't do anything different than it does anywhere else in the world — the femtocell looks just like any other cell tower to the phone, and your phone connects to it when the femtocell's signal is stronger than the outside cell tower's signal.

This means you don't need to choose a special mobile phone to use a femtocell — any cell phone can work with femtocells. The only limitation is the type of cell phone network the phone is designed to work with (GSM or CDMA). If you have a CDMA phone (for example, from Verizon or Sprint), it can connect only to a CDMA femtocell. GSM phones (AT&T or T-Mobile) can connect only to GSM femtocells.

Like FMC, femtocells aren't something that you can just pick up at the local electronics super-store and install — they'll be something that your cell phone company sells, rents, or gives you to improve your coverage. An example of an early femtocell is Samsung's CDMA Ubicell, which can be seen at the following URL (just search on the page for *femtocell*): www.samsung.com/us/business/telecommunication/.

If you can't yet get (or don't want) FMC service and you're not willing to wait until femtocells become available from your mobile phone provider, consider an in-home cell phone extender. These devices use an antenna placed outside your home or in a window to boost the power of incoming phone signals. Essentially a cell phone extender gives you inside the house the signal strength you have out in the driveway. Danny's been using zBoost from Wi-Ex (www.wiex.com) and he's had great results. This is a cheap ($399) way of getting the signal to reach all the nooks and crannies of your home. Just remember, a cell phone extender won't help if you have no signal *outside* the house.

Understanding FMC (Fixed Mobile Convergence)

The next big thing in wireless and VoIP is here now and it's called *fixed mobile convergence,* or FMC. FMC is the combination of mobile (cellular) and VoIP into a single device. With FMC you can use your phone as a cellular phone anywhere you have coverage, and when you're in range of a Wi-Fi access point and broadband connection, your phone can automatically switch over to the Wi-Fi network.

Using home phones on the cellular network

For certain types of calls (such as international calls) or for certain users (folks who burn through all their minutes each month), cell phone calls can be expensive. The opposite side of this equation is that for in-country, in-plan minutes, cell phone calls are essentially free. You pay a flat rate every month and get a certain number of minutes that don't cost you any more (no long-distance charges, no per-minute charges, and so on). And many cell phone plans include freebies such as free nights and weekends or unlimited in-network calls. So many folks end up using their cell phones in the house for almost all calls, just as a moneysaving device.

To support this, a sort of reverse form of FMC has arisen: home cordless phones that connect to your cell phone (via Bluetooth) and let you leave your mobile phone on the charger while you make calls from in the home.

An example of this is GE's Cell Fusion DECT 6.0 phone (www.home-electronics.net/ge/pc/view Prd.asp?idcategory=2&idproduct=3). This phone system (which costs about $150 for a dual handset kit) uses the DECT system (as the name implies) for transmissions between the handset and the base station. The cool feature that sets this phone apart is its ability to *pair* (or make a network connection) with up to two Bluetooth-enabled cell phones. When you've paired the phone to your mobile, you can simply press a button labeled Cell on the Cell Fusion phone whenever you want to place a call and use some of your free cell phone minutes instead of paying for long distance. Incoming calls to your cell phone will also ring to the Cell Fusion phone — no more digging through your purse or briefcase in a desperate attempt to grab the cell phone before the call goes to voicemail. Pretty neat stuff.

Why would you want to switch to the Wi-Fi network? Well the biggest reason is to save money. Mobile phones are relatively cheap when you're in your local (or nationwide) calling area, making domestic phone calls, and within your monthly allowance of minutes. When you roam outside your calling area, try making a call internationally, or go beyond your *bundled* minutes, you'll find that your cell phone company is pretty darned good at separating you from your money.

Another reason why FMC makes sense is the simple fact that cell phone coverage isn't always that great *inside* many buildings. Big public buildings tend to have special small cellular base stations inside the building (so you can make calls from that hotel lobby, convention center, or shopping mall), but individual homes and apartments often have lousy indoor coverage. (Pat has to stand in his driveway to make calls on one of his cell phones — it's a good thing he lives in sunny San Diego and not some place cold come January.) FMC can alleviate this problem by switching your phone over to your in-home Wi-Fi network when its signal is stronger than your mobile phone carrier's signal. FMC isn't something you just do on your own — you need a mobile phone that supports it, and you need your mobile phone provider's network to support the service so that calls are routed to the right place at the right time, based on whatever rules are set up for the service. Support from the mobile phone carrier is important, too, to ensure that you can *roam* from one network to another. FMC should allow you to start a call in your home office using the Wi-Fi network, and continue the call as you walk outside, get in your car, and start driving towards a meeting — as you leave the range of your Wi-Fi network, your phone will automatically switch over to the cellular network, and your phone provider will transparently and automatically *reroute* the call so that you can keep talking without losing your connection (or even hearing anything that makes you think you've switched networks).

FMC, as we said, is the *next* big thing, but a few carriers are already offering the service. In the U.S., T-Mobile (www.tmobile.com) is the first to offer an FMC service to consumers. T-Mobile's Hot Spot @ Home (www.theonly phoneyouneed.com/) combines an FMC-capable (dual-mode cellular and Wi-Fi) phone with your broadband Internet access and a Wi-Fi access point to offer FMC service. (You can use your own AP or buy one through T-Mobile — as we write, T-Mobile is giving away the router to promote the service!)

The Hot Spot @ Home service from T-Mobile has two levels. If you need only improved coverage, you can pick up one of T-Mobile's dual-mode phones and use the minutes already in your plan for any calls you make from a Wi-Fi connection. If you're also trying to save money, you can add an unlimited calling plan — any calls in the U.S. are free when placed over the Wi-Fi network. T-Mobile is currently charging $20 per month for the unlimited calling service.

You can place (and receive) Wi-Fi calls from your home network and from any of T-Mobile's thousands of public hot spots. (We discuss these in Chapter 16.) You can also make Wi-Fi calls from any other hot spot (though T-Mobile doesn't provide support for these calls if you're having trouble getting connected). T-Mobile's phones work with WEP and WPA encrypted Wi-Fi networks, but they don't work with Wi-Fi networks that require a Web browser to establish a connection or that use WPA-Enterprise (802.1X) authentication. (Check out Chapter 9 if you're unsure what all these encryption acronyms mean.)

All the mobile operators are examining FMC solutions. When combined with your Wi-Fi network and broadband Internet connection, FMC stands a good chance of letting you say goodbye to analog phones forever.

Chapter 14

Other Cool Things You Can Network

*T*he wireless age is upon us, with all sorts of new devices and capabilities that you can add to your network to save you time and enhance your lifestyle. After you have your wireless local area network in place, which we show you how to do in Parts II and III, you can do a nearly unlimited number of things. It sort of reminds us of the Dr. Seuss book *Oh, the Places You'll Go!*

In this chapter, we introduce you to some of the neater things that are available now for your wireless home network. In Chapter 19, we talk about the things that are coming soon to a network near you! Together, with the gaming, A/V, and phone discussions in Chapters 11, 12, and 13, respectively, you see why we say that wireless home networking isn't just for computers anymore.

In this chapter, we give you an overview of many new products, but we can't give much specific information about how to set up these products. In general, you have to provide your service set identifier (SSID) and WPA passphrase (or WEP key, if your network doesn't support WPA). That should be 95 percent of what you need to do to set up your device for your wireless network. In this chapter and in Chapter 19, we feel that it's important to expose you to the developments happening now so that you can look around and explore different options while you wirelessly enable your home. To say that your whole house will have wireless devices in every room within the next few years is *not* an understatement — it's truly coming on fast (so hold on tight!).

The wireless-enablement of consumer goods is spreading faster than a wild-fire. As we write, products are coming out daily. If you're interested in seeing what else has popped up since we wrote this book check out our book update site (www.digitaldummies.com).

Making a Connection to Your Car

For many people, their cars are more than mechanisms to get them from point A to point B. Some folks spend a considerable amount of time each day commuting — we know people who spend one and a half hours in the car *each way* in a commute. For others, like those with RVs, their vehicles represent entire vacation homes.

If you think about the things you do in your car — listen to music, talk on the phone, let your kids watch movies — they're not all that different from things you do around the house. Because your home's wireless connection can reach outside your walls and into your driveway or garage, your car can go online with your home network and access data ranging from your address book on your PC to your latest MP3s in your stereo. You can download them to your car, thus simplifying your life and making the car truly a second home. (No more calls home asking "Honey, can you look on my computer for the number for . . . ?")

Your car's path to wireless enlightenment

Although you may think that wireless is a new topic for your car, your car has been wirelessly enabled for years. Your car stereo gets wireless AM/FM signals from afar and, with the advent of satellite radio, now even farther than ever. (See the nearby sidebar, "Satellite radio versus digital radio.") Wireless phone options — cellular and Bluetooth-based technologies — are quickly filtering into the car. (We discuss Bluetooth and cars more in Chapter 15.) And then there's the new wave of electronic toll systems that predominantly use short-range wireless technology to extract from your bank account that quarter (or dollar) every time you cross a toll bridge. Wireless is all over your car, but not centralized on any sort of wireless backbone like it is for your home.

Your car is also becoming more outfitted for computing and entertainment devices and functionality as manufacturers add, as standard and optional features, such items as CD and DVD playback systems, global positioning systems (GPSes), and even computers to operate your car.

All this spells opportunity for wireless. Bluetooth and 802.11 technologies are infiltrating the car and providing you with the opportunity to create the same wireless backbone as in your home — a universal wireless network that any device or function can access to talk to other parts of the car, such as your stereo, and to points outside the car. In fact, your wireless *home* network plays an important part in helping consolidate and integrate your *car's* wireless network with devices inside the car and to connect it with your home's network as these two areas converge.

The response has been a flurry of activity by auto manufacturers and others to network enable cars with wireless phone, data, video, audio, and control mechanisms that resemble the same efforts going on inside your house by other consumer goods manufacturers. In fact, you're starting to see entire product lines that include home and car wireless network products.

For years, efforts to wirelessly sync the car to other places had been going full steam ahead — that is, until the iPod came along. The iPod offers portability of entire music collections in ways that had not been seen before, and the focus shifted from trying to get music into your car wirelessly to just carrying it into the car on your iPod. We think this is a temporary swing to an extreme, and that the ideal solution is in the middle — a computer presence in the car that can reach out and synchronize with the home, and yet have connectivity to portable devices via Bluetooth, 802.11, and other technologies.

Yet portable devices (such as Zunes) aren't going away anytime soon. The best solution is not to build a bunch of different hardwired connections into the car, but rather to build a car that can modularly accept them and make the best wireless connection for the user. At the same time, we think that network connectivity in car devices — whether it be Wi-Fi in the garage or in an "information filling station" at your local drug store, or cellular broadband data on the road — is absolutely the best way to go moving forward.

Although it's tempting to focus on linking iPod and Zunes and cell phones to your car, we think that approach is shortsighted. So we cover both approaches, one with more of an eye to the future than the other.

Synching your car with devices in the car

By far the most common approach today to integrating music players and other content devices to the car's audio system has been through FM transmitters — small add-on accessories that take the output from the device's headphone jack and transmit it over an available FM frequency so your car's stereo can be tuned into it. Simple, quick, and cheap. Whether you're talking about an iPod, Zune, or other unit, you can find a range of FM transmitters for $10 and up. Companies such as Griffin Technology (www.griffintechnology. com) are known for their MP3 player accessories.

In the wireless realm, Parrot (www.driveblue.com) offers a number of retrofit Bluetooth-enabled music controllers that capture the music sent by your Bluetooth stereo mobile phone or MP3 player and redirect it to the vehicle's speakers (which automatically mute anything else playing). You can scroll through the titles via a simple LCD screen that attaches to your dashboard. The Parrot MK6100, for instance, is about $250.

Satellite radio versus digital radio

Your wireless home isn't always just about 802.11 technologies — other forms of wireless can enhance your home, and satellite radio is one of them, particularly for your car. If you're like us, you live where there isn't a whole lot of programming you want to listen to. Check out satellite radio, which offers a huge number of stations (more than 100) beamed to your house or car from a handful of geostationary satellites hovering above the equator. We find a ton more diverse and just plain interesting stuff coming across these space-based airwaves than we find on our local radio. Satellite radio services, from startups such as XM Radio or SIRIUS, require you to (gasp) *pay* for your radio (about $12.95 per month).

Check out the Web sites of the two providers (XM Radio, www.xmradio.com; and SIRIUS, www.sirius.com) to find the programming you prefer. Then, get your hands on a satellite radio tuner. (You can find a bunch of models listed on each company's Web page.) The majority of these satellite tuners are designed for in-car use (because people tend to listen to the radio most while they're driving), but XM Radio offers some cool tuners (from Sony and Delco) that can do double duty: You put these tuners in your car, and when you get home, pull them out and plug them into your A/V receiver or into a portable boom box.

We like the Delphi XM SkyFi3 (http://xmradio.com/shop — click the On the Go menu, $159) which is an iPod-like portable XM receiver that can also store as much as 10 hours worth of XM content, so you can catch up on those car hack shows you missed! XM Radio has also launched a version of its service that wirelessly transmits weather conditions to a specialized receiver as well, although it's expensive at $99 per month. (For that price, you can get a good PDA with wireless EVDO access from a carrier such as Sprint, www.sprint.com, and get all the weather plus Internet access — that's probably a

better deal.) Within the realm of affordable luxuries, XM also offers live and up-to-date traffic reports in many cities (the service works with a number of built-in and aftermarket GPS navigations systems) for $3.99 a month on top of your radio subscription.

Tip: Check out the annual pricing plans. You can save a good deal of money by paying in advance for a whole year. Also, each of these two satellite radio companies offers family plans for multiple receivers, where the price per extra receiver subscription can drop to as low as $6.99 per month — pretty good if you have lots of kids. However, Sirius and XM Radio are considering a corporate merger — if this is approved by legislators, we're not sure what will happen to programming and pricing plans.

Now you may not want to spend the extra dollars needed to get digital satellite radio into your car. Lucky for you, a free over-the-air (broadcast from terrestrial antennas) alternative known as HD Radio (www.hdradio.com) is available. This is a local broadcast service that allows local AM and FM stations to broadcast a second channel using a newer digital radio technology. As a user, you get free reception and better audio quality (the HD Radio folks claim that FM broadcasts will sound as good as a CD, and AM broadcasts will sound as good as regular FM broadcasts). A number of car manufacturers are adding HD Radio to cars at the factory (either as a standard feature or as an option), and you can easily add HD Radio to your existing car stereo (a number of these solutions are listed on the HD Radio Web site).

HD Radio is still new, but most big cities have a dozen or more stations up and running. The great thing about HD Radio (besides the free part) is that it doesn't interfere with traditional AM and FM stations, so having an HD Radio in your car just opens up the radio band to provide you with more stations. And the digital transmission system helps improve the transmission quality — so you're much less likely to have the signal fade as you drive across town.

By the way, the neatest feature of HD Radio hasn't made it to the car yet (you can also buy in-home HD Radio receivers). This feature, called iTunes Tagging, lets you press a "tag" button on your HD Radio when you hear a song you like. The tag is saved to your iPod, which is docked in the HD Radio, so the next time you're syncing your iPod with your computer, you can purchase the song from the iTunes Store. With the increasing number of car audio systems that can dock an iPod, we expect that this feature will eventually make it into cars.

Another cool Parrot product is the RK8200 Bluetooth Car Stereo, a headend unit that replaces your current stereo in your car but has a USB port, an SD card reader, an line-in jack, an iPod connector, and A2DP Bluetooth support — note *no* CD player. This revolutionary product has 2GB of onboard memory (plus whatever you can add via the SD card port), enough for hundreds of songs. Even more, the faceplate comes off to reveal a compartment where you can dock your iPod or cell phone for even more accessible content. The RK8200 costs about $240.

So you have plenty of options for retrofitting your car to work with your gadgets. But what's more interesting to us is where the new car models are taking us. Ford, for instance, has unveiled its new Bluetooth-powered Sync system, a Microsoft Auto software system that controls all sorts of in-car audio equipment. Sync is powered by a small in-dash computer running Windows Automotive, with 256MB of RAM and a 400-MHz StrongArm processor. It allows users to interface their mobile phone, music player, or digital storage device with their Ford's audio system. The devices will be controlled by voice commands, steering-wheel mounted controls, or the car's audio controls.

You can use the car's audio system to read back text messages sent to portable devices. It will also synchronize your contact information from devices, and will even be able to distinguish most ring tones loaded onto mobile phones. You can even link to the car through a USB port for recharging your portable devices.

Ford first offered the Sync system on the 2008 models of Focus, Fusion, Five Hundred, Edge, Freestyle, Explorer, and Sport Trac; the Mercury Milan, Montego, and Mountaineer; and the Lincoln MKX and MKZ. Ford says it will put the system in all its future products as an optional accessory.

The move by Ford is an acknowledgment of the fast pace of the consumer products industry. Instead of trying to create a leading edge dashboard device that will be stale in a few years, they created an infrastructure that enables software upgrades remotely but also allows car owners to link their leading-edge devices into the car. Expect to see more of this approach as the car reaches out and uses other devices to bring flexibility and connectivity to the car's audio and visual entertainment infrastructure. Ford has a year-long exclusive on this Microsoft technology in the U.S. market, and then it will be available to other manufacturers too.

Synching your car stereo with home

The major area where 802.11 is just beginning to show up is in third-party add-ons to the car — a typical precursor to manufacturers directly bundling these add-ons into the car (in-car VCRs started the same way). One example is in the A/V arena. We show in Chapter 12 how simple it is to synchronize your audio and video server across the house and over the Internet — why not with your car, too? (See Figure 14-1.)

A confluence of approaches are available, each struggling to win. Until recently, the ability to store content in the car (as opposed to on devices you take to the car, such as the iPod) has been frowned on by the same people who sue college students for downloading songs for frat parties. However, a new trend towards digital rights management (DRM) free content is making it popular again to think about having a massive hard drive in your car that synchronizes with the home whenever it's in range.

Figure 14-1:
Linking your car with your wireless home network is a matter of having your car's access point or wireless client log on to and sync with the wireless home network.

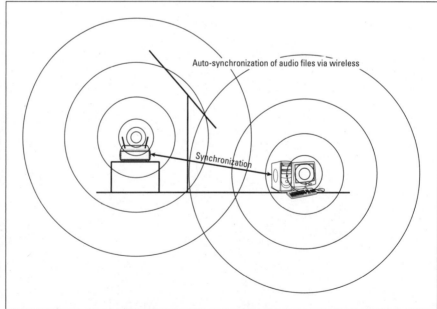

Our favorite product for this was the Rockford Fosgate 802.11b-based car product, Omnifi (www.omnifimedia.com), which was, sadly, sold only until late 2005. Omnifi allows you to wirelessly transfer tunes from your home PC to the car, where they can be played on your existing car stereo. The Omnifi has an installable hard drive that can store as many as 20GB of files; the home component is a stand-alone receiver capable of streaming media dispatched from the PC (see Figure 14-2). We were sorry to see this product taken off the market because it's really the only (shipping) retrofit, auto-updating, automobile-based Wi-Fi wireless system we've seen. You can still find it on eBay and in various online stores.

Omnifi eliminates the legwork (the need to burn CDs or load your iPod) to listen to digital music in the car. It gives consumers the ability to download and transfer music and programs from the Internet to the PC hard drive to the consumer's car and home stereo and theater systems — using wireless technologies. You can also subscribe to services such as audiobooks, from www.audible.com, so that you can listen to your favorite mystery book while you drive down the road. iTunes work as well. Very cool.

Other vendors say that they're entering the marketplace, so expect your car to become a hot zone for wireless technologies soon. Delphi Corporation, a well-known brand in car electronics, has been working with several partners to bring home-car integration to the market. It has shown prototype Wi-Fi enabled devices that sync with cable set-top boxes in your living room, and is working to bring audio and video downloads to the car.

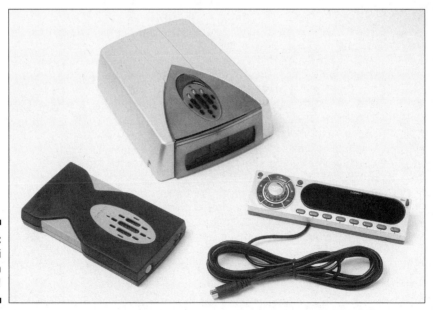

Figure 14-2:
The Omnifi
system in
your car!

Another manufacturer, Z-App Systems (www.zappsys.com), announced a home Wi-Fi audio system called the AL-1 in January 2007. The AL-1 (which will have a list price of $499) is the centerpiece of a family of Wi-Fi music gear. One part of this family, the MP-1, will bring your car into the Wi-Fi era by automatically synchronizing a copy of the music stored on your AL-1 onto the MP-1's internal hard drive via the Wi-Fi connection. This system isn't on the market yet, and we don't even know what the price will be, but it's worth keeping an eye on the Web site if Wi-Fi music is what you need for your car!

Other car manufacturers have likewise shown prototypes of various systems, but the Omnifi remains the only mass market product we've seen that's explicitly designed for the home-car linkage. It remains your best bet, if you can find one.

If you want to build a full-fledged car computer, check out the section later in this chapter, "Getting online with your own car PC."

Turning your car into a hot spot

In Chapter 16, we talk about cellular data services that you can access with your laptop when you're on the go — or from home if you're sitting on the couch. With unlimited data access, you can hop on the Internet anywhere. EV-DO is a popular data service offered by companies such as Sprint (www.sprint.com) and Verizon (www.verizon.com); AT&T offers a similar service called HSDPA (also discussed in Chapter 16).

Some brainy folks thought to marry these data services with Wi-Fi to create instant Wi-Fi hot spots anywhere you want — in your car, on your boat, or in the middle of a park. New devices called wireless WAN routers (where WAN means wide area network) interface with your cellular data service on the one hand and your Wi-Fi network on the other.

There's no one name for these routers. You can also find them as EV-DO routers, HSDPA routers, 3G routers, or wireless cellular routers — but *not* wireless mobile routers — these are usually just Wi-Fi travel routers. Consumer-grade versions are in the $200 to $300 range, and commercial ones can cost more than $500.

You need to get the model that is compatible with your network provider. Kyocera has an 802.11n version called the KR2 Mobile Router (www.kyocera-wireless.com, $200) that supports EV-DO services with PCMCIA, ExpressCard, and USB connections. D-Link has its 3G Mobile Router DIR-450 (www.dlink.com, $200) for EV-DO as well, but at the time of this writing it was 802.11g.

The Linksys entry is an 802.11g-based WRT54G3G model (www.linksys.com, $220). Most Wi-Fi router makers will have at least one wireless cellular router in their product line.

Be sure to check the card compatibility chart online for any wireless cellular router you purchase. It likely will not work with any card not explicitly on the list, and similar model numbers also likely will not work. Wireless cellular routers lag in support for the most recent cards, so if you buy a new card from your carrier, it might not be supported for several months.

You might want Wi-Fi in your car without all the complications of router and EV-DO service configuration. AutoNet Mobile (www.autonetmobile.com) will soon be offering a consumer-friendly EV-DO Wi-Fi service as a complete turnkey package (including the monthly EV-DO service). This self-contained unit is plug and play — AutoNet Mobile acts as your service provider and preconfigures everything so all you have to do is plug it into a DC power supply (in other words, a cigarette lighter) in your car (and pay a monthly fee) and you're online with Wi-Fi.

AutoNet Mobile expects to launch their product/service combo to consumers some time in soon. Initially, they are selling their product only to the Avis rental car company for you to rent when you want Wi-Fi in your rental car as well as in your hotel room.

What can you do with a portable wireless router? Just about anything you want. Stick it in your car and you can have Wi-Fi access for anyone in your car — and those around you. You can even have a virtual party with the cars in front of and behind you, linked via Wi-Fi.

An enterprising guy named Mike Outmesguine decided to put one in his backpack so he could always have a hot spot wherever he went. He and his friends can play multiplayer games while sitting in the middle of a nice park, courtesy of this solar-powered portable contraption. (How's that for trying to be the center of attention wherever you go!)

To build a Wi-Fi hot spot knapsack yourself, you need three major components: a wireless WAN router, such as the KR2 device; a cellular data PC Card, such as the Sprint EV-DO PCMCIA Card; and a Voltaic Systems solar-charging backpack or case (www.voltaicsystems.com, $200). That and about $35 of additional items from Radio Shack, and you're ready to hit the trail wirelessly (see Figure 14-3). Check out Mike's step-by-step *Popular Science* magazine article:

```
www.popsci.com/popsci/how20/6a278ca927d05010vgnvcm1000004e
                    ecbccdrcrd.html
```

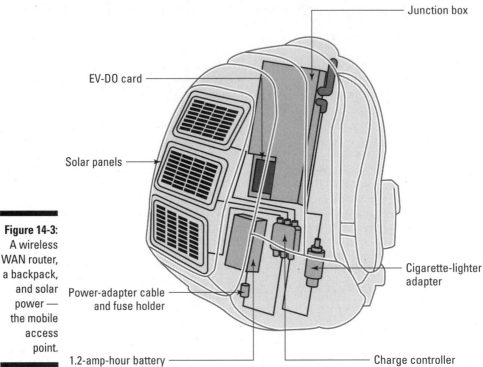

Junction box

EV-DO card

Solar panels

Figure 14-3:
A wireless
WAN router,
a backpack,
and solar
power —
the mobile
access
point.

Power-adapter cable
and fuse holder

Cigarette-lighter
adapter

1.2-amp-hour battery

Charge controller

Getting online with your own car PC

Pretty soon, downloading audio or video to the car won't be enough — you'll
want a full-fledged PC on board. Luckily for you, some cool, wireless-capable
auto PCs are now on the market.

With a PC in your car (we don't recall seeing any of those plastic traffic signs
in any car windows saying "PC on Board" — do you?), you can mimic your
wireless home network in your car, almost in its entirety. You can sync with
your PC for audio and video to play over your car's radio and video display
system. You can play computer games over those same systems. You can
access your address books and calendars, just like at your desk. You can
use wireless keyboards. You can link to your wireless cellular router to surf
the Internet.

Colloquially known as a *carputer* — a computer designed to be installed in a
car — these small-footprint devices use less power and are better prepared
for the rugged car experience. When we say *small,* we mean it: We've seen

them no bigger than a paperback book. After you install one, you use a wireless keyboard, touch-screen interface, remote control, and other similar devices to run specific applications on your PC.

Carputers are definitely in the hobbyist stage, in the sense that you install one and then keep adding devices. We've seen setups with Wi-Fi cameras, multiplayer gaming, and other such fun stuff scattered throughout the car.

It starts with the basic unit, however, and you can find a couple of good online sources for basic parts and systems: CarCPU.com (www.carcpu.com) and MP3Car.com (www.mp3car.com). You can get additional accessories to boost your enjoyment of your car PC. A wireless keyboard makes it simple to interface with the PC for text-oriented tasks (as is common with kids' games) and for surfing the Internet. You can wirelessly connect to the Internet while driving by using a cellular data PC Card, like the Sierra Wireless AirCard 750.

So, you can now pull up to a hot spot and log on. (Check out Chapter 16 for more about hot spots.) Or autosync when you enter your garage. It's just a matter of time until your passengers can play games car-to-car with another wirelessly enabled car while driving down the road.

Installing your car PC is both easy and hard. It's easy in the sense that you screw the unit to your car and run power to the unit. It's hard in the sense that other than the wireless connections, any connections to your car stereo or video system may entail running wires, just like with the audio wireless car servers we describe earlier in this chapter. After you have all this in place, though, using a different application is just a matter of installing new software on your car PC. It's just like with your home PC: After you install your printer, monitors, and all the other parts of the system, the hard work is done. Just install new software to do new things.

What does it cost to try out a carputer? Beginner packages, which include a computer, keyboard, dashboard mountable monitor, and miscellaneous gear are less than $1,000. Then you install software from the Web; a wide range is available, from free, program-it-yourself code libraries up to full-fledged software and hardware packages like those from StreetDeck (www.streetdeck.com), which run around $2,100.

 Putting a PC in your car is a fun project. Once installed, you can do all sorts of things with it. Many user interfaces replace the existing car stereo. If you need to remove your car's stereo system to do the install, we highly recommend www.carstereohelp.com — with instructions for each car's make and model — to find out how to safely and correctly take your dashboard apart. Also check out the wiki on car computing at MP3car.com (www.mp3car.com/wiki/index.php/Main_Page), where you can find a great overview of lots of resources for outfitting your car with tech gear. And the forums at MP3car.com are a great place to ask questions.

Networking your navigation system

In-car GPS navigation systems are one of the hottest areas in the consumer electronics business. Car manufacturers charge premiums of $1,000 or $2,000 (or more!) for fancy integrated navigation systems that pick up your current location (and other things such as which direction you're heading and your speed) and use a DVD database to map your location and provide you with point-to-point driving directions, local points of interest (POI), and more.

Even more GPS navigation systems are sold as aftermarket add-ins to the car, with manufacturers such as TomTom (www.tomtom.com), Garmin (www.garmin.com), and Magellan (www.magellangps.com) each selling millions of portable GPS systems every year.

Most navigation systems are *not* networked in a meaningful way — yes, they pick up incoming radio signals from the GPS satellites, but they don't have real-time communications with a network to enhance their functionality. The one exception here is the small (but growing) number of navigation systems that can pick up real-time traffic information from sources such as XM Radio (discussed earlier in the chapter).

Networking navigation systems makes a lot of sense because things change. Perhaps the new shortcut road that wasn't built when you bought your nav system has been completed (this would save you a ton of time, if only your nav system knew this and could route you accordingly), or a bridge is closed for a six-month repair period (you wouldn't have to turn around and backtrack if only your nav system knew this), or you're looking for a Japanese restaurant, and you'd have to drive only 3 miles instead of 12 (if only your nav system knew about the new Bento Box joint that opened up last summer). You get the picture — up-to-date information can make a navigation system much more useful.

Manufacturers *are* adding some networking capabilities to their nav systems in an offline way. Most portable nav systems can be plugged into your PC (via a USB cable) to receive updated maps and POI listings on a periodic basis. The folks at TomTom have taken this concept one step further in two ways:

- ✔ By creating an online community called TomTom Map Share: Map Share lets you feed your real world experiences (like that bridge that's closed) back into the user community. TomTom gathers this information and provides updated map information that can be downloaded to your nav system whenever you sync it with your PC.

- ✔ By integrating with Google Maps (maps.google.com): You can search Google Maps on your PC, and with a simple button-click send that location to your TomTom navigation system. The next time you sync your nav system, the destination will be there.

These offerings from TomTom are great, but they still require you to lug the GPS system into your home to sync things, and they require you to think about your navigation needs ahead of time rather than as events occur.

A new startup company in Silicon Valley called Dash Navigation (www.dash.net) is bringing to market a *two-way Internet connected* navigation system called the Dash Express. Dash Express uses a combination of Wi-Fi and GPRS (a slightly slower but widely available cellular data system) to create a navigation system that's always up-to-date wherever you are. With the two-way wireless Internet connection, the Dash Express can

- ✔ **Always be up-to-date:** The system constantly receives updated map and POI information over the Internet connection (Wi-Fi when at home, GPRS on the road).

- ✔ **Tap into the gigantic database of maps and address that Yahoo! provides on the Internet:** Dash Express lets you do live searches of Yahoo!'s Local Search (local.yahoo.com) from the nav unit itself. You can find POIs based on keyword searches, and even search for people's addresses and phone numbers.

- ✔ **Get real-time traffic data from "feet on the street":** This is perhaps the most far-out aspect of Dash Express. Dash Express systems automatically tap into a real-time traffic network that feeds your own and all other Dash users' current location and speed information into an anonymous system that combines user data with other traffic data sources to send updated traffic info back to your nav system. Ever hear an announcer on the radio say, "the I-5 is clear throughout the county" while you're on the I-5 stopped dead? Dash uses this real-world driver data to improve the traffic reports and keeps this from happening. (If only they could just get rid of the traffic for us!)

- ✔ **E-mail your nav system:** Because your Dash Express is on the Internet, it has an e-mail address. Have somewhere you need to be this afternoon? Shoot your Dash an e-mail before you get in the car, and that destination will be loaded in the system waiting for you. You can even give out the e-mail address to friends, so if your buddies change the restaurant where you're meeting them, they can send you the location while you're on the road heading there!

As we write, Dash Express isn't on the market, but it's on the way. You can preorder the unit from Dash's Web site for $599. The network subscription will add another $12.95 per month, but we think that's a bargain considering the convenience the system will provide. (You can use Dash Express as a stand-alone, non-networked nav system without the subscription, but the real magic here is in the network connectivity.)

Are navigation systems the hub of the car?

Earlier in this chapter we discuss the car PC — it's a neat way to add a lot of information and entertainment (often called *infotainment*) features to your car. Of course, not everyone is ready to put a PC in their car (at least not on their own). If, however, you look at what car navigation systems can do today, you'll see that a lot of what you might want from a car PC is easily available in today's fancier navigation systems.

What can a nav system bring to your car? Well, of course they bring GPS-based navigation (they'd be pretty useless if they didn't). They also bring a nice big color screen (again, a no-brainer). But what else is available in the nav-based infotainment realm? Try these features on for size:

✔ **Music servers:** Many navigation systems have hard drive or flash memory systems that not only hold map and POI data but also provide room to store your own media. MP3 and other music files can be synced to your navigation system when it's connected to your PC, and then played back in the car through an FM transmitter or auxiliary audio connection into your car stereo.

✔ **Document viewing:** A number of nav systems can be uploaded with detailed travel guides, reference materials, and even dictionaries. Going on a trip? Upload a travel guide and quickly pull up a description and guide to the tourist highlights for your location!

✔ **Hands-free calling:** Most nav systems, beyond the least expensive, include a Bluetooth hands-free phone system (like the

ones we discuss in Chapter 15). You can leave your phone in your pocket and make and receive calls using the built-in microphone on your nav system and either a speaker built into the system or your car stereo's speakers.

✔ **Text messaging:** A few navigation systems, when connected via Bluetooth to your mobile phone, can display incoming text messages (SMS messages) on your navigation screen. Most systems don't let you type replies (for safety reasons), but this is a great way to have your friends in the convoy to the big alumni homecoming game let you know they're pulling over in two miles for some BBQ.

Navigation systems may also have a built-in DVD or other video player (MPEG, WMV), or even a photo viewer so you can upload pictures of the kids and have them up on the screen when you're not actively navigating. As we've mentioned, a number of navigation systems can also receive traffic information broadcasts and automatically route you around the worst traffic (though if you live in Southern California, like Pat, there's really *no* getting around traffic!).

What this functionality needs to become really useful is network connection that brings a live, real-time element into the equation. The Dash Express system we discuss has this built in. We suspect that other manufacturers will take advantage of the Bluetooth connection to mobile phones to add this functionality by simply taking advantage of the fast 3G connection built into many of today's phones.

Choosing wireless gear for your car

The integration of external wireless connectivity options to cars is in its infancy. However, if you're shopping for auto-based audio and video gear, look for the following:

- ✔ **PC Card (PCMCIA) slots:** You get the ultimate in flexibility with PC Card slots because you can put any card you want into the system. You need these for connecting to your home when parked in the yard and accessing the Internet when traveling. Ideally, you would have two PC Card slots because it probably will be a while before many dual-mode Wi-Fi/cellular cards are on the market.

- ✔ **FM modulator:** Some systems have an optional FM modulator that enables you to merely tune into an unused FM band in your area and broadcast your music from the server to your stereo system. Because some audio and video systems require you to have specific receivers (that is, your actual audio component where you listen to the music) for your car to make full use of the new functionality, it can get expensive to install a system. FM modulators make it easy to put in a system without changing out your stereo; you lose some of the onscreen reporting that comes with a hard-wired installation, but you still get access to the music (which is the important part). Many new iPod players use FM modulation to link to your car.

- ✔ **Upgradeable storage hard disk space:** Look for systems that allow you to add storage space. Storage is getting cheaper and coming in smaller form factors all the time. You probably want to keep adding storage space as your audio and video collections increase.

- ✔ **Lots of interfaces:** After your system is installed, you want to plug a number of things into it. Make sure that you have a good supply of USB, FireWire, Ethernet, PC Card, serial, and RCA ports. Also look for an SD Card interface so you can easily transfer info and add storage if you need to. You may have already installed a VHS tape deck or DVD player in your car; if you did, you may be able to easily install an audio server or a video server right beside it and use available In jacks on the video player to feed your existing screen and audio system.

All in all, expect a wireless LAN in your car soon — it just makes sense.

"Look, Ma, I'm on TV" — Video Monitoring over Wireless LANs

The heightened awareness for security has given rise to a more consumer-friendly grade of video monitoring gear for your wireless network, too — this stuff used to be the exclusive domain of security installers. You can get network-aware 802.11g videocameras that contain their own integrated Web servers, which eliminates the need to connect a camera directly to your computer. After installation, you can use the camera's assigned Internet Protocol (IP) address on your network to gain access to the camera, view live streaming video, and make necessary changes to camera settings.

Network cameras are much more expensive than cameras you attach to your PC because they need to contain many of the elements of a PC to maintain that network connection. Expect to pay from $100 to more than $1,000 for network cameras; the more expensive versions offer pan-tilt-zoom capabilities and extra features such as two-way audio, digital zoom, and motion detection ($200 is the average price for a well-equipped camera).

D-Link is the leading vendor of wireless-based video surveillance. It has a special line of SecuriCam products designed just for surveillance, as well as a large number of other wireless and wired network camera products. Its DCS-6620G Wireless G 10x Optical Zoom Internet Camera (www.dlink.com, $700) is on the higher end of their product line (see Figure 14-4). This 802.11g camera has motorized pan-tilt-zoom (so that you can look around an area and zoom in), two-way audio support (so that you can hear people and talk to them as well), dual-motion MJPEG and MPEG-4 support (so that you can stream video using different bandwidth levels and quality), extreme low-light sensitivity (so that you can take pictures in dark rooms), and a frame capture rate of up to 30 fps. You can remotely monitor your camera using a Web-based interface or through the D-Link IP surveillance software. Your cameras can be accessed via the Web, with as many as ten simultaneous users viewing the live feed. Using the IP surveillance program, you can monitor and manage as many as 16 cameras, set recording schedules, configure motion-detection settings, and change settings to multiple cameras — all from one place.

Figure 14-4:
The D-Link SecuriCam DCS-6620G wireless network camera.

Not to leave motorcyclists out!

The wireless bug is hitting motorcyclists too. Leading motorcycle helmet designers are adding Bluetooth to their products so that motorcyclists can talk on the phone while they ride. If you're a cyclist and love your helmet now, you can get a Bluetooth kit and just add it — it's not that hard of a project. The InterPhone hands-free and intercom Bluetooth helmet kit (from many online shops such as www.cellularaccessory.com, $135) can be used to provide Bluetooth in your helmet (in fewer than five minutes, says the manufacturer). Parrot (www.driveblue.com) sells a hands-free kit (SK4000, $150) that allows the motorcyclist to place phone calls, listen to FM radio, stream music wirelessly via a Bluetooth stereo-enabled device, or transfer music via a mini-USB cable. The SK4000 uses Parrot's multi-user voice recognition software, which will recognize a contact's name when you speak it and dial the number automatically. Also, the Text-To-Speech (TTS) voice synthesis feature on the Parrot SK4000 reads contact names from the user's phonebook through the earpiece and will also audibly identify radio stations to help the driver select a station.

The other end of the pricing spectrum for D-Link is the DCS-G900 ($120), which is an 802.11g-based camera offering simple, basic streaming video to the Web. The image is static, depending on where you point and focus the camera when you install it.

D-link has the best selection of wireless cameras — you can probably find the perfect camera for your needs there.

Go to www.dlink.com/products/liveDemo/?model=DCS-5300W for a live demo of the D-Link DCS-5300 camera. See what it's like to pan, tilt, and zoom!

Panasonic also has a large lineup of cameras. Its BL-C30A wireless network camera (www.panasonic.com, $299) allows as many as 20 simultaneous viewers to see as many as 15 frames per second (fps) of live-motion video at 320 x 240. Resolution goes up to 640 x 480 at 15 fps. Through a Web-based interface, you can perform remote pan and tilt functions and click to eight preset angles. Panasonic offers a stand-alone unit, the BL-WV10A TV Adapter ($499), that will stream your Panasonic images to your TV set.

Love pets? Panasonic has been specializing in the remote pet experience with a series of products marketed as petcams. For instance, its high-end KX-HCM110A PetCam Network Camera with 2-Way Audio ($329) allows you to see and talk to your pets from far away and see their reactions. (In truth, an IP camera with two-way audio can do the same.) Panasonic also sponsors a YouTube for pet lovers at www.seemypetcam.com. You can upload your pet's IP wireless camera videos for others to see!

You can also get cameras from other players, such as Linksys (www.linksys. com), Hawking Technologies (www.hawkingtech.com), and TRENDnet (www.trendware.com). You will often find videocameras bundled into other packages; Hawking's Net-Vision HNC290G Wireless-G Network Camera ($115) interworks with its Hawking HomeRemote Wireless Home Automation System HRGZ1 Gateway ($180), which enables you to turn lights on and off in the house remotely. Often you'll find packages of three or four cameras for a lower bundled price as well.

Installing a wireless network camera is incredibly simple. These network devices usually sport both an RJ-45 10Base-T wired network interface along with an 802.11b/g air interface. Installing the camera usually involves first connecting the camera to your network via the wired connection and then using the provided software to access your camera's settings. Depending on how complicated the camera is (whether it supports the ability to pan, to e-mail pictures on a regular basis, or to allow external access, for example), you may need to set any number of other settings.

Security varies tremendously among videocamera offerings. If security is important to you (as it should be!), you should check the technical specs of any camera before you buy. Panasonic's BL-C30A, for instance, is an older model, and has only 40/64/128-bit WEP encryption to help protect your wireless network from illegal intrusion. The D-Link cameras top out at WPA as of this writing too. TrendNet's TV-IP312W Wireless 2-Way Audio Day/Night Internet Camera Server (www.trendware.com, $220), on the other hand, supports 64/128-bit WEP, WPA-PSK, and WPA2-PSK. (We talk more about WEP and WPA in Chapters 6 and 9, if you need to know more.) Look for a camera that has at least WPA2 Personal (PSK) on board — over time more cameras will have this.

To allow anyone from outside your home's LAN to view your camera feed directly (that is, not from a window pane published on your Web page), you need a static WAN IP address. Although you can probably get such an address from your broadband connection provider, it will probably be pricey. More likely, you will use a *dynamic DNS service (DDNS),* which allows you to assign a permanent Web address to the camera. A DDNS is easier to remember than an IP address and is static. Your camera vendor should help you do this as part of the setup process. D-Link, for example, has its own free DDNS service (www.dlinkddns.com) that you can activate during your setup process. Panasonic has its free Viewnetcam.com.

One of the cameras we like is the Linksys WVC200 Wireless-G Pan/Tilt/Zoom Video Camera (www.linksys.com, $270) because it shows the camera's IP address in an LCD on the front of the camera. This makes debugging and setup issues easier. However, don't pay for the Linksys SoloLink $19.95 DDNS service — check out free service such as DynDNS (www.dyndns.com/ services/dns/dyndns/) if Linksys is still charging for SoloLink when you read this. The WVC200 also supports only WEP and WPA as of this writing, not

WPA2. While we prefer WPA2, WPA is more than adequate as far as network security goes — we strongly recommend you skip over systems that only support WEP.

Wondering about 802.11n? As we write, most of the IP cameras are still 802.11g or b, but some n-based devices are coming on the market. SmartVue's S4 product line (www.smartvue.com) sports an 802.11n chipset, but is pricey — each professional grade camera retails at around $1,300. Over time, everyone will move to 802.11n — it just makes sense.

The wireless communication doesn't have to be all 802.11 based, although we would argue that it makes sense to use standards-based gear whenever you can. Danny likes his X10 FloodCam (www.x10.com, $99), which videotapes all activity around the house, night and day, and sends the color images to a VCR or PC. That system uses 2.4 GHz to send the signals, but it's not standardized wireless LAN traffic. We believe that over time, many of these systems will move to 802.11 or Bluetooth as chip and licensing costs continue to come down.

Controlling Your Home over Your Wireless LAN

Another area of wireless activity is home control. If you got excited about going from the six remote controls on your TV set to one universal remote control, you ain't seen nothin' yet. (And if you still have those six remote controls, we have some options for you, too.)

The problem with controlling anything remotely is having an agreed-on protocol between the transmitter and receiver. In the infrared (IR) space, strong agreement and standardization exist among all the different manufacturers of remote controls, so the concept of universal remote control is possible for IR. (IR remotes are the standard for the majority of home audio and video equipment.) But there has not been the same rallying around a particular format in the *radio frequency* (RF) space, thus making it difficult to consolidate control devices except within the same manufacturer's line. And then you have issues of controlling nonentertainment devices, such as heating and air-conditioning and security systems. Those have different requirements just from a user interface perspective.

The advent of 802.11 technologies, ZigBee, Z-Wave, and Bluetooth — as well as touchscreen LCDs and programmable handheld devices — offers the opportunity to change this situation because, at the least, manufacturers can agree on the physical transport layer of the signal and a common operating system and platform. We're now starting to see the first moves toward collapsing control of various home functions to a few form factors and standards. We talk about these topics throughout this section.

See me, feel me, hear me, touch me

Cool new handheld devices — namely, Web tablets and stand-alone touch-screens, are sporting IR interfaces and can become remotes for your whole home. (*Whole home* means that you can use it anywhere that your wireless net reaches for a broad range of devices anywhere in your home; check out Chapter 1 for more details about whole-home networks.)

You're probably familiar with touchscreens if you've ever used a kiosk in a mall to find a store or in a hotel to find a restaurant. Touch panels are smaller (typically 6- to 10-inch screens) and are wall mounted or simply lie on a table; you touch the screen to accomplish certain tasks.

Touch panels have become a centerpiece for expensive home control installa-tions. They allow you to turn the air conditioning on and off, set the alarm, turn off the lights, select music, change channels on the TV — and the list goes on. These are merely user interfaces into often PC-driven functionality that can control almost anything in your house — even the coffee maker.

Crestron (www.crestron.com) rules the upper end of touch-panel options with an entire product line for home control that includes wireless-enabled touch panels. The Crestron color touch panel systems are to die for (or at least to second-mortgage for). We would say, "The only thing these touch panels cannot do is let the dog out on cold nights," but if we said it, someone would retort, "Well, actually, they can."

Crestron's Isys i/O WiFi, TPMC-8x is a modified tablet-style PC with an 8.4-inch screen. This product runs a specially modified version of Windows and communicates using 802.11b/g/a. With this device, you can control your home theater and home automation system, turn on lights, and basically control anything in an automated house. You can also listen to music files and view streaming video directly on the tablet itself!

Crestron is definitely high end: The average installation tops $50,000. But if you're installing a home theater, a wireless computing network, a slew of A/V, and home automation on top of that, you probably will talk to Crestron at some point.

A popular, lower-cost alternative to Crestron is Control4 (www.control4. com). Control4 makes a line of home entertainment, control, and automation devices, ranging from home controllers that can centrally control all the devices in a home, home theater controllers, which centralize control of your home theater components, whole-home audio distribution systems, and ZigBee lighting and HVAC (heating, ventilation and air conditioning) controllers.

Control4 uses widely adopted standards such as Ethernet, 802.11, and ZigBee to keep its prices down while still offering the kind of space-age automation that used to be in the realm of only the truly wealthy. It's the home control system "for the rest of us" (just like our *For Dummies* book)!

To keep tabs on all your automated and remotely controlled systems, Control4 offers touchscreens such as the 10.5-inch wireless touchscreen (shown in Figure 14-5). This device uses 802.11g and that big color screen to show you the status all sorts of devices and systems in your home, and the 802.11g Wi-Fi connection can send control commands back to your Control4 home or home theater controllers from anywhere in the house.

If you're interested in home automation and linking the various aspects of your home, try *Smart Homes For Dummies,* 3rd Edition (Wiley). It's the best book on the topic. (Can you tell that Pat and Danny wrote it?)

Figure 14-5: Control4's wireless touch-screen can control all sorts of devices in your home.

Doing your wireless control less expensively

You don't need to spring for a $50,000 Crestron installation (or even a $5,000 to $10,000 Control4 installation) to get wireless control over devices in your home. That's because the advent of ZigBee and Z-Wave (discussed in Chapter 3) have brought lower, commodity prices to wireless control systems.

Maximizing your entertainment with macros

The most advanced remote controls can interface with your A/V gear through *macros*. Select Watch TV, for example, and the remote sequentially goes through all the motions to turn on the TV, turn on the home theater receiver, select the right inputs on the TV and home theater receiver, turn on the satellite receiver or cable set-top box, and do anything else that's required to watch television. You can program the remote by simply plugging it into your PC or Mac (with a USB cable) and then selecting the components you use from vast libraries of components available online from the remote's manufacturer. Answer a few questions about the configuration of your particular system (for example, do you listen to the TV through the TV's speakers or through your home theater receiver?) and you're on your way to one-remote Zen. Examples of remotes that use macros are Logitech's Harmony line of remotes (www.logitech.com).

If you can forgo the fanciness and limit your ambitions, you can find *universal remote controls* (the kind of programmable all-in-one remotes that many folks buy for their home theater) that can move beyond the TV and DVD player and control other systems in your house without wires.

An example here is Monster Cable's tidily named Home Theater and Lighting Controller 300 featuring OmniLink (www.monstercable.com). This $500 remote provides all the high-end home theater remote control features you'd ever want (including the ability to use macros, or a series of sequential commands that let you do a complex task with a single push of a button), and adds into the mix wireless lighting controls using the Z-Wave technology standard (a mesh wireless control network, which we discuss in Chapter 3).

Monster sells their own line of Z-Wave lighting control modules (manufactured for them by the giant electrical company Leviton, www.leviton.com), including both dimmers and switches. These control modules are available as plug-ins (you plug them into an outlet and then plug a lamp into them) and in-wall switches (you replace an existing switch). Monster also offers an in-wall controller that can be used with the remote control, so you can turn lights on and off or dim them throughout the home from a single wall switch.

Sit, Ubu, Sit . . . er, Speak!

Your wireless network can help with your pet tricks, too! Although we're not sure that this is what the pet trainer meant when she said that she would teach your dog to speak, speak he can if he's Sony's AIBO robotic dog. For seven years, Sony lead the market in robotic trainable dogs, until in 2005 it "put down" the line in a cost-cutting move. We don't usually write about discontinued toys, but this one is so exciting (and still widely available on eBay) that we decided to tell you about it.

Now you can say, "Beam me up Scotty!"

Every once in a while, technology meets our imagination and you're ecstatic. It didn't happen for us with any of the *Star Wars* light-saber toys — "Lighted clear plastic tubes not laser beam be," as Yoda would say. Nor can any of the existing robotic dinosaurs really shake the earth yet like a true Tyrannosaurus Rex. (We actually think this is coming soon: A life-sized *Jurassic Park* has to appear sometime in the next decade.)

But we were awed into silence with a working *Star Trek: The Original Series (TOS)* "communicator" that allows us to send and receive cellular phone calls. These are rare — each is custom made from *Star Trek* toy parts by a guy who, at the time of this writing, sells them only on eBay for around $350. It pairs with any Bluetooth-capable phone, allowing you to make calls like any member of the Enterprise crew. It even is voice controllable — "Contact Starfleet Command, Uhura!"

A button on the back turns it on/off, accepts and rejects calls, and initiates voice commands. The two buttons on the control panel, under the grill, turn the volume up and down. The blue LED indicates pairing, the red LED indicates battery status, and the green LED illuminates whenever the grill is open. You get 8 to 10 hours of talk time and 400 hours of standby.

But what's really cool is that when you flip it open, you hear the familiar grill opening chirps, just like on the show! *Star Trek* purists will be upset to know that the moiré in the middle of the device does not spin. Apparently, it was impossible to include the motor with the Bluetooth electronics and speaker.

Working tricorders and communicator pins *(Star Trek: The Next Generation)* must be right around the corner. Sorry, these are available only in Federation Territory. (We can hear the Klingons shouting "ghuy'cha'" now!)

Don't be misled and think of this as a cute expensive toy — this is one incredible robot. If you don't know much about the AIBO, check out its Web site (http://support.sony-europe.com/aibo/) to find out about this robotic puppy. It's neat how Sony has wirelessly enabled its robo-dog with an AIBO wireless LAN 802.11b card. Your pooch roves about, constantly linked to your wireless home network. With AIBO Messenger software, AIBO can read your e-mail and home pages. AIBO tells you when you receive e-mail in your inbox. AIBO reads your e-mail messages to you. ("Hey, Master, you got an e-mail from your girlfriend. She dumped you.") You can send an e-mail to AIBO asking it to take a picture on demand and send it back to you via e-mail. AIBO can read as many as five preregistered Web sites for you. And AIBO reminds you of important events.

With AIBO Navigator software, your computer becomes AIBO's remote-control unit. From the cockpit view on your PC, you can experience the world from AIBO's eyes in real time. (You know, there are just some things that a dog sees that we would rather not see!)

Through the control graphical user interface on your PC, you can move your AIBO anywhere you want. By using the sound transmission feature, you can make AIBO speak from a remote location.

We're not sure that you're ready to start telling people that your dog has an SSID ("AIBONET"), but this is one good example of robots now using your wireless home highway. Above all, make sure that you follow the security suggestions we give you in Chapter 9. (Can you imagine taking control of your neighbor's unsecured AIBO — now, *that* could be fun!) You can find out more about setting up an AIBO on your wireless LAN at the Web site listed previously.

A mint condition, state-of-the-art, last-generation ERS-7M3 AIBO will run you $3,000 or more, but if you want the cutting edge of wireless toys, you cannot afford to be without an AIBO!

Wirelessly Connect Your Digital Cameras

When the first Wi-Fi connected cameras came on the market, we were jealous beyond belief. We hate cables (which is why we try to wirelessly connect everything we can). The problem was that only a few cameras had Wi-Fi (or any other wireless) on board, and it was not worth throwing away a perfectly good working camera because we were lazy about cables.

Well now, we can be lazy and happy with a brilliant product from Eye-Fi (www.eye.fi). Eye-Fi offers an SD memory card outfitted with Wi-Fi on board — how cool is that? Simply pop the card in your camera, take pictures, and watch the pictures upload automatically as soon as you return to your home network. Worried about security? No need — the Eye-Fi supports static WEP 40/104/128, WPA-PSK, and WPA2-PSK security. (See Chapter 9 if you need some background on these abbreviations.)

You can automatically load pictures to sharing and printing Web sites, including Kodak Gallery, Shutterfly, Wal-Mart, Snapfish, Photobucket, Facebook, Webshots, Picasa Web Albums, SmugMug, Flickr, Fotki, TypePad, VOX, dotPhoto, Phanfare, Sharpcast, and Gallery. The Eye-Fi Service intelligently downloads your photos from your camera, handles log-ins and passwords for the site, and resizes pictures (if your site requires it) — all over a wireless connection. Photo uploads are free and unlimited because they are using your home's Wi-Fi and Internet connections.

The Eye-Fi card uses 802.11g technology, so it is backward compatible to 802.11b and forward compatible to 802.11g supporting 802.11n devices. A 2GB card costs about $99 retail — and the great thing about these is that you don't need to buy as large a card because it can be offloaded more easily and more often. Just too great a product to resist!

Chapter 15

Using a Bluetooth Network

*M*ost of the time, when people talk about wireless networks, they're talking about wireless local area networks (LANs). LANs, as the name implies, are *local,* which means that they don't cover a wide area (like a town or a city block). Wide area networks (WANs), like the Internet, do that bigger job. For the most part, you can think of a LAN as something that's designed to cover your entire house (and maybe surrounding areas, such as the back patio).

Another kind of wireless network is being developed and promoted by wireless equipment manufacturers. The *personal area network* (PAN) is designed to cover just a few yards of space and not a whole house (or office or factory floor or whatever). PANs are typically designed to connect personal devices (cell phones, laptop computers, handheld computers, and personal digital assistants) and also as a technology for connecting peripheral devices to these personal electronics. For example, you could use a wireless PAN technology to connect a mouse and a keyboard to your computer without any cables under the desk for your beagle to trip over.

The difference between LANs and PANs isn't clear cut. Some devices may be able to establish network connections by using either LAN or PAN technologies. The bottom-line distinction between LANs and PANs is this: If something connects to a computer by a network cable, its wireless connection is usually a LAN; if it connects by a local cable (such as USB), its wireless connection is usually a PAN.

In this chapter, we discuss the most prominent wireless PAN technology: Bluetooth, which we introduce in Chapter 3. The Bluetooth technology has been in development for years and years. We first wrote about it in our first edition of *Smart Homes For Dummies* (Wiley Publishing, Inc.) in 1999. For a while, it seemed that Bluetooth might end up in the historical dustbin of wireless networking — a great idea that never panned out — but these days Bluetooth seems to be everywhere. Watch a few TV cell phone ads and you hear the term — or check out the ads for new Lexus, Toyota, BMW, or Acura cars, which have Bluetooth built right in for hands-free cell phone operation.

The most common use of Bluetooth these days is connecting mobile phones to hands-free systems. You've probably also seen an even more popular example of Bluetooth in action: the cool cordless Bluetooth headsets that let you leave your phone in your pocket while making a call. Now you can finally talk on the cell phone and use both hands to gesticulate!

Discovering Bluetooth Basics

Let's get the biggest question out of the way first: What the heck is up with that name? Well, it has nothing to do with what happens when you chew on your pen a bit too hard during a stressful meeting. Nor does it have anything to do with blueberry pie, blueberry toaster pastries, or any other blue food. Bluetooth — www.bluetooth.com is the Web site for the industry group — is named after Harald Blåtand (Bluetooth), king of Denmark from A.D. 940 to 981, who was responsible for uniting Denmark and Norway. (We're a little rusty on our medieval Scandinavian history, so if we're wrong about that, blame our high school history teachers. If you're a Dane or a Norwegian, feel free to e-mail us with the story!) The idea here is that Bluetooth can unite things that were previously un-unitable.

The big cell phone (and other telecommunications equipment) manufacturer Ericsson was the first company to promote the technology (back in the 1990s, as we mention earlier), and other cell phone companies joined in with Ericsson to come up with an industry de facto standard for the technology. The *Institute of Electrical and Electronics Engineers* (IEEE) — the folks who created the 802.11 standards that we talk about throughout this book — have since become involved with the technology under the auspices of a committee named 802.15.

The initial IEEE standard for PANs, 802.15.1, was adapted from the Bluetooth specification and is fully compatible with Bluetooth 1.1, the most common variant of Bluetooth. (There are 1.2, 2.0 + EDR, and now 2.1 + EDR versions of the technology, as discussed in Chapter 3. They're compatible with Bluetooth 1.1 and add some additional features and performance.)

If you're looking for a few facts and figures about Bluetooth, you've come to the right chapter. Here are some of the most important things to remember about Bluetooth:

✔ **Bluetooth operates in the 2.4 GHz frequency spectrum.** It uses the same general chunk of the airwaves as do 802.11g and 802.11n. (This means that interference between the two technologies is indeed a possibility, though 802.11n draft 2.0 is designed to sense Bluetooth transmissions and switch to different channels so they don't interfere.)

✔ **The Bluetooth specification allows a maximum data connection speed of 723 Kbps.** A few of the most recent Bluetooth specifications can go much faster (2.1 Mbps for Bluetooth 2.0 and 3.0 Mbps for Bluetooth 2.1, with a proposed Bluetooth 3.0 that can go up to 480 Mbps), but many Bluetooth devices still use the slower speed specification — and Bluetooth 3.0 won't exist for a few more years. Compare this with the 248 Mbps of 802.11n. Bluetooth is much slower than wireless LAN technologies for now.

✔ **Bluetooth uses much lower power levels than do wireless LAN technologies (802.11).** Thus, Bluetooth devices have a much smaller effect, power-wise, than 802.11 devices. This is a huge deal for some of the small electronic devices because Bluetooth eats up a whole lot less battery life than 802.11 systems. The proposed Wibree specification of Bluetooth will use even less power than the current version; it's designed to be used in wireless-enabled watches and will increase the battery life of your cell phone Bluetooth headset five times what it is today.

Because Bluetooth uses a lower power level than 802.11, it can't beam its radio waves as far as 802.11 does. Thus, the range of Bluetooth is considerably less than that of a wireless LAN. Theoretically, you can get up to 100 meters (these are called *Class 1* devices), but most Bluetooth systems use less than the maximum allowable power ratings, and you typically see ranges of 30 feet or less with most Bluetooth gear — which means that you can reach across the room (or into the next room), but not all the way across the house.

✔ **Bluetooth uses a peer-to-peer networking model.** This means that you don't have to connect devices back through a central network hub like an access point (AP). Devices can connect directly to each other using Bluetooth's wireless link. The Bluetooth networking process is highly automated; Bluetooth devices actively seek out other Bluetooth devices to see whether they can connect and share information.

✔ **Bluetooth doesn't require line of sight between any connected devices.** Bluetooth uses radio signals that can pass through walls, doors, furniture, and other objects. So you don't need to have a direct line of sight like you do with infrared systems.

✔ **Bluetooth can also connect multiple devices in a point-to-multipoint fashion.** One *master* device (often a laptop computer or a PDA) can connect with as many as seven slave devices simultaneously in this manner. (*Slave* devices are usually things such as keyboards and printers.)

The really big deal you should take away from this list is that Bluetooth is designed to be a low-power (and low-priced!) technology for portable and mobile devices. Bluetooth (do they call it *Bleutooth* in France?) isn't designed to replace a wireless LAN. It's designed to be cheaply built into devices to allow quick and easy connections.

Some of the PAN applications that Bluetooth has been designed to perform include

- **Cable replacement:** Peripheral devices that use cables today — keyboards, mice, cell phone headsets, and the like — can now cut that cord and use Bluetooth links instead.

- **Synchronization:** Many people have important information (such as address books, phone number lists, and calendars) on multiple devices (such as PCs, PDAs, and cell phones), and keeping this information *synchronized* (up-to-date and identical on each device) can be a real pain. Bluetooth (when combined with synchronization software) allows these devices to wirelessly and automatically talk with each other and keep up-to-date.

- **Simple file sharing:** If you've ever been at a meeting with a group of technology geeks (we go to these meetings all the time, but then, we're geeks ourselves), you may have noticed these folks pulling out their Windows Mobile and Palm PDAs and doing all sorts of contortions with them. What they're doing is exchanging files (usually electronic business cards) via the built-in infrared (IR) system found on Palms. This system is awkward because you need to have the Palms literally inches apart with the IR sensors lined up. Bluetooth, because it uses radio waves, has a much greater range, which doesn't require direct IR alignment — and is much faster to boot.

Look for even more cool applications in the future. For example, Bluetooth could be used to connect an electronic wallet (on your cell phone) to an electronic kiosk. For example, a soda machine could be Bluetooth enabled, and if you wanted a soda, you wouldn't need to spend ten minutes trying to feed your last, raggedy dollar bill into the machine. You would just press a button on your PDA or cell phone, and it would send a buck from your electronic wallet to the machine and dispense your soda.

Another common future application may be customized information for a particular area. Ever go to one of those huge conferences held in places like Las Vegas? The booth numbers tend to go from 0 to 20,000, and the convention floor is about the size of 50 football fields — in other words, it's difficult to find your way around. With Bluetooth, you can simply walk by an info kiosk and have a floor map and exhibitor display downloaded to your phone. We're hoping that this feature is in place next time we go to the Consumer Electronics Show; we hate being late for appointments because we're spending an hour searching for a booth.

Bluetooth Mobile Phones

The first place where Bluetooth technology is taking off is in the cell phone world. This statement probably shouldn't be a surprise because Sony Ericsson, a huge cell phone maker, was the initial proponent of the technology, and other huge cell phone companies, such as Nokia, are also proponents.

Today just about every new phone being announced (except for the cheap-o ones) included Bluetooth technology. Sony Ericsson, Nokia, Motorola, Samsung, and Siemens, among others, are all selling Bluetooth-enabled phones. The adoption of the technology has been spectacular. A few years ago, Bluetooth was a rarity; now it's a standard.

You can do many things with Bluetooth in a cell phone, but the five most common applications are

- ✔ **Eliminate cables:** Many people use headsets with their cell phones. It's much easier to hear with an earpiece in your ear than it is to hold one of today's miniscule cell phones up to your ear — and much more convenient. The wire running up your torso, around your arm, and along the side of your head into your ear is a real pain, though. (Some people go to great lengths to keep from being tangled up in this wire — check out the jackets at www.scottevest.com.) A better solution is to connect your headset wirelessly — using Bluetooth, of course. Literally dozens of Bluetooth headsets are on the market, from specialized headset manufacturers such as Plantronics (www.plantronics.com) and Jabra (www.jabra.com), as well as from the cell phone manufacturers themselves.

- ✔ **Synchronize phone books:** Lots of us keep a phone book on our PC or PDA — and most of us who do have been utterly frustrated by the difficulty we face when we try to get these phone books onto our cell phones. If you can do it at all, you end up buying some special cable and software and then you still have to manually correct some of the entries. But with Bluetooth on your cell phone and PC or PDA, the process can be automatic.

- ✔ **Get pictures off your camera phone:** Many new cell phones are camera phones with a built-in digital camera. The cell phone companies promote this concept because they can charge customers for multimedia messaging services (MMS) and allow people to send pictures to other cell phone customers. But if your PC has Bluetooth capabilities, you can use Bluetooth to send the picture you just snapped to your PC's hard drive (or even use Bluetooth to transfer the file directly to a buddy's cell phone when he or she is within range — for free!).

✔ **Go hands-free in the car:** Face it — driving with a cell phone in your hands isn't safe. Using a headset is better, but the best choice (other than not using your phone while driving) is to use a completely hands-free system, which uses a microphone and the speakers from your car audio system. This used to take a costly installation process and meant having someone rip into the wiring and interior of your car. If you bought a new phone, you probably needed to have the old hands-free gear ripped out and a new one installed. No more — Bluetooth cars are here, and they let you use any Bluetooth-enabled cell phone to go hands-free. Just set the phone in the glove box or dashboard cubbyhole and don't touch it again. Keep your hands and eyes on the road!

If your current car isn't outfitted with Bluetooth, don't despair. Dozens of Bluetooth retrofit kits are available on the market — ranging from simple speaker/microphone devices that plug into your 12-volt power source (the lighter, in other words) to custom-installed, fully integrated systems that can even use your car's steering wheel controls.

✔ **Get your laptop on the Internet while on the road:** We think that the best way to connect your laptop to the Internet when you're out of the house is to find an 802.11 hot spot (we talk about them in Chapter 16), but sometimes you're just not near a hot spot. Well, worry no more because if you have a cell phone and laptop with Bluetooth, you can use your cell phone as a wireless modem to connect to the Internet. With most cell phone services, you can establish a low-speed, dial-up Internet connection for some basic stuff (such as getting e-mail or reading text-heavy Web pages). If your cell phone system (and plan) includes a high-speed option (one of the 2.5 or 3G systems we talk about in Chapter 16), you can get online at speeds rivaling (although not yet equaling) broadband connections such as DSL — all without wires!

Some cell phones have Bluetooth capabilities but have been artificially limited by the cell phone companies. For example, some Bluetooth phones have had their software configured by your cell phone company in such a way that you can't use the phone as a modem for your laptop, as described in the preceding bullet. There's no easy way to know this up front — but it's a good reason to read the reviews in sources such as CNET (www.cnet.com) before taking a leap.

Bluetooth Smartphones and PDAs

In addition to cell phones, the other category of device that's seeing a great deal of action in the Bluetooth arena is the PDA category. The term *PDA* (personal digital assistant) encompasses a wide range of handheld computing devices — and therefore, PDAs are also often referred to as *handhelds*.

The most common types of PDAs are

✔ **PDAs that use the ACCESS Garnet operating system (OS):** These PDAs run the Garnet operating system (formerly Palm OS) — which is an older but still useful and user-friendly OS. You can find Palm PDAs on Palm Computing's Web site (www.palm.com) and also by searching the Web site of ACCESS (www.access-company.com), the spin off that develops the OS.

✔ **Handhelds that use the Microsoft Windows Mobile operating system:** Windows Mobile handhelds are typically (though not always) a bit more expensive and faster than ACCESS OS PDAs. The major manufacturers of Windows Mobile systems include Hewlett-Packard (www.hp.com), Toshiba (www.toshiba.com), and Samsung (www.Samsung.com) — even Palm makes a Windows Mobile version of its smartphone. In many ways, down to the user interface, Windows Mobile models tend to mirror Windows-based desktop and laptop computers in a smaller, shrunken-down form.

✔ **Smartphones:** As we mention earlier in this chapter, in the section "Discovering Bluetooth Basics," the line between PDAs and cell phones becomes more blurry with each passing day, and in fact *smartphones,* which combine a PDA and a cell phone in one device, are taking over the PDA world. Companies such as Palm are building cell phones and PDAs in one (the famous Treo phones), and other companies such as Samsung (www.samsung.com) sell Windows Mobile–based combos. Some smartphone devices use entirely different operating systems (such as Symbian, Blackberry, or even the open-source Linux operating system used on many business server computers). Even Apple is in the smart-phone business with the release of the Apple iPhone. This multimedia mobile phone device has not only Bluetooth but also Wi-Fi and EDGE built into it. The iPhone uses an optimized version of the OS X operating system. This phone generated so much hype that even though it's less than 1 percent of the smartphone market — which is less than a half percent of the total cell phone market — we have to mention it here because it's just too cool to leave out.

Despite the variations among the PDA world, there's also a commonality — PDAs work much better as connected devices that can talk to computers and other PDAs. And, because PDAs and cell phones are increasingly *converging,* or taking on the same functionality, any of the applications we discuss in the preceding section may come into play with a PDA.

In particular, the synchronization application we discuss in the preceding section is especially important for PDAs because they tend to be mobile, on-the-road-again (thanks to Willie Nelson) extensions of a user's main PC. Most PDAs now require either a *docking cradle* (a device you physically set the PDA in, which is connected via a cable to the PC), or at least a USB or another cable to synchronize contacts, calendars, and the like with the PC. With Bluetooth, you just need to have your PDA in the same room as the PC, with no physical connection. You can even set up your PDA to automatically synchronize when it's within range of the PC.

Accordingly, we've begun to see Bluetooth functionality built into an increasing number of PDAs. For example, the newest Palm model, the Tungsten E2, includes a built-in Bluetooth system, as does the Nokia N800 Internet tablet (a handheld internet browsing device for when you just can't be bothered to turn on that computer).

You can also buy some cool Bluetooth accessories for handhelds. One big issue with handhelds is the process of entering data into them. Most either have a tiny keyboard (a thumb keyboard, really, which is too small for using all your fingers and touch typing) or use a handwriting system, where you use a stylus and write in not-quite-plain English on the screen. Both systems can work well if you spend the time required to master them, but neither is optimal, especially if you want to do some serious data entry — like writing a book! In that case, you really need a keyboard. Check out the Freedom Input Bluetooth keyboards (www.freedominput.com). These devices, available for PDAs, Windows Mobile devices, and smartphones, are compact (some even fold up) but give you a nearly full-size typing area.

If you already own a PDA and it doesn't have Bluetooth built in, what can you do? Do you really have to go and replace that old PDA with a new model? Maybe not. Several manufacturers are selling add-on cards for existing PDAs that enable Bluetooth communications. For example, Socket Communications (www.socketcom.com) sells Compact Flash (CF) Bluetooth cards for Windows Mobile PDAs. Speaking more generally, most PDAs and smartphones have a memory card slot — SD, Compact Flash, or memory stick — that is most often used to expand the amount of memory in the PDA but can be used for other purposes. You can find Bluetooth cards in these memory card formats. With the increasing number of devices already enabled with Bluetooth and Wi-Fi, it will be harder and harder to find these memory card format wireless adapters in the near future.

Getting a Bluetooth card installed and set up on your PDA is easy. The first thing you may have to do is to install some Bluetooth software on your handheld. If this step is required, you simply put the software CD in your PC and follow the onscreen instructions, which guide you through the process of setting up the software. After the software is on your PC, it should be automatically uploaded to your PDA the next time you sync it (using your cable or cradle). After the software is on your PDA, just slide the Bluetooth card into the PDA. The PDA recognizes it, and then may guide you through a quick setup wizard-type program. (Or it may not — this process is so automated that you may not notice anything happening.) That's it — you're Bluetooth-ed!

After you get Bluetooth hardware and software on your PDA, you're ready to go. By its nature, Bluetooth is constantly on the lookout for other Bluetooth devices. When it finds something else (such as your Bluetooth-equipped PC or a Bluetooth printer) that can "talk" Bluetooth, the two devices communicate and inform each other of their capabilities. If there's a match (such as you have a document to print and a nearby printer has Bluetooth), a dialog box pops up on your screen through which you can do your thing. Pairing Bluetooth devices is usually easy. In some cases (such as syncing mobile phone address books with your PC), you need to finesse some software on one side or the other. With a Bluetooth headset for your cell phone, for example, you tell your phone to find the device. Then you enter a four-digit code into your phone so it knows to talk to only that headset and the headset knows it's dedicated to only that phone. Although we find that pairing Bluetooth is pretty simple, it's always wise to consult the owner's manual and the Web sites of the software and hardware companies involved.

Check out the section "Understanding Pairing and Discovery," at the end of this chapter, for more details on making Bluetooth connections.

Other Bluetooth Devices

Cell phones and PDAs aren't the only devices that can use Bluetooth. In fact, the value of Bluetooth would be considerably lessened if they were. It's the *network effect* — the value (to the user) of a networked device that increases exponentially as the number of networked devices increases. To use a common analogy, think about fax machines (if you can remember them — we hardly ever use ours any more). The first guy with a fax machine found it pretty useless, at least until the second person got hers. As more and more folks got faxes, the fax machine became more useful to each one of them simply because they had many more people to send faxes to (or receive them from).

Bluetooth is the same. Just connecting your PDA to your cell phone is kind of cool, in a geek-chic kinda way, but it doesn't set the world on its ear. But when you start considering wireless headsets, printers, PCs, keyboards, and even global positioning system (GPS) receivers — check out Telenav (www.telenav.com) GPS navigation software and receivers from GlobalSat (www.globalsat.com) — the value of Bluetooth becomes much clearer. In this section, we discuss some of these other Bluetooth devices.

Printers

We talk about connecting printers to your wireless LAN in Chapter 10, but what if you want to access your printer from all the portable devices that don't have wireless LAN connections built into them? Or, if you don't have your printer connected to the wireless LAN, what do you do when you want to quickly print a document that's on your laptop? Well, why not use Bluetooth?

You can get Bluetooth onto your printer in two ways:

✔ **Buy a printer with built-in Bluetooth.** This item is relatively rare as we write, and it looks as though Wi-Fi enabled printers will replace these completely over time. An example comes from HP (www.hp.com), with its DeskJet 450wbt printer ($349 list price). In addition to connecting to laptops, PDAs, and other mobile devices using Bluetooth, this Mac- and Windows-compatible printer can connect to your PC with a standard USB cable. So, you can connect just about any PC or portable device directly to this printer, with wires or wirelessly.

✔ **Buy a Bluetooth adapter for your existing printer.** Many printer manufacturers are focusing on building printers with built-in Wi-Fi, but that doesn't have to stop you. Belkin, for example, offers a Bluetooth printer adapter, the F8T031 (about $75), that plugs into the USB port and works with most inkjet printers.

Audio systems

An area where Bluetooth is starting to make some inroads is in the realm of audio systems. This really should come as no surprise, considering that cell phone audio (for example, hands-free and headset systems) is where the vast majority of Bluetooth action occurs.

What we're talking about here is Bluetooth devices that carry higher-quality audio signals — hi-fi (as opposed to Wi-Fi), as it were. Well, this is an exciting new area for the Bluetooth world because Bluetooth is designed for audio and supports relatively high-quality digital audio transmissions.

You may find Bluetooth audio devices in two distinct places:

✔ **Headphones:** Many of us now carry iPods or other portable digital audio players (MP3 players, as they're commonly known) wherever we go. You can identify us by our ubiquitous (at least among the 80 percent or so of MP3 player owners who use iPods) white headphone cords snaking up out of our pockets and into our ears. Well it's time to cut *that* cord too. With systems like the Jabra Wireless Headphones ($13, www.Jabra. com), you can be up to 30 feet from your iPod while grooving to the latest single from White Stripes. The Jabra BT620s system even includes integrated controls so that you can not only listen but also adjust the volume, pause, or skip to the beginning of *Blue Orchid.* It even works as a headset for your music-capable smartphone and will stop the music so you can answer a call without missing a beat — so to speak.

✔ **Speaker systems:** If you have a stereo or multichannel audio system in your house, you know the Achilles' heel of all such systems: those ugly speaker wires running from the back of your receiver or amplifier to the speakers. For home theater systems, this problem is particularly acute because you have speakers in the *back* of the room (we wrote *Home Theater For Dummies* and even we have trouble dealing with that speaker wire run). Well, Bluetooth can come to the rescue. Many manufacturers make Bluetooth speaker systems that work with your Bluetooth-enabled devices. Companies such as iBluon and Motorola manufacture Bluetooth transmitters that take the signal from your stereo's headset Out jack. So cut the cord and still enjoy your music.

Keyboards and meeses (that's plural for mouse!)

Wireless keyboards and mice have been around for a while (Danny has been swearing by his Logitech wireless mouse for years and years), but they've been a bit clunky. To get them working, you have to buy a pair of radio transceivers to plug into your computer, and then you have to worry about interference between your mouse and other devices in your home. With Bluetooth, things get much easier. Danny recently upgraded to the Bluetooth version of his Logitech mouse. He also attached a Bluetooth presenter mouse that works at the same time — Bluetooth is the only way to connect more than one mouse to a single computer — so he can work out and scroll through his e-mail. (Unfortunately, you can't connect more than one keyboard to a computer, but if you have a Bluetooth keyboard it's easy enough to pick it up and take it with you.) If your PC (or PDA, for that matter) has Bluetooth built in, you don't need to buy any special adapters or trans-ceivers. Just put the batteries in your keyboard and mouse and start working. You probably don't even need to install any special software or drivers on your PC to make this work. For example, if you have a Mac, check out the Apple Wireless Keyboard and Mouse (www.apple.com/keyboard). They are slickly designed (of course — they're from Apple!) and go for months on their batteries without any cords.

If your PC isn't already Bluetooth equipped, consider buying the Logitech diNovo Media Desktop Laser (www.logitech.com, about $199). This system includes both a full-function wireless keyboard — one of those cool multi-media models with a ton of extra buttons for special functions (such as audio volume and MP3 fast forward and rewind) — and a detached media pad that acts as a hand remote or numeric keyboard with a built-in calculator. It also includes a wireless optical mouse (no mouse ball to clean) with the cool four-way scrolling feature, and a Bluetooth adapter that plugs into one of your PC's USB ports. This adapter turns your PC into a Bluetooth PC. In other words, it can be used with any Bluetooth device, not just with the keyboard and mouse that come in the box with it. This kit is a great way to unwire your mouse and keyboard *and* get a Bluetooth PC, all in one fell swoop.

The diNovo Media Desktop Laser is easy to set up. You just plug the receiver into a USB port on the back of your computer and install the keyboard and mouse driver software. (This isn't a Bluetooth requirement; rather, it allows you to use all the special buttons on the keyboard and the extra mouse buttons.) You must have an up-to-date version of Windows XP (simply use the built-in Windows XP software update program).

Bluetooth adapters

A large number of laptops and an increasing number of desktop computers —
like most of the Apple product line — have built-in Bluetooth. However, if
your PC doesn't, you need some sort of adapter, just like you need an 802.11
adapter to connect your PC to your wireless LAN. The most common way
to get Bluetooth onto your PC is by using a USB adapter (or *dongle*). These
compact devices (about the size of your pinkie — unless you're in the NBA,
in which case, we say *half* a pinkie) plug directly into a USB port and are
self-contained Bluetooth adapters. In other words, they need no external
power supply or antenna. Figure 15-1 shows the D-Link DBT-120 USB
Bluetooth adapter.

Figure 15-1:
The D-Link
USB
Bluetooth
adapter
is tiny —
about the
size of a
small pack
of gum.

 Because Bluetooth is a relatively low-speed connection (remember that the
maximum speed is only 732 Kbps in most cases, and a maximum of 3 Mbps
for the fastest USB devices), USB connections will always be fast enough for
Bluetooth. You don't need to worry about having an available Ethernet, PC
Card, or other high-speed connection available on your PC.

 Because many people have more USB devices than USB ports on their computers, they often use USB *hubs,* which connect to one of the USB ports on
the back of the computer and connect multiple USB devices through the hub
to that port. When you're using USB devices (such as Bluetooth adapters)
that require power from the USB port, you should plug them directly into the
PC itself and not into a hub. If you need to use a hub, make sure that it's a
powered hub (with its own cord running to a wall outlet or power strip).
Insufficient power from an unpowered hub is perhaps the most common
cause of USB problems.

If you have lots of USB devices, using a USB hub is simple. We've never seen
one that even required special software to be loaded. Just plug the hub (use
a standard USB cable — there should be one in the box with the hub) into
one of the USB ports on the back of your PC. If it's a powered hub (which we

recommend), plug the power cord into your power strip and into the back of the hub (a designated power outlet is there), and you're ready to go! It's easy as can be. Now you can plug any USB device you have (keyboard, mouse, digital camera, printer — you name it) into the hub and away you go.

Street prices for these USB Bluetooth adapters generally run under $40, and you can find them at most computer stores (both online and the real brick-and-mortar stores down the street). Vendors include companies such as D-Link (www.dlink.com), Belkin (www.belkin.com), and Sony (www.sony.com).

Understanding Pairing and Discovery

A key concept to understand when you're dealing with a Bluetooth device (like a cell phone or cordless headset) is pairing. *Pairing* is simply the process of two Bluetooth-enabled devices exchanging an electronic *hand-shake* (an electronic "greeting" where they introduce themselves and their capabilities) and then "deciding," based on their capabilities and your preferences (which you set up within the Bluetooth preferences menu on your device), how to communicate.

A typical Bluetooth cell phone has three key settings you need to configure to pair with another Bluetooth device:

- ✔ **Power:** First, you need to make sure that Bluetooth is turned on. Many phones (and other battery-powered devices) have Bluetooth turned off by default, just to lower power consumption and maximize battery life. On your phone's Bluetooth menu, make sure that you have turned on the power.

- ✔ **Discoverable:** With most Bluetooth devices (such as cell phones or PCs and Macs), you can configure your Bluetooth system to be *discoverable,* which means that the device openly identifies itself to other nearby Bluetooth devices for possible pairings. If you set your device to be discoverable, it can be found — if you turn off this feature, your phone can still make Bluetooth connections, but only to devices with which it has previously paired.

  This setting has different names on different phones. On Pat's Motorola phone, it's Find Me; yours may be different.

  Some phones and other devices aren't discoverable *all the time.* For example, Pat's RAZR phone becomes discoverable for 60 seconds when you select Find Me.

- ✔ **Device name:** Most devices have a generic (and somewhat descriptive) name identifying them (like Motorola V3 RAZR). You can modify this name to whatever you want ("Pat's phone," for example) so that you recognize it when you establish a pairing.

(Un)plugging into Bluetooth access points

Although most people use Bluetooth to connect to devices in a *peer-to-peer* fashion — connecting two devices directly by using a Bluetooth airlink connection — in some situations you may want to be able to connect Bluetooth devices to your wireless home network itself (or to the Internet through your wireless home network). Enter the Bluetooth access point. Like the wireless access points we discuss throughout this book, Bluetooth access points provide a means of connecting multiple Bluetooth devices to a wired network connection.

Bluetooth APs, like the Belkin Bluetooth Access Point with USB Print Server ($199), have a high-powered Bluetooth radio system (which means that they can reach as far as 100 meters, although your range is limited by the range of the devices you're connecting to the AP, which is typically much shorter) and connect to your wireless home network with a wired Ethernet connection. The Belkin AP also includes a USB print server, so you can connect any standard USB printer to the AP and share it with both Bluetooth devices and any device connected to your wireless home network (including 802.11 devices — as long as your wireless home network is connected to the same Ethernet network).

Moving forward, we expect to see access points with both 802.11 *and* Bluetooth functionality built in — multipurpose access points that can connect to any wireless device in your home.

One other important Bluetooth concept affects the ability of two Bluetooth devices to talk to each other: Bluetooth profiles. A *profile* is simply a standardized *service,* or function, of Bluetooth. There are more than two dozen profiles for Bluetooth devices, such as *HFP* (Hands Free Profile) for hands-free cell phone use, or *FTP* (File Transfer Profile) for sending files (like pictures or electronic business cards) from one device to another.

For two devices to communicate using Bluetooth, they *both* must support a common profile (or profiles). And, for two Bluetooth devices to not only communicate but also do whatever it is that you want to do (such as send a picture from your camera to your Mac), they both need to support the profile that supports that function (in this case, the FTP profile).

Making all this happen is, we're sorry to tell you, highly dependent on the particular Bluetooth devices you're using. And because more than a thousand Bluetooth devices are available, we can't account for every possibility here. This is one of those times where you should spend a few minutes reading the manual (sorry!) and figuring out exactly which steps your device requires. (We hate having to tell you that, but it's true.)

We don't totally leave you hanging here though. Here are some generic steps you need to take:

1. **Go to the Bluetooth setup or configuration menu of both devices and do the following:**

   a. **Turn on the Bluetooth power.**

   b. **(Optional) Customize your device name to something you recognize.**

   c. **Make the devices discoverable.**

   Typically, you set up one device to be discoverable and the other to "look" for discoverable devices. For example, you may press a button on a Bluetooth cordless headset to make it discoverable, and invoke a menu setting on your phone to allow it to discover compatible Bluetooth devices.

   One device notifies you with an alert or onscreen menu item that it has discovered the other, and asks whether you want to pair. For example, if you press the button on your headset, your cell phone displays a message asking whether you want to pair.

2. **Confirm that you do indeed want to make your device discoverable by pressing Yes or OK (or whatever positive option *your* device offers).**

3. **Enter the passkey and press Yes or OK.**

   Most Bluetooth devices use a *passkey* (numeric or alphanumeric code), which allows you to confirm that it's your device that's pairing and not the device belonging to the guy in the trench coat who's hiding behind a newspaper across the coffee shop. You find the passkey for most devices in their manuals (drat! — the dreaded manual pops up again). In some cases (like pairing with a PC or Mac), one device generates and displays a passkey, which you then enter into the other device.

   Your devices verify the passkey and pair. That's all you have to do in most cases — you now have a nice wireless Bluetooth connection set up, and you're ready to do whatever it is you want to do with Bluetooth (like talk on your phone hands free!).

 After you've paired two devices, they *should* be paired for good. The next time you want to connect them, you should only have to go through Steps 1 and 2 (maybe even just Step 1) and skip the whole passkey thing. Bluetooth devices are supposed to mate for life (like penguins). Sometimes, however, Bluetooth is a bit funky and things don't work as you had planned. Don't be surprised if you have to repeat all these steps next time you want to connect. A great deal of work is going on to make Bluetooth more user friendly, and making pairing easier and more consistent is the primary focus.

Chapter 16

Going Wireless Away from Home

*T*hroughout this third edition of *Wireless Home Networking For Dummies*, we focus (no big surprise here) on wireless networks in your home. But wireless networks aren't just for the house. For example, many businesses have adopted wireless networking technologies to provide network connections for workers roaming throughout offices, conference rooms, and factory floors. Just about every big university has built a campuswide wireless network that enables students, faculty, and staff members to connect to the campus network (and the Internet) from just about every nook and cranny on campus. Entire cities are beginning to go "unwired," by setting up metropolitan Wi-Fi networks that provide free or cheap wireless access to residents, workers, and visitors.

These networks are useful if you happen to work or teach or study at a business or school that has a wireless network. But you don't need to be in one of these locations to take advantage and get online wirelessly. You can find tens of thousands of *hot spots* (places where you can log on to publicly available Wi-Fi networks) across the United States (and the world, for that matter).

In this chapter, we give you some background on public hot spots, and we discuss the various types of free and for-pay networks out there. We also talk about tools you can use to find a hot spot when you're out of the house. Finally, we talk in some detail about some of the bigger for-pay hot spot providers out there and how you can get on their networks. The key thing to remember about hot spots — the really cool part — is that they use 802.11 wireless networking equipment. In other words, they use the same kind of equipment you use in your wireless home network, so you can take basically any wireless device in your home (as long as it's portable enough to lug around) and use it to connect to a wireless hot spot.

Discovering Public Hot Spots

A wide variety of people and organizations have begun to provide hot spot services, ranging from individuals who have opened up their wireless home networks for neighbors and strangers to multinational telecommunications service providers who have built nationwide or worldwide hot spot networks containing many hundreds of access points. There's an in-between here, too. Perhaps the prototypical hot spot operator is the hip (or wannabe hip) urban cafe with a digital subscriber line and an access point (AP) in the corner. In Figure 16-1, you can see a sample configuration of APs in an airport concourse, which is a popular location for hot spots because of travelers' downtime when waiting for flights (or the everlasting gobstopper that is the TSA line).

Many hot spots now use 802.11g, though it's not uncommon to still run across 802.11b hot spots. As we write, no hot spots that we know of are using 802.11n (though we're sure a café or two somewhere in the world have upgraded). The key thing to keep in mind is that if you have an 802.11b, g, or n network adapter in your laptop or other device, you should be able to connect. *Note:* If your laptop or handheld computer has an 802.11a-only network adapter, you can't connect to the vast majority of hot spots (we've *never* seen an 802.11a hot spot). Luckily, most folks who have 802.11a in their laptops have it in the form of a dual-band 802.11a/b/g network adapter, so they won't have problems connecting to an 802.11g hot spot. Head to Chapter 2 for a refresher on the 802.11 Wi-Fi standards.

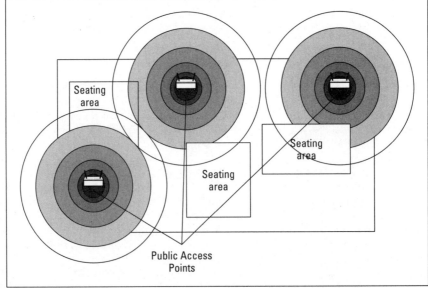

Figure 16-1:
An airport concourse is a perfect location for a hot spot, using several access points.

Of the myriad reasons that someone (or some company or organization) may open up a hot spot location, the most common we've seen include

- ✔ **In a spirit of community-mindedness:** Many hot spot operators strongly believe in the concept of a connected Internet community, and they want to do their part by providing a hop-on point for friends, neighbors, and even passers-by to get online. For an example of this, check out a service provider called *Fon* (www.fon.com/en/), which has built a worldwide network of hot spots around this principle.

- ✔ **As a municipal amenity:** Not only individuals want to create a connected community. Many towns, cities, and villages have begun exploring the possibility of building municipality-wide Wi-Fi networks. A cost is associated with this concept, of course, but they see this cost as being less than the benefit the community will receive. For example, many towns are looking at an openly accessible downtown Wi-Fi network as a way to attract business (and businesspeople) to downtown areas that have suffered because of businesses moving to the suburbs.

- ✔ **As a way to attract customers:** Many cafes and other public gathering spots have installed free-to-use hot spots as a means of getting customers to come in the door and to stay longer. These businesses don't charge for the hot spot usage, but they figure you will buy more double espressos if you can sit in a comfy chair and surf the Web while you're drinking your coffee — in many cases, the business provides you with free access after you buy something.

- ✔ **As a business in and of itself:** Most of the larger hot spot providers have made public wireless LAN access their core business. They see that hot spot access is a great tool for traveling businesspeople, mobile workers (such as sales folks and field techs), and the like. They've built their businesses based on the assumption that these people (or their companies) will pay for Wi-Fi access mainly because of the benefits that a broadband connection offers them compared with the dial-up modem connections they've been traditionally forced to use while on the road.

Another group of hot spot operators exists that we like to call the *unwilling* (or *unwitting!*) hot spot operators. These are often regular Joes who have built wireless home networks but haven't activated any of the security measures we discuss in Chapter 9. Their access points have been left wide open, and their neighbors (or people sitting on the park bench across the street) are taking advantage of this open access point to do some free Web surfing. Businesses, too, fall in this category: You would be shocked at how many businesses have unsecured access points — in many cases their IT people don't even know about it. It's all too common for a department to install its own access point (a *rogue access point*) without telling the IT staff that they've done so.

Going onto one of these not-really-a-hot-spot hot spots with your PC is an iffy legal proposition. On the one hand, if you're sitting somewhere (such as in your home) and your computer automatically associates itself with someone's unsecured AP, there's no real harm. But the jury's still out if you actively seek out and get onto someone's unsecured access point that they *haven't* explicitly set up as a hot spot. A small number of people have been arrested for theft of service, trespassing, and other charges for using someone's Wi-Fi without permission. For the most part, these cases have revolved around something else — for example, someone lurking in front of a home or business with a laptop, or someone doing something illegal online over another person's network.

We tend to divide hot spot operators into two categories: free networks, or *freenets,* which let anyone associate with the hot spot and get access without paying, and *for-pay* hot spots, which require users to set up an account and pay per use or a monthly (or yearly) fee for access. In this section, we talk a bit about these two types of operators, as well as a third type of operator who could fit into either category — the municipal/metro hot spot (or hot zone) operator.

Freenets and open access points

Most open access points are just that: individual access points that have been purposely (or mistakenly) left open for others to use. Because this is essentially an ad hoc network created by individuals, without any particular organization behind them, these open hot spots can be hard to find. (***Note:*** This is different from an ad hoc network that doesn't use an access point; refer to Chapter 7.) In some areas, the owners of these hot spots are part of an organized group, which makes these hot spots easier to find. But in other locations, you need to do some Web research or use some special programs on your laptop or handheld computer to find an open access point.

The more organized groups of open access points — often called *freenets* — can be found in many larger cities. You can find a list of freenets at www. freenetworks.org. One of the biggest of these freenets is NYCwireless (www. nycwireless.net), a freenet serving Manhattan, Brooklyn, and other areas of the metro New York City region. Similar informal and grassroots networks exist in other big cities.

A growing number of businesses are offering free hot spot services as well. These range from entire shopping malls or even city blocks offering the service as an amenity to attract customers to restaurants and cafes which simply have an access point turned on out of neighborliness. A growing number of chain restaurants (such as Panera Bread) now offer free Wi-Fi hot spots in all their locations.

The folks at Wi-Fi Planet (one of our favorite sources of industry news) run the Web site Wi-FiHotSpotList.com (www.wi-fihotspotlist.com), which lets you search through its huge worldwide database of hot spots. You can search by city, state, or country. Wi-FiHotSpotList.com includes both free and for-pay hot spots, so it's a comprehensive list.

Another great site is JiWire (www.jiwire.com). This site includes a comprehensive listing of free and for-pay hot spots, a great Wi-Fi news site (Wi-Fi Net News), and even special software you can download to help you locate hot spots without being online (just enter the address and you can search a locally stored database on your PC).

You have much more luck finding freenets and free public access points in urban areas. The nature of 802.11 technologies is such that most off-the-shelf access points reach a few hundred feet with any kind of throughput. So, when you get out of the city and into the suburbs and rural areas, chances are that an access point in someone's house won't reach any place you're going to be — unless that house is right next door to a park or other public space. There's just a density issue to overcome. In a city, where numerous access points may be on a single block, you have much better luck getting online.

Although these lists are good, none of them is truly comprehensive because many individuals who have open hot spots haven't submitted them. If you're looking for a hot spot and haven't found it through one of these Web sites (or one of the many, many others online), try using one of the hot spot–finding programs we discuss in the upcoming section "Tools for Finding Hot Spots."

Some of the hot spots you find by using these tools, or some of the online Web pages that collect the reports of people using these tools, are indeed open, albeit unintentionally. We don't get involved in a discussion of the morality or ethics of using these access points to get online. We would say, however, that some people think that locating and using an open access point is a bad thing, akin to stealing. So, if you're going to hop on someone's access point and you don't know for sure that you're meant to do that, you're on your own.

For-pay services

Although we think that freenets are an awesome concept, if you have an essential business document to e-mail or a PowerPoint presentation that you absolutely have to download from the company server before you get to your meeting, you may not want to rely solely on the generosity of strangers. You may even be willing to pay to get a good, reliable, secure connection to the Internet for these business (or important personal) purposes.

Trust us: Someone out there is thinking about how he can help you with that need. In fact, a bunch of companies are focusing on exactly that business. It's the nature of capitalism, right? The concluding sections of this chapter talk about a few of these companies, but for now, we talk just in generalities. Commercial hot spot providers are mainly focused on the business market, providing access to mobile workers and road-warrior types. Many of these providers also offer relatively inexpensive plans (by using either prepaid calling cards or pay-by-the-use models) that you may use for nonbusiness connectivity (at least if you're like us, and you can't go a day without checking your mail or reading DBR — www.dukebasketballreport.com — even when you're on vacation).

Unless you're living in a city or town right near a hot spot provider, you probably don't pick up a hot spot as your primary ISP, although in some places (often, smaller towns), ISPs are using Wi-Fi as the primary pipe to their customers' homes. You can expect to find for-pay hot spot access in lots of areas outside the home. The most common include

- Hotel lobbies and rooms
- Coffee shops and Internet cafes
- Airport gates and lounges
- Office building lobbies
- Train stations
- Meeting facilities

Basically, anywhere that folks armed with a laptop or a handheld computer may find themselves is a potential for a hot spot operator to build a business.

Pretty soon, you will even be able to (once again) plug into a Wi-Fi network on an airplane. A few years back, Boeing (you know, the folks who make jets) started a service called Connexion by Boeing, which was designed to provide Wi-Fi service to plane passengers (connecting them to a satellite Internet connection). Unfortunately, the costs of this service far outstripped the revenues gained from paying customers, and Boeing shut down the service. Well, JetBlue airlines launched (in December 2007) a *free* Wi-Fi service on selected flights, and a company called Aircell (www.aircell.com) has announced deals with both American Airlines and Virgin America to provide Wi-Fi services sometime in 2008. So stay tuned!

The single biggest issue that has been holding back the hot spot industry so far — keeping it a huge future trend rather than a use-it-anywhere-today reality — has been the issue of roaming. As of this writing, no single hot spot operator has anything close to ubiquitous coverage, though a few companies (such as Boingo) are making deals and getting closer. Instead, dozens of different hot spot operators, of different sizes, operate in competition with each other. As a user, perhaps a salesperson who's traveling across town to several different clients in one day, you may run into hot spots from three or four providers — and need accounts from each of those providers.

Opening up to your neighbors

When we say, "opening up to your neighbors," we're not talking about group therapy or wild hot tub parties. Wireless networks can carry through walls, across yards, and potentially around the neighborhood. Although wireless LANs were designed from the start for in-building use, the technology can be used in outdoor settings. For example, most college campuses are now wired with dozens or hundreds of wireless access points so that students, staff members, and professors can access the Internet from just about anywhere on campus. At UC San Diego, for example, freshmen are outfitted with wireless personal digital assistants (PDAs) to schedule classes, send e-mails and instant messages, and even find their friends at the student center (by using a locator program written by a student). Many folks are adapting this concept when it comes to access in their neighborhood by setting up community wireless LANs.

Some creators of these community LANs have taken the openness of the Internet to heart and have opened up their access points to any and all takers. In other areas, where broadband access is scarce, neighbors pool money to buy a T1 or other business-class, high-speed Internet line to share it wirelessly.

We think that both concepts make a great deal of sense, but we have one warning: Many Internet service providers (ISPs) don't like the idea of you sharing your Internet connection without them getting a piece of the action. Beware that you may have to pay for a more expensive commercial ISP line. Before you share your Internet connection, check your ISP's Terms of Service (TOS) or look at the listing of wireless-friendly ISPs on the Electronic Frontier Foundation's Web page (http://w2.eff.org/Infrastructure/Wireless_cellular_radio/wireless_friendly_isp_list.html). The same is true of DSL, fiber-optic, and cable modem providers. Your usage agreement with the provider basically says that you won't do this, and ISPs are starting to charge high-use fees to lines that have *extranormal* traffic (that is, those lines that seem like a bunch of people on the broadband line are sharing the connection). One ISP that not only allows you to share your Internet connection by hot spot but also encourages it is Speakeasy (www.speakeasy.net).

This situation is much different than the cell phone industry, in which you can pretty much take your phone anywhere and make calls. The cell phone providers have elaborate roaming arrangements in place that allow them to bill each other (and in the end, bill you, the user) for these calls. Hot spot service providers haven't reached this point. However, a couple of trends will help bring about some true hot spot roaming:

- ✔ **Hot spot aggregators, such as Boingo Wireless, are bringing together thousands of hot spots.** Boingo (founded by Sky Dayton, who also founded the huge ISP EarthLink), doesn't operate any of its own hot spots but instead has partnered with a huge range of other hot spot operators, from little mom-and-pop hot spot operators to big operations, such as Wayport. Boingo provides all the billing and account management for users. Thus, a Boingo customer can go to any Boingo partner's hot spot, log on, and get online. (We talk about both Boingo and Wayport in more detail later in this chapter.)

✔ **Cell phone companies are getting into the hot spot business.** Led by T-Mobile (which has hot spots in almost every Starbucks coffee shop), cell phone companies are beginning to buy into the hot spot concept by setting up widespread networks of hot spots in their cellular phone territories. Although these networks aren't yet ubiquitous — the coverage isn't anywhere close to that of the cellular phone networks yet — they're getting better by the day.

Besides improving coverage and solving the roaming problem, commercial hot spot providers are beginning to look at solutions that provide a higher grade of access — offering business class hot spot services, in other words. For example, they're exploring special hot spot access points and related gear that can offer different tiers of speeds (you could pay more to get a faster connection) or that can offer secure connections to corporate networks (so that you can safely log on to the office network to get files).

In the following section, we talk about some of the most prominent commercial hot spot providers operating in the United States. We don't spend any time talking about the smaller local hot spot providers out there, although many of them are hooking up with companies like Boingo. We're not down on these smaller providers, but we're aiming for the maximum bang for our writing buck. If you have a local favorite that meets your needs, go for it!

Understanding metro Wi-Fi

A final category of Wi-Fi hot spot is the *metro-wide hot spot* (or *hot zone*) that a number of cities have begun to launch. Cities as big as Philadelphia and San Francisco and as small as Addison, Texas (population, 14,166), have or are building metro Wi-Fi hot zones. (We're sure that even smaller towns are doing the same thing, but are flying beneath the press radar!)

A metro-wide hot spot is a city-wide network of access points connected back to a broadband Internet connection. This network can be built for any number of reasons, including:

✔ As a network for the city/metro area government and public services, providing Internet access on the go for police, fire, public works, and other officials

✔ As a means of providing broadband access to residents in their homes (most common in areas where other broadband services are not widely available)

✔ As a public amenity to all (residents, visitors, and the like) for outdoor access to the Internet

✔ Finally, and most commonly, some combination of the preceding

Metro Wi-Fi networks can be free, subscription based (for a fee), or (as is often the case) a combination of the two. For example, many cities are proposing a free advertising-supported low-speed service and a higher speed service for a monthly service fee.

The main thing to keep in mind about metro-wide Wi-Fi networks is that although they work *technically* (meaning, it's possible to build the network and run it successfully), the *business case* for such a network is often difficult to make. Metro Wi-Fi networks are expensive to build and expensive to operate, and a number of cities have bit off more than they could chew and scaled back their plans. The rise of high-speed broadband services from mobile phone companies (*3G* services) has also made the need for metro-wide Wi-Fi a bit less acute. In the long term, metro-wide Wi-Fi may never be as big or as prevalent as folks thought it would be a few years ago. Even Google has scaled back or slowed down their plans to build such networks for cities.

Using T-Mobile Hot Spots

The biggest hot spot provider in the United States — at least in terms of companies that run their own hot spots — is T-Mobile (http://hotspot.t-mobile.com). T-Mobile has hot spots up and running in more than 8,600 locations, primarily at Starbucks coffee shops throughout the United States. T-Mobile got into the hot spot business when it purchased the assets of a start-up company named Mobilestar, which made the initial deal with Starbucks to provide wireless access in these coffee shops.

T-Mobile has branched out beyond Starbucks and is also offering access in American Airlines Admirals Clubs in a few dozen airports as well as in a handful of other locations. T-Mobile charges $29.99 per month for unlimited national access if you sign up for a year and $39.99 monthly if you pay month to month. If you have a phone from T-Mobile, you can add the unlimited plan to your monthly bill for $19.99. You can also pay by the day (about $10) or by the hour ($6 per hour).

T-Mobile also offers some corporate accounts (for those forward-thinking companies that encourage their employees to drink quadruple Americanos during working hours — Danny, are you listening?), prepaid accounts, and pay-as-you-go plans.

To try out T-Mobile hot spots for free, register on the T-Mobile site, at hotspot.t-mobile.com.

T-Mobile, like most hot spot companies, uses your Web browser to log you in and activate your service. You need to set the service set identifier (SSID) in your wireless network adapter's client software to `tmobile` to get on the network. (Check out Part III of this book for information on how to do that on your laptop or handheld.) If you're using a Windows XP or Vista PC, you can also download a T-Mobile connection manager software client at http://client.hotspot.t-mobile.com/.

One cool feature of T-Mobile hot spots is that they have begun to support WPA and 802.1x security (refer to Chapter 9), so you can connect to them and feel safe and secure about your wireless connections.

Using Wayport Hot Spots

Another big commercial hot spot provider is Wayport (www.wayport.com). Wayport has made business travelers its number-one focus: The company has more than 7,000 hot spots around the world. Besides just offering Wi-Fi access, Wayport offers wired Internet access in many hotels and airports. (You see Wayport Laptop Lane kiosks in many airports when you scurry from your security strip search to the gate.)

Like T-Mobile, Wayport offers a range of service plans, ranging from one-time, pay-as-you-go plans using your credit card to prepaid calling card plans. You can sign up as an annual customer for $29.95 per month (if you sign up for a year's worth of service; otherwise, it's $49.95 for a month-to-month plan) to get unlimited access to any Wayport Wi-Fi location nationwide. Wayport also offers corporate plans, so consider bribing your IT manager if you travel often.

Like T-Mobile, Wayport uses your Web browser to authenticate you and collect your billing information. You need to set your SSID to `Wayport_Access` to get logged on to the access port.

Using Boingo Hot Spots

When Boingo (www.boingo.com) was launched in 2002, it made a big splash because it was the first company to bring a solution to the hot spot roaming issue. Boingo doesn't own its own network of hot spots; instead, it has partnered with a number of other hot spot providers (including Wayport, which we discuss in the preceding section). Boingo provides you, the user, with some software, and gives you access to all the hot spots of its partners with a single account, a single bill, and not much hassle on your part.

As of this writing, Boingo has more than 100,000 hot spots up and running on its network. Like the other providers, Boingo offers monthly plans ($21.95 for unlimited access in North America, $39.00 for global access) as well as pay-as-you-go plans and corporate accounts. (Keep buttering up your IT manager!)

The big difference between Boingo and most other services is that Boingo uses its own software to control and manage the connection process. You download the Boingo software (available for most Windows and Mac computers and also for Pocket PC handhelds) and use the software to sign on to a Boingo hot spot. This arrangement allows Boingo to offer a more consistent user experience when you roam around using its service. Boingo is also taking advantage of this software to offer a Virtual Private Network, or VPN, service for business customers. *VPN* is a secured network connection that others can't intrude on. (Refer to Chapter 9 for more information on VPNs.)

We talk a bit more about Boingo software in the following section because you can use it to sniff out open access points, regardless of whether they're Boingo's.

Tools for Finding Hot Spots

When you're on the road looking for a freenet, a community hot spot, or a commercial provider, here are a few ways that you can get your laptop or handheld computer to find available networks:

- ✔ **Do your homework:** If you know exactly where you're going to be, you can do some online sleuthing, find available networks, and write down the SSIDs or WPA passphrases or WEP keys (if required) before you get there. We talk about these items in more detail in Chapter 9. Most hot spots don't use WPA or WEP (it's too hard for their customers to figure out), but you can find the SSID on the Web site of the hot spot provider you're planning to use. Just look in the support or how-to-connect section.

- ✔ **Look for a sign:** Providers that push open hot spots usually post some prominent signs and otherwise advertise this service. Most are providing you with Wi-Fi access as a means of getting you in the door as a paying customer, so they find a way to let you know what they're up to.

- ✔ **Rely on your network adapter's client software:** Many network adapter software systems give you a nice pull-down list of available access points. In most cases, this list doesn't provide details about the access points, but you can use trial-and-error to see whether you can get online.

- ✔ **Use a network sniffer program:** These programs work with your network adapter to ferret out the access points near you and provide a bit of information about them. In this section, we describe sniffers from two companies: Netstumbler.com and Boingo. (***Note:*** In most cases, *network sniffer programs* are used to record and decode network packets — something the highly paid network analysts at your company may use. In this case, we're referring to programs that are designed solely for wireless LANs and that sniff out radio waves and identify available networks.)

We find sniffer programs to be handy because they're a great way to take a quick survey of our surroundings when we're on the road. For example, Pat was recently staying at a hotel that belonged to a chain partnered with Wayport, but Wayport hadn't officially started offering service yet — and the hotel staff was clueless. No problem! A quick session using the Network Stumbler software (see the following subsection), and — lo and behold! — the Wayport access point in the lobby was up and running. With a quick flip of the wallet (to pull out his prepaid card), Pat was up and running on high-speed wireless Internet. Take that, dial-up!

Network sniffer programs are also a good way to help you evaluate the security of your own network. In fact, they're the main reason why the developers of Network Stumbler created the program. After you implement some of the security steps we discuss in Chapter 9, you can fire up your favorite sniffer program and see whether you've been successful.

Netstumbler.com

The granddaddy of wireless network sniffer programs is Network Stumbler (www.netstumbler.com), which is a Windows program (it works with Windows 95, 98, Me, 2000, and XP) that connects to the PC Card network adapter in your laptop and lets you survey the airwaves for available Wi-Fi access points. Network Stumbler lists all available access points and gives you relatively detailed information about things such as the SSID and Media Access Control (MAC) address of the AP, whether WEP is enabled, and the relative power of the signal. You can even combine Network Stumbler with a GPS card in your laptop to figure out exactly where you and the access point are located.

Network Stumbler doesn't work with every Wi-Fi card. You can find a list of compatible cards on the Netstumbler.com Web site.

Figure 16-2 shows Network Stumbler in action in Pat's house, tracking down his two access points (and one of his neighbor's APs, too!).

If you use a Pocket PC handheld computer, the folks at Netstumbler.com have a program for you: Mini Stumbler, available at the same Web site (www.net-stumbler.com). A similar program called MacStumbler (www.macstumbler.com) is available for Mac OS X computers.

In fact, a growing number of these network sniffer programs are available, and most of them are free to download. You can find a list at the Personal Telco Project at http://wiki.personaltelco.net/index.cgi/WirelessSniffer.

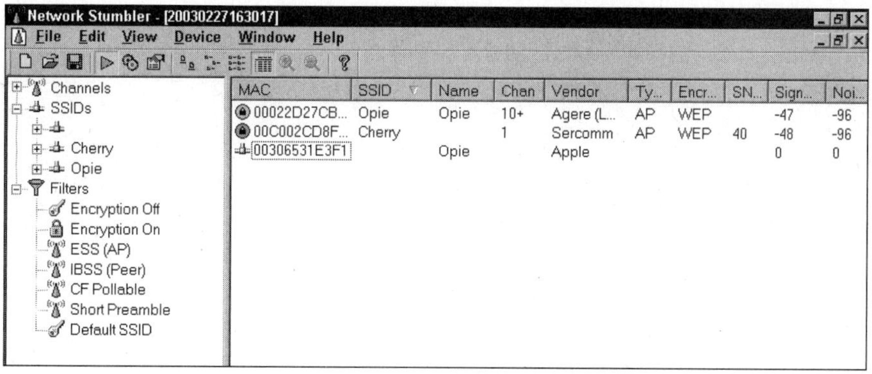

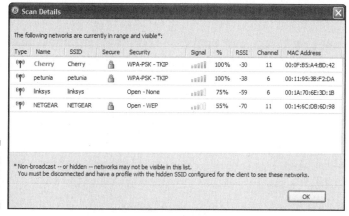

Figure 16-2: Netstumbling Pat's house — lots of access there!

Boingo

You can also use the Boingo client software (available at www.boingo.com) as a network sniffer program (as long as you're using a compatible operating system and network adapter). The primary purpose of this software is to manage your connections to the Boingo network, but Boingo has also designed the software (and encourages the use of it) as a means of finding and connecting to freenets and other public open networks.

You can even use the Boingo software as a manager for all your Wi-Fi network connections. If you have a wireless network at home, one or more in the office, plus some public networks you want to connect to, try out the Boingo software. Figure 16-3 shows the Boingo software in action.

Figure 16-3: Go! Go! Boingo!

Staying Secure in a Hot Spot Environment

As we mention earlier in the chapter, most Wi-Fi hot spots, whether they be free or for pay, utilize no network security and encryption (this is simply because it's easier for users to get online without trying to figure out WPA passphrases and the like). There are some exceptions (for example, T-Mobile uses WPA and 802.1x authentication on their hot spots), but the vast majority of hot spots are completely without encryption.

What this means to you, as a user of a hot spot, is that everything that you send and receive from your laptop is "in the clear." Anyone else in Wi-Fi range could intercept your transmissions and read them. If that doesn't give you pause, it should!

The lack of hot spot encryption also could lead to a situation where you unwittingly log onto a "fake" hot spot with a similar SSID to the one you're trying to log onto. In this *evil twin* attack, some bad person sets up an access point with an SSID such as Starbucks right near the Starbucks where you think you're logging into a T-Mobile hot spot. You log on and they capture everything you do online (for example, online banking and Webmail passwords). Not a good situation.

You can do a few things to secure yourself in a hot spot environment. The first (and best) is to use a Virtual Private Network (or VPN). Using a VPN in a hot spot gives you three distinct benefits:

- A VPN provides security even without airlink encryption (WPA or WEP) by encrypting *all* your inbound and outbound traffic. Even though someone could freely "read" and copy all your Wi-Fi signals, those signals would be protected by the VPN's encryption and would be nothing but gibberish to the end user.

- A VPN provides privacy and anonymity online (even beyond the bounds of the hot spot) by making your public "face" on the Internet an IP address in your VPN provider's network rather than your own IP address. This means that any online tracking (both the benign and the malign kinds) that relies on your IP address would never be able to associate *you* with your actual IP address. This benefit could also apply at home or anywhere you go online.

- A VPN provides you better access to the Internet in locations where certain Web sites or Internet applications (such as VoIP, discussed in Chapter 13) are imposed by the government or other organizations. For example, many western travelers in China find that they can't access Web sites that they normally view (for example, some parts of Wikipedia are blocked). A VPN lets you "tunnel" through national firewalls and do what you want to do on the Internet without being blocked.

Securing your Wi-Fi with WiTopia

Our favorite hosted VPN service comes from the folks at WiTopia, with their Personal VPN service. For $39.99 a year, WiTopia will secure your Wi-Fi traffic by routing it through an encrypted *VPN tunnel,* which keeps your data from prying eyes all the way from your Mac or PC (or iPhone, more on this in a moment) to WiTopia's secure server (from which it then makes its way onto the wild world of the Internet).

You can get two types of VPNs from WiTopia:

- An SSL VPN, which uses the same technology (secure sockets layer) that secure Web pages use to encrypt all your data traffic.

- A PPTP VPN, which uses the same technology used by many big corporations in their VPNs. (PPTP stands for point to point tunneling protocol.)

The SSL VPN has been WiTopia's traditional product, built around an open source software effort called (appropriately) OpenVPN (www. openvpn.net). The WiTopia folks added PPTP VPN support in 2007 as a way of adding support for even more clients, including the famous Apple iPhone. Mac and Windows users can download the OpenVPN software from WiTopia's Web site; for PPTP VPNs, users simply take advantage of the PPTP VPN client software built into most operating systems (including Windows XP and beyond, Mac OS X, and Apple's version of OS X for the iPhone and iPod Touch).

As we write, WiTopia is offering users a choice of either VPN system for $39.99 a year, but eventually they plan to sell different versions of Personal VPN at different prices for the PPTP and SSL variants. Either way, it's a good deal and a great way to secure your network.

Many corporations provide VPN services for their remote (work at home) and mobile workers. If yours does, make sure you use it in hot spots. If you don't have access to a corporate VPN, consider subscribing to a VPN service such as WiTopia's Personal VPN (www.witopia.net) or HotSpotVPN (www.hotspotvpn.com). These are *hosted* VPN services, which provide you with a secure and reliable VPN solution over the Internet for a monthly or annual fee. For more information about WiTopia, check out the sidebar titled "Securing your Wi-Fi with WiTopia."

If you can't (or don't want to) bother with a VPN service in unsecured hot spots, you should practice safe browsing. That means you should pay close attention to the SSID you are connecting to and make sure it is the one you mean to connect to. Don't connect to a free public Wi-Fi network unless that's actually the SSID advertised for the hot spot you're in!

You should also use secured/encrypted connections whenever possible. That means, for example, connecting to secure Web pages and checking your browser to make sure you have actually done so whenever you're doing something sensitive online (such as online banking or even e-mail). Make sure that you are connected to a Web site with an *https* rather than *http* prefix to the URL. When you're on the secured site, click the lock icon in your browser (it's typically up in the address bar of your browser, or in the bottom-right corner on the status bar, depending on which browser you're using). Check the certificate that pops up and make sure the name of the business in the certificate is the one you think you're connected to.

If you use Google's Gmail service (http://mail.google.com), navigate to the site using https (in other words, go to https://mail.google.com) and you'll be securely connected to it.

If your ISP supports it, you can also configure your e-mail client to use a secure login, so when you download e-mail you'll be using an encrypted connection. How you set this up depends on both your e-mail client and your ISP's configuration, so search your ISP's Web site support section for "Secure IMAP" or "Secure POP."

No matter what you do for security in a hot spot, always be aware that you are in a *public* place using unsecured airwaves. People can eavesdrop on your Wi-Fi signal and they can probably also "shoulder surf" and just read your screen. Keep that in mind!

Dealing with Hot Spots on Mobile Devices

A number of mobile devices — by that we mean smartphones and PDAs — are now equipped with built-in Wi-Fi capabilities. You can also find Wi-Fi built into handheld gaming devices (such as the Nintendo DS), in music/video players such as Apple's iPod Touch and Microsoft's Zune, and in VoIP and Skype phones (as discussed in Chapter 13).

Due to the portable nature of these devices, you'll find that you're *more* likely to have them tucked away in your pocketbook (or "man purse" . . . oops, we mean trendy messenger bag) when hot spot access is available.

Getting online with one of these devices is easy when there's an open hot spot available to you. In fact, most of them will automatically associate with the hot spot and get you online. (***Note:*** How this works is a device-by-device process, so read the manual if you don't know how to connect to a Wi-Fi network with your particular portable device.)

Where this process gets to be a bit difficult is when you're in a location that requires you to register to get online (either as a way of making a payment or just to register with a free hot spot for access). Typically, hot spots that require registration do so in one of two ways:

✔ **Using a captive portal:** A *captive portal* is a system that automatically directs you to a registration Web page before allowing you unfettered access to the Internet over a hot spot connection. This process works fine *if* your mobile device has a built-in Web browser but is stopped dead in its tracks if you're using a device without a Web browser (such as a Wi-Fi Skype phone).

Not all mobile device Web browsers support captive portal systems, usually due to a lack of JavaScript functionality in the browser.

✔ **Using client software:** A smaller number of hot spots require (or offer as an option) a software client that handles user authentication and authorization. With a client installed on your device, you can bypass the requirement to load a Web page and get yourself on the network without the hassle. For example, Boingo offers client software for Windows Mobile and Nokia Series 60 smartphones, as does Boingo's partner Skype (this software allows you to make free or inexpensive calls using Wi-Fi rather than your cellular connection).

So the bottom line here is that you'll need either a Web browser, a special bit of client software, or an open hot spot to get online with your mobile device. We wish we had a better answer here, but, in fact, this is a major issue in the hot spot industry today.

On the Go with EV-DO!

If you're a wireless power user — and you tend to travel on the main thoroughfares and metro areas — you may be interested in another on-the-road option (heck, you can even use it while you're at home!) for wireless connectivity: wireless WAN services. These *wireless wide area network services* are offered by cellular carriers in more and more places around the United States as they build out their networks for the next generation of audio and video (yes, TV on your phone) services.

Wireless WAN services come in different flavors depending on the technology each carrier is deploying and where each flavor is available. Some of the most common of these connections are

✔ **1xRTT:** Stands for *single carrier (1x) radio transmission technology,* a 3G (third-generation) wireless technology based on the *CDMA* (code division multiple access, if you must know) platform. (1xRTT is also referred to as *CDMA2000.*) 1xRTT has the capability to provide speeds of as much as 144 Kbps (but usually in the 60 Kbps–90 Kbps range). Carriers such as Sprint and Verizon offer this service.

- ✔ **EV-DO:** Stands for *Evolution Data Only.* This CDMA-based wireless data platform, the fastest wireless WAN technology available on the mass market, is capable of transmitting more than 2 Mbps, but typically is in the 400 Kbps–700 Kbps range. It's offered by Sprint and Verizon.

- ✔ **GPRS/EDGE:** The competitor to CDMA is a European standard named *Group System for Mobile Communications,* or *GSM* for short. The high-speed WAN version of GSM is called *GPRS* (General Packet Radio Service) and is offered by AT&T and T-Mobile in the United States. GPRS is often described as 2.5G — that is, a technology between the second (2G) and third (3G) generations of mobile telephony. Although speeds can theoretically top 170 Kbps, a more likely range is 30 Kbps–70 Kbps — not that fast. A slightly faster version, called *EDGE,* is widely available across the United States as well.

- ✔ **HSDPA:** The 3G variant of CDMA, as we mention earlier, is EV-DO; GSM has its own 3G variant called *HSDPA* (High Speed Downlink Packet Access). HSDPA offers download speeds as fast as 3.6 Mbps and is widely available in Europe but less so (to date) in the U.S. AT&T has launched the service in several cities and should eventually reach all its major markets with the service (we'd guess by the end of 2008).

- ✔ **WiMAX:** The up-and-coming wireless WAN technology is called *WiMAX* (Worldwide Interoperability for Microwave Access), which some people believe could act as your home's broadband connection, too, because it can hit speeds of up to 70 Mbps! Wow, we can't wait. Look for actual services you can purchase based on WiMAX starting in 2008.

Using these data services on your laptop is easy. You just plug your PC Card or Express card into your laptop (just like an 802.11 PC Card or Express card) and launch your carrier's cellular access program. You're online, surfing away.

Wireless WAN chips are starting to ship in laptops now, in the same way that Intel seeded the growth of the Wi-Fi space with 802.11 capabilities embedded on the motherboard (with its Centrino products). So you can, if you want to, order a Dell or Sony laptop with Verizon EV-DO on board (Wi-Fi too!) — no hassling with PC Cards any more!

Of course it's not just laptops that can utilize these services. Most new phones (and all new smartphones) have at least a built-in 2.5G data capability. Smartphones include e-mail client software, Web browsers, instant messaging client software, and more. Plus, in many cases, you can connect your phone to your laptop using a USB cable or a Bluetooth connection (see Chapter 15 for more on Bluetooth) and use the phone as a broadband wireless modem for your laptop computer.

The biggest issues for these services are now cost (an unlimited plan sets you back $60–$80 per month, and that's on top of whatever you pay for your mobile voice services) and availability (mostly in the major metro areas and on interstate highways). Still, if you can get it, it's great. We love our Sprint EV-DO service!

Part V
The Part of Tens

The 5th Wave   By Rich Tennant

"We take network security here very seriously."

In this part . . .

*P*art V is the one you've been waiting for, right? We
have four top-ten lists here that we hope you will find
interesting as well as helpful: ten frequently asked questions about wireless home networking; ten ways to
improve the performance of your wireless home network;
and ten way-cool devices that you will (eventually)
connect to your wireless home network; and ten sources
for additional info on wireless networking.

Chapter 17

Ten FAQs about Wireless Home Networks

*W*ireless networks are increasingly easy to set up, configure, and connect to. But they are far from foolproof and dead simple. Despite some great efforts by vendors and industry organizations to simplify the wireless buying, installing, and using experience, things can get a bit confusing, even to those in the know.

In this chapter, we look at ten issues we hear the most often when friends and family ask us for help with getting started in the wireless LAN world. We talked to our helpful friends at several of the most popular vendors of wireless networking equipment and asked them what *they* hear (or what their customer service reps, sales partners, and others close to real-life users hear). Here's what we have put together (we spend the rest of the chapter answering these questions, by the way!):

✔ Which standard is right for me?

✔ Should I invest in 802.11g or draft 802.11n?

- ✔ I can connect to the Internet by using an Ethernet cable but not by using my wireless local area network (LAN). What am I doing wrong?
- ✔ How do I get my video games to work on my wireless LAN?
- ✔ My videoconferencing application doesn't work. What do I do?
- ✔ How do I secure my network from hackers?
- ✔ What is firmware, and why might I need to upgrade it?
- ✔ Isn't Network Address Translation (NAT) the same as a firewall?
- ✔ How can I find out my Internet Protocol (IP) address?
- ✔ If everything stops working, what can I do?

If you don't see in this list the particular question you're asking, we recommend that you at least skim through this chapter anyway. You never know: You may find your answer lurking where you least expect it, or you may come across a tidbit of information that may come in handy later. And, throughout this chapter, we also steer you to where in the book we further discuss various topics — which may in turn lead you to your answer (or to other tidbits of information that come in handy later). What we're saying is that reading this chapter can only help you. Also check out Chapter 18, where we give you some troubleshooting tips.

If you're new to *Wireless Home Networking For Dummies,* this chapter is a great place to start because you get a good overview to the things many people ask (when they haven't read the manual or this book!), and you can get to some meat (we hope you're not vegetarian!) of the issues surrounding wireless. Don't feel bad if you feel like you're reading the book backward. Just don't read it upside down.

We firmly believe in the power of the Web and of using vendor Web sites for all they're worth. Support is a critical part of this process. When you're deciding on a particular piece of equipment for your home network, take a look at the support area on the vendor site for that device. Look at the frequently asked questions (FAQs) for the device; you may find some of those hidden gotchas that you wish you had known about *before* buying the gear.

Q: Which standard is right for me?

As we discuss in Chapters 2 and 4 (among other places), several standardized version of Wi-Fi wireless network exist: 802.11b, 802.11a, 802.11g, and 802.11n. When you shop for wireless networking equipment, you find that the vast majority of wireless gear on the market is based on the 802.11g standard. That's a good thing because it makes it easier to choose gear — we absolutely recommend that you choose equipment that's compatible with (and Wi-Fi certified for) 802.11n. Notice we did not say 802.11g (no, it's not a typo). 802.11n draft 2 equipment is fully compatible with 802.11g equipment and will fully replace 802.11g within the next year or two.

The bottom line is that 802.11n is not only a safe recommendation but also a good one. Although it's far from perfect (the state of the art *always* moves forward), 802.11n provides a combination of range, compatibility, and speed that makes it good enough for most people. You are not going to find more speed or range than 802.11n draft 2 systems offer.

Q: Should I consider buying one of the enhanced 802.11g (Turbo, MIMO, or Pre-N) systems rather than standard 802.11n?

Before the current draft 2 802.11n systems hit the market in 2007, most manufacturers launched Wi-Fi products that were faster (and longer range) than standard 802.11g systems and used proprietary (meaning not standards-based) variations of 802.11g. These systems are often labeled with marketing terms such as Turbo, MIMO, or something similar (every manufacturer uses a different term) that indicates these are 802.11g routers on steroids.

We've used a number of these systems, and for the most part they work well, *when they are used in a network of the same equipment.* In other words, these systems work well in a network in which everything (routers, adapters, and so on) is from that same manufacturer using the same proprietary technology. These systems also work fine with standard 802.11g (or even 802.11b) equipment, but the full range and speed benefits are realized only in a homogeneous network.

Our only problem with these systems comes into play when we look forward. 802.11n systems are now on the marketplace, offering similar or greater speed and range benefits, and these benefits will work with *any* other 802.11n certified gear, from any manufacturer. So if you choose an 802.11n system instead of one of these proprietary systems, and then buy a new laptop next year (with built-in 802.11n), you'll be able to get the extra speed and range on that laptop without buying any extra equipment (which may or may not be available at that point).

 We think that manufacturers are still selling enhanced 802.11g gear mainly to continue supporting customers who've invested in these technologies over the past few years. If you're building a new network, it makes a lot of sense to invest the small extra amount in an 802.11n system instead of in one of these older systems.

Q: I can connect to the Internet by using an Ethernet cable but not by using my wireless LAN. What am I doing wrong?

You're almost there. The fact that everything works for one configuration but not for another rules out many problems. As long as your AP and router are the same device (which is most common), you know that the AP can talk to your Internet gateway (whether it's your cable modem, digital subscriber line [DSL] modem, or dial-up routers, for example). You know that because, when you're connected via Ethernet, there's no problem. The problem is then relegated to being between the AP and the client on the PC.

Most of the time, this is a configuration issue dealing with your service set identifier (SSID) and your security configurations with Wi-Fi Protected Access (WPA2) or Wired Equivalent Privacy (WEP). Your SSID denotes your service area ID for your LAN, and your WEP controls your encryption keys for your data packets. Without both, you can't decode the signals traveling through the air.

Bring up your wireless configuration program, as we discuss in Chapter 7, and verify again that your SSID is set correctly and your WPA2 passphrase or WEP key is correct. Most configuration programs will find all the wireless transmitters in your area. If you don't see yours, you have set up your AP in stealth mode so it does not broadcast its name. If that's the case, you can try typing the word **any** into the SSID to see whether it finds the AP, or you can go back to your AP configuration using a wired connection and copy the SSID from the AP's configuration screen — keep in mind that SSIDs are case sensitive.

If neither of those issues is the problem, borrow a friend's laptop with a compatible wireless connection to see whether his or her card can find and sign on to your LAN when empowered with the right SSID and WPA2 or WEP code. If it can, you know that your client card may have gone bad.

If a card (or any electronics, generally speaking) is going to go bad, most have technical problems within the first 30 days.

If your friend's PC cannot log on, the problem may be with your AP. At this point, we have to say "Check the vendor's Web site for specific problem-solving ideas and call its tech-support number for further help."

Q: How do I get my video games to work on my wireless LAN?

This question has an easy answer and a not-so-easy answer. The easy answer is that you can get your Xbox, PlayStation 2, or GameCube onto your wireless LAN by linking the Ethernet port on your gaming device (if necessary, by purchasing a network adapter kit to add an Ethernet port on your system) with a wireless bridge — which gets your gaming gear onto your wireless network in an easy fashion. You just need to be sure to set your bridge to the same SSID and WEP key or WPA passphrase as your LAN.

That's the easy part, and you should now be able to access the Internet from your box.

The tough part is allowing the Internet to access your gaming system. This requirement applies to certain games, two-way voice systems, and some aspects of multiplayer gaming. You may need to open certain ports in your router to enable those packets bound for your gaming system to get there. This process is called *port forwarding* (or something like that — vendors love to name things differently among themselves). Port forwarding basically says to the router that it should block all packets from accessing your system except those with certain characteristics that you identify. (These types of data packets can be let through to your gaming server.) We talk a great deal about this topic in Chapter 11, in the section about dealing with port forwarding, so be sure to read up on that before tinkering with your router configuration.

If this process is too complex to pull off with your present router, consider just setting up a demilitarized zone (DMZ) for your gaming application, where your gaming console or PC sits fairly open to the Internet. (We discuss setting up a DMZ in Chapter 11.) This setup isn't a preferred one, however, for security reasons, and we recommend that you try to get port forwarding to work.

Our esteemed tech editor has a great suggestion if you're having issues with port forwarding: a Web site called www.portforward.com. Check it out!

Q: My videoconferencing application doesn't work. What do I do?

In some ways, videoconferencing is its own animal in its own world. Videoconferencing has its own set of standards that it follows; typically has specialized hardware and software; and, until recently, has required special telephone lines to work.

The success of the Internet and its related protocols has opened up videoconferencing to the mass market with IP standards-based Web cameras and other software-based systems becoming popular.

Still, if you have installed a router with the appropriate protection from the Internet bad guys, videoconferencing can be problematic for all the same reasons as in gaming, which we mention in the preceding section. You need to have packets coming into your application just as much as you're sending packets out to someone else.

Wait a minute. You may be thinking "Data packets come into my machine all the time (like when I download Web pages), so what are you saying?" Well, those packets are requested, and the router in your AP (or your separate router, if that's how your network is set up) knows that they're coming and lets them through. Videoconferencing packets are often unrequested, which makes the whole getting-through-the-router thing a bit tougher.

As such, the answer is the same as with gaming. You need to open ports in your router (called port forwarding) or set up your video application in a DMZ. Again, Chapter 11 can be a world of help here.

Q: How do I secure my network from hackers?

Nothing is totally secure from anything. The adage "Where there's a will, there's a way" tends to govern most discussions about someone hacking into your LAN. We tend to fall back on this one instead: Unless you have some major, supersecret hidden trove of something on your LAN that many people would simply kill to have access to, the chances of a hacker spending a great deal of time to get on your LAN is minimal. This statement means that as long as you do the basic security enhancements we recommend in Chapter 9, you should be covered. This does not mean you are safe from maliciousness. Even if hackers care nothing for the contents of your computer, they care a lot about using the processing power of that computer for their own ends. Nasty software called viruses, or Trojans, can get to your computer in many ways. These programs give hackers control of your computer unbeknownst to you so they do other more malicious things such as sending more spam e-mail or infecting more machines.

You can secure the following parts of your network by taking the following actions:

- **Your Internet connection:** You should turn on, at minimum, whatever firewall protection your router offers. If you can, choose a router that has stateful packet inspection (SPI). You should also use antivirus software and seriously consider using personal firewall software on your PCs. Using a firewall in both your router and on your PC is defense in depth: After the bad guys get by your router firewall's Maginot line, you have extra guns to protect your PCs. (For a little historical perspective on defense strategies, read up on Maginot and his fortification.)

- **Your airwaves:** Because wireless LAN signals can travel right through your walls and out the door, you should strongly consider turning on WPA2 (and taking other measures, which we discuss in Chapter 9) to keep the next-door neighbors from snooping on your network.

Q: What is firmware, and why might I need to upgrade it?

Any consumer electronics device is governed by software seated in onboard chip memory storage. When you turn on the device, it checks this memory to find out what to do and loads the software in that area. This software turns the device on and basically tells it how to operate.

This *firmware* can be updated through a process that's specific to each manufacturer. Often, you see options in your software configuration program for checking for firmware upgrades.

Some folks advocate never, ever touching your firmware if you don't need to. Indeed, reprogramming your firmware can upset much of the logical innards of the device you struggled so hard to configure properly in the first place. In fact, you may see advice on a vendor site, such as this statement from the D-Link site: "Do not upgrade firmware unless you are having specific problems." In other words: If it ain't broke, don't fix it. Many times, a firmware upgrade can cause you to lose all customized settings you've configured on your router. Although not all vendor firmware upgrades reset your settings to their defaults, many do. Also, it's always best to do a firmware upgrade with a *wired* connection to the router — if you lose the wireless signal during the upgrade, you could be forced to totally reset your router — the router might even become inoperable. Be careful!

Despite those warnings, we say "Never say never." Most AP and router vendors operate under a process of continuous improvement, by adding new features and fixing bugs regularly. One key way that you can keep current with these standards is by upgrading your firmware. Over time, your wireless network will fall out of sync with the latest bug fixes and improvements, and you will have to upgrade at some point. When you do so, follow all the manufacturer's warnings.

In Chapter 9, we discuss Wi-Fi Protected Access 2 (WPA-2). Many older APs and network adapters will be able to use WPA-2, but only after their firmware has been upgraded.

Q: Is NAT the same as a firewall?

If you find networking confusing, you're not alone. (If it were easy, we would have no market for our books!) One area of confusion is Network Address Translation (NAT). No, NAT isn't the same as a firewall. It's important to understand the difference to make sure that you set up your network correctly. Firewalls provide a greater level of security than NAT routers and, thanks to dropping hardware costs, are generally available in all routers these days. The quality of the firewall built into your AP is not necessarily related to the price of the AP. We recommend checking the reviews of any hardware you are looking to purchase from sites such as www.cnet.com.

Often, you hear the term *firewall* used to describe a router's ability to protect LAN IP addresses from Internet snoopers. But a true firewall goes deeper than that, by using SPI. SPI allows the firewall to look at each IP address and domain requesting access to the network; the administrator can specify certain IP addresses or domain names that are allowed to be let in while blocking any other attempt to access the LAN. (Sometimes you hear this called *filtering.*)

Firewalls can also add another layer of protection through a Virtual Private Network (VPN). It enables remote access to the private network through the use of secure logins and authentication. Finally, firewalls can help protect your family from unsavory content by enabling you to block content from certain sites.

Firewalls go well beyond NAT, and we highly recommend that you have a firewall in your home network. Check out Chapter 9 for more information on firewalls.

Q: How can I find out my IP address?

First off, you have two IP addresses: a public IP address and a private IP address. In some instances, you need to know one or the other or both addresses.

Your *private* IP address is your IP address on your LAN so that your router knows where to send traffic in and among LAN devices. If you have a LAN printer, that device has its own IP address, as does any network device on your LAN.

The address these devices have, however, is rarely the public IP address (the address is the "Internet phone number" of your network), mostly because public IP addresses are becoming scarce. Your Internet gateway has a public IP address for your home. If you want to access from a public location a specific device on your home network, you typically have to enable port forwarding in your router and then add that port number on the end of your public IP address when you try to make a connection. For example, if you had a Web server on your network, you would type the address 68.129.5.29:80 into your browser when you tried to access it remotely — 80 is the port used for HTTP servers.

You can usually find out your wide area network (public IP address) and LAN (private IP address) from within your router configuration software or Web page, such as http://192.168.1.100. You may see a status screen; this common place shows your present IP addresses and other key information about your present Internet connection.

If you have Windows XP, you can find your computer's private IP address by choosing Start⇨Run. When the Run dialog box pops up, type **cmd** and then click OK. In the window that opens, type **ipconfig** at the command prompt and then press Enter. You see your IP address and a few other network parameters.

If you have Windows Vista, you can find your private IP by clicking the Windows icon (where the Start button used to be in Windows XP), choosing Control Panel, and then choosing Network and Sharing Center. In the Network and Sharing Center, you can access your network status, which will give you your IP address. Keep in mind that Vista security is different from Windows XP. You need to have Administrator access to be able to get to the Network and Sharing Center.

This IP address is your *internal,* or *private,* IP address, not the public address that people on the Internet use to connect to your network. If you try to give this address to someone (perhaps so that they can connect to your computer to do videoconferencing or to connect to a game server you're hosting), it doesn't work. You need the public IP address that you find in the configuration program for your access point or router. A number of Web sites are available to help you determine your *external,* or public, IP address (for example, whatismyip.com).

Q: If everything stops working, what can I do?

The long length of time it can take to get help from tech support these days leads a lot of people to read the manual, check out the Web site, and work hard to debug their situation. But what happens if you have tried everything and it's still a dead connection — and tech support agrees with you?

In these instances, your last resort is to reset the system back to its factory defaults and start over. Typically you reset your router by pressing a small, recessed button on the back or bottom of the router. (Check your router's manual — you may have to do this step for a particular length of time, or with another step such as unplugging and replugging the power cord on your router.) If you do this, be sure to upgrade your firmware while you're at it because it resets your variables anyway. Who knows? The more recent firmware update may resolve some issues that could be causing the problems.

Resetting your device is considered a drastic action and should be taken only after you have tried everything else. Make sure that you at least get a tech-support person on the phone to confirm that you *have* tried everything and that a reset makes sense.

Chapter 18

Ten Ways to Troubleshoot Wireless LAN Performance

Although troubleshooting any piece of network equipment can be frustrating, troubleshooting wireless equipment is a little more so because there's so much that you just can't check. After all, radio waves are invisible. That's the rub with improving the throughput (performance) of your wireless home network, but we're here to help. And don't get hung up on the term *throughput* (the effective speed of your network); when you take into account retransmissions attributable to errors, you find that the amount of data moving across your network is *lower* than the *nominal* speed of your network. For example, your PC may tell you that you're connected at 54 Mbps, but because of retransmissions and other factors, you may be sending and receiving data at about half that speed.

The trick to successfully troubleshooting anything is to be logical and systematic. First, be logical. Think about the most likely issues (no matter how improbable) and work from there. Second, be systematic. Networks are complicated things, which mandate a focus on sequential troubleshooting on your part. Patience is a virtue when it comes to network debugging.

Perhaps hardest of all is making sense of performance issues — the subject of this chapter. First, you can't get great performance reporting from consumer-level access points, or APs. (The much more expensive ones sold to businesses are better at that.) Even so, debugging performance based on performance data in arrears is tough. Fixing performance issues is a trial-and-error, real-time process. At least most wireless client devices have some sort of signal-strength meter, which is one of the best sources of information you can get to help you understand what's happening.

Signal-strength meters (which are usually part of the software included with your wireless gear) are the best way to get a quick read on your network. These signal-strength meters are used by the pros, says Tim Shaughnessy at NETGEAR: "I would highlight it as a tool." We agree.

It's a good idea to work with a friend or family member. Your friend can be in a poor reception "hole" with a notebook computer and the wireless utility showing the signal strength. You can try moving or configuring the access point to see what works. Just be patient — the signal meter may take a few seconds to react to changes (count to ten after each change, it's what we do to make sure we are not rushing the process).

Because not all performance issues can be tracked down (at least not easily), in this chapter we introduce you to the most common ways to improve the performance of your wireless home network. We know that these are tried-and-true tips because we have tried them ourselves. We're pretty good at debugging this stuff by now. We just can't seem to figure out when it's not plugged in! (Well, Pat can't. Read the "Check the obvious" sidebar to see what we mean.)

Move the Access Point

A wireless signal degrades with distance. You may find that the place you originally placed your access point, or AP, doesn't really fit with your subsequent real-world use of your wireless local area network. A move may be in order.

After your AP is up and working, you will probably forget about it — people often do. APs can often be moved around and even shuffled aside by subsequent gear. Because the access connection is still up (that is to say, working), sometimes people don't notice that the AP's performance degrades when you hide it more or move it around.

Check the obvious

Sometimes, what's causing you trouble is something simple — which you can fix simply. For example, one of us (and we won't say who — *Pat*) was surprised that his access point just stopped working one day. The culprit was his beagle, Opie, who had pulled the plug out of the wall. As obvious as this sounds, it took the unnamed person *(Pat)* an hour to figure it out. Now, if someone told you, "Hey, the AP just stopped working," you would probably say "Is it plugged in?" The moral: Think of the obvious and check it first.

Here are a few more "obvious" things to check:

Problem: The power goes out and then comes back on. Different equipment takes different lengths of time to reset and restart, which causes the loss of connectivity and logical configurations on your network.

Solution: Sometimes, you need to turn off all your devices. Leave them all off for a minute or two, and then turn them all back on, working your way from the Internet connection to your computer — from the wide area network (WAN) connection (your broadband modem, for example) back to your machine. This process allows each device to start up with everything upstream properly in place and turned on.

Problem: Your access point is working fine, with great throughput and a strong signal footprint, until one day it all just drops off substantially. No hardware problem. No new interferers installed at home. No new obstructions. No changes of software. Nothing. The cause: Your next-door neighbor got an access point and is using his on the same channel as yours.

Solution: This problem is hard to debug in the first place. How the heck do you find out who is causing invisible interference — by going door to door? "Uh, pardon me; I'm going door to door to try to debug interferers on my access point. Are

you suddenly emitting any extraneous radio waves? No, I'm not wearing an aluminum foil hat. Why?" Often, when debugging performance issues, you need to try many of the one-step solutions, such as changing channels, to see whether they have an effect. If you can find the solution, you have a great deal of insight into what the problem was. (If changing channels solved the problem, someone nearby was probably using the same channel, and you can then start tracking down who that is!)

The wireless utility for the adapter may have a tab, called a *site survey* or *station list*, that lists the APs in range. The tab may show your neighbor's access point and the channel it's on.

APs that follow the 802.11n draft 2.0 standard dynamically switch channels when there's too much interference. The 802.11n equipment we have seen does not even give you an option to choose a channel because of this dynamic switching capability. Keep in mind that the higher speed of these APs is achieved by combining channels so they can send and receive data on more than one channel at a time and can use more than one antenna to send and receive data. To take full advantage of the dynamic nature of 802.11n, you need an 802.11n AP or router as well as an 802.11n network adapter in your computer.

Before you chase a performance issue, make sure that you *have* one. The advertised rates for throughput for the various wireless standards are misleading. What starts out at 54 Mbps for 802.11g is really more like a maximum of 36 Mbps in practice (and less as distance increases). For 802.11n, it's more like 125 Mbps at best, rather than the 248 Mbps you hear bandied about. You *occasionally* see high levels (like when you're within a few yards of the access point), but that's rare. The moral: If you think that you should be getting 248 Mbps but you're getting only 100 Mbps, consider yourself lucky — very lucky.

Speed: What to expect

Many of the newest technologies use multiple methods to greatly increase the effective speed and range of wireless connections. Unfortunately, much of that speed boost can be lost if you're in an area with lots of radio interference. If you have lots of noise in the area or many networks fighting for open channels, the base speed of what you're using — 54 Mbps for n and 11 Mbps for g — is the best you can hope for.

Make sure that other gear isn't blocking your AP, that it isn't flush against a wall (which can cause interference), that its vertical orientation isn't too close to the ground (more interference), and that it isn't in the line of sight of radio wave interference (such as from microwaves and cordless phones). Even a few inches can make a difference. The best location is in the center of your desired coverage area (remember to think in three dimensions!) and on top of a desk or bookcase. For more about setting up APs, check out Chapter 6.

Move the Antenna

Remember the days before everyone had cable or satellite TV? There was a reason why people would fiddle with the rabbit ears on a TV set — they were trying to get the antenna into the ideal position to receive signals. Whether the antenna is on the client or on the access point, the same concept applies: Moving the antenna can yield results. Because different antennas have different signal coverage areas, reorienting them in different declinations (or angles relative to the horizon) changes their coverage patterns. A strong signal translates to better throughput and performance.

Look at it this way: The antenna creates a certain footprint of its signal. If you're networking a multistory home and you're not getting a great signal upstairs, try shifting your antenna to a 45° angle, to increase a more vertical signal — that is, to send more signal to the upstairs and downstairs and less horizontally.

Change Channels

Each access point broadcasts its signals over portions of the wireless frequencies called *channels*. The 802.11g standard (the most common system at the time we wrote this chapter) defines 11 channels in the United States that overlap considerably, leaving only 3 channels that don't overlap with each other. The IEEE 802.11a standard specifies 12 (although most current products support only 8) nonoverlapping channels. The 802.11n draft 2.0 proposal uses the same 11 channels as 802.11g at 2.4 GHz and the 12 channels of 802.11a at 5 GHz in the United States, again with overlapping channels.

802.11n is designed to work with all the previous standards. The dynamic switching of channels on either frequency available to it means you have a lot less to configure during setup. Some single-frequency APs still give you the option to choose channels at the beginning, but they don't necessarily have to stay on that channel as they work.

This situation affects your ability to have multiple access points in the same area, whether they're your own or your neighbors'. Because channels can overlap, you can have the resulting interference. For 802.11g access points that are within range of each other, set them to different channels, five apart from each other (such as 1, 6, and 11), to avoid inter-access point interference. We discuss the channel assignments for wireless LANs further in Chapter 6.

Check for Dual-Band Interference

Despite the industry's mad rush to wirelessly enable every networkable device it makes, a whole lot hasn't been worked through yet, particularly interoperability. We're not talking about whether one vendor's 802.11g PC Card works with another vendor's 802.11g access point — the Wi-Fi interoperability tests usually make sure that's not a problem (unless one of your products isn't Wi-Fi certified). Instead, we're talking about having Bluetooth (see Chapter 15 for more on this technology) working in the same area as 802.11b, g, and n, or having older 802.11a APs and 802.11b, g, and n APs operating in the same area. In some instances, like the former example, Bluetooth and 802.11b, g, and n operate in the same frequency range, and therefore have some potential for interference. Because 802.11a and 802.11b, g, and n operate in separate frequency bands, they're less likely to be exposed to interference.

Some issues also exist with how the different standards are implemented in different products. Some APs that support 802.11g and n, for example, really support one or the other — not both simultaneously. If you have all g in your house, that's great. If you have all n, that's great. If you have some n and the access point detects that g is in the house, it could downshift to g rates. You may be all set, but then your neighbor upstairs may buy a g network adapter (because you've said "Sure, no problem, you can share my Internet connection."). He's not only freeloading, but he also could be forcing your whole access point to shift down to the lower speeds.

To be fair, many of these very early implementation issues have gone away while vendors refined their solutions. Check out how any multimode access point that you buy handles dealing with more than one variant of 802.11 at the same time. Most newer APs compartmentalize their signals so that they can allow the faster 802.11n signals to connect at full (or nearly full) speed, while still allowing older 802.11g signals on the network, which is very nice and almost necessary.

Check for New Obstacles

Wireless technologies are susceptible to physical obstacles. In Chapter 4, Table 4-1 tells you the relative attenuation of your wireless signals (radio frequency, or RF) as they move through your house. One person in our neighborhood noticed a gradual degradation of his wireless signal outside his house, where he regularly sits and surfs the Net (by his pool). The culprit turned out to be a growing pile of newspapers for recycling. Wireless signals don't like such masses of paper.

Move around your house and think about it from the eyes of Superman, using his X-ray vision to see your access point. If you have a bad signal, think about what's in the way. If the obstacles are permanent, think about using a HomePlug or other powerline networking wireless access point (which we discuss in Chapter 3) to go around the obstacle by putting an access point on either side of the obstacle.

Another way to get around problems with obstacles is to switch technologies. In some instances, 802.11n products could provide better throughput and reach than your old 802.11g when it comes to obstacles. Many draft 2.0 products use special radio transmission techniques that help focus the signal into the areas containing your wireless client devices. These aimed signals can help you overcome environments that just don't work with regular Wi-Fi gear. If you're in a dense environment with lots of clutter and you're using 802.11g, switching to 802.11n may provide some relief.

Install Another Antenna

In Chapter 5, we point out that a detachable antenna is a great idea because you may want to add an antenna to achieve a different level of coverage in your home. Different antennas yield different signal footprints. If your access point is located at one end of the house, putting an omnidirectional antenna on that access point is a waste because more than half the signal may prove to be unusable. A directional antenna better serves your home.

Antennas are inexpensive relative to their benefits and can more easily help you accommodate signal optimization because you can leave the access point in the same place and just move the antenna around until you get the best signal. In a home, there's not a huge distance limitation on how far away the antenna can be from the access point.

802.11n systems, with their special MIMO transmission technologies, are typically designed to use only the antenna that came with the system. You can't just slap any old antenna onto an 802.11n AP or router. For the most part, this isn't a problem, simply because 802.11n has significantly better range than older systems such as 802.11g.

Use a Signal Booster

Signal boosters used to be offered when 802.11g came out a few years ago. The concept was that if you have a big house (or lots of interference), you can add a *signal booster,* which essentially turns up the volume on your wireless home network transmitter. Unfortunately, it does nothing for the wireless card in your computer, and that was the great failing in this product. Your base station would be stronger, but your workstation's signal would be the same. So, you could see your base station better, but couldn't communicate with it any better because your wireless card was at the same signal strength.

A signal booster was supposed to improve the range of your access point. The 802.11g products now typically have a range of 100 to 150 feet indoors mainly because 802.11g products operate at a relatively low frequency. 802.11a products have an even shorter reach — up to 75 feet indoors — because the higher frequencies that 802.11a use lose strength faster with distance than do the lower frequencies used by 802.11g. The 802.11n products from companies such as Belkin reach at least another 25 to 50 feet, and many products using MIMO also achieve better range.

The signal range of the APs now on the market is steadily increasing because manufacturers are creating more efficient transceiver chipsets. We recommend reading the most recent reviews of products because products truly are improving monthly.

You can still find signal boosters for sale on eBay from companies such as Linksys, which sold the WSB24 Wireless Signal Booster that piggybacked onto a Linksys wireless access point (or wireless access point router).

Signal boosters have pretty much been discontinued, and even though your can still get them, we strongly recommend staying away from them because you have many other options that are more versatile and compatible with what you already have and that keep you up-to-date with the newest technologies.

If you happen to come across one of these — or someone gives you one — you should know that signal boosters are *mated* devices, which means they're engineered for specific products. Vendors have to walk a fine line when boosting signals in light of federal limits on the aggregate signal that can be used in the unlicensed frequencies. For example, the Linksys Wireless Signal Booster was certified by the Federal Communications Commission (FCC) for use with the WAP11 Wireless Access Point and BEFW11S4 Wireless Access Point Router only. Linksys says that using the WSB24 with any other product from either Linksys or another vendor voids the user's authority to operate the device.

The main reason that companies such as Linksys sold their signal boosters for use with only their own products is certification issues. The FCC has to approve any radio transmission equipment sold on the market. A great deal of testing must be done for a piece of gear to get certified, and the certification testing must be done for the complete system — and vendors usually do this expensive testing only with their own gear.

As some reviews have pointed out, however, you *could* use the WSB24 with any wireless LAN product that operates in the 2.4 GHz band — notably, 802.11g products. You couldn't use it with 802.11a or any dual-band 2.4/5 GHz products; its design couldn't deal with the higher frequency.

Add an Access Point

Adding another access point (or two) can greatly increase your signal coverage, as shown in Figure 18-1. The great thing about wireless is that it's fairly portable — you can literally plug it in anywhere. The main issues are getting power to it and getting an Ethernet connection (which carries the data) to it.

The first item is usually not a problem because many electrical codes require, in a residence, that power outlets be placed every eight feet. The second issue (getting the Ethernet connection to your AP) used to be a matter of running all sorts of wiring around the house. Depending on the actual throughput you're looking to provide, however, you may be able to set up another AP by using the HomePlug, DS2, or even wireless repeater functionality that we mention in Chapter 3 and elsewhere in this chapter. We don't repeat those options here, but know that you have those options when you're moving away from your office or other place where many of your network connections are concentrated.

After you get the connectivity and power to the place you want, what do you need to consider when you're installing a *second* AP? Choose the right channel: If you have auto channel selection in your AP, you don't need to worry because your AP's smarts handle it for you. If you're setting the channel manually, don't choose the same one that your other AP is set to.

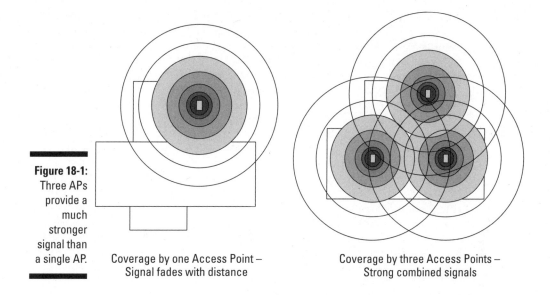

Figure 18-1:
Three APs
provide a
much
stronger
signal than
a single AP.

Coverage by one Access Point –
Signal fades with distance

Coverage by three Access Points –
Strong combined signals

Carefully choose which channels you use for each of your access points. Make sure that you have proper spacing of your channels if you have 802.11g access points (which have overlapping bands). Read the section "Change Channels," earlier in this chapter, for more information on channels.

Add a Repeater or Bridge

Wireless repeaters are an alternative way to extend the range of an existing wireless network instead of adding more APs. We talk earlier in this book (refer to Chapter 2) about the role of bridges and repeaters in a wireless network. The topic of bridges can be complex, and we don't want to rehash it here — be sure to read Chapter 2 for all that juicy detail.

Not many stand-alone repeaters are on the consumer market. However, what's important for our discussion is that repeater capability is finding its way into the AP firmware from many AP vendors. A wireless AP *repeater* basically does double duty — it's an AP as well as a wireless connection back to the main AP that's connected to the Internet connection.

Meraki Networks (meraki.com) has created the Meraki Mini ($50), the ultimate smart AP. If you use one connected to an Ethernet connection from your wireless network, you get a simple wireless AP running 802.11b/g. You add another unit by plugging it into an electrical connection within range of the first unit. The second unit will find the first and, using a sophisticated mesh routing technology, will increase the range of the first AP and increase the capacity as well. Meraki is selling these supersmall APs (about the size of a deck of cards) for communities. While you can buy a couple for yourself, they want to sell these to whole neighborhoods so you and your friends can build your own wireless mesh network. At its most basic level, a repeater simply regenerates a wireless network signal to extend the range of the existing wireless LAN. You set the two devices to the same channel with the same service set identifier (SSID), thus effectively broadening the collective footprint of the signal.

If you have throughput performance issues because of interference or reach, putting an AP into repeating mode may help extend the reach of your network.

However, it's not clear that adding a repeater helps actual throughput in all situations, unfortunately. Some testing labs have cited issues with throughput at the main AP because of interference from the new repeating AP (which is broadcasting on the same channel). Others note that the repeater must receive and retransmit each frame (or burst of data) on the same RF channel, which effectively doubles the number of frames that are sent. This effectively cuts throughput in half. Some vendors have dealt with this through software and claim that it's not an issue.

It's hard at this juncture to make a blanket statement about the basic effectiveness of installing an AP in repeater mode, particularly versus the option of running a high-quality Ethernet cable to a second AP set on a different channel. If you can do the latter, that's preferable.

When you're using the bridging and repeating functions of APs and bridges, we recommend that you use products from the same manufacturer at both ends of the bridge, to minimize any issues between vendors. Most companies support this functionality only between their own products and not across multiple vendors' products.

Check Your Cordless Phone Frequencies

The wireless frequencies at 2.4 GHz and 5.2 GHz are unlicensed (as we define in Part I of this book), which means that you, as the buyer of an AP and operator of a wireless broadcasting capability, don't need to get permission from the FCC to use these frequencies as long as you stay within certain power and usage limitations as set by federal guidelines. It also means that you don't have to pay any money to use the airwaves — because no license is required, it doesn't cost anything.

Many consumer manufacturers have taken advantage of free radio spectrums and created various products for these unlicensed frequencies, such as cordless phones, wireless A/V connection systems, RF remote controls, and wireless cameras.

A home outfitted with a variety of Radio Shack and X10.com gadgets may have a fair amount of radio clutter on these frequencies, which can cut into your network's performance. These sources of RF energy occasionally block users and access points from accessing their shared air medium.

As home wireless LAN use grows, people report more interference with home *X10 networks,* which use various wireless transmitters and signaling over electrical lines to communicate among their connected devices. If you have an X10 network for your home automation and it starts acting weird (such as the lights go on and off and you think your house is haunted), your LAN might be the source of the problem. A strong wireless LAN in your house can be fatal to an X10 network.

At some point, you have to get better control over these interferers, and you don't have many options. First, you can change channels, like we mention earlier in this chapter. Cordless phones, for example, use channels just like your local area network does; you can change them so that they don't cross paths (wirelessly speaking) with your data heading toward the Internet.

Second, you can change phones. If you have an 802.11n or g network operating at home on the 2.4 GHz band, consider one of the newer 5 GHz cordless phones for your house. ***Note:*** An old-fashioned 900 MHz phone doesn't interfere with either one, but finding one these days is a miracle.

You may find that your scratchy cordless phone improves substantially in quality and your LAN performance improves too. Look for other devices that can move to other frequencies or move to your 802.11 network. As we discuss in Chapter 19, all sorts of devices are coming down the road that will work *over* your 802.11 network and not compete with it. Ultimately, you need to keep the airwaves relatively clear to optimize all your performance issues.

At the end of the day, interference from sources outside your house is probably your own fault. If your neighbor asks you how your wireless connection works, lie and tell her that it works horribly. You don't want your neighbor getting one and sending any stray radio waves toward your network. Do the same with cable modems. You don't want your neighbor's traffic slowing you down because it's a shared connection at the neighborhood level. Interference is a sign of popularity — it means that lots of other people have caught on. Keep it your little secret.

Chapter 19

More Than Ten Devices to Connect to Your Wireless Network in the Future

*W*e tell you throughout this book to think about the big picture — to think about more than just networking your home computers. In Chapter 10, we talk about adding various peripheral devices (such as a printer) to your home network. In Chapters 11 and 12, we talk extensively about all the gaming gear and audiovisual equipment that you would want to hook into your wireless home network. In Chapter 13, we talk about using newfangled phone gear over wireless networks. In Chapter 14, you hear about lots of things you can connect today, ranging from cameras to cars.

Clearly, the boom is on among the consumer goods manufacturers to wirelessly network enable everything with wireless processing chips. You get the convenience (and cool factor) of monitoring the health of your gadgets, and vendors want to sell you add-on services to take advantage of that wireless chip. This transformation is happening to everything: clocks, sewing machines, automobiles, toaster ovens — even shoes. If a device can be added to your wireless home network, value-added services can be sold to those who want to track their kids, listen to home-stored music in the car, and know when Fido is in the neighbor's garbage cans again.

In this chapter, we expose you to some things that you could bring to your wireless home network soon. Many of these products already exist. Expect in coming years that they will infiltrate your home. Like the Borg says on *Star Trek,* "Prepare to be assimilated."

Your Bathtub

Yup, wireless toys are everywhere now, having traversed their way into the innermost sanctuary of your home: the bathroom. We're not talking *Psycho*-type shots of people in the shower — we're interested in how to get audio, video, and data into the bathroom so that you can enjoy your privacy even more than you do today.

Not too many homes are wired for computer and video in the bathroom. (We've even seen a creative retrofit solution from Google, jokingly launched on April Fools Day — the Google TiSP service, www.google.com/tisp/index.html). Wireless may be the only way to get signals — like a phone signal — to some of these places. We have seen wireless-enabled toilets (don't ask) and all sorts of wireless controls for lighting in the bathroom to create just the right atmosphere for that bath.

It's the wireless enablement of the bathtub itself that gets us excited. Luxury bathing combined with a home entertainment bathing center in one outfitted bathroom set is probably the ultimate for a wireless enthusiast.

Jacuzzi (www.jacuzzi.com) is the leader in this foray. They have 42-inch plasma TVs in hot tubs and LCDs in the shower. These days, Jacuzzi sells the only wireless waterproof remote control (Aquasound) we've seen, but it's what comes with the remote control that gets us. The Jacuzzi Affinity hot tub (Figure 19-1) comes standard with a built-in stereo/CD system, complete with four speakers as well as an integrated 9-inch television. The multichannel unit is waterproof and includes a remote control. Cable ready, this feature allows you to enjoy the morning news or your favorite movie. A digital control panel offers easy access to the whirlpool operation, underwater lighting, and temperature readout. Talk about wired! All these features cost a mere $12,919 retail, but you can find it for a street price of a mere $7,000 or so. Oh, and you get the hot tub part too — three fixed back jets per person and five fully directional jets around the perimeter.

The problem is that most homes aren't wired for audio or video in their bathroom. That's where your wireless home network comes into play. You can use the same wireless A/V extension devices used to link your PC and your stereo system to reach into the bathroom and bring your Affinity online.

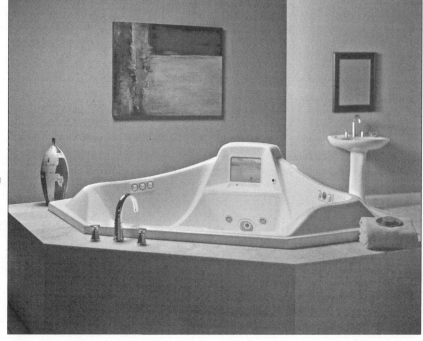

Figure 19-1:
The Jacuzzi
Affinity hot
tub can
add to your
home's
wireless
entertain-
ment.

You can also get wireless speakers designed for the humidity and tempera-
tures found in the bathroom — note that they're water *resistant,* not waterproof, so don't expect to drop them in the water and have them work. You
can, though, check out underwater speakers, like those from Lubell Labs
(www.lubell.com).

You can creatively get wireless into your bathroom in other ways, but you
have to be careful about humidity and exposing electronics directly to water.
Check out what this bloke did in his bathroom: www.chasingparkedcars.
com/bathroom/index.html. We think that there will be more and more retrofit
electronics for the bathroom over time, making it easier to add a TV to your
shower, for instance. The electronic technologies are changing too fast to
embed them into devices such as showers that will be around for 20 years.

Your Car

In Chapter 15, we discuss how cars are sporting Bluetooth interfaces to
enable devices to interact with the car's entertainment and communications
systems. In Chapter 14, we discuss the range of aftermarket devices you
can buy now that provide 802.11-based connectivity between your home's
wireless LAN and your car, whenever it's in range. (We guess that makes your
garage a really big docking station!)

OnStar calling

Car manufacturers are sensing a business opportunity in providing connectivity to your car. Perhaps the most well-known service is OnStar (www.onstar.com), offered on a number of GM and other vehicles. OnStar offers emergency car services, such as the ones from the American Automobile Association (AAA), with GPS and two-way cellular communications thrown in. You can not only make cell phone calls with the system, but also get GM to unlock your car doors. It's a factory-installed-only option, so you can't get it if it's not in your car when you bought it. You have to pay monthly service fees that start at $18.95 per month, or $199.00 per year. You can add turn-by-turn instructions for another $10.00 per month.

Other car manufacturers are following suit. BMW offers the similar BMW Assist, for example. We expect all car manufacturers to offer something similar within a few years — it makes too much sense. Check out some of the short movies on how OnStar has gotten people out of sticky situations at www.onstar.com/us_english/jsp/idemo/index.jsp.

Because most cars already have a massive computing and entertainment infrastructure, reaching out and linking that infrastructure to both the Internet and your wireless home network is simply a no-brainer.

A wireless connection in the car enables you to talk to your car via your wireless network. Now, before you accuse us of having gone loony for talking to our car, think about whether your lights are still on. Wouldn't it be great to check from your 40th-floor apartment rather than head all the way down to the parking garage? Just grab your 802.11g-enabled handheld computer, surf to your car's own Web server, and check whether you left the lights on again. Or perhaps you're filling out a new insurance form and forgot to check the mileage on your car. Click over to the dashboard page and see what it says.

You can also, on request, check out your car's exact location based on GPS readings. (*GPS* is a location-finding system that effectively can tell you where something is, based on its ability to triangulate signals from three or more satellites that orbit the Earth. GPS can usually spot its target within 10–100 meters of the actual location.) You can, again at your request, even allow your dealer to check your car's service status via the Internet. You can also switch on the lights or the auxiliary heating, for example, call up numbers in the car telephone or addresses in the navigation system, and unlock and lock the car — all from the wireless comfort of your couch (using some of those neat touch-panel remote controls that we talk about in Chapter 14). Just grab your wireless Web tablet, surf, and select. Pretty cool. The opportunities to wirelessly connect to your automobile are truly endless.

Your car could also talk to other cars. If all cars were interconnected, information could be daisy-chained from car to car, alerting users of obstructions in the road or braking ahead. (Of course, this would never be used to alert people that police speed traps are ahead!) Expect cars to become outfitted with at least a Wi-Fi bridge on board as a standard offering, driven in part by the increasing availability of Wi-Fi at the city level and at hotspots. The same capabilities that would allow a car to log into a citywide Wi-Fi network would also enable cars to establish peer-to-peer networks, communicating constantly. Once car-to-car communications are established, group viewing, talking, and listening can't be too far away. That'll make those college road trips to the beach more interesting! Products such as Pepwave's CarFi (www.pepwave.com) have no wide area data connections (like the mobile routers we discuss in Chapter 14). They just do Wi-Fi well.

Look for the following near-term applications for wirelessly linking your car to your home:

- ✔ **Vehicle monitoring systems:** These devices — usually mounted under a seat, under the hood, or in the trunk — monitor the speed, acceleration, deceleration, and various other driving and engine performance variables so that you can determine whether your kids are racing down the street after they nicely drive out of your driveway. When your car is parked in your driveway, the information is automatically uploaded to your PC over your wireless home network.

  Devices such as Davis Instruments Corporation's DriveRight (www.davisnet.com, $375) and RoadSafety International's RS-1000 Teen Driver System (www.roadsafety.com, $295) can link to your home's network via any USB wireless client device.

- ✔ **E-commerce:** It's iTunes meets Wi-Fi — you hear a great new song on your radio. Maybe you didn't catch the artist or song title. You push the Buy button on your audio system, which initiates a secure online transaction, and a legal copy of the song is purchased and downloaded to the car at the next wireless hot spot your car senses. From now on, you can listen to the song over and over again, just like you would with a CD. When you get home, you can upload it to your home's audio system. Currently there are *home* HD Radio systems (see Chapter 14 for more on HD Radio) that can support this functionality with an attached iPod and the Apple iTunes Store — we expect that this functionality will move to the car before too long.

- ✔ **Remote control:** Use remote controls for your car to automatically open minivan doors or turn on the lights before you get in. A remote car starter is a treat for anyone who lives in very hot or cold weather (get that heater going before you leave your home). Fancier remote controls, such as the AutoCommand Remote Starters and Security products from DesignTech International (www.designtech-intl.com, around $200), have a built-in car finder capability as well as a remote headlight control. AutoCommand can be programmed to automatically start your vehicle at the same time the next day, at a low temperature, or at a low battery voltage.

Okay, so these aren't necessarily new and don't require a wireless home network. But when you can use wireless networks to connect these devices to the rest of your home's other systems, you can start experiencing a whole home network. Imagine using that wireless connection to link to your home automation system, such as the one we discuss in Chapter 14. When you utter "Start the car," the system communicates with the car and gets it into the right temperature setting — based on the present temperature outside (it gets its readings from its Davis Instruments backyard wireless weather station (www.davisnet.com/weather/products/index.asp).

Look soon for neat combinations between car monitoring systems and the Bluetooth capabilities on cell phones to be able to distinguish which phones (and therefore which people) are traveling around in your car!

Your Home Appliances

Most attempts to converge the Internet and home appliances have been prototypes and concept products — a few products are on the market, but we would be less than honest if we said that the quantities being sold were anything but mass market yet. LGE (www.lge.com) was the first in the world to introduce the Internet refrigerator — a Home Network product with Internet access capability — back in June 2000 (see Figure 19-2). LGE soon introduced other Internet-based information appliance products in the washing machine, air conditioner, and microwave areas. The Internet refrigerator is outfitted with a 15-inch detachable LCD touch screen that serves as a TV monitor, computer screen, stereo, and digital camera all in one. You can call your refrigerator from your cell phone, PDA, or any Internet-enabled device.

LGE also has an Internet air conditioner that allows you to download programs into the device so that you can have preprogrammed cooling times, just like with your heating system setbacks. Talk to your digital home theater to preprogram something stored on your audio server to be playing when you get home. It's all interrelated, by sharing a network in common. Wireless plays a part by enabling these devices to talk to one another in the home.

As of this writing, LGE sells a next-generation multimedia refrigerator (model LSC27991, $3,800) that is more like a TV that happens to have a refrigerator behind it. The refrigerator has two screens, one in each door, and is wirelessly enabled for weather alerts (powered by Ambient Devices' wireless alerting network technology; see the sidebar "The wireless orb knows all"). However, all TV and DVD connections are standard wired connections.

Figure 19-2:
The first LGE Internet refrigerator was wirelessly enabled.

Samsung (www.samsung.com/us/) has the RH269LBSH Digital Network Refrigerator, which is equipped with Internet access, a videophone, and a TV. In addition to storing food, consumers can send and receive e-mail, surf the Net, and watch a favorite DVD by using the refrigerator's touchscreen control panel, which also serves as a detachable wireless-enabled handheld computer. Pretty neat.

All this is still pricey though — you may spend $4,000 or more on an Internet refrigerator. Sadly, due to this high cost and other reasons, these connected home appliances have not really taken off. The market demand has not been there for the all-in-one products — people still seem tied to their TVs and PC screens as separate from the appliances. Indeed, the latest moves by the consumer electronics and appliances industry seems more focused on making TVs more functional.

More wireless changes are coming too. With recent developments in radio frequency identification (RFID), Near Field Communications (NFC), and other low-power and low-priced technologies, you may indeed get to the point where your kitchen monitors all its appliances (and what's in them — "We need more milk").

The wireless orb knows all

Ambient Devices (www.ambientdevices.com) offers wireless products that make tangible interfaces to digital information. This sounds broad, but so are their product offerings. They offer glowing orbs that change colors based on stock prices; umbrellas whose handles glow when it's going to rain; weather displays that tell you, at a glance, what the weather is going to be for the next 7 days; even an "Energy Joule" that tells you the current price of electricity and your consumption at a specific outlet. The key to their ability to do this is their wireless network. All products tune into the wireless Ambient Information Network to receive broadcasted data. Our favorite product is the Ambient Orb, the colorful globe that we've programmed to tell us when we've sold more books on Amazon.com!

Your Entertainment Systems

In Chapter 12 we talk about ways you can connect your entertainment systems (your home theater, TV, and audio equipment) to your wireless network. Today that primarily means getting content from your PC and/or the Internet into those devices using *media adapters* that connect to your wireless network on one end and to your TV or audio gear on the other end.

In the not-so-distant future, however, you'll be able to skip the extra gear because wireless will be built right into your audio/visual gear. Read on for some examples of how this will happen.

Wi-Fi networking will be built into receivers and TVs

Hewlett-Packard has released a Wi-Fi ready television. The HP MediaSmart TV (www.hp.com) is a high-definition LCD TV with wireless Ethernet capabilities on board. Through this television, you can access CinemaNow (www.cinema now.com) and Live365 (www.live365.com) to download movies and music instantly. You can also use an HP Snapfish account to store photos online and have them play directly on the TV anytime. Other TV vendors are rushing to offer Internet-connected TVs as well, with the ability in some cases to insert a CableCARD to supplant your cable TV box. Expect to see Internet connectivity to be standard soon in most higher-end TVs. As an interim step, Sony offers an *external* device called the DMX-NVI BRAVIA Internet Video Link (www.sony.com, $299). This device (which needs a Wi-Fi Ethernet bridge to go wireless, see Chapter 12) provides a mechanism to access a variety of Internet content on your shiny new BRAVIA LCD HDTV. We expect Sony to move this functionality into the TV eventually and to add a fast 802.11n wireless connection as well.

Other gear in your home theater is also going wireless. For instance, Denon (www.denon.com) has its AVR-4308CI Advanced 7.1 Channel Home Theater/ MultiMedia A/V Receiver with Ethernet networking and 802.11b/g Wi-Fi on board. The Wi-Fi not only gives you access to streaming media but also lets you log in remotely to your receiver.

802.11n, which we cover in detail in Chapter 2, has been designed specifically to support multimedia networking among all the devices in the home. We expect to see this become standard in at least midrange and high-end A/V gear in the next few years.

Cables? Who needs them?

Another and quite different wireless change looming on the horizon is wireless cabling. You may not care much about wireless cabling until you put that 50-inch LCD on the wall and realize that there's an HDMI cable coming down the wall — serious spousal issues on *that* one!

Wireless HDMI comes to the rescue. Wireless HDMI is exactly what it sounds like — a wireless high-definition multimedia interface that links your HDMI port on your TV to your HDMI output on your satellite box, A/V receiver, PS3, or whatever. Wireless HDMI is not a standard per se, but many early implementations are coming to market using ultra wideband (UWB) under the WiMedia standard. Early wireless HDMI chipsets can use the WiMedia UWB standard to deliver more than 300 Mbps of sustained throughput for in-room coverage. The theoretical maximum throughput of UWB is 480 Mbps. At this rate, Wireless HDMI will have to compress the HD signal.

A group of consumer electronics kingpins got together in 2005 to form the WirelessHD Consortium aimed at developing a noncompressed wireless standard for high-definition audio/video transmission. Instead of UWB, the WiHD standard uses the 60 GHz band to offer HD content without the need for compression. Instead of providing up to 300 Mbps using UWB, WiHD reportedly will transmit at 5 Gbps.

Wireless HDMI technologies will be available to consumers first. The first WiHD products will hit the market sometime in 2008. Gefen, for instance, has its Wireless HDMI Extender (www.gefen.com, $699), offering transmission of high-definition video (for you video geeks, the system supports up to 1080p at 30 fps, or 1080i at 60 fps, at distances up to 33 feet). Gefen does compress the signal, using lossy JPEG 2000 compression, and the resulting image quality will be less than that of wired HDMI. However, until there's more experience with the product in the field (in different wireless environments), we won't know how much is lost. For $699, we're counting on it being minimal!

Other major brands are getting into the wireless HDMI business as well, and we're expecting the current high prices to drop considerably over the next few years as we move along the chip volume production curve and as competing WiHD products come to market.

The wireless cable experience is not limited to HDMI though. We expect to see short-distance, high-capacity wireless technologies actually turn the mess of wires behind your stereo gear into a totally wireless network with logical configurations done on your browser or through your TV set. Want to connect your DVD player to your receiver? No problem; just configure the wireless ports on both machines to see each other and you're done. We're excited about this development, which we hope will happen in the next three to five years.

Your Musical Instruments

Band gear has been wireless for some time. You can get wireless mics, guitars, and other musical instruments. But what is new is the bevy of musical gear that is coming on the market, designed for hopping on your wireless LAN and making your life fun. We're talking wireless band mayhem!

Guitar Hero (www.guitarhero.com, $90), the runaway success from Activision, jump-started this trend in our minds. A simple wireless guitar with buttons instead of strings allows even the most unmusically minded player to play with the best bands on Earth.

Rock Band (www.rockband.com, $170) takes it a step higher by taking the four key instruments one needs to make a band (guitar, bass, drums, vocals), and builds them into a highly playable (and addictive) game. Each person plays their respective role in the game, using their wireless instruments, and drums, strums, bangs, and yells their way into rock history. As we write, the first versions of this game are coming out for the latest gaming platforms, such as the PS3 and Xbox 360, but PC versions are expected as well. It's only a matter of time before you are virtually playing with other players all over the globe via the Internet.

A wireless home backbone enables fast access to online music scores, such as those from www.score-on-line.com.

Other musical instruments are also growing more complex and wireless. With ConcertMaster, from Baldwin Piano (www.gibson.com/en-us/Divisions/Baldwin/), your wireless home LAN can plug into your ConcertMaster Mark II–equipped Baldwin, Chickering, or Wurlitzer piano and play almost any musical piece you can imagine. You can plan an entire evening of music, from any combination of sources, to play in any order — all via a wireless RF remote control.

The internal ConcertMaster Library comes preloaded with 20 hours of performances in five musical categories, or you can create as many as 99 custom library categories to store your music. With as many as 99 songs in each category, you can conceivably have nearly 50,000 songs onboard and ready to play. Use your wireless access to your home's Internet connection to download the latest operating system software from Baldwin's servers. The system can accept any wireless MIDI interface. Encore!

You can record on this system too. A one-touch Quick-Record button lets you instantly save piano performances, such as your child's piano recital. You can also use songs that you record and store on a CD or USB flash drive with your PC to use in editing, sequencing, and score notation programs.

Your Pets

GPS-based tracking services can be used for pets, too! Just about everyone can identify with having lost a pet at some point. The GPS device can be collar-based or a subdermal implant. This device can serve as your pet's electronic ID tag; it also can serve as the basis for real-time feedback to the pet or its owner, and perhaps provide automatic notification if your dog goes out of the yard, for example.

Globalpetfinder.com is a typical example of a GPS-enabled system (www. globalpetfinder.com, $290). With this system, you create one or more circular virtual fences defined by a GPS location. Your home's address, for example, is translated by its online site into a GPS coordinate, and you can create a fence that might be 100 feet in radius. If your pet wanders outside this fence, you're alerted immediately and sent the continuously updated location of your pet to the two-way wireless device of your choice — cell phone, PDA, or computer, for example. You can find your pet by dialing the collar's phone number, and it replies with the present location. If you're using a PDA with a graphical interface, such as a Treo or Blackberry, you can see the location on a street map. You have to pay a monthly subscription fee for the service — to cover the cell costs — which ranges from $18 to $20 per month. If your dog runs away often, go for the Escape Artist Peace of Mind plan!

The 802.11 technologies are making their way into the pet-tracking arena as well. Several companies are testing prototypes of wireless clients that would log onto neighborhood Wi-Fi APs and send messages about their positions back to their owners. Although the coverage certainly isn't as broad as cellular service, it certainly would be much less expensive. So your LAN may soon be part of a neighborhood wireless network infrastructure that provides a NAN — *neighborhood area network* — one of whose benefits is such continual tracking capability for pets.

Checking out new wireless gadgets

The merging of wireless and other consumer goods is a major economic trend. You can expect that you will have many more options in the future to improve your life (or ruin it) using Wi-Fi devices. Here are three great places to keep track of the latest and greatest in new wireless products:

✔ **Gizmodo** (www.gizmodo.com): Gizmodo tracks all the leading-edge gadgets of any type. This site is fun to visit, just to see what someone has dreamed up. As we write this chapter, there's a neat story about glow-in-the-dark light bulbs that still provide luminescence after they're turned off — that's emergency lighting! For your wireless fancy, all sorts of articles on new wireless wares

appear each week; just be prepared — many are available only in Asia. Rats!

✔ **Engadget** (www.engadget.com): Engadget was founded by one of the major editors from Gizmodo. It largely mimics Gizmodo but with meatier posts and reader comments for many articles.

✔ **EHomeUpgrade** (www.ehomeupgrade.com): EHomeUpgrade covers a broader spectrum of software, services, and even industry trends, but hardcore wireless is a mainstay of its fare as well.

You can't go wrong checking these sites regularly to see what's new to put in your home!

Your Robots

Current technology dictates that robots are reliant on special algorithms and hidden technologies to help them navigate. For example, the Roomba robotic vacuum cleaner, from iRobot (www.irobot.com, $119–$499), relies on internal programming and virtual walls to contain its coverage area. The Friendly Machines Robomow robotic lawnmower relies on hidden wiring under the ground (www.friendlymachines.com, $1,100 to $1,500).

iRobot also has been busy shaking up the home with robots for floor washing (Scooba, $299–$499), shop sweeping (Dirt Dog, $129), pool cleaning (Verro, $799–$1,099), and gutter cleaning (Looj, $99–$169). They even have a robot (ConnectR, $499) for remote visitation — you can remotely control ConnectR to roam your house and send back audio and video — who needs a dog anymore?

As your home becomes even more wirelessly connected, devices can start to triangulate their positions based on home-based homing beacons of sorts that help them sense their position at any time. The presence of a wireless home network will drive new innovation into these devices. Most manufacturers are busy designing 802.11 and other wireless technologies into the next versions of their products.

The following list highlights some other product ideas that manufacturers are working on now. We can't yet offer price points or tell you when these products will hit the market, but expect them to come soon:

- **Robotic garbage taker-outers:** Robotic firms are designing units that take the trash out for you, on schedule, no matter what the weather — simple as that.

- **Robotic mail collectors:** A robotic mail collector goes and gets the mail for you. Neither snow, nor rain, nor gloom of night, nor winds of change, nor a nation challenged can stay them from the swift completion of their appointed rounds. New wirelessly outfitted mailboxes tell you (and the robots) when your mail has arrived.

- **Robotic snow blowers:** Manufacturers are working to perfect robotic snow blowers that continually clear your driveway and sidewalks while snow falls.

- **Robotic golf ball retrievers:** These bots retrieve golf balls. Initially designed for driving range use, they're being modified for the home market.

- **Robotic guard dogs:** Robots that can roam areas and send back audio and video feeds are coming to the market. These new versions of man's best friend can sniff out fires or lethal gases, take photos of burglars, and send intruder alerts to homeowners' cell phones. Some have embedded artificial intelligence (AI) to act autonomously and independently. Check out the dragonlike Sanyo Banryu or its R2D2-like successor TMSUK's Mujiro Rigurio, the Mitsubishi Wakamaru, Takenaka Engineering's Mihari Wan, and others emerging even as we write this book.

- **Robotic gutter cleaners:** A range of spiderlike robots is available that can maneuver on inclines, such as roofs, and feature robotic sensors and arms that can clean areas.

- **Robotic cooks:** Put the ingredients in, select a mode, and wait for your dinner to be cooked — it's better than a TV dinner, for sure.

- **Robotic pooper scoopers:** The units we have discovered roam your yard in search of something to clean up and then deposit the findings in a place you determine.

The world is still getting used to robots and their limitations. More than one company has canceled its robotic development programs until the market is more rational about its expectations. Early household robots were panned in the market because people expected them to act like people — to cook them dinner and scratch their backs on demand. The market success of the iRobot purpose-built robots has shown that buyers want robots that do something and do it well.

Still, the quest for the all-purpose android remains strong. For this reason, you're more likely to see humanoid robots demonstrating stuff such as skipping rope at special events rather than cooking dinner in your kitchen. Products such as Honda's ASIMO (Advanced Step in Innovative Mobility, world.honda.com/ASIMO/) are remarkable for the basic things they can do, such as shake hands and bow, but the taskmasters we mention in the preceding list can help you with day-to-day chores.

For years, we watched Sony's cute Aibo robotic dog go through seven generations of development, evolving into a wireless-enabled, 1,000-word barking companion that was simply fun to play with. Then the disastrous news hit that Sony had canceled the product for good. As we write, there are rumors of a PlayStation-enabled Aibo, the Aibo PS. The Wi-Fi capable AIBO PS would be completely controllable through a Sony PSP or PlayStation 3. Search online when you read this and see whether this rumor became reality. If so, you'd have a lot of fun with this new Aibo in your home.

Your Apparel

Wireless is making its way into your clothing. Researchers are already experimenting with *wearables* — the merging of 802.11 and Bluetooth directly into clothing so that it can have networking capabilities. Want to synch your PDA? No problem: Just stick it in your pocket. All sorts of companies are working on waterproof and washerproof devices for wirelessly connecting to your wireless home network. Burton (the snowboard people) and Motorola have a line of Bluetooth-enabled jackets called Audex (direct.motorola.com/ens/audex/default.asp, $350). The Audex Motorola Jacket series sports built-in Bluetooth wireless stereo speakers and a wired iPod connection — so it's up to you whether to listen to tunes or answer incoming calls. Dada Footware has launched its wireless Code M shoe line (www.dadafootwear.com, $199) that stores music and workout coaching and plays it either out loud or via Bluetooth to wireless headsets. We have even seen jackets that display advertisements on their backs and T-shirts that show the strength of any Wi-Fi wireless signal available (www.thinkgeek.com/tshirts/generic/991e/).

Wireless technology will also infiltrate your clothing through radio frequency identification tags, or RFIDs, which are very small, lightweight, electronic, read-write storage devices (microchips) half the size of a grain of sand. They listen for radio queries and, when pinged, respond by transmitting their ID codes. Most RFID tags have no batteries because they use the power from the initial radio signal to transmit their responses; thus, they never wear out. Data is accessible in real time through handheld or fixed-position readers, using RF signals to transfer data to and from tags. RFID applications are infinite, but when embedded in clothing, RFIDs offer applications such as tracking people (such as kids at school) or sorting clothing from the dryer (no more problems matching socks or identifying clothes for each child's pile).

Having wireless fun with geocaching

Geocaching is an entertaining adventure game based around the GPS technology. It's basically a wireless treasure hunt. The idea is to have individuals and organizations set up caches all over the world; the GPS locations are then posted on the Internet, and GPS users seek the caches. Once they're found, some sort of reward may be there; the only rule is that if you take something from the cache, you need to leave something behind for others to find later. Check out what caches are near you: www.geocaching.com.

Want to find out more about GPS? Visit a couple of fun GPS tracking (pun intended!) sites, such as www.gps-practice-and-fun.com and www.gpsinformation.net.

A technology of great impact in our lifetime is GPS, which is increasingly being built into cars, cell phones, devices, and clothing. GPS equipment and chips are so cheap that you will find them everywhere. They're used in amusement parks to help keep track of your kids. There are already prototypes of GPS-enabled shoes (the initial application has been to protect prostitutes).

Most GPS-driven applications have software that enables you to interpret the GPS results. You can grab a Web tablet at home while on your couch, wirelessly surf to the tracking Web site, and determine where Fido (or Fred) is located. Want to see whether your spouse's car is heading home from work yet? Grab your PDA as you walk down the street, log on to a nearby hot spot, and check it out. Many applications are also being ported to cell phones, so you can use those wireless devices to find out what's going on.

GPS-based devices — primarily in a watch or lanyard-hung form factor — are available that can track people.

Many perimeter-oriented child-safety devices emit an alarm if your child wanders outside an adjustable safety zone (such as wanders away from you in the mall). For instance, the GigaAir Child Tracking system ($190) is a two-piece, battery-powered system that consists of a clip-on unit worn by the child and a second pager-size unit carried by the parent or guardian. The safety perimeter is set by the parent and can be as little as 10 feet and as much as 75 feet. The alarm tone also acts as a homing device to help a parent and child find each other after it has gone off — important for those subway rush hours in New York City. Many other person-locator products are on the market, such as a more removal-resistant unit from ionKids (www.brick housesecurity.com/vbsik.html, $200) and a GPS Kid Locator Tracker Backpack (www.spyshops.ca, $900).

Note that there is a difference between a tracking device and a locator device. Tracking devices will tell where someone has been, but only after the device returns to you. A popular example is the GPS Trackstick (www.trackstick. com). A locator device, on the other hand, will remotely tell you where it is at any particular time. GPS-enabled phones and services are examples of these. Don't buy one expecting the other!

Various possible monthly fees are associated with personal tracking and location devices. Some don't have any fees; they involve short-range, closed-system wireless signals. Some charge a monthly fee, just like a cell phone plan. Some charge per-use fees, like per-locate attempts. Be sure to check the fine print when you're buying any sort of wireless location device to make sure you don't have lots of extra fees that go along with it. (That's why we like 802.11-based products. They're cheap and often don't have these fees. But then again, they don't have the range that some of these other systems do.)

Applied Digital Solutions (www.digitalangel.com) is on the leading edge. The company has developed the VeriChip, which can be implanted under the skin of people in high-risk (think kidnapping) areas overseas. This chip is an implantable, 12mm x 2.1mm radio frequency device, about the size of the point of a ballpoint pen. The chip contains a unique verification number.

Although watches are a great form factor for lots of wireless connectivity opportunities, they have been hampered by either wired interface require-ments (like a USB connection) or an infrared (IR) connection, which requires line of sight to your PC. Expect these same devices to quickly take on Bluetooth and 802.11 interfaces so that continual updating — as with the Microsoft Smart Personal Objects Technology (SPOT) model (direct.msn.com) — can occur.

Creating wireless connectivity via jewelry bears its own set of issues because of the size and weight requirements of the host jewelry for any wireless system. The smaller the jewelry, the less power the wireless transmitter has to do its job. The less power, the shorter the range and the more limited the bandwidth and application of the device.

Cellular Jewelry (www.cellularjewelry.com) offers bracelets, watches, pens, and other devices that flash when you receive a phone call. Tired of missing calls when that phone is in your purse or jacket pocket? These devices — which work well only with GSM phones, not CDMA ones — alert you in a visual fashion, and in a fashionable way too!

Wearables are going wireless — MP3 sunglasses, Wi-Finder purses, GPS belts — you name it, someone has thought of it! Check out the Engadget wearables blog, at wearables.engadget.com.

Everything in Your Home

Did we leave anything out? Well, yes, in fact we have. That's because *everything* in your home that uses electricity can potentially be wirelessly enabled to a *home control and automation network*. In Chapter 3 we talked a little bit about ZigBee and Z-Wave, two wireless technologies that are hitting the market today and are designed around very low-cost and low-power chips that can be embedded in any electrically powered device in the home. Other low-price and low-power wireless technologies, such as Wibree, are also in the works and can expand your home's wireless control network.

Where you'll use ZigBee and Z-Wave

Low power means short distance. It also means small. You'll be using technologies such as ZigBee and Z-Wave to do things such as allow lamps to be controlled by your PC and to tell you whether or not your doors are locked.

Energy management is a huge potential application for these technologies. Consider the following implementations of lower power chips:

✔ Allowing electric and gas meters to talk to your household energy hogs and tell them when it's less expensive to do their chores (such as run the laundry). Your meter can also talk to the home's wireless network to communicate usage back to the central station (so no one has to come by your house to check the meter).

✔ Installing programmable controllable thermostats (PCT) designed to improve energy efficiency and electric service consumption. Using their wireless connections, they can reach out to sensors in the house to drive more efficient use of energy zones and time-of-day setbacks.

✔ Using sensor-outfitted outlets for each appliance to monitor them for energy usage and to report back to central in-home energy control programs — programs you can monitor on your television or PC.

Z-Wave, and to a lesser extent ZigBee, are also focused on home automation. Because they are wireless, these technologies allow you to install, upgrade, and network your home control system without wires. You can configure and run multiple systems from a single remote control. You can also receive automatic notification if there's something unusual happening in the house (like your oven is on at 2:00 A.M.).

As your wireless backbone becomes pervasive in the home, expect lots of ZigBee and Z-Wave products to form the last few feet of these connections because their lower cost pushes them into smaller places around the house. This is truly the next wave of wireless expansion in your house.

Because they use *mesh networking* technologies, where signals can bounce from device to device throughout the home (like a frog crossing a pond on top of lily pads), the more ZigBee or Z-Wave devices you have in your home, the better the network works (a frog can hop across a pond covered with lily pads a lot more easily than it can get across a pond with the pads spread far apart). If your power utility puts ZigBee or Z-Wave in your home for energy-savings purposes, you can take advantage of these devices when you add your own home control and automation devices. Remember, with mesh networking systems, the more you have, the better they work!

Introducing Wibree

A new, even lower-powered (think watch batteries, not AC power) technology is arriving that can embed wireless control and networking in *anything:* Wibree. Think of Wibree as a low-power option for Bluetooth; Wibree and Bluetooth technology are complementary technologies. Wibree even uses the same antenna and 2.4 GHz frequency band as Bluetooth.

Bluetooth technology (which we discuss in Chapter 15) is well suited for streaming and data-intensive applications such as file transfer, and Wibree is designed for applications where ultra-low-power consumption, small size, and low cost are needed. So Wibree in many cases picks up where Bluetooth leaves off.

Whereas your cell phone might talk to your car via Bluetooth, your car keys might have Wibree inside them. That way, when you lose your keys, you can search the house for them by querying Wibree gateways to see if anyone detects them.

Bluetooth and Wibree are *wireless personal area networks* (WPANs) with a star topology, and thus are truly designed for PAN. ZigBee, driven by its focus on wireless monitoring, lighting control, energy conservation, and so on, is a mesh technology in which one fixed device communicates wirelessly with another. So you might see all of these in your home.

How might you use Wibree?

- ✔ **Sports and wellness:** Sports watches that connect to sensors located on the body, shoes, and other fitness gear can gather data on heart rate, distance, speed, and acceleration and send the information to a mobile phone.

- ✔ **Healthcare:** Wibree-driven sensors can be built into stand-alone health-monitoring devices that can send vital health-related information (blood pressure, glucose level) to Bluetooth-Wibree dual-mode devices (such as mobile phones and personal computers), which can process this information and send alerts to the mobile phones of patients and caretakers.

✔ **Office and mobile accessories:** You can use Wibree's small size and ability to extend battery life in office and mobile accessories. These can also use Wibree to avoid dongles for connectivity, which add an extra component and raise the overall cost.

✔ **Entertainment:** Remote controls, gaming accessories, and other entertainment devices can use Wibree's sensor technologies to interact with one another.

✔ **Watches:** Watches and wrist-top devices can use Wibree to connect them to mobile phones and accessories. Now you can use your watch to control that inbound call, or to send a quick alert via text messaging.

You'll see a lot of Bluetooth-Wibree dual-mode implementation, where Wibree functionality is integrated with Bluetooth for a minor incremental cost by utilizing key Bluetooth components. Examples of devices that would benefit from the Bluetooth-Wibree dual-mode implementation are mobile phones and personal computers.

Chapter 20

Top Ten Sources for More Information

*W*e've tried hard in this book to capture all that's happening with wireless networks in the home. However, we can't cover everything in one book, and so, in fairness to other publications, we're leaving some things for them to talk about on their Web sites and in their print publications. (Nice of us, isn't it?)

We want to keep you informed of the latest changes to what's in this book, so we encourage you to check out the *Wireless Home Networking For Dummies* site, at www.digitaldummies.com, where you can find updates and new information.

This chapter lists the publications that we read regularly (and therefore recommend unabashedly) and that you should get your hands on as part of your wireless home networking project. Many of these sources provide up-to-date performance information, which can be critical when making a decision about which equipment to buy and what standards to pursue.

The Web sites mentioned also have a ton of information online, but you may have to try different search keywords to find what you're looking for. Some publications like to use the term *Wi-Fi,* for example, and others use *802.11.* If you don't get hits on certain terms when you're searching around, try other ones that you know. It's rare to come up empty on a search about wireless networking these days. All sites listed here are free.

CNET.com

CNET.com (www.cnet.com) is a simple-to-use, free Web site where you can do apples-to-apples comparisons of wireless equipment. You can count on finding pictures of what you're buying, editor ratings of the equipment, user ratings of the gear, reviews of most devices, and a listing of the places on the Web where you can buy it all — along with true pricing. What's great about CNET is that it covers the wireless networking aspect of Wi-Fi as well as the consumer goods portion of Wi-Fi (such as home theater, A/V gear, and phones). It's your one-stop resource for evaluating your future home wireless purchases.

Get started at CNET in its Wi-Fi Networking section, which at the time this book was written was at http://reviews.cnet.com/networking-wifi/?tag=co. There, you find feature specs, reviews, and price comparisons of leading wireless gear. (CNET even certifies listed vendors, so you know that they pass at least one test of online legitimacy.)

What we especially like is the ability to do a side-by-side comparison so that we can see which product has which features. By clicking the boxes next to each name, you can select that gear for comparison shopping. You can also filter the results by price, features, support, and other factors at the bottom of the page. Then just click Compare to receive a results page.

At wireless.cnet.com, the CNET editors provide feature stories focused on wireless use in practical applications. Overall, we visit this solid site often before buying anything.

CNET, like many other sites, now supports RSS feeds. If you don't know about RSS, you will soon: Most news and information sites offer RSS feeds to tell you what's happening on their Web sites. An *RSS feed* is an electronic feed that contains basic information about a particular item, like the headline, posting date, and summary paragraph about each news item on the site. You use a program called an RSS reader, such as NewsGator Online (www.newsgator.com) or any of dozens of other free RSS readers, to reach out and access these feeds regularly. You find RSS readers that load into your e-mail program, browser, and instant messaging program, for example. All these readers allow you to scan the headlines and click the ones you want to read. You could set up an RSS reader to access the RSS feeds of each of these sites in this chapter to stay current on everything wireless. We highly recommend RSS. By the way, the Google of the RSS world is the Syndic8 (www.syndic8.com) site. There, you can find a massive listing of user-submitted and Syndic8-authenticated RSS feeds. Just enter your keyword in the Search area and Syndic8 displays all the listings of available publications and sources with that phrase in their descriptions. Check it out!

Amazon.com, Shopping.com, Pricegrabber.com, and more

What? Learn about wireless on a shopping site? Ah, but you can glean a broad range of information from these sites that will help you in your purchase and evaluation of wireless technologies. Amazon.com will show you multiple pictures — usually the front and back — that you can use to see what sort of LEDs, LCDs, and ports you are getting. The user reviews are always helpful — we usually read the negative reviews to try to find the pitfalls and do more research on those using Google.

Amazon.com, Shopping.com, and Pricegrabber.com are great for telling you what other people are interested in and what's popular — although what everyone else is buying is not always a good indicator of quality. All three sites will help you find out where you can buy the products and who has the cheapest pricing, although Amazon.com is more focused on selling on Amazon first and foremost. Shopping.com and Pricegrabber.com are more intent on linking you to other vendors and are a good resource as you start comparison shopping.

Wi-Fi Planet, WiFi-Forum, and More

Wi-Fi Planet (www.wi-fiplanet.com/) is a great resource for keeping up with industry news and getting reviews of access points, client devices, security tools, and software. Look for the tutorial section, where you can find articles such as "TiVo and Wi-Fi — Imperfect Together" and "Used Routers Can Create Whole New Problems."

One of the more interactive parts of Wi-Fi Planet is its forum, where you can ask questions to the collective readership and get answers. (You can ask a question, and the system e-mails you with any responses — very nice.) The forum has General, Security, Troubleshooting, Interoperability, Standards, Hardware, Applications, VoIP, and WiMAX sections. The discussions are tolerant of beginners, but can get quite sophisticated in their responses. All in all, it's a great site for information. (Wi-Fi Planet also has RSS feeds!)

Another forum that tends to get a lot of traffic is the WiFi-Forum (www.wifi-forum.com), which runs out of London and has a more international clientele.

The Wi-Fi Net News site (www.wifinetnews.com/) is a great site for finding out what's going on in the wireless world. You may have heard about *Weblogs,* or *blogs*: They're link-running, rambling commentaries that people keep online about topics near and dear to their hearts.

Unless you want to track the wireless industry, though, you probably wouldn't want to check this site daily, but it's a great resource for when you want to see what the latest news is about a particular vendor or technology. We follow this site every day for interesting news and product or service developments.

Check out these other Weblogs about wireless topics: FierceWireless (www.fiercewireless.com) and Daily Wireless (www.dailywireless.org). By the way, almost all Weblogs offer RSS feeds!

PC Magazine and PC World

The venerable *PC Magazine* (www.pcmag.com) is the go-to publication for PC users. This magazine regularly and religiously tracks all aspects of wireless, from individual product reviews to sweeping buyer's guides across different wireless segments to updates on key operating system and supporting software changes. If you have a PC, you should be subscribing to this magazine.

We really like the First Look sections of the publication, which offer you immediate insight on new product announcements and give you hands-on, quick reviews of the latest developments on the market. This site is great for the products you've heard were coming. *PC Magazine* is usually one of the first to review these products.

A one-year subscription (25 issues) runs only $20. You can subscribe to either electronic or print issues, which is nice if you want to catch up on your reading on the go but don't want to carry a bag of publications.

PC World (www.pcworld.com) is likewise a great resource. We'd be hard-pressed to say whether it's better or worse than *PC Magazine* — the reviews, articles, and overall networking coverage are definitely as good in either magazine.

Electronic House Magazine

Electronic House (www.electronichouse.com) is one of our favorite publications because you can read lots of easy-to-understand articles about all aspects of an electronic home, including articles on wireless networking and all the consumer appliances and other non-PC devices that are going wireless. It's written for the consumer who enjoys technology.

Electronic House magazine includes articles on wireless home networking, wireless home control, and subsystems such as residential lighting, security, home theater, energy management, and telecommunications. It also regularly looks at new and emerging technologies using wireless capabilities, such as wireless refrigerators and wireless touchpanels, to control your home.

The magazine costs $19.95 per year for ten issues. Back issues are $5.95 each or six issues for $30 (plus shipping), so you can catch up on what you've missed (we always love doing that). You definitely want to subscribe to this one!

Its Web site is also packed with great articles and ideas, and it's a fabulous site for finding out how other people have adapted wireless devices into their home. A bevy of slideshows demonstrate all sorts of homes that have been remade into themed spaces — we love the *Star Trek* slideshows about homeowners who have remodeled their homes to look like the *Enterprise!* No visible wires there!

You can sign up for newsletters that will tell you about the latest articles on their site — we always find ourselves clicking through on some topic. Check them out at www.electronichouse.com/eh/newsletters/.

Practically Networked

Practically Networked (www.practicallynetworked.com) is a free site run by the folks at Internet.com. It has basic tutorials on networking topics, background information on key technologies, and a troubleshooting guide. The site can contain some dated information (such as the troubleshooting guide), but it does have monitored discussion groups, where you can get some good feedback, and the reviews section gives you a listing of products with a fairly comprehensive buyer's-guide-style listing of features.

ExtremeTech.com

Ziff Davis Media has a great site (www.extremetech.com) with special sections focused on networking and wireless issues. There's heavy traffic at the discussion groups, and people seem willing to provide quick and knowledgeable answers. (You can find some seriously educated geeks in these groups.) Check out the links to wireless articles and reviews by ExtremeTech staff.

The site can be difficult to navigate because the layout is a little confusing. We recommend that you visit the OS, Software and Networking area, where wireless topics are covered in fair detail. And, if you're having a problem that you just can't seem to crack, check out the discussion groups on this site.

Fan sites

All the wireless products seem to have their own sets of fans. Some fans go a little further and set up Web sites geared toward telling all about their favorite products. The most popular brand of wireless gear has long been that made by Linksys (now a division of Cisco, the huge networking equipment vendor). So it's no surprise that Linksys gear comes with its own unofficial support site, with forums, tips and tricks, and even links to specialized *firmware* that can make your access point do neat tricks, such as act as part of a *mesh network* to expand the coverage of your Internet connection across several access points. Check out the site at www.linksysinfo.org. If you have a different brand, don't despair. Do a Google search or check out some of the sites listed in this section for forums or vendor-specific pages, or go to www.broadbandreports.com and look in the Hardware by Brand forums there.

Network World

Network World (www.networkworld.com) is the leading publication for networking professionals, and although this site is geared primarily to businesses, it has lots of content about wireless because so much of the technology first appeared in commercial venues. The site has detailed buyer's guides that show the features and functionality of wireless LAN products — and almost all this information is applicable for your home. Importantly, you can also search the site for more content on Wi-Fi and 802.11 as well as on Bluetooth and WiMAX. The publication has a large reporting staff and stays on top of everything networking related.

Wikipedia

For having content maintained by the masses on the Internet, *Wikipedia* (www.wikipedia.org) is not all that bad. Anyone can update information on *Wikipedia,* and there have been lots of publicly discussed instances where vendors wrote bad things about other vendors on the site. But as a whole, it's pretty good. Its wireless coverage includes topics such as the following:

- ✔ **Wi-Fi:** en.wikipedia.org/wiki/Wi-Fi
- ✔ **Wireless access points:** n.wikipedia.org/wiki/Access_Point
- ✔ **IEEE 802.11n:** en.wikipedia.org/wiki/802.11n

It's a great tool to get a high-level idea of any topic, with substantial avenues offsite for more detailed information. What we like most about *Wikipedia* is that we usually find neat links to other related topics in the External Links section of each page — links we probably would not find elsewhere.

Other Cool Sites

We can't list here all the sites we regularly visit, but lots of good information is out there. This section lists some other sites worth looking at.

Tech and wireless news sites

The following sites provide daily news coverage focused on the technology industry in general, or on wireless technologies in particular. We make them part of our everyday Web surfing routine — you may want to as well!

- ✔ **SearchMobileComputing.com:** searchmobilecomputing.techtarget.com
- ✔ **TechWeb:** www.techweb.com
- ✔ **ZDNet:** www.zdnet.com

Industry organizations

The creation and maintenance of standards has driven wireless to very low price points and great interoperability. Here are some organizations pushing for change in wireless — each site has info about wireless and networks:

- ✔ **Bluetooth SIG:** www.bluetooth.com
- ✔ **Freenetworks.org:** www.freenetworks.org
- ✔ **IEEE 802 home page:** www.ieee802.org
- ✔ **Wi-Fi Alliance** (formerly WECA): www.wi-fi.org
- ✔ **WiMAX Forum:** www.wimaxforum.org
- ✔ **Wireless LAN Association:** www.wlana.org

Roaming services and Wi-Finder organizations

As we mention in Chapter 16, a range of potential services is available that you can use to log on when you're on the road. Most of these have sections of their sites devoted to helping you find out where you can log on near you. Here are some frequently mentioned services and initiatives:

- ✔ **Boingo Wireless:** www.boingo.com
- ✔ **iPass:** www.ipass.com

- ✔ **JiWire:** www.jiwire.com
- ✔ **Wi-Fi HotSpot List:** www.wi-fihotspotlist.com

Manufacturers

Some of these firms are more oriented toward business products, but many of them have great educational FAQs (frequently asked questions) and information that are helpful for people trying to read everything they can (which we support!):

- ✔ **3Com:** www.3com.com
- ✔ **Actiontec:** www.actiontec.com
- ✔ **Alvarion:** www.alvarion.com
- ✔ **Apple:** www.apple.com/airportextreme
- ✔ **Belkin:** www.belkin.com
- ✔ **Buffalo Technology:** www.buffalotech.com
- ✔ **Cisco:** www.cisco.com
- ✔ **D-Link:** www.d-link.com
- ✔ **Hewlett-Packard:** www.hp.com
- ✔ **Intel:** www.intel.com
- ✔ **Intermec:** home.intermec.com
- ✔ **Linksys:** www.linksys.com
- ✔ **Macsense:** www.macsense.com
- ✔ **Microsoft:** www.microsoft.com
- ✔ **NETGEAR:** www.netgear.com
- ✔ **Proxim:** www.proxim.com
- ✔ **Sierra Wireless:** www.sierrawireless.com
- ✔ **SMC Networks:** www.smc.com

Index

• *B* •

• C •

• D •

• *F* •

• *G* •

• **S** •

BUSINESS, CAREERS & PERSONAL FINANCE

0-7645-9847-3

0-7645-2431-3

Also available:
- Business Plans Kit For Dummies
  0-7645-9794-9
- Economics For Dummies
  0-7645-5726-2
- Grant Writing For Dummies
  0-7645-8416-2
- Home Buying For Dummies
  0-7645-5331-3
- Managing For Dummies
  0-7645-1771-6
- Marketing For Dummies
  0-7645-5600-2

- Personal Finance For Dummies
  0-7645-2590-5*
- Resumes For Dummies
  0-7645-5471-9
- Selling For Dummies
  0-7645-5363-1
- Six Sigma For Dummies
  0-7645-6798-5
- Small Business Kit For Dummies
  0-7645-5984-2
- Starting an eBay Business For Dummies
  0-7645-6924-4
- Your Dream Career For Dummies
  0-7645-9795-7

HOME & BUSINESS COMPUTER BASICS

0-470-05432-8

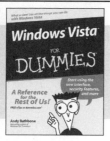

0-471-75421-8

Also available:
- Cleaning Windows Vista For Dummies
  0-471-78293-9
- Excel 2007 For Dummies
  0-470-03737-7
- Mac OS X Tiger For Dummies
  0-7645-7675-5
- MacBook For Dummies
  0-470-04859-X
- Macs For Dummies
  0-470-04849-2
- Office 2007 For Dummies
  0-470-00923-3

- Outlook 2007 For Dummies
  0-470-03830-6
- PCs For Dummies
  0-7645-8958-X
- Salesforce.com For Dummies
  0-470-04893-X
- Upgrading & Fixing Laptops For Dummies
  0-7645-8959-8
- Word 2007 For Dummies
  0-470-03658-3
- Quicken 2007 For Dummies
  0-470-04600-7

FOOD, HOME, GARDEN, HOBBIES, MUSIC & PETS

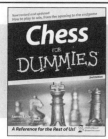

0-7645-8404-9

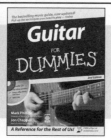

0-7645-9904-6

Also available:
- Candy Making For Dummies
  0-7645-9734-5
- Card Games For Dummies
  0-7645-9910-0
- Crocheting For Dummies
  0-7645-4151-X
- Dog Training For Dummies
  0-7645-8418-9
- Healthy Carb Cookbook For Dummies
  0-7645-8476-6
- Home Maintenance For Dummies
  0-7645-5215-5

- Horses For Dummies
  0-7645-9797-3
- Jewelry Making & Beading For Dummies
  0-7645-2571-9
- Orchids For Dummies
  0-7645-6759-4
- Puppies For Dummies
  0-7645-5255-4
- Rock Guitar For Dummies
  0-7645-5356-9
- Sewing For Dummies
  0-7645-6847-7
- Singing For Dummies
  0-7645-2475-5

INTERNET & DIGITAL MEDIA

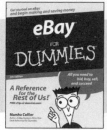

0-470-04529-9

0-470-04894-8

Also available:
- Blogging For Dummies
  0-471-77084-1
- Digital Photography For Dummies
  0-7645-9802-3
- Digital Photography All-in-One Desk Reference For Dummies
  0-470-03743-1
- Digital SLR Cameras and Photography For Dummies
  0-7645-9803-1
- eBay Business All-in-One Desk Reference For Dummies
  0-7645-8438-3
- HDTV For Dummies
  0-470-09673-X

- Home Entertainment PCs For Dummies
  0-470-05523-5
- MySpace For Dummies
  0-470-09529-6
- Search Engine Optimization For Dummies
  0-471-97998-8
- Skype For Dummies
  0-470-04891-3
- The Internet For Dummies
  0-7645-8996-2
- Wiring Your Digital Home For Dummies
  0-471-91830-X

* Separate Canadian edition also available
† Separate U.K. edition also available

Available wherever books are sold. For more information or to order direct: U.S. customers visit www.dummies.com or call 1-877-762-2974.
U.K. customers visit www.wileyeurope.com or call 0800 243407. Canadian customers visit www.wiley.ca or call 1-800-567-4797.

SPORTS, FITNESS, PARENTING, RELIGION & SPIRITUALITY

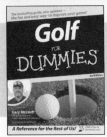

0-471-76871-5

0-7645-7841-3

Also available:

- Catholicism For Dummies
  0-7645-5391-7
- Exercise Balls For Dummies
  0-7645-5623-1
- Fitness For Dummies
  0-7645-7851-0
- Football For Dummies
  0-7645-3936-1
- Judaism For Dummies
  0-7645-5299-6
- Potty Training For Dummies
  0-7645-5417-4
- Buddhism For Dummies
  0-7645-5359-3

- Pregnancy For Dummies
  0-7645-4483-7 †
- Ten Minute Tone-Ups For Dummies
  0-7645-7207-5
- NASCAR For Dummies
  0-7645-7681-X
- Religion For Dummies
  0-7645-5264-3
- Soccer For Dummies
  0-7645-5229-5
- Women in the Bible For Dummies
  0-7645-8475-8

TRAVEL

0-7645-7749-2

0-7645-6945-7

Also available:

- Alaska For Dummies
  0-7645-7746-8
- Cruise Vacations For Dummies
  0-7645-6941-4
- England For Dummies
  0-7645-4276-1
- Europe For Dummies
  0-7645-7529-5
- Germany For Dummies
  0-7645-7823-5
- Hawaii For Dummies
  0-7645-7402-7

- Italy For Dummies
  0-7645-7386-1
- Las Vegas For Dummies
  0-7645-7382-9
- London For Dummies
  0-7645-4277-X
- Paris For Dummies
  0-7645-7630-5
- RV Vacations For Dummies
  0-7645-4442-X
- Walt Disney World & Orlando
  For Dummies
  0-7645-9660-8

GRAPHICS, DESIGN & WEB DEVELOPMENT

0-7645-8815-X

0-7645-9571-7

Also available:

- 3D Game Animation For Dummies
  0-7645-8789-7
- AutoCAD 2006 For Dummies
  0-7645-8925-3
- Building a Web Site For Dummies
  0-7645-7144-3
- Creating Web Pages For Dummies
  0-470-08030-2
- Creating Web Pages All-in-One Desk
  Reference For Dummies
  0-7645-4345-8
- Dreamweaver 8 For Dummies
  0-7645-9649-7

- InDesign CS2 For Dummies
  0-7645-9572-5
- Macromedia Flash 8 For Dummies
  0-7645-9691-8
- Photoshop CS2 and Digital
  Photography For Dummies
  0-7645-9580-6
- Photoshop Elements 4 For Dummies
  0-471-77483-9
- Syndicating Web Sites with RSS Feeds
  For Dummies
  0-7645-8848-6
- Yahoo! SiteBuilder For Dummies
  0-7645-9800-7

NETWORKING, SECURITY, PROGRAMMING & DATABASES

0-7645-7728-X

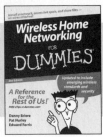

0-471-74940-0

Also available:

- Access 2007 For Dummies
  0-470-04612-0
- ASP.NET 2 For Dummies
  0-7645-7907-X
- C# 2005 For Dummies
  0-7645-9704-3
- Hacking For Dummies
  0-470-05235-X
- Hacking Wireless Networks
  For Dummies
  0-7645-9730-2
- Java For Dummies
  0-470-08716-1

- Microsoft SQL Server 2005 For Dummies
  0-7645-7755-7
- Networking All-in-One Desk Reference
  For Dummies
  0-7645-9939-9
- Preventing Identity Theft For Dummies
  0-7645-7336-5
- Telecom For Dummies
  0-471-77085-X
- Visual Studio 2005 All-in-One Desk
  Reference For Dummies
  0-7645-9775-2
- XML For Dummies
  0-7645-8845-1

HEALTH & SELF-HELP

0-7645-8450-2

0-7645-4149-8

Also available:
- Bipolar Disorder For Dummies
  0-7645-8451-0
- Chemotherapy and Radiation
  For Dummies
  0-7645-7832-4
- Controlling Cholesterol For Dummies
  0-7645-5440-9
- Diabetes For Dummies
  0-7645-6820-5* †
- Divorce For Dummies
  0-7645-8417-0 †

- Fibromyalgia For Dummies
  0-7645-5441-7
- Low-Calorie Dieting For Dummies
  0-7645-9905-4
- Meditation For Dummies
  0-471-77774-9
- Osteoporosis For Dummies
  0-7645-7621-6
- Overcoming Anxiety For Dummies
  0-7645-5447-6
- Reiki For Dummies
  0-7645-9907-0
- Stress Management For Dummies
  0-7645-5144-2

EDUCATION, HISTORY, REFERENCE & TEST PREPARATION

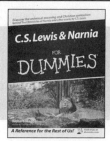

0-7645-8381-6

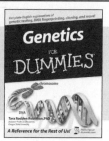

0-7645-9554-7

Also available:
- The ACT For Dummies
  0-7645-9652-7
- Algebra For Dummies
  0-7645-5325-9
- Algebra Workbook For Dummies
  0-7645-8467-7
- Astronomy For Dummies
  0-7645-8465-0
- Calculus For Dummies
  0-7645-2498-4
- Chemistry For Dummies
  0-7645-5430-1
- Forensics For Dummies
  0-7645-5580-4

- Freemasons For Dummies
  0-7645-9796-5
- French For Dummies
  0-7645-5193-0
- Geometry For Dummies
  0-7645-5324-0
- Organic Chemistry I For Dummies
  0-7645-6902-3
- The SAT I For Dummies
  0-7645-7193-1
- Spanish For Dummies
  0-7645-5194-9
- Statistics For Dummies
  0-7645-5423-9

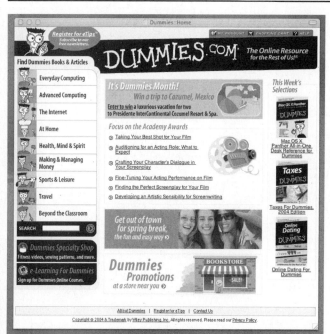

Get smart @ dummies.com®

- **Find a full list of Dummies titles**
- **Look into loads of FREE on-site articles**
- **Sign up for FREE eTips e-mailed to you weekly**
- **See what other products carry the Dummies name**
- **Shop directly from the Dummies bookstore**
- **Enter to win new prizes every month!**

* Separate Canadian edition also available
† Separate U.K. edition also available

Available wherever books are sold. For more information or to order direct: U.S. customers visit www.dummies.com or call 1-877-762-2974.
U.K. customers visit www.wileyeurope.com or call 0800 243407. Canadian customers visit www.wiley.ca or call 1-800-567-4797.